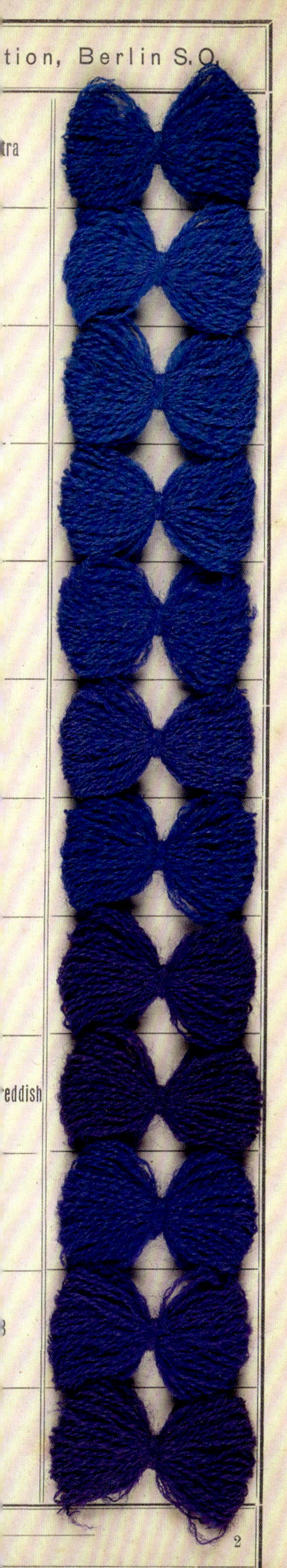

No.	Dye	No.	Dye
49	2% Guinea Fast Violet 10 B	61	3% Ponceau 3 R
50	1% Victoria Blue B	62	3% Ponceau 2 R
51	1% Victoria Blue R	63	3% Ponceau R
52	1% Victoria Blue 4 R	64	3% Ponceau G
53	3% Acid Magenta S	65	3% Victoria Scarlet G
54	3% Bordeaux B	66	3% Victoria Scarlet R
55	3% Bordeaux R	67	3% Victoria Scarlet 2 R
56	3% Bordeaux S	68	3% Victoria Scarlet 3 R
57	3% Bordeaux SF	69	3% Victoria Sarlet 4 R
58	3% Brilliant Bordeaux S	70	1.5% Ponceau B O extra
59	3% Azo Rubine S	71	3% Crystal Ponceau 6 R
60	3% Azo Rubine SG	72	3% Ponceau SS

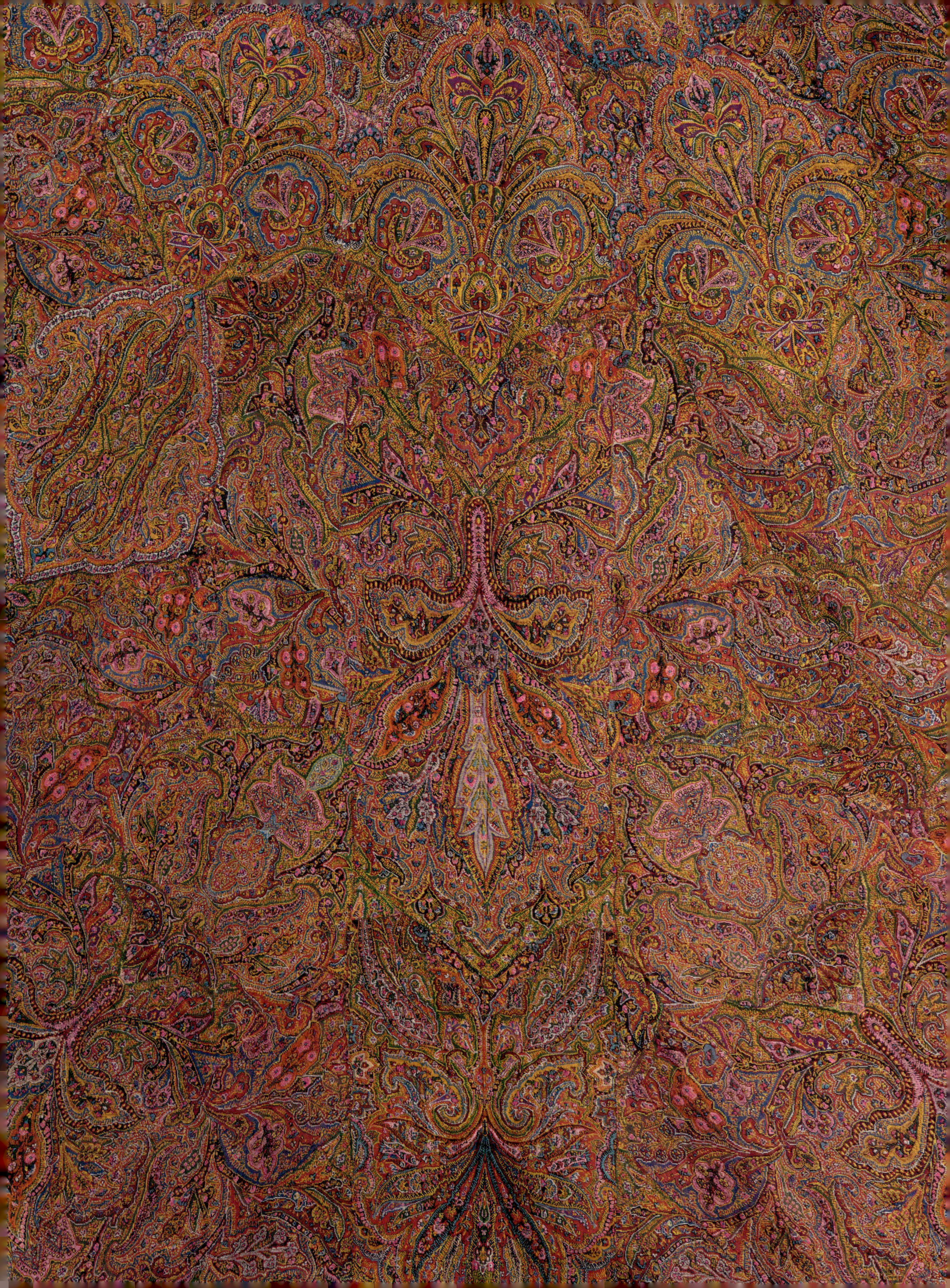

COLOUR REVOLUTION

Victorian Art, Fashion & Design

Edited by

Charlotte Ribeyrol, Matthew Winterbottom
and Madeline Hewitson

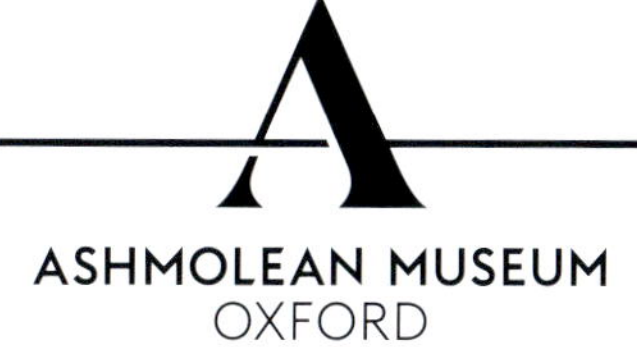

ASHMOLEAN MUSEUM
OXFORD

colour revolution: victorian art, fashion & design
21 September 2023 to 18 February 2024

Stefano Evangelista, Lena Fritsch, Tea Ghigo, Colin Harrison, Madeline Hewitson, Clare Pollard, Elizabeth Prettejohn, Charlotte Ribeyrol and Matthew Winterbottom have asserted their moral rights to be identified as the authors of this work.

British Library Cataloguing in Publications Data
A catalogue record for this book is available from the British Library

isbn: 978-1-910807-57-6

Catalogue designed by Stephen Hebron

Printed and bound in Great Britain by Gomer Press

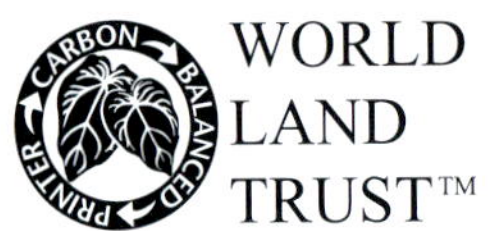

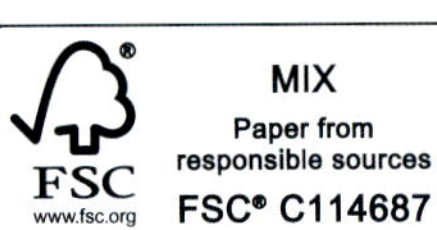

www.carbonbalancedprinter.com
Registration No. CBP2275

For further details of Ashmolean titles please visit:
www.ashmolean.org/shop

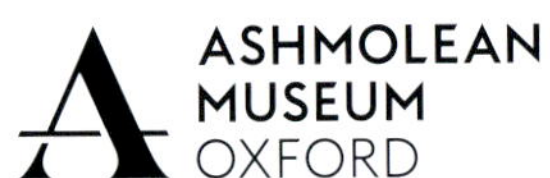

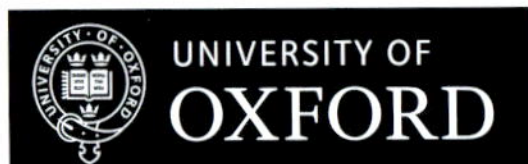

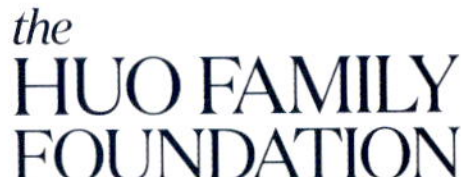

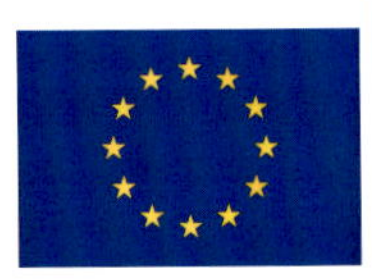

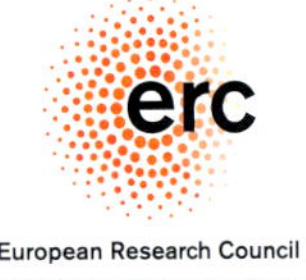

This research undertaken for the Chromotope project received funding from the European Research Council (ERC) under the European Union's Horizon 2020 research and innovation programme (Grant agreement No. 818563)

Exhibition supported by:
Mr Barrie and Mrs Deedee Wigmore
The Patrons of the Ashmolean Museum
The Huo Family Foundation
Kathryn Uhde
Albert Dawson Educational Trust
Henry Moore Foundation
Dr Lee MacCormick Edwards Charitable Foundation
The Anson Charitable Trust

We are most grateful to all our lenders who are supporting our exhibition, especially private lenders who prefer to remain anonymous, and the following:

Manchester Art Gallery
Fashion Museum Bath
Victoria and Albert Museum
The Bodleian Libraries, University of Oxford
The Trustees of the British Museum
The Hunterian, University of Glasgow
Birmingham Museums Trust on behalf of Birmingham City Council
Guildhall Art Gallery, City of London Corporation
Joan Hart Collection
Tate
The President and Fellows of Trinity College Oxford
The British Library
The Devonshire Collections, Chatsworth
The Metropolitan Museum of Art
National Galleries Scotland
National Museums Liverpool, Walker Art Gallery
National Trust, Cragside
Society of Antiquaries of London (Kelmscott Manor)
Amgueddfa Cymru – National Museum of Wales
Collection of Prof. Shane Butler
The Faringdon Collection Trust, Buscot Park
Government Art Collection
Historic Royal Palaces
Museum of the History of Science, University of Oxford
Museu de Montserrat
Trustees of the De Morgan Foundation
Oriel College, University of Oxford
Pitt Rivers Museum, University of Oxford
RIBA Collections, The Royal Institute of British Architects
Jody Sperling
The Whitworth, The University of Manchester
The New Art Gallery Walsall, Permanent Collection
Williamson Art Gallery and Museum, Birkenhead
Private Collection, Classé au titre des monuments historiques par arrêté du 24 janvier 2002

Contents

Foreword

Xa Sturgis
Director, Ashmolean Museum

This catalogue, and the exhibition it accompanies, seeks to blow away the grimy smog of early industrialisation that colours many people's picture of Victorian Britain. It explores the revolutionary and technological-driven explosion of colour production and use that occurred in the middle years of the nineteenth century. As importantly, it seeks to recapture the excitement and anxiety that accompany all such revolutions, as artists, makers and writers embraced, responded to and resisted the new chromatic possibilities. In doing so it help us to look afresh at Victorian artistic production with eyes and minds alert to the extent to which their making and meaning rely upon their use and choice of colour.

The catalogue and exhibition are two of many outputs from a major collaborative research project *Chromotope: the nineteenth-century chromatic turn* supported by the Ashmolean's first (and possibly last) grant from the European Research Council. They emerge from a wide ranging, international and cross-disciplinary collaboration of the most fruitful kind and we are indebted to all collaborators on the project both within the Ashmolean and beyond. I would particularly like to thank the Ashmolean's curators of the exhibition Matthew Winterbottom and Madeline Hewitson and above all their collaborator Charlotte Ribeyrol (Professor of 19th-Century British Literature at Sorbonne University) the research project's 'Principal Investigator' for the energy and acuity she has brought to every aspect of the project and for her unfailing curiosity of mind and generosity of spirit.

If the research project has depended upon wide-ranging collaboration so too has the exhibition itself. So thank you to the many lenders, both institutional and private, for being willing to part with so many treasured objects for the duration of this show. There are many coups to be celebrated within the exhibition, among them the reuniting of the three chromatically distinct versions of a single composition by Albert Moore reassembled for the first time since they left his studio in 1875, thanks to the imaginative generosity of two private lenders and the National Galleries of Scotland.

The exhibition has also been fortunate in its supporters and I would, once again, like to shout my thanks to Barrie and Deedee Wigmore for their exceptional support of the Museum, and our nineteenth-century collections over many years. This exhibition is one of many fruits of this support as the Ashmolean builds both its collection of Victorian decorative arts and its reputation as a centre for the study of this area. But, of course, they are not alone and my thanks are also extended to The Huo Family Foundation; Kathryn Uhde; The Henry Moore Foundation; the Dr Lee MacCormick Edwards Charitable Foundation; The Anson Charitable Trust and the Patrons of the Ashmolean Museum for their invaluable support of the exhibition and this catalogue.

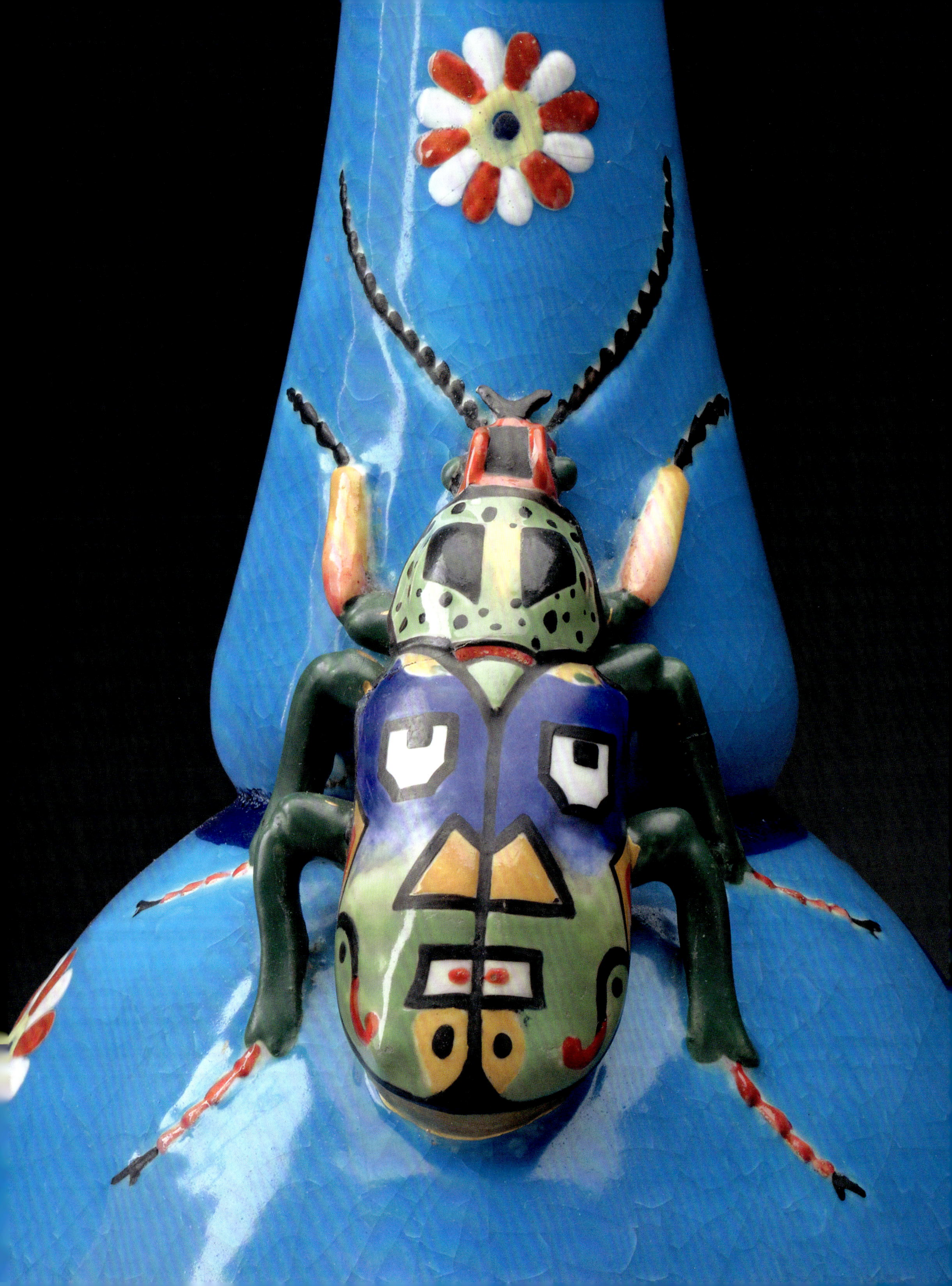

Acknowledgements

This catalogue and the exhibition it accompanies has been a work of fruitful collaboration. As part of the European Research Council funded project, *Chromotope: the nineteenth-century chromatic turn* we have benefitted from innumerable contributions from curators, conservators, scholars and colleagues. Firstly, we would like to thank the partners of *Chromotope*: Sorbonne Université, the VALE research team, Trinity College, Oxford and the Conservatoire des Arts and Métiers (CNAM) as well as members of the Chromotope team: Irene Bilbao, Anne-Laure Carre, Kelly Domoney, Christopher Doogue, Arnaud Dubois, Stefano Evangelista, Clotilde Ferroud, Tea Ghigo, Stella Granier, Colin Harrison, David Howell, Julie Legangneux, and Alessandra Ronetti.

We are also grateful to the authors of individual catalogue essays and in particular, Liz Prettejohn for her preface and support of the exhibition since its inception.

We are indebted to our generous private lenders, lending institutions and their many members of staff that supported research and loans including Lucy Baxter, Claire Breay, Julie Brown, Ann Bukantas, Shane Butler, Stephen Calloway, Andrea Clarke, Caroline Corbeau-Parsons, Max Donnelly, Andrew Dunning, Philip Grover, Sarah Hardy, Joan Hart, Kathy Haslam, Caroline Hedengren, Stephanie Herdrich, Olivia Horsfall Turner, Carol Jacobi, Charlotte Keenan, Julie-Anne Lambert, Miles Lambert, Patricia de Montfort, Victoria Osbourne, Katherine Pearce, Laura-Maria Popoviciu, Judy Rudoe, Emma Sillett, Colin Simpson, Jody Sperling, Siân Stephenson, Matthew Storey, Eleanor Summers, Joyce Townsend, and Florence Tyler.

We have benefitted from many experts who kindly shared their knowledge of particular artists and objects, notably Cassandra Albinson, Megan Aldridge, Tim Barringer, Geoffrey Batchen, Judith Bronkhurst, Barbara Bryant, Mark Eastment, Donato Esposito, Margaretta Frederick, Catherine Futter, Elizabeth St. George, Charlotte Gere, Cora Gilroy-Ware, Erica Hirschler, Olivia Holder, Merlin Holland, Frederick Ilchman, Jessica Insley, David Kastan, Martin Levy, Sophie Lynford, Jan Marsh, Meghan Melvin, Peter Miall, Stephanie Moser, Marenka Thompson-Odlum, Phillipe and Carine Pieters, Katherine (Kerry) Roeder, Malcolm Rogers, Lesley Scott, Richard Trainor, Peter Trippi, Susan Weber, William Whyte, Bernard Williams, Hannah Williamson, Robert Wilson, and Barbara Veith. We would also like to acknowledge speakers and delegates at the 'Glowing Colour' conference held at Worcester College, Oxford in June 2019 for their ideas, questions and conversations that helped to shape the exhibition.

Our sincere thanks go to our colleagues in the Western Art department for their ongoing support. This also extends to members of the Conservation, Photographic Studio and Publications departments for bringing this catalogue to life and in such beautiful form. We also want to recognise the tireless work of our Exhibitions, Interpretation and Registrars teams to bring the exhibition to fruition.

Finally, a personal thank you to our families for their love and encouragement. From Matthew, thank you Alessandro. From Charlotte, thank you Arnaud, Louis and Valentin. And from Madeline, thank you Michael.

Opposite: detail of fig. 64

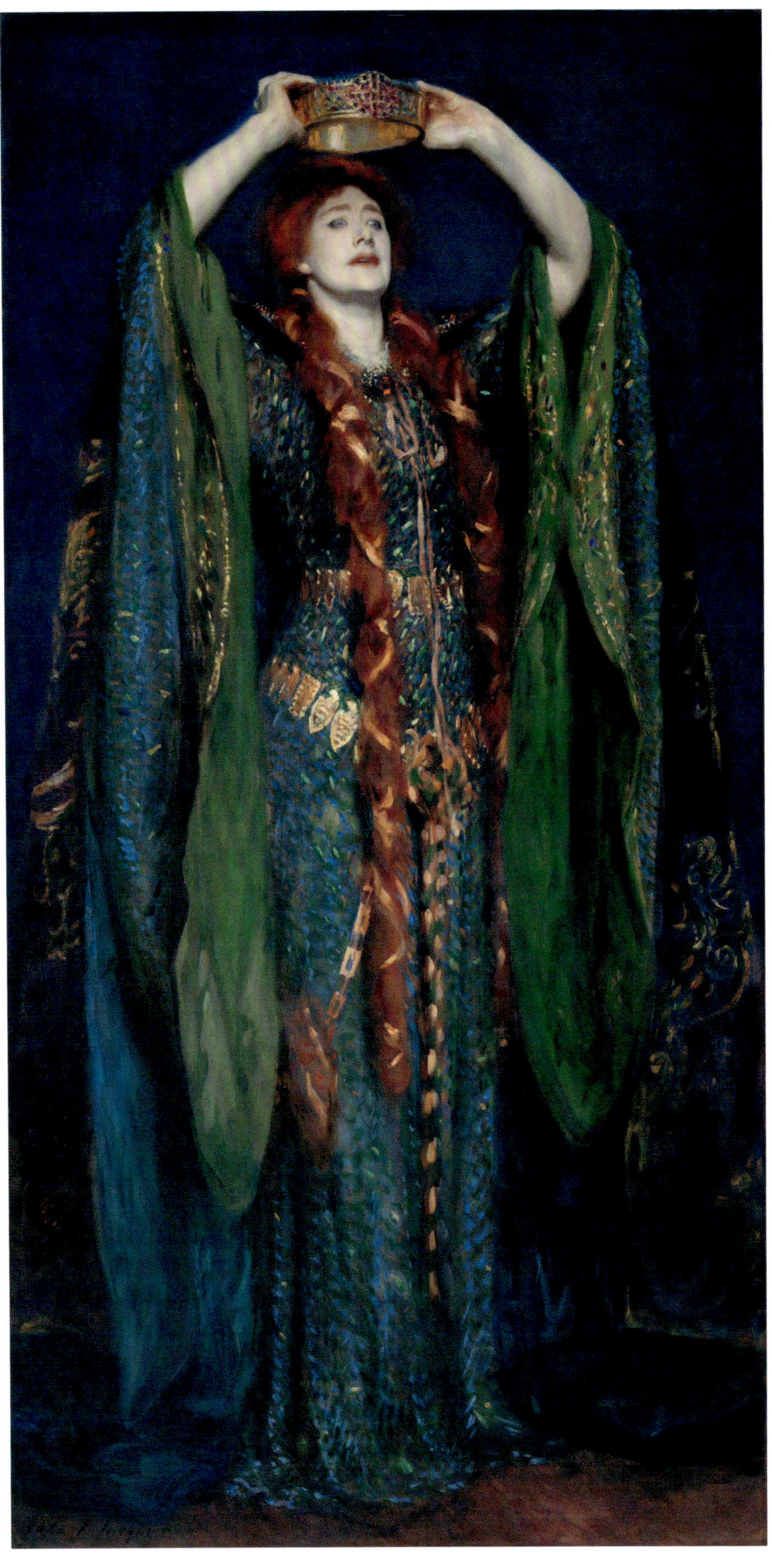

Fig. 1 John Singer Sargent (1856–1925), *Ellen Terry as Lady Macbeth*, 1889. Oil on canvas. Tate, N02053

Preface

Elizabeth Prettejohn

'As the sun colours flowers, so art colours life': it may come as a surprise that this motto adorned the London studio of one of the Victorian era's leading classical painters, Lawrence Alma-Tadema, so famous for his careful scholarship, archaeological precision and meticulous drawing. Compare the youthful words of another Victorian classicist, Frederic Leighton, writing in 1860 to his German teacher and mentor, Eduard von Steinle: 'in spite of my fanatic preference for colour I promised myself to be a draughtsman before I became a colourist'. Classical form might provide the foundation on which these artists built their practice, but it is colour that generates energy and joie de vivre.

'Colour', in Tadema's motto, is a verb – not a thing, but an action, one that propels both nature and art. In this exhibition those two worlds – the one external to us, the other created by human hands – are in constant interplay. The hummingbird becomes a necklace or a fan; the Pre-Raphaelite painter eschews artistic convention to see the colours of the natural world anew; the documentation of scientific fact is transformed into illustrations or photographs of astonishing beauty. Natural and synthetic colours may be difficult to tell apart, and they adorn or enliven everything from earthenware and jewellery to books and manuscripts, slippers and socks.

The mobility or lability of colour was of course nothing new in the Victorian period; it was, indeed, at the heart of the traditional dichotomy in art theory between the reliability of design and the vagaries of colour – between intellectual *disegno* and sensuous *colorito*, in the terminology of the Renaissance historian and theorist Giorgio Vasari. Yet there are good reasons for calling attention to Victorian Britain, with its networks of global connections, as something like a vast laboratory for experimentation in colour. As the essays in this catalogue will explore in more detail, the spirit of experimentation moved fluidly between and among spheres of activity – science, art, technology, industry, fashion, literature. The individuals who populate the following pages are each eminent in their own fields – William Henry Perkin the chemist, Sarah Angelina Acland the photographer, William Burges the architect, Loïe Fuller the dancer – yet they are also prepared to experiment in other disciplines, from archaeology and natural history to new print technologies and theatrical spectacles. To take just one typically complex example, the serpentine dance of iridescent green that conjured Lady Macbeth for audiences at the Lyceum Theatre in 1888 was the result of a collaboration between a supplier of beetle-wing cases, a costume designer (Alice Comyns Carr), an actor (Ellen Terry), and a theatrical manager (Henry Irving), immortalised subsequently by a painter (John Singer Sargent) who must have drawn on all the resources of the artist's colourman (fig. 1). Colour often opened a conduit or built a bridge between disciplines in a Victorian world where professionals in one sphere were not afraid to venture into another, or to share their expertise in unexpected forms of collaboration.

One could say that all these Victorian individuals were artists in some sense, and yet the contribution of professional painters is worth emphasis. Already in 1830, the startling natural observation of John Constable's *Water Meadows near Salisbury* had come under attack as 'a nasty green thing'. The French artists and critics who first encountered British paintings in large numbers, at the Universal Exposition of 1855 in Paris, were startled, and at times shocked, by both the brightness and the juxtapositions of colours, unsanctioned by previous art theory or academic practice. For the seasoned critic Théophile Gautier – in fact an admirer – the riot of 'impossible colour associations' in a British painting almost needed to be translated into a black and white engraving to make it intelligible to French eyes. Some blamed the English climate: French critics were able to sense a radical approach to perception among British artists – an intensity in the effort to observe the natural world without bias or prejudice. French critics did not yet know how this new approach had been encouraged by the writings of John Ruskin, but rumours began to circulate about the programmatic aims of the new group of artists who called themselves 'Pre-Raphaelites'. 'I am really astounded by Hunt's sheep', wrote Eugène Delacroix, the French artist himself renowned as a colourist, in a journal entry of 30 June 1855, with reference to William Holman Hunt's brilliantly coloured *Strayed Sheep*, on display in the Exposition; earlier that month Delacroix had marvelled at the sensitive observation of John Everett Millais's *Order of Release*, noting particularly the red patches on the feet of the sleeping baby – a detail carefully observed from life, though not sanctioned by art theory. Hunt's picture made such a powerful impact that the French art critic Robert de La Sizeranne was still referring to its 'blood-red sheep in indigo bushes' in the 1890s. British colour seemed to impress itself indelibly on the French memory. When Jean des Esseintes, the archetypal aesthete of Joris-Karl Huysmans's novel, *À Rebours* of 1884, imagines what it might be like to visit London, memories of British paintings seen at the universal expositions of previous decades come irresistibly to mind: the 'silvery green tints' of moonlight in Millais's *Eve of St Agnes*, shown in Paris in 1867, and the 'strange colours' of George Frederic Watts's paintings, 'streaked with gamboge and indigo … brushed by an anaemic Michelangelo and retouched by a Raphael drowned in blue'.

The references to Old Master painting, in Huysmans's 'decadent' novel, may seem to move away from the attentiveness to external nature so conspicuous in the art of the earlier Victorian period. Yet this exhibition also shows how inspiration could come from the colours of artefacts and artworks of past ages. The Pre-Raphaelite artists have often been accused of inconsistency in their espousal of both truth-to-nature and reverence for early Renaissance art, but that is a misconception. The new approach to perception that made them see the colours of nature afresh also permitted them to see anew the colours of old art: the bright and light colours of early artists such as Fra Angelico, and the bold juxtapositions of jewel-like hues in the painting of northern European artists such as Van Eyck. These vibrant colours were in striking contrast to the subdued tones – the brown trees and discoloured varnishes – in Old Master paintings of the seventeenth century, formerly revered as precedents for the art student, now disparaged in Ruskin's *Modern Painters* as conventional and falsifying to the colours of the natural world. Paradoxically, the rebellious younger generation of Victorian artists refreshed the colours of their own, modern art by studying the even Older Masters of the fifteenth century and earlier.

In the lectures on aesthetics of the German philosopher G.W.F. Hegel, complexity of colour is characteristic of the latest stage in the development of the arts – the romantic art-form, or what we might call modern art. Victorian artists and designers were prepared to call on all manner of modern technologies in their colour explorations. That is one reason why their works looked so modern, and at times shockingly so, to the art critics of France and other countries. But the new colour technologies emerged as part of what might be seen as an even more profound revolution in ways of seeing colour – a revolution that affected the way the Victorians saw art, including the art of the distant past, as well as nature.

The word 'revolution' should not be used lightly: revolutions are shattering events with disturbing consequences. As the critical responses indicate, the Victorian colour revolution could indeed disturb or shock viewers, even experienced critics well-versed in art theory and practice. A reaction in the next generation tended to reinstate quieter colour harmonies as the sign of 'good taste', from Ben Nicholson's white reliefs to the pared-down aesthetic of the Bauhaus or Scandinavian design. One might ask, indeed, whether colour has a large share of the blame for the nagging doubts about Victorian taste, which – a century and two decades after Queen Victoria's death – still haunt the writings of many art critics and the decisions of many curators. Victorian colour evinces to a high – or, for some of its critics, excessive – degree all the qualities that have made colour suspect in traditional art theory: its appeal to children and the uneducated, its changefulness, its seductiveness, its refusal to stay within bounds.

It requires some bravery, then, to explore Victorian colour in the form of an exhibition, which, after all, keeps the revolution going. If visitors find the colours on display at times disturbing, that will be a sign that the exhibition has fulfilled its aims. Perhaps, though, we can learn most from the artists who revelled in colour – like Leighton, who planned to reward himself for his industry in learning to draw by indulging his native predilection for colour, or Tadema, who filled his studio with hues of both nature and craft: 'As the sun colours flowers, so art colours life.'

1

GLOWING COLOUR

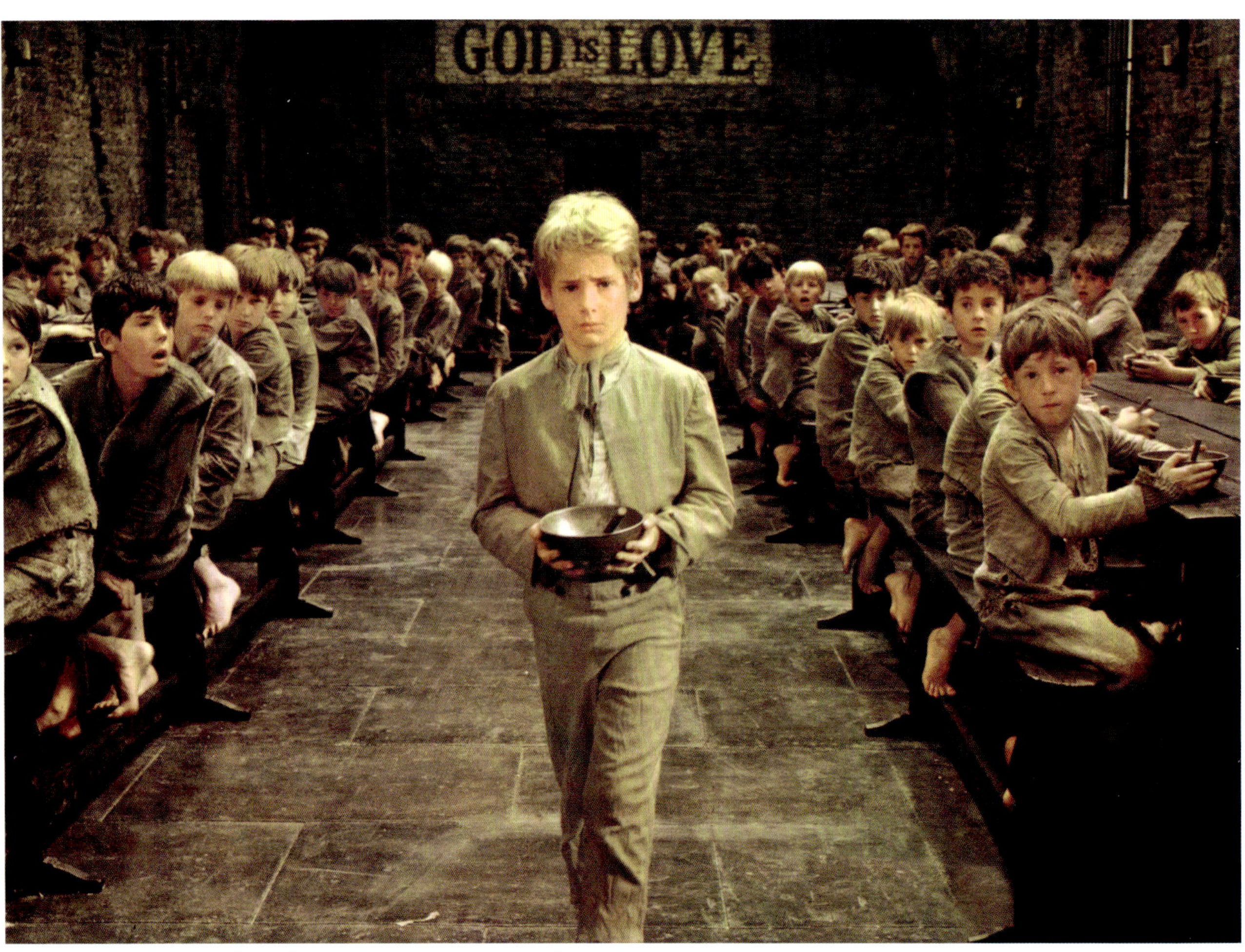

Fig. 2 Still from the 1968 film, *Oliver!*, directed by Carol Reed and starring Mark Lester in the title role

‘The Age of Colour’: Victorian Britain (1837–1901)

Matthew Winterbottom and Charlotte Ribeyrol

Colour is not something that many of us today associate with Victorian Britain. We often think of smoggy, polluted cities, gloomy interiors and sombre clothes. This distorted view is perpetuated by contemporary films and media that frequently portray the era as dark and colourless (fig. 2). In fact, nothing could be further from the truth. As the following chapters will reveal, this was one of the most colourful periods in British history. Colour in all its rainbow hues was appreciated and used as never before. Our Victorian ancestors started a ‘Colour Revolution’[1] that created the modern technicolour world we live in today.

Our distorted view is partly down to the Victorians themselves. Rapid industrialisation created huge, filthy cities and a new urban poor living in appalling conditions. It was this world, evoked so brilliantly by writers such as Charles Dickens, that have helped shape our perceptions of the entire period:

> It was a town of red brick, or of brick that would have been red if the smoke and ashes had allowed it; but as matters stood, it was a town of unnatural red and black like the painted face of a savage. It was a town of machinery and tall chimneys, out of which interminable serpents of smoke trailed themselves for ever and ever, and never got uncoiled. It had a black canal in it, and a river that ran purple with ill-smelling dye, and vast piles of building full of windows where there was a rattling and a trembling all day long, and where the piston of the steam-engine worked monotonously up and down, like the head of an elephant in a state of melancholy madness. It contained several large streets all very like one another, and many small streets still more like one another, inhabited by people equally like one another, who all went in and out at the same hours, with the same sound upon the same pavements, to do the same work, and to whom every day was the same as yesterday and to-morrow, and every year the counterpart of the last and the next.[2]

This monotony and monochromy of modern urban life is well captured by Gustave Doré’s engraving of London, which features an ominous steaming train in the distance (fig. 3).

The critic John Ruskin also described his own times as ‘one seamless stuff of brown’, compared to the life ‘interwoven with white and purple’ of the Middle Ages. ‘They were the ages of gold: ours are the ages of umber’, he wrote.[3] Ruskin’s early concerns about the catastrophic social and environmental

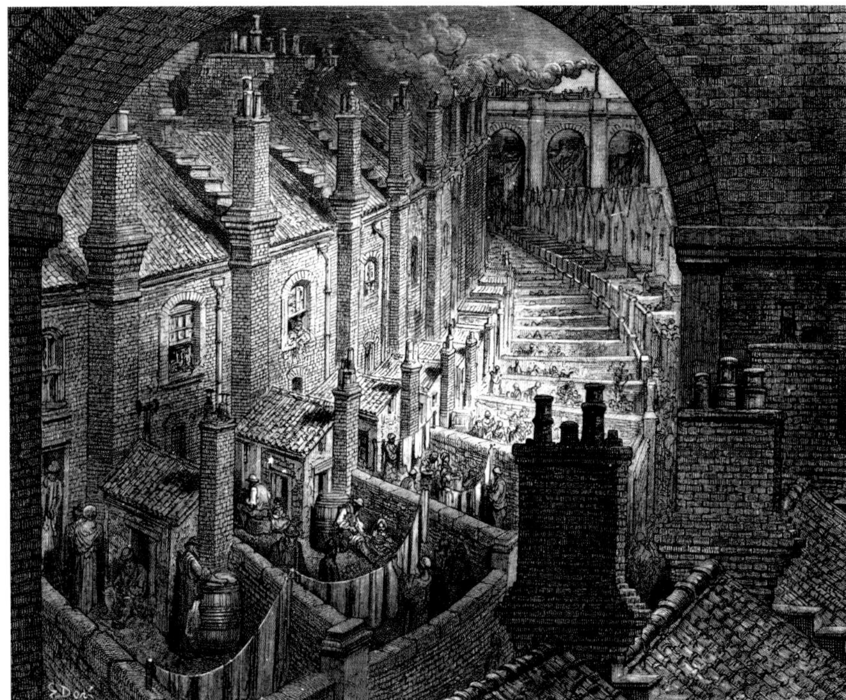

Fig. 3 Gustave Doré (1832–1883), 'Over London by Rail', from *London: A Pilgrimage*, 1872. Wood engraving. Science Museum Group London

consequences of industrialisation are still relevant today. Even Oxford – where Ruskin lived and worked for most of his life – was affected, despite being far from the industrial heartlands:

> The first time I recognized the clouds brought by the plague-wind as distinct in character was in walking back from Oxford, after a hard day's work, to Abingdon, in the early spring of 1871 … For the sky is covered with grey cloud; – not rain-cloud, but a dry black veil, which no ray of sunshine can pierce; partly diffused in mist, feeble mist, enough to make distant objects unintelligible, yet without any substance, or wreathing, or colour of its own … It looks partly as if it were made of poisonous smoke; very possibly it may be: there are at least two hundred furnace chimneys in a square of two miles on every side of me.[4]

Britain was then in the vanguard of the Industrial Revolution. Its population doubled between 1801 and 1851, and doubled again between 1851 and 1901. Millions poured into her growing cities to work in the new factories. In 1801 only 17 percent of Britain's population lived in towns and cities. By 1851 this had increased to 51 percent, and for the first time in history more people lived in cities than the countryside. By 1891, an astonishing 72 percent of British people were urban dwellers. While this rapid industrialisation did bring appalling pollution, disease and slums, it also brought unprecedented wealth and power for Britain and its Empire.

The following poem by 'A Lancashire Lady' was written during the so-called Cotton Famine of the 1860s, when many of Lancashire's mills halted production due to the shortage of American cotton caused by the Civil War. While acknowledging that the terrible pollution caused by the mill chimneys has eased, the writer here pleads for them to start working again so the starving workers can be paid:

Traveller on the Northern Railway!
Look and learn, as on you speed;
See the hundred smokeless chimneys,
Learn their tale of cheerless need.

Ah! perchance the landscape fairer
Charms your taste, your artist-eye;
Little do you guess how dearly
Costs that now unclouded sky.

'How much prettier is this county!'
Says the careless passer-by;
'Clouds of smoke we see no longer,
What's the reason? – Tell me why.

'Better far it were, most surely,
Never more such clouds to see,
Bringing taint o'er nature's beauty,
With their foul obscurity.'

Thoughtless fair one! from yon chimney
Floats the golden breath of life;
Stop that current at your pleasure!
Stop! and starve the child – the wife.

Ah! to them each smokeless chimney
Is a signal of despair;
They see hunger, sickness, ruin,
Written in that pure, bright air.

...

Rather pray that peace, soon bringing
Work and plenty in her train,
We may see these smokeless chimneys
Blackening all the land again.'[5]

Such was the duel-edged nature of the Industrial Revolution. It simultaneously 'blackened the land' but brought colour to the masses.

This was not just a metaphor: in 1856 chemist William Perkin succeeded in turning coal – the very stuff of the Industrial Revolution – into colour. This discovery was soon followed by a rainbow of new, coal tar-based aniline dyes which were first publicly displayed at the London International Exhibition of 1862 – a pivotal event which led the *New York Times* correspondent to write with irony about the bright hues flaunted by modern fashionistas across the world:

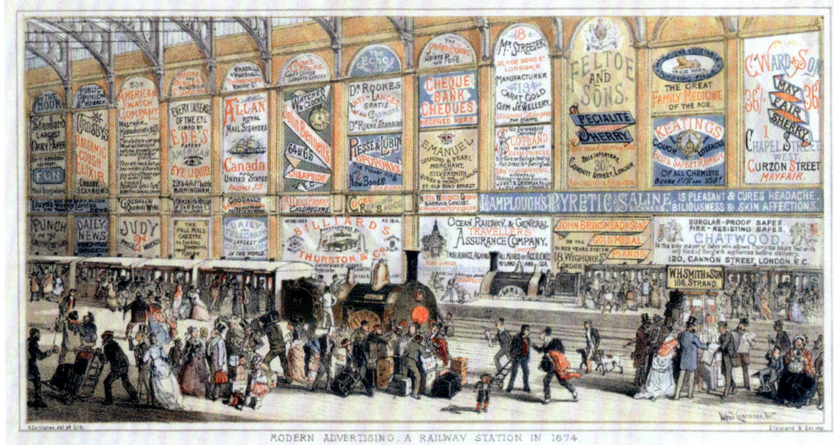

Fig. 4 Alfred Concanen (1835–1886), *Modern Advertising: A Railway Station, in 1874*. Coloured lithograph. Showing a busy railway station. The station walls are covered in posters, advertising everything from sherry to medical remedies and magazines

> Does it ever occur to Angelina, as she floats magnificently down Broadway, in all the lustre of youth and fashion, that the exquisite dress she wears, and whose faultless sheen seems to be robbed from the dewy blushes of Spring, is in fact dipped and steeped in the essence of vile, smoky, stinky, crackly English coal? … Yes, frightful as it may seem, our wives and sweethearts are gradually becoming carboniferous, and the day may not be far distant when we shall have to hand them to dinner with a pair of tongs.[6]

By 1862, the Colour Revolution had indeed transformed the experience of colour for all sections of society, from the clothes people wore to the food they ate (fig. 4).[7] This was the 'Age of Colour',[8] which soon spread from Britain across the world, as importations of pigments and dye stuffs from the colonies were disrupted by the cheaper aniline dyes.

So why is the Victorian age still perceived today in terms of blackness and bleakness? This may be because Queen Victoria herself has skewed our view on the era. The 40 years she spent in black mourning dress following the death of her beloved Prince Albert in 1861 have fixed a morbid image of her in the popular imagination (fig. 5). Before her husband's death the queen had enjoyed wearing colourful clothes, but – unlike her many later mourning dresses – few of these dresses have survived. The queen helped popularise the new aniline dyes in the late 1850s and famously wore bright purple to the wedding of her eldest daughter in 1858. She and Prince Albert even enjoyed dressing up in colourful fancy dress for the balls they held at Buckingham Palace in the 1840s and 1850s (fig. 6). The royal couple commissioned an extraordinary new ballroom for Buckingham Palace that was decorated with colourful Renaissance-style decoration by Ludwig Grüner. Shut up following the death of Prince Albert – and blackened by 40 years of London's filthy air – the ballroom's colourful decoration was replaced by Edward VII in the early twentieth century with an anodyne scheme in white and gold.

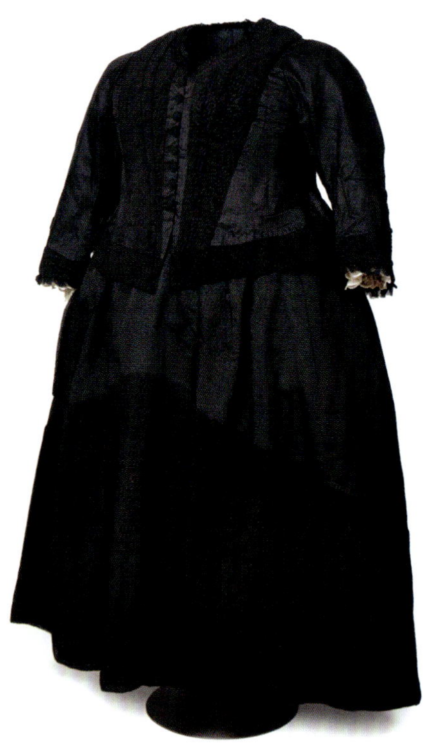

Fig. 5 Queen Victoria's mourning dress, *c.*1890. Black silk. Historic Royal Palaces

Our distorted, monochromatic view of the Victorians is also shaped by the advent of photography. While allowing us to see the actual faces of our ancestors for the first time, early monochrome photographs could not convey the rich colours of the world in which they lived. Compare the monochrome photograph of Louise, Duchess of Devonshire, wearing her Queen Zenobia dress in 1897 with the extraordinary colours of the surviving dress (figs 7, 8). While it is true that men's clothing did get progressively more sombre from the 1840s onwards, women's clothes were often brilliantly coloured – sometimes shockingly so (fig. 9). Within the confines of their own homes, even men might indulge in colourful smoking jackets or slippers, challenging our traditional view of nineteenth-century 'men in black' (see pp. 96–7).[9]

The Colour Revolution was not just about the invention of new synthetic colours, but a broader cultural phenomenon which affected colour perception as well as colour production. Discussions about the properties of light and spectral colours which Isaac Newton had explored in *Opticks* (1704) were no longer confined to scientific circles. Following in the footsteps of Newton and

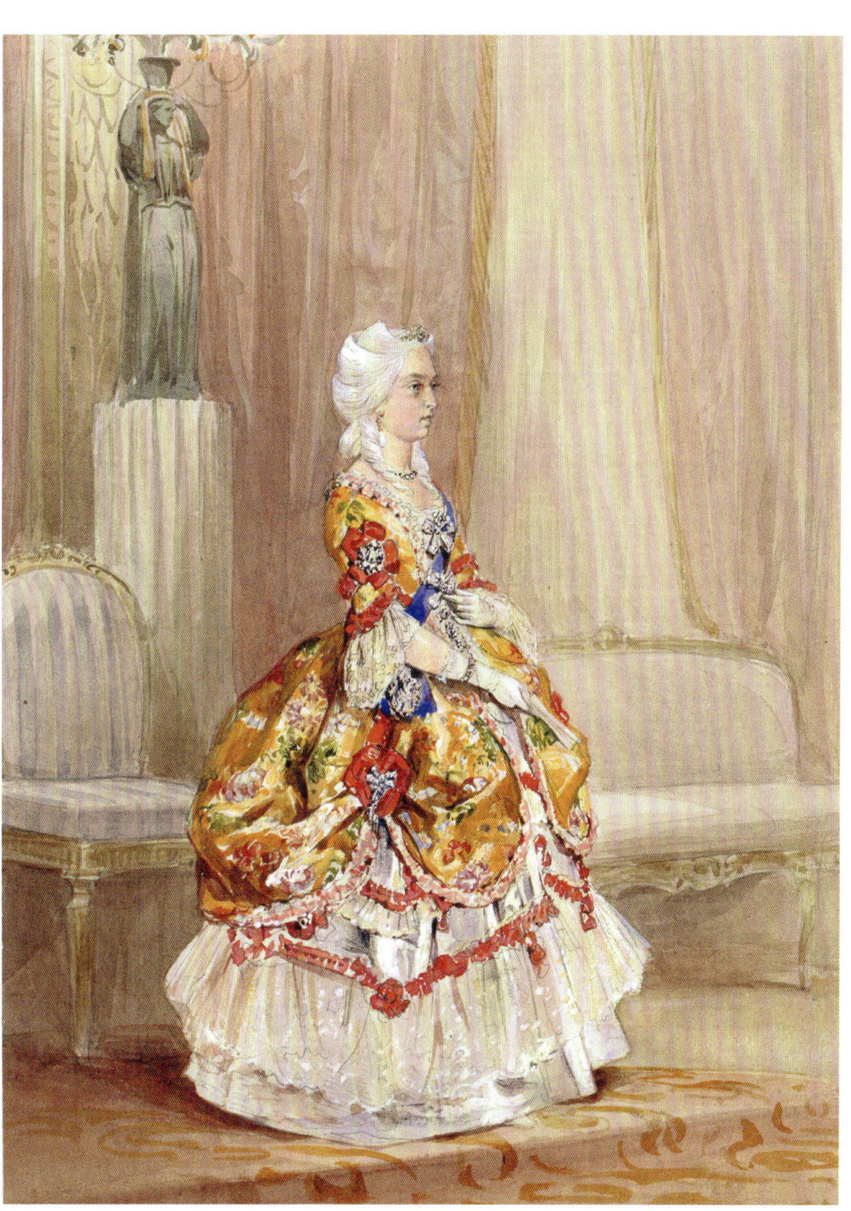

Fig. 6 Louis Hague (1806–1885), *Queen Victoria in costume for the 1745 Fancy Ball, 6 June 1845*, 1845. Watercolour and bodycolour over pencil. Royal Collection Trust, RCIN 913347

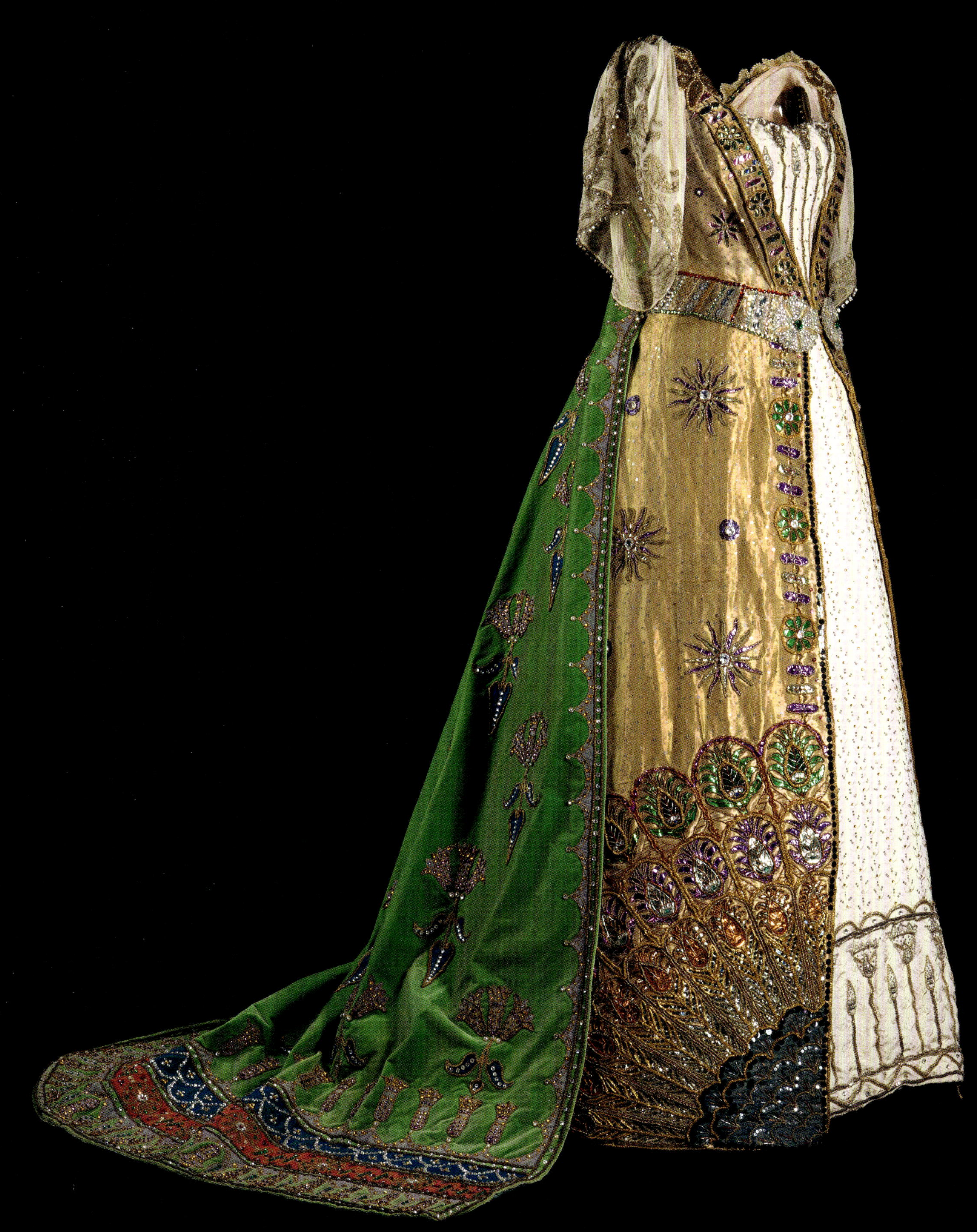

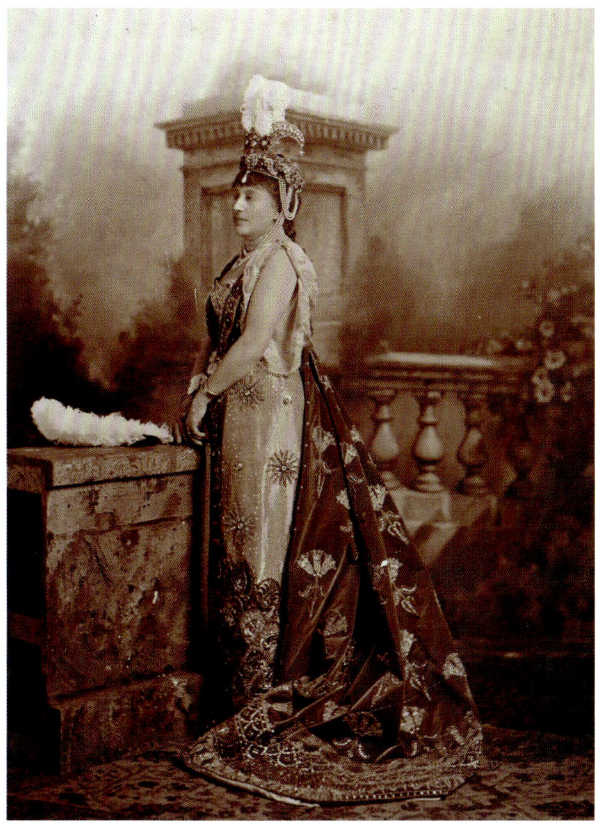

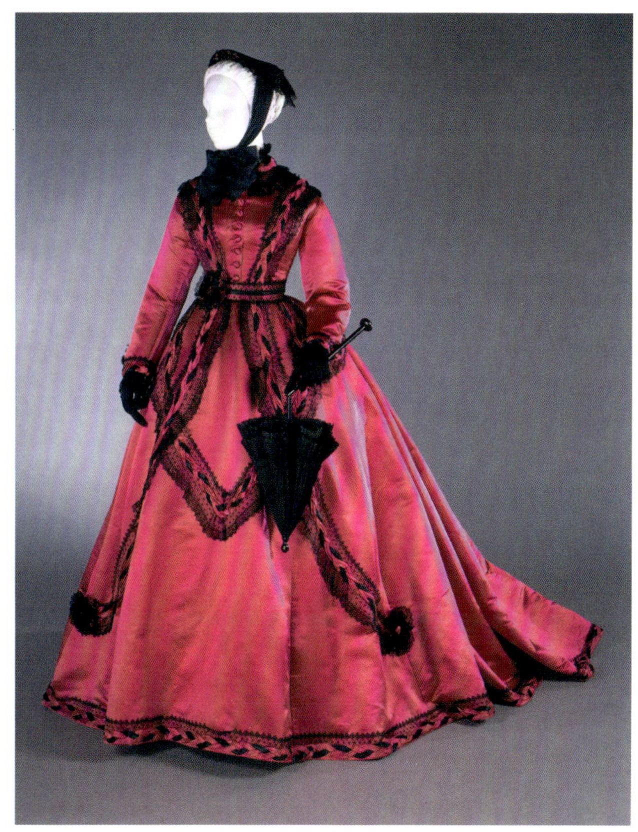

Opposite: Fig. 7 Queen Zenobia dress by House of Worth, Paris. Worn by Louise, Duchess of Devonshire, to the Devonshire House Ball in 1897. The Devonshire Collections, Chatsworth

Above left: Fig. 8 The Duchess of Devonshire as Zenobia, Queen of Palmyra, by James Lafayette (1853–1923), 1897. Photogravure. National Portrait Gallery, London, NPG AX4100

Above right: Fig. 9 Dress, possibly American, *c.*1866–8. Magenta silk satin with black silk satin and black cotton lace. Philadelphia Museum of Art

Thomas Young's trichromatic theory, which established the existence of three types of photoreceptors in the eye, the Scottish mathematician and physicist James Clerk Maxwell further analysed the mechanisms of colour vision. In 1861, he used his findings to create the first durable colour photograph of a tartan ribbon using red, green and blue filters (fig. 10). From 1899 E. Sanger Shepherd introduced a slightly modified, three-colour process, so that for the first time amateur photographers could attempt their own colour photographs. Sarah Acland, the daughter of Ruskin's friend Sir Henry Acland, was a pioneer in this field (see pp. 74–7).

Although colour photography would only reach a much wider audience after the Lumière brothers patented the autochrome in 1903,[10] scientific investigation into colour perception – coupled with technological progress – fed into popular culture throughout the nineteenth century. This was due to the invention, or improvement, of pre-film animation devices such as magic lanterns, phenakistoscopes, chromatropes or zoetropes (fig. 11), which turned the modern world into a fascinating kaleidoscope.

The multiplication of colour stimuli in everyday life was, however, also causing concern. As scientists strove to understand the workings of the 'colour sense' – and what was perceived at the time as the 'pathologies' of colour-blindness, or synaesthesia – it soon became apparent that the way colour was consumed needed to be more closely monitored.[11] The fear of the effect of colour on the supposedly more impressionable masses was heightened by new types of

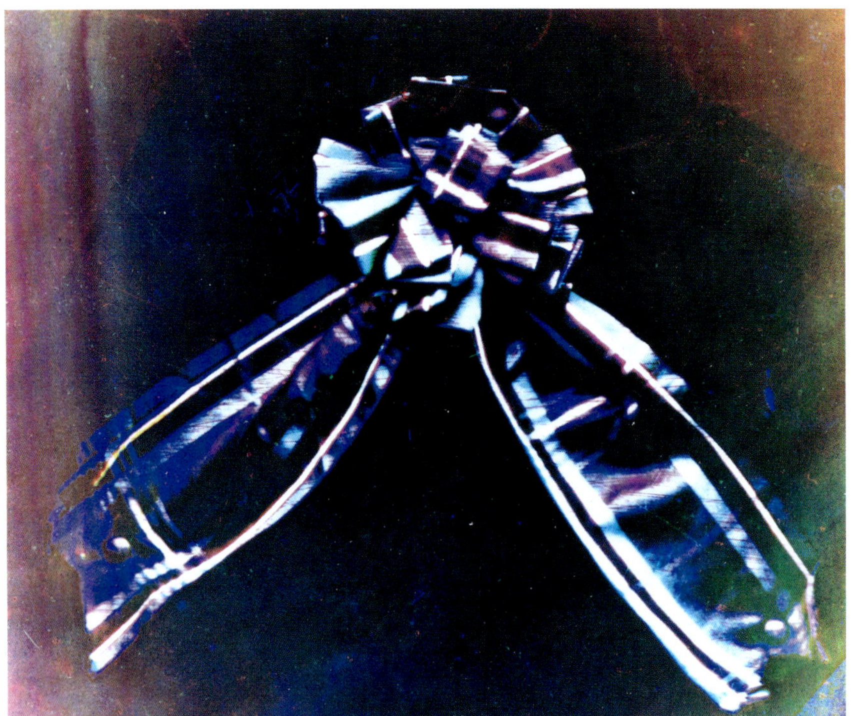

Fig. 10 Colour photograph of a tartan ribbon by James Clerk Maxwell (1831–1879) and Thomas Sutton (1819–1875), *c.*1930s (original 1861). Science Museum Group

lighting, which could make certain hues appear more garish and alluring. The success of the proto-cinematic performances of the 'Electric Fairy' Loïe Fuller, who used both coloured gel filters and coloured lights for her 'magical' dances, was further evidence of the highly sensual appeal of colour.[12]

The emergence of a new type of colourful visual culture therefore required more control. This may explain why so many essays and manuals offering guidance on how colours should be arranged (in clothes or at home – the two often being related) were published during this period.[13] *The Principles of Harmony and Contrast of Colours* (1839) devised by French chemist Michel Eugène Chevreul (fig. 12) is possibly the clearest example of a new urge to classify colour. Its starting point was a complaint from the weavers at the Gobelins Dye Works about the dullness of the black dyes produced by the dyeing department, of which Chevreul was in charge. Having tested the questionable wools, he found that the quality of the dye was not at fault: the blacks looked dull not because of their chemical composition, but because of their juxtaposition with certain other colours. Chevreul's essay and colour wheel (fig. 13) would later become hugely influential in Impressionist and Neo-Impressionist circles.[14] But even before these 'Principles' were translated into English in 1854, Mary Philadelphia Merrifield, a British art and fashion writer who made a name for herself by translating medieval colour treatises, discussed Chevreul's impact in an article on Owen Jones's polychrome decoration for the 1851 Crystal Palace (fig. 14). This important text – 'The Harmony of Colours as Exemplified in the Exhibition' – not only highlights the modernity of Jones's colour scheme, but also reveals the newly acquired expertise of women in the chromatic field.[15]

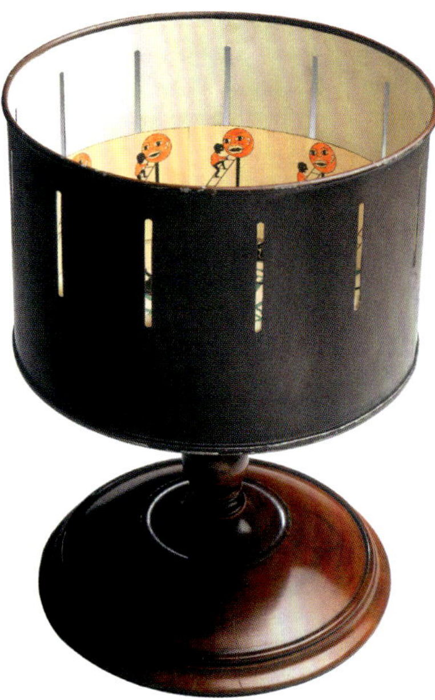

Fig. 11 Victorian zoetrope, National Science Museum Group

Right: Fig. 12 Michel Eugène Chevreul (1776–1889) *De la loi du contraste simultané des couleurs*, 1839. Bodleian Library, University of Oxford, (Vet.) 1856 d.10 (Atlas)

Far right: Fig. 13 'Premier cercle chromatique renfermant les couleurs franches', from Michel Eugène Chevreul (1776–1889), *Des couleurs et de leurs applications aux arts industriels à l'aide des cercles chromatiques*, 1864

DE LA LOI

CONTRASTE SIMULTANÉ

DES COULEURS

M. E. CHEVREUL,

Atlas.

PARIS.

PITOIS-LEVRAULT ET Ce, LIBRAIRES,

CERCLE CHROMATIQUE

Mr CHEVREUL

RENFERMANT

LES COULEURS FRANCHES

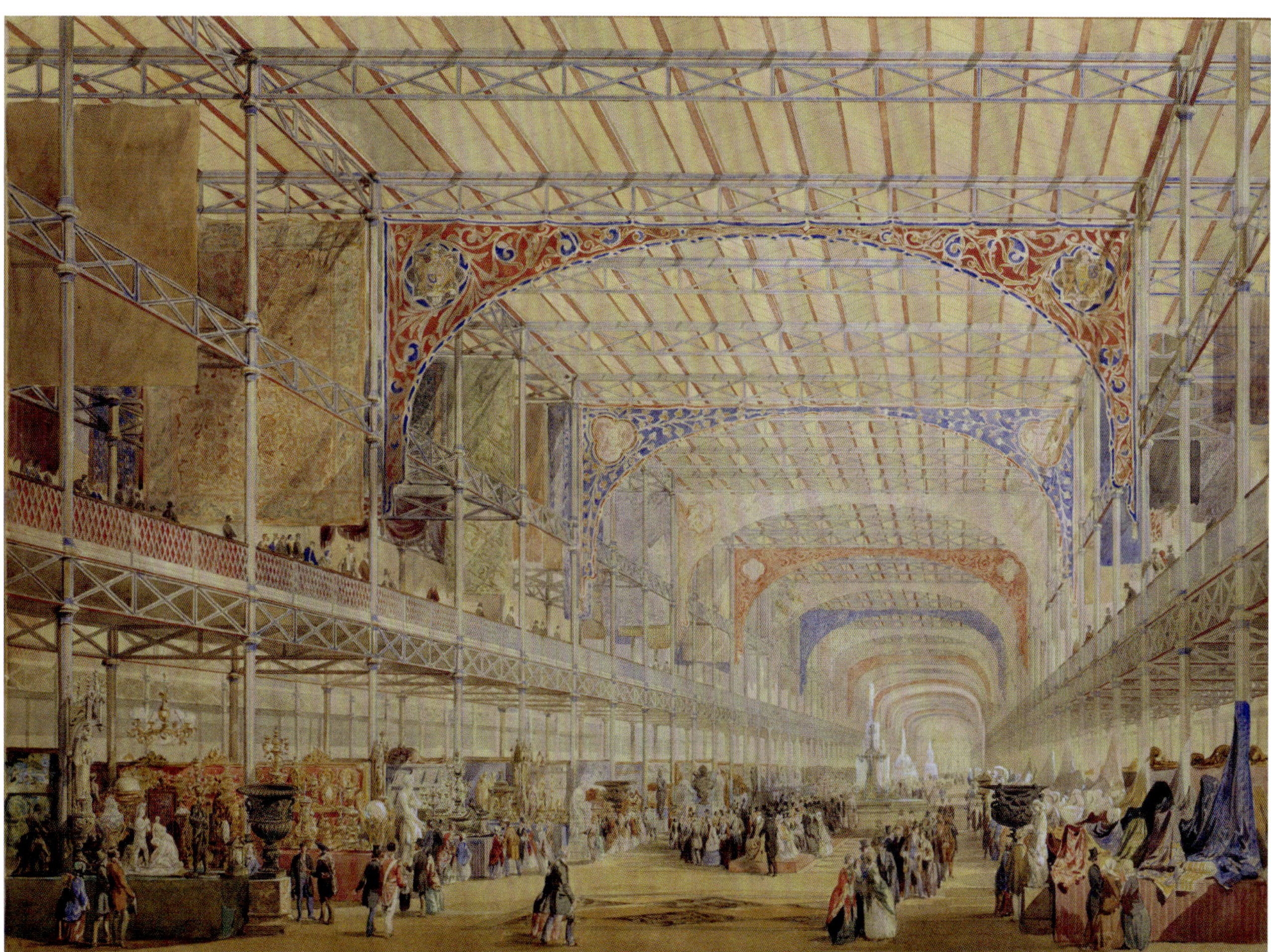

Fig. 14 William Simpson (1823–1899), *Interior of the Crystal Palace*, *c.*1851. Watercolour. Victoria and Albert Museum, London, 546-1897

GOETHE'S

THEORY OF COLOURS;

TRANSLATED FROM THE GERMAN:

WITH NOTES BY

CHARLES LOCK EASTLAKE, R.A., F.R.S.

"Cicero varietatem proprìè in coloribus nasci, hinc in alienum migrare existimavit. Certè non alibi natura copiosius aut majore lasciviâ opes suas commendavit. Metalla, gemmas, marmora, flores, astra, omnia denique quæ progenuit suis etiam coloribus distinxit; at venia debeatur si quis in tam numerosâ rerum sylvâ caligaverit."

CELIO CALCAGNINI.

LONDON:
JOHN MURRAY, ALBEMARLE STREET.
1840.

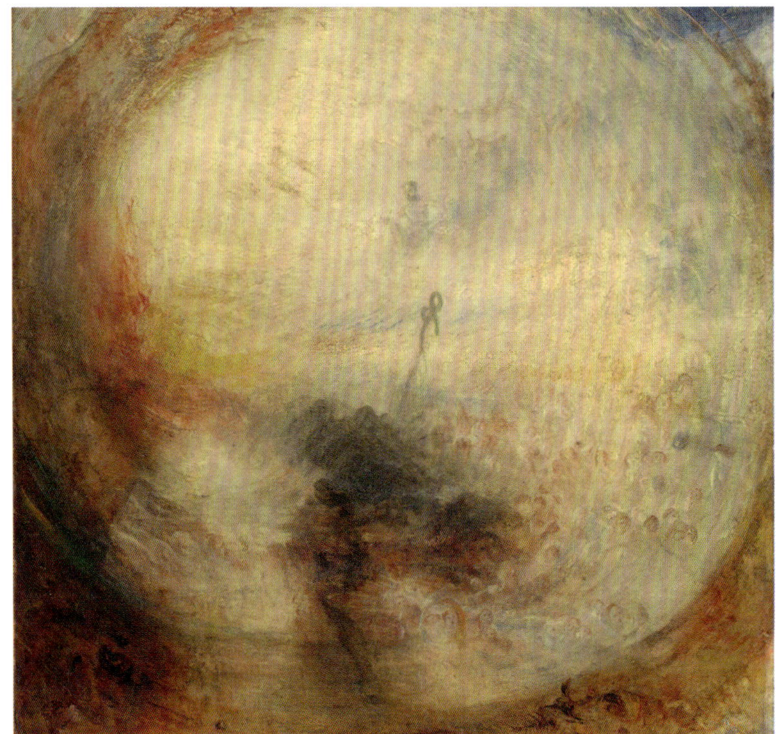

As the experience of colour changed, attitudes towards colour evolved. Since the Renaissance, colour had been considered secondary to design. It was seen as less intellectual, feminine, 'primitive' and even dangerous.[16] Even Johann Wolfgang von Goethe in his *Theory of Colours* (1810) claimed that 'savage nations, uneducated people, and children have a great predilection for vivid colours'.[17] Goethe's text (fig. 15) was nonetheless a romantic rebellion against Newton's objective attempts at measuring colour, introducing the key idea that hue also had a physiological and psychological effect on the mind and mood of the observer. This greatly influenced Joseph Mallord William Turner, who read *Theory of Colours* in Charles Lock Eastlake's 1840 translation, and even directly referenced 'Goethe's theory' in some of his works (fig. 16).

With a similarly Romantic distrust of scientific classifications – and their 'unweaving' of the beautiful rainbow of nature – Ruskin celebrated the sacredness of colour. He argued that colour was a divine gift from God that should be celebrated and embraced just as it had been during the Middle Ages in stained glass, illuminated manuscripts and sumptuous textiles. Leaving all 'rules' aside, Ruskin believed that the beautiful – God-given – colours of the natural world should inspire and guide the 'instinct' of the colourist.[18]

Ruskin was therefore particularly careful to distinguish the colours of modernity from the colours of the past. He loved colour, but hated anilines because of their industrial origin. Similarly, William Morris advocated the use of ancient organic pigments. This explains why he could admire the beautiful purple of Arthur Hughes's *April Love* (of which he was the first owner) (fig. 83, p. 90), while loathing the newly invented mauve. The problem, simply, was not

Above left: Fig. 15 Johann Wolfgang von Goethe (1749–1832), *Goethe's Theory of Colours; translated from the German: with notes by Charles Lock Eastlake*, 1840. Bodleian Library, University of Oxford, Fielder J.1120

Above right: Fig. 16 J.M.W. Turner (1775–1851), *Light and Colour (Goethe's Theory) – The Morning after the Deluge – Moses Writing the Book of Genesis*, 1843. Oil on canvas. Tate, N00532 the hue itself but the material composition of the colour. Hughes's purple was not aniline; pigment analysis has revealed that it was a mixture of organic red madder and cobalt blue.[19]

The new understanding of colour production and colour perception during this period is often said to have fostered abstraction in painting, and Impressionism in particular. But the works of the Pre-Raphaelites and their followers tell a different story: their figurative paintings in jewel-like hues indicate nostalgia for more meaningful, age-old colouring practices. The Victorian age was indeed not just a period of industrial progress, but one marked by revivals, whether Greek or Gothic. The fascination with ancient colours – including those of the Assyrian, Egyptian or Pompeiian past – was fostered by archaeological excavations, which in turn fuelled the imagination of artists like Edward Poynter and Lawrence Alma-Tadema (fig. 121, p. 141).

And yet the Colour Revolution did not entail a simplistic opposition between past and present. Many Victorian painters and writers were in fact deeply engaged in this scientific, technological and chromatic turning-point. Some artists welcomed modern pigments, as shown by the toxic emerald green used by John Everett Millais for *The Woodman's Daughter* (fig. 17).[20] Oscar Wilde himself flaunted an aniline-dyed green carnation at the première of *Lady Windermere's Fan* (1892), and yet claimed in the *Picture of Dorian Gray* (1891) that one should 'never trust a woman who wears mauve' because the common dye was seen as vulgar as well as potentially unstable.[21] Such 'coloristic snubbery'[22] was widespread in *fin-de-siècle* artistic circles as aesthetes rejected gaudy anilines in favour of more subtle artistic colours or tertiary hues. These were defined by designer Christopher Dresser in the colour section of his *Principles of Decorative Design* (1873) as the mixture of two secondary colours such as olive, citrine or russet. In the age of mass-produced and mass-consumed colour, the complex, poetic names of these tertiary hues were evidently intended to act as 'class markers.'[23]

This conflict between the colours of the past and the coal-tar based hues of modernity strikingly converged at the 1862 International Exhibition, where the newly created firm of Morris, Marshall, Faulkner & Co. first exhibited. Although now 'almost forgotten',[24] this exhibition not only displayed Japanese artefacts and the new range of Perkin's aniline dyes for the first time, but also presented monuments to the polychromy of the past – from John Gibson's polychrome statue *The Tinted Venus* (fig. 95, p. 106) and Minton's majolica fountain, to John Bell's *Daughter of Eve*, which translated skin colour into bronze electrotype (fig. 112, p. 127). Moreover, the show, visited by millions, received attention from all sections of society in Britain, as well as unprecedented international media coverage in colour thanks to the new technique of chromolithography. This technique, invented in 1837 by Godefroy Engelmann, was not the first colour printing process, but it was the first to use aniline inks and to enable standardised polychrome printing on an industrial scale. The London publisher Day & Son was a leader in the field. The firm, which had printed Owen Jones's *Grammar of Ornament* (fig. 18), with its distinct, flat-colour style, was one of the first British printers to adopt steam-powered presses in the early

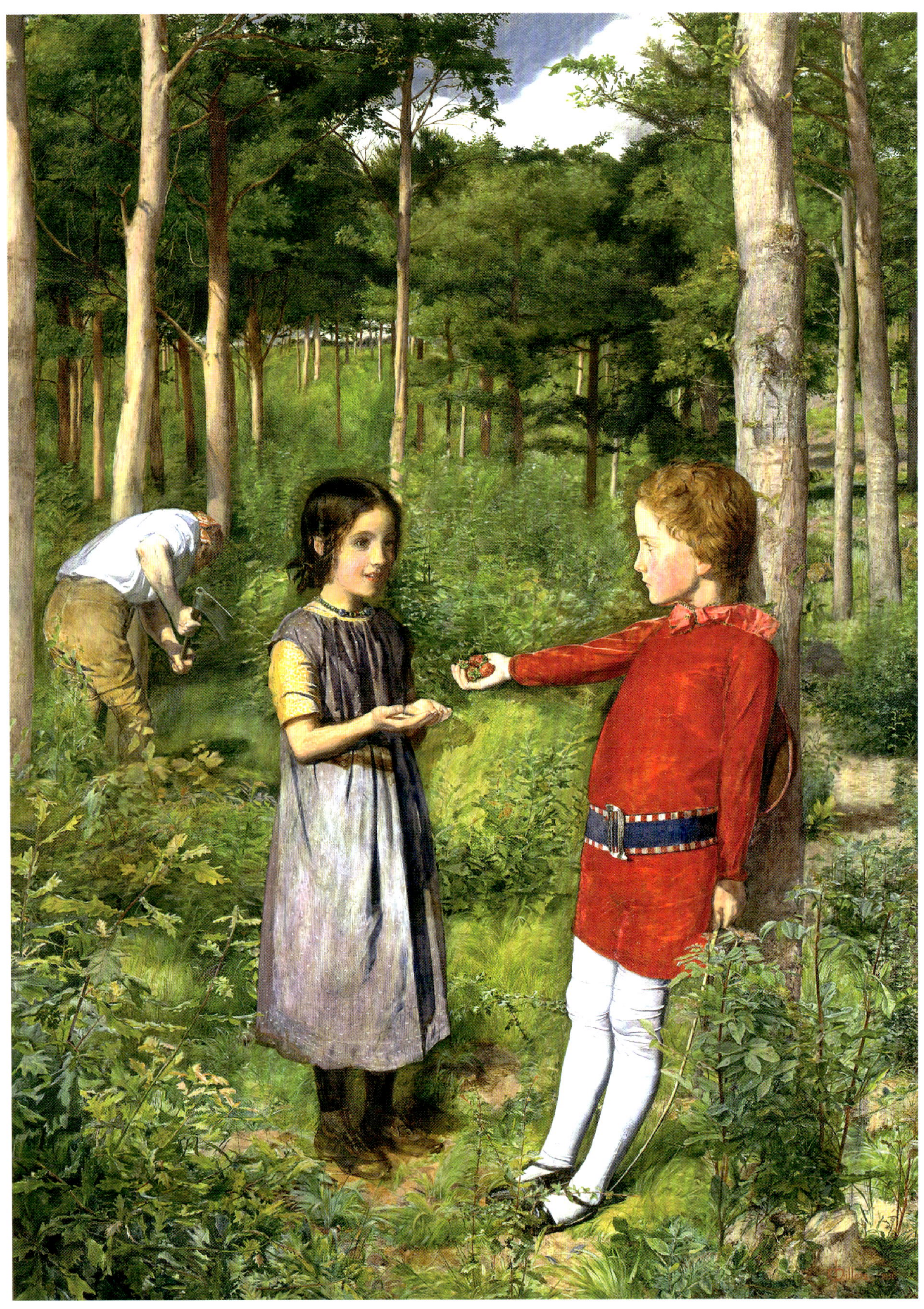

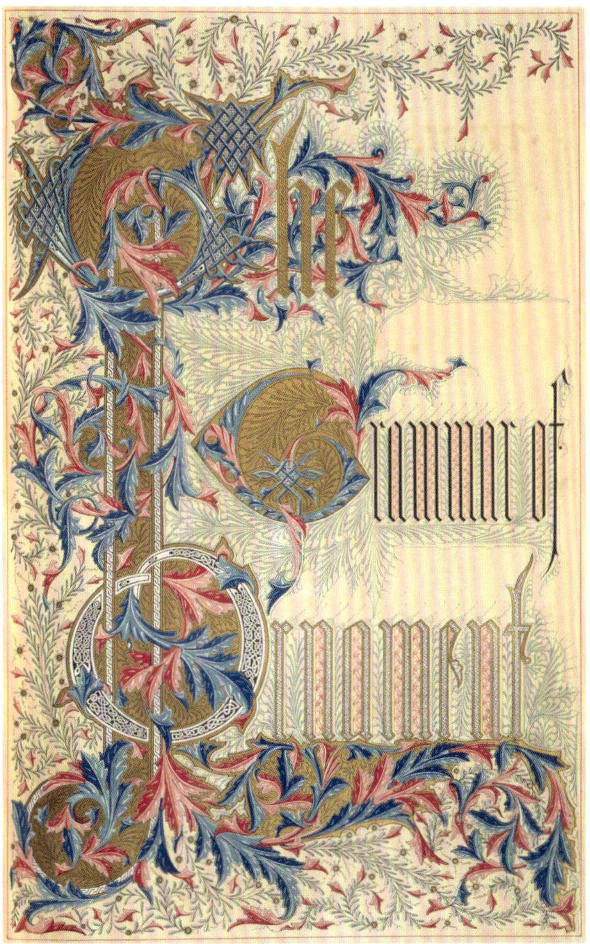

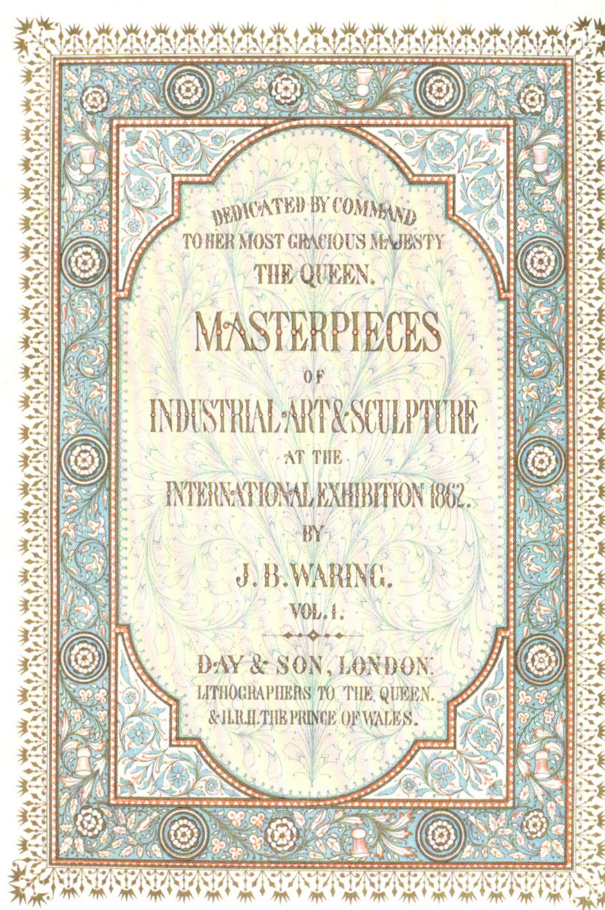

Opposite: Fig. 17 John Everett Millais (1829–1896), *The Woodman's Daughter*, 1851. Oil on canvas. Guildhall Art Gallery, City of London Corporation

Above left: Fig. 18 Owen Jones (1809–1874) and Francis Bedford (1815–1894), *Grammar of Ornament*, 1856, frontispiece. Chromolithograph. Metropolitan Museum of Art, New York, gift of Friends of the Thomas J. Watson Library

Above right: Fig. 19 J.B. Waring (1823–1875), *Masterpieces of Industrial Art & Sculpture at the International Exhibition, 1862*, 1863, frontispiece. Chromolithograph. Bodleian Library, University of Oxford, Johnson b.67

1860s, as shown by John Burley Waring's three-volume tome *Masterpieces of Industrial Art & Sculpture at the International Exhibition, 1862*, (fig. 19). A 'visual symptom of a new era of consumerism in Britain', the technique enabled colour printing to become much cheaper and – more importantly – to bring 'color [sic] to all aspects of printed life, from books and magazines to greetings cards and calendars, from food packaging and sheet music to scientific illustrations, charts, and maps, as well as reproductions of paintings'.[25] By 1892 *The British and Colonial Printer and Stationer* even claimed that 'throughout the length and breadth of the kingdom there is not one domicile into which the chromo has not penetrated'[26], which confirms how far colour had become the sign of modernity.

It is this complex, multifaceted history of nineteenth-century colour which this exhibition and catalogue tells, using a selection of artworks – paintings, textiles, ceramics, sculpture and photography – to reflect the kaleidoscope of the Victorian chromatic experience.

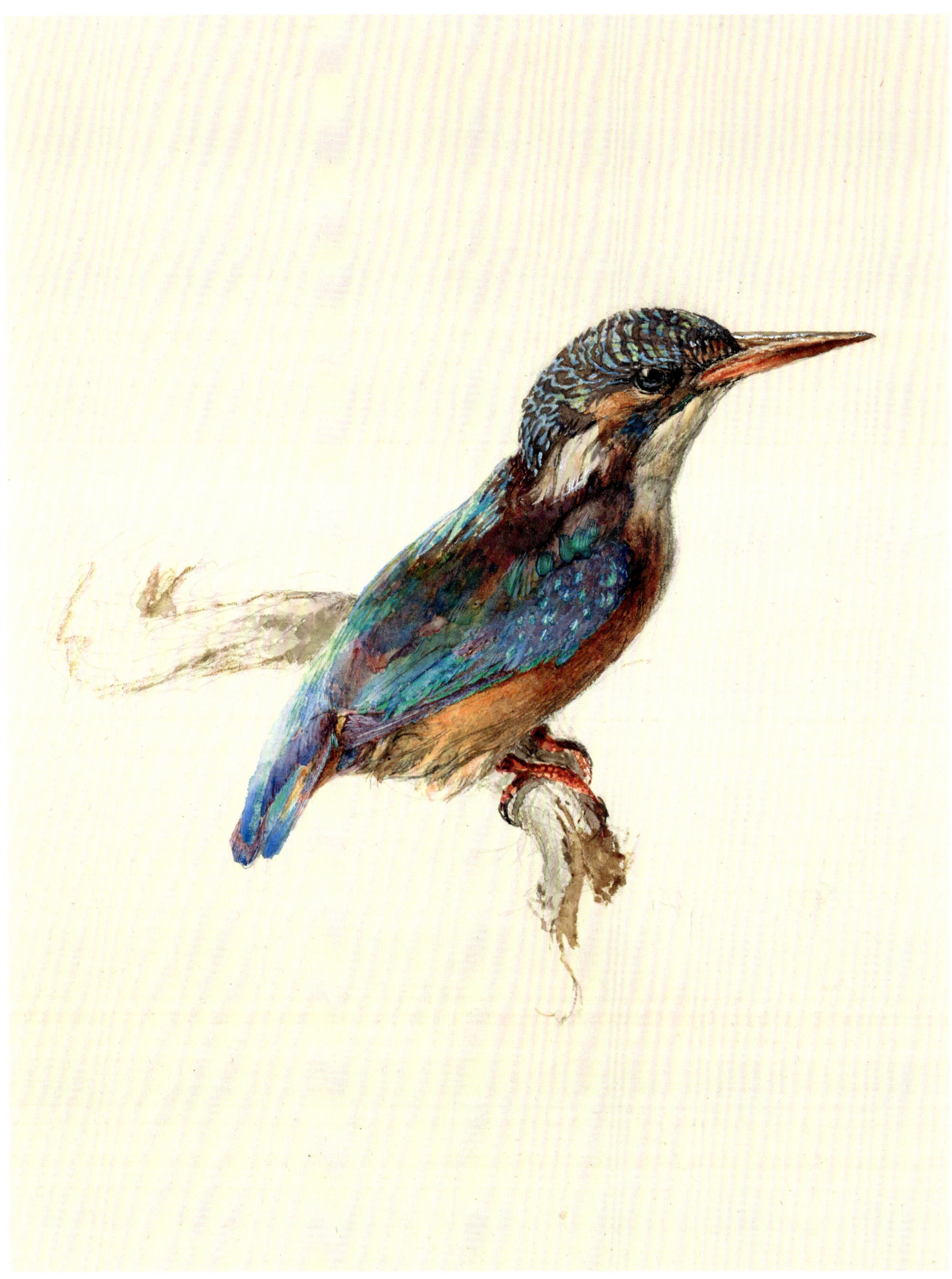

Colour in Ruskin's Teachings

Colin Harrison

From the mid-1840s until the mid-1880s, one of the most persistent strains in Ruskin's astonishingly varied output was his interest in the practical teaching of drawing. It began with informal advice to individual correspondents, and culminated in the formation of two great teaching collections: one compiled during his first period as Slade Professor in the University of Oxford and officially transferred to the University in 1875; the other given in the same year to the Guild of St George, which Ruskin founded in 1871 in Walkley, Sheffield. Here, the museum combined copies of the Old Masters, original drawings and watercolours, and medieval manuscripts with specimens of geology and an extensive library, with the intention of improving the lives of the local workmen and providing inspiration and stimulation. The collections at Oxford were intended to encourage students and townspeople to copy works of art not to become artists, but to understand the work and their surroundings. They include a bewildering variety of works on paper, from cheap book illustrations and master engravings by Albrecht Dürer, to some of Ruskin's most prized watercolours by J.M.W. Turner and a large number of his own drawings, many made especially for his lectures. The most highly coloured are Ruskin's own – he naturally kept back his greatest Turners, such as the *Pass of Faido* (Morgan Library, New York), but included, for example, the extraordinary kaleidoscope that is his *Study of the Kingfisher with Dominant Reference to Colour* (fig. 20), and a whole range of studies of architecture in Florence, Verona and Venice that emphasised the coloured stones of the churches and municipal buildings. However, the preponderance of monochrome objects in the Oxford collections reflects Ruskin's inability to articulate and develop fully his ideas on colour and how to teach it, perhaps because he remained too close to this subject. Indeed, neither of the drawing manuals he published nor the many editions of the catalogues of his teaching collections offer a comprehensive course in how to become even an accomplished copyist, let alone an original artist.

As has frequently been observed, Ruskin broadly followed the tradition promoted by Giorgio Vasari in the Renaissance in separating the constituents of a work of art into *disegno* and *colore* – design and colour – and contrasting the Schools of Florence, which embodied the former, and Venice, typically seen as the heart of colour.[27] Unlike Vasari and the first president of the Royal Academy, Sir Joshua Reynolds, who maintained the superiority of Michelangelo and design over Titian and colour, Ruskin admired both, though he was intellectually and emotionally attracted to colour. Indeed, in the successive volumes of *Modern Painters* (1843–60) he frequently maintained that, for example, 'to colour perfectly is the rarest and most precious (technical)

Fig. 20 John Ruskin (1819–1900), *Study of a Kingfisher, with dominant Reference to Colour*, before 1872. Pencil, watercolour and bodycolour. Ashmolean Museum, WA.RS.RUD.201

power an artist can possess.'[28] His *Elements of Drawing*, published in 1857, was a very successful drawing manual: clear, concise and well written. However, as Ruskin's editors, E.T. Cook and Sir Alexander Wedderburn, noted, it was by no means complete – Ruskin in later years said to a pupil: 'They were all wrong. They were only one side of the matter. *The Elements of Drawing* are not complete, and therefore they are misguiding and wrong.'[29] In fact, the volume was intended to be only the first of two, the second to deal mostly with colour. It is significant that they were based on the lessons that Ruskin had been giving in the Working Men's College in London from 1856, only in outline and shading, and leaving the application of colour to Dante Gabriel Rossetti. The manual comprises a series of three letters in which Ruskin laid out the basic principles for becoming an accomplished draughtsman, concentrating on outline and shading, but including lessons in laying in flat tints in watercolour from a block of cobalt blue. However, he warns against leaving a drawing unfinished: 'if … an artist restricts himself to outline, he is a bad draughtsman, and his work is bad. There is no exception to this law.'[30] The third letter, 'On Colour and Composition', finally addresses the third element of a drawing – colour – but does not develop the instruction very fully, since this was largely reserved for the second volume, and the chapter is generally devoted to composition. Ruskin wrote: 'You ought to love colour, and to think nothing quite beautiful or perfect without it; and if you really do love it, for its own sake, and are not merely desirous to colour because you think a painting a finer thing than a drawing, there is some chance you may colour well.'[31] Unfortunately, for Ruskin, most amateur artists do not have the capacity to colour well, for the 'chances are more than a thousand to one against your being right both in form and colour with a given touch'. He believed that the minutely detailed coloured drawings he later made for his Drawing School were not the province of an amateur artist, who should satisfy himself in making colour sketches as *aides-mémoire*. His practical advice on materials is conventional – even his advocacy of 'Chinese white', once contentious among professional watercolourists, had become widely accepted. He does, however, explain the relationship of colour to perspective, noting that 'it is a favourite dogma among modern writers on colour that "warm colours" (reds and yellows) "approach" or express nearness, and "cold colours" (blue and grey) "retire" or express distance'. This, he argues, is quite wrong, for colours of themselves 'are ABSOLUTELY inexpressive respecting distance.'[32] It should be noted that, unlike the instruction given at the South Kensington School and its counterparts all over the country, and codified in William Dyce's *Drawing Book of the Government Schools of Design* (1842–3), Ruskin encouraged the use of watercolour at an early stage, and rejected the official doctrine which reduced drawing to a mechanical process of imitation.[33]

In the early 1870s, Ruskin began reworking *The Elements of Drawing* in connection both with his work at Oxford, where he had been elected Slade Professor in 1869, and as part of the scheme he was devising for the recently established Guild of St George. This ultimately became *The Laws of Fesole*, a thorough revision of *The Elements of Drawing* which again was published incomplete, for Ruskin always intended it to be illustrated with reproductions of some of the works in his Drawing School. In the autumn of 1871 Ruskin began to send George Allen drawings to engrave for what he called 'The Oxford Art School Series'; some of these examples were from the Rudimentary Series itself, and his intention was that these would 'be issued to the public from the Oxford schools, with a short text to each number to replace my *Elements of Drawing*'.[34] In fact, *The Laws of Fesole* was based on the teaching collections at Oxford, and can only be understood with them in mind. They thus complement Ruskin's first Slade lectures, published as *Lectures on Art* (1870) and *Lectures on Landscape* (delivered 1871, published 1898), and there is considerable overlapping between the three.[35] In *The Laws of Fesole*, Ruskin makes even more explicit his belief that there are 'three divisions of the art of painting': outline, colour and shade, in order of difficulty. He devotes an entire chapter to 'The Twelve Zodiacal Colours', reminding his reader that 'all objects appear to the eye merely as masses of colour', and that shadows are coloured just as much as lights.[36] The technical discussion of the juxtaposition of the twelve colours of the rainbow owes much to George Field, the leading colour theorist of the nineteenth century, and to Ruskin's own observations. He goes on to repeat his discouraging conviction that the amateur should not aspire to produce finished drawings, only sketches.

These lectures can be supplemented by the catalogues of the teaching collections at Oxford. The first published catalogue of any series was the *Catalogue of Examples*, subsequently augmented and divided into the Standard Series and the Reference Series. Nos. 2 and 3 of the former offer a contrasting pair of watercolours by Turner, *The Junction of the Greta and Tees at Rokeby* (fig. 21) and the *Scene on the Loire* (fig. 22). Whereas the latter is 'wholly painted in solid colour', the former 'is painted wholly in transparent; and the two drawings together show the complete management of colours soluble in water'.[37] In his *Lectures on Landscape* of 1871, Turner explained that he had given the University the Loire drawings in 1861 for two reasons: firstly for their 'infallible decision' and secondly for 'their extreme modesty in colour'. He continued: 'They are, beyond all other works that I know existing, dependent for their effect on low, subdued tones; their favourite choice in time of day being either dawn or twilight, and even their brightest sunsets produced chiefly out of grey paper.'[38] Much earlier, in a lecture to the Architectural Association in 1857, Ruskin had recommended his audience 'rise early, always watch the sunrise and the way the clouds break from the dawn'.[39] Among many studies by Ruskin of clouds and sunrises in Oxford, *Study of Dawn: The First Scarlet on the Clouds* (Ashmolean, WA.RS.ED.003) elicits a special commentary in the third edition of the catalogue of the Educational Series: 'I would request any student, who finds by the pleasure he takes in colour … to set aside a quarter of an hour of every morning, as a part of its devotions, for the observance of the sun-rise, and always to have pencil and colour at hand to make note of anything more than usually beautiful.'[40]

Ruskin's teachings on colour in his didactic works are fragmentary and contradictory. This is nowhere more apparent than in his inclusion in the Educational Series of 25 plates from Turner's *Liber Studiorum*. In *Modern*

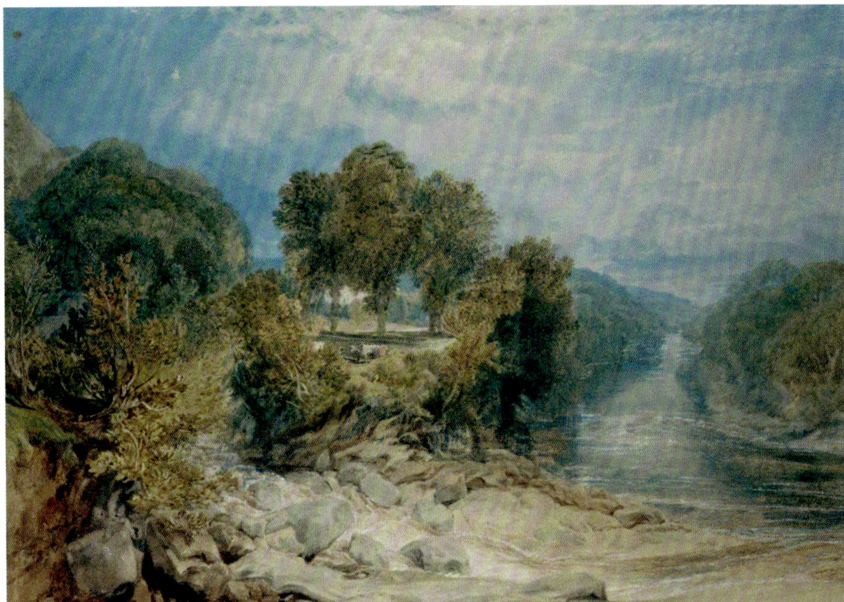

Fig. 21 J.M.W. Turner (1775–1851), *The Junction of the Greta and Tees at Rokeby*, 1816–18. Watercolour over graphite. Ashmolean Museum, WA.RS.STD.002

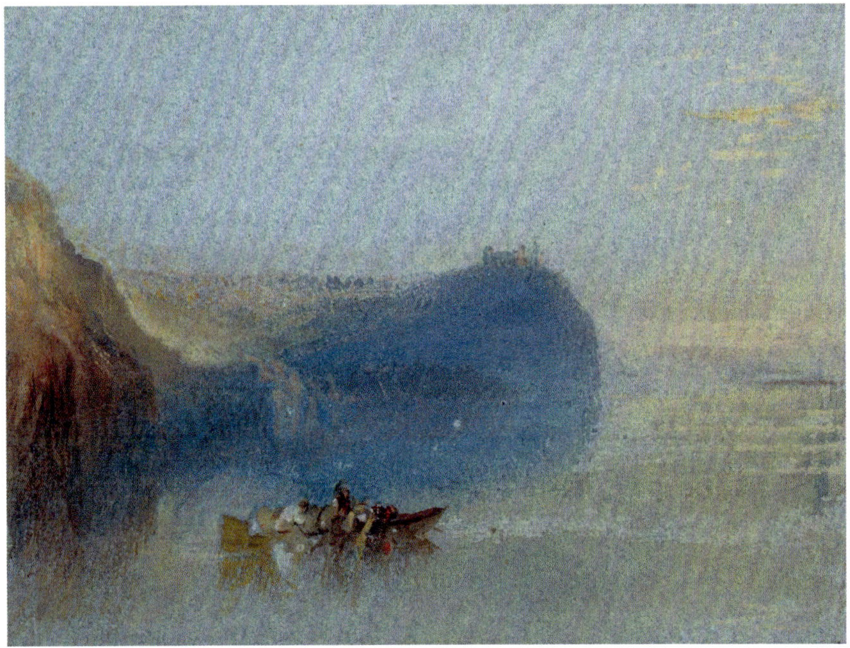

Fig. 22 J.M.W. Turner (1775–1851), *Scene on the Loire*, 1826–30. Watercolour and bodycolour. Ashmolean Museum, WA.RS.STD.003

Painters he had frequently referred to the series, and in *Lectures on Art* he used them to illustrate the 'chiaroscuro of landscape', being much more suitable than a photograph, which may record some pertinent facts, but are entirely mechanical, and show nothing of the moral side of art. Ruskin's interpretation of their qualities can also be seen in his own monochrome studies of landscape in the teaching collections, many dating from the late 1840s and early 1850s, when he adopted the early Pre-Raphaelites' minutely detailed vision. Such celebrated drawings as *Study of Gneiss Rock, Glenfinlas* (1853) and *The Glacier des Bossons,*

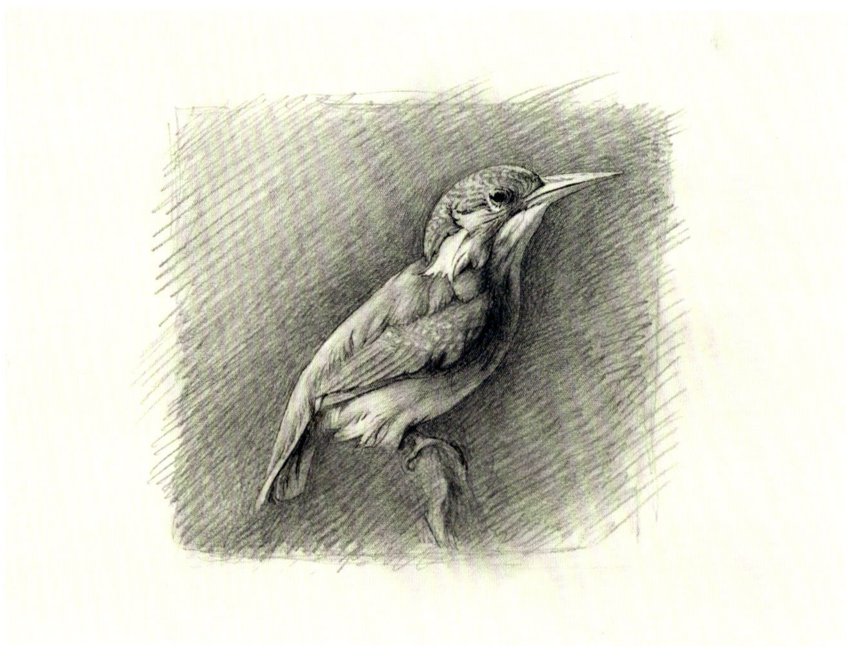

Fig. 23 John Ruskin (1819–1900), *Study of a Kingfisher, with dominant Reference to Shade*, before 1872. Pen and ink over graphite. Ashmolean Museum, WA.RS.RUD.202

Chamouni (1849) offered approachable examples for copying, and Ruskin thought so highly of them that he had some reproduced in black and white photographs and distributed to students.

One of the most celebrated drawings by Ruskin in Oxford is *Study of a Kingfisher, with dominant Reference to Colour* (fig. 20), usually seen in isolation as one of the most brilliantly coloured and technically accomplished of the artist's drawings. However, in many ways, it epitomised Ruskin's teaching of drawing, for it was placed in the ninth cabinet of the Rudimentary Series, devoted to 'Exercises in Colour with Shade, on Patterns of Plumage and Scale', and should be considered with its four companions, one a complementary *Study of a Kingfisher, with dominant Reference to Shade, but local colour still kept note of, as an element of shade* (fig. 23). Together, they offer the student a complete lesson in mastering the elements of Ruskin's teaching.

Fig. 24 J.M.W. Turner (1775–1851), *Venice: San Giorgio Maggiore – Early Morning*, 1819. Watercolour. Tate, D15254

Turner's Paintings of Venice

Colin Harrison

On 12 August 1891, Edmond de Goncourt wrote in his diary that a painting of Venice he had seen that day in the possession of Camille Groult was:

> One of the ten that have delighted my eyes the most. For this Turner is liquid gold, and within it an infusion of purple … Ah! This Salute, this Doge's Palace, this sea, this sky with the pink translucency of Pagodite, all as if seen in an apotheosis of the colour of precious stones! And of colour in droplets, in tears, in fusings … And the beauty of the painting is made of something that is not taught in any book written by a teacher of aesthetics, it is made of energy, of riotous colouring, of exaggeration in the cooking.[41]

In spite of the fact that the painting was probably a fake, Goncourt's reaction typifies the intense fascination with the colour of Turner's late Venetian paintings, which was by this date almost universal. So, a few years later, Paul Signac made a pilgrimage to London to see Turner's paintings, and marvelled at the late work on display at the National Gallery, especially the artist's use of 'colour for colour's sake'. He also made a scribbled copy of one of Turner's paintings of the Salute, which he inscribed 'this poor little prayer to our God Turner'.[42] The apotheosis of this view of Turner as an abstract artist, especially in his late views of Venice, came in an exhibition at the Museum of Modern Art in New York in 1966, organised and catalogued by the painter and critic Lawrence Gowing. In his foreword, Monroe Wheeler claimed that 'in his forties, [Turner] found himself revolutionizing his art, eliminating from it linear draughtsmanship and classical composition; glorifying only light and shade, by the sole means of colour'.[43] To achieve this effect, the paintings were displayed without frames, with a tiny handful of early works, and a preponderance of Venetian subjects, in both oils and watercolours, from the 1830s and 1840s.

Naturally, with such a thesis, Gowing seized upon critic William Hazlitt's derogatory description in 1816 of Turner's works as 'too much abstractions of aerial perspective, and representations not properly of the objects of nature, as of the medium through which they were seen', to claim that, when Turner first arrived in Venice in 1819, he was very much affected by the spirit of the city, which the painter Henry Fuseli had called 'the birthplace and the theatre of colour', to 'make drawings entirely of colour, with no other substance'.[44] Yet, although Turner exhibited views of Venice almost annually from 1835 until 1846, it is clear that he intended them to be evocations of specific views – embodying reflections on historical truth – rather than simply blazing abstractions of colour. Their commercial success confirms that this is how many of his contemporaries viewed them.

Turner spent a total of less than four weeks sketching in Venice, on three visits in 1819, 1833 and 1840. Paul Hills noted the city's particular appeal: 'No city built on land can offer so brilliant an arrangement and so strange an intermingling and intensifying of the colour of the sky and the colour of the buildings on the surface of its thoroughfares.'[45] Turner had eagerly read Byron's *Childe Harold*, published in 1818, and its romantic view of the city in terminal decline pervaded the painter's work ever after – as Ruskin wrote in his autobiography: 'My Venice, like Turner's, had been chiefly created for us by Byron.'[46] Even before Turner had been to Venice he made two remarkable watercolours reproduced in James Hakewill's *Picturesque Tour of Italy* (1819); these were based on the author's own pencil drawings.[47] During his first visit of a few days in late summer 1819 on a tour primarily devoted to Rome, Turner concentrated on making pencil sketches of specific architectural details – A.J. Finberg noted that 'it would take up too much time to colour in the open air – [Turner] could make fifteen or sixteen pencil sketches to one coloured'. However it is the four limpid watercolours in the 'Como and Venice' sketchbook that are regarded as the artist's exceptional work during the period.[48] Specialists disagree over whether they were all made in front of the motif or partly from memory, but they generally agree on Turner's novel depiction of light falling on buildings, or his illumination of them from behind (fig. 24). Although Turner had obviously fallen for the faded charms of Venice during this visit, his sketches resulted in only a handful of works prepared in his studio in London, including two illustrations for Samuel Rogers's *Italy, a Poem* (1830) and *Poems* (1834).[49] More notable were two oil paintings shown at the Royal Academy in 1833: *Ducal Palace, Venice* (untraced) and *Bridge of Sighs, Ducal Palace and Custom-House, Venice: Canaletti painting* (Tate). The exhibition enjoyed great success, partly due to newspaper coverage of Turner's wish to outdo his rival Clarkson Stanfield.[50] According to the *Morning Chronicle* (6 June 1833), it was painted in two or three days after the artist heard that Stanfield was exhibiting a similar view. While this is unlikely, contemporary critics judged Turner's work favourably, *The Spectator* describing it as 'a most brilliant gem. The emerald waters, the bright blue sky, and the ruddy hue of the Ducal Palace, relieved by the chaste whiteness of the stone buildings around'. For Turner, it was a tribute to his great predecessor of Venetian painting, Canaletto.

Turner made his second visit to Venice in 1833 at the expense of his patron, H.A.J. Munro of Novar, who intended to commission a painting or watercolour based on his sketches. The visit was characteristically short but, together with the earlier studies, provided Turner with material for major oil paintings shown at the Royal Academy from 1834 to 1840. Although the financial arrangements are not clear, Munro bought Turner's *Venice, from the Porch of the Madonna della Salute* at the Royal Academy in 1835 (fig. 25). The brilliance of colour – showing the buildings almost dissolving into their reflections in the Grand Canal – was almost universally appreciated by contemporaries. By contrast, Turner's view of Venice shown the following year, *Juliet and her Nurse* (private

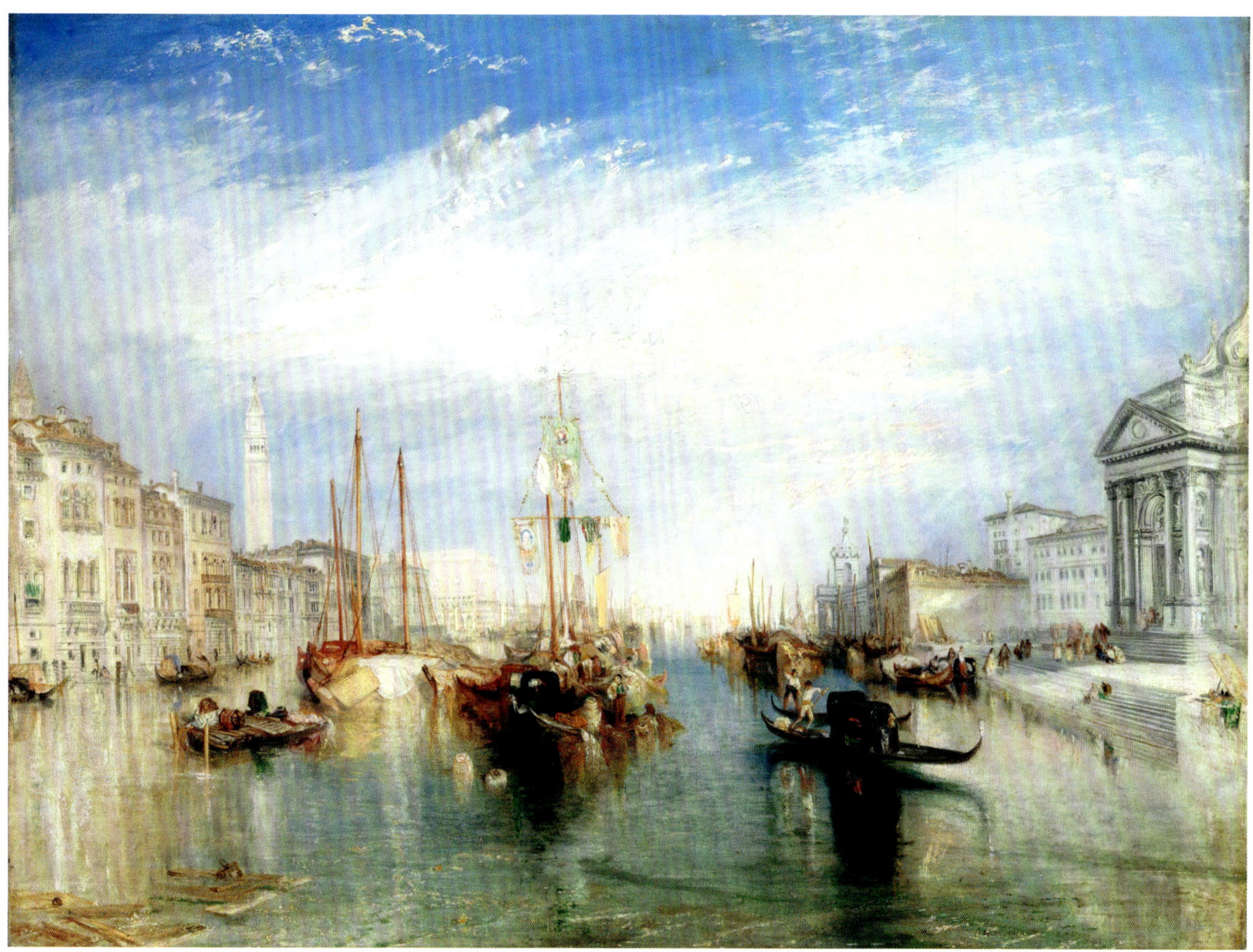

Fig. 25 J.M.W. Turner (1775–1851), *Venice, from the Porch of Madonna della Salute*, c.1835. Oil on canvas. Lent by The Metropolitan Museum of Art, Bequest of Cornelius Vanderbilt, 1899 (99.31)

collection), was the subject of such a severe review by the Rev. John Eagles that it inspired the teenage John Ruskin to write his first defence of Turner.[51] Eagles, in *Blackwood's Magazine*, contended that the picture was 'a strange jumble … neither sunlight, moonlight, nor starlight, nor firelight … a composition as from models of different parts of Venice, thrown higgledy-piggledy together, streaked blue and pink and thrown into a flour tub'. Turner discouraged Ruskin from publishing his riposte, in which he defended the painting in poetic and whimsical terms, identifying the mists rising above the city as 'aetherial spirits, souls of the mighty dead breathed out of the tombs of Italy into the blue of her bright heaven, and wandering in vague and infinite glory around the earth they have loved'.

Commercial considerations may have encouraged Turner to spend two weeks in Venice in the late summer of 1840, from 20 August to 3 September – he had recently exhibited two Venetian subjects at the Royal Academy, one commissioned by John Sheepshanks, so he knew there was a strong market for such pictures.[52] As usual, he worked assiduously, using a number of 'roll' sketchbooks, which were wide and narrow, with soft covers that could be rolled up and put into his pocket. Turner filled these with the usual pencil sketches of architectural compositions and details and, exceptionally, a sequence of about

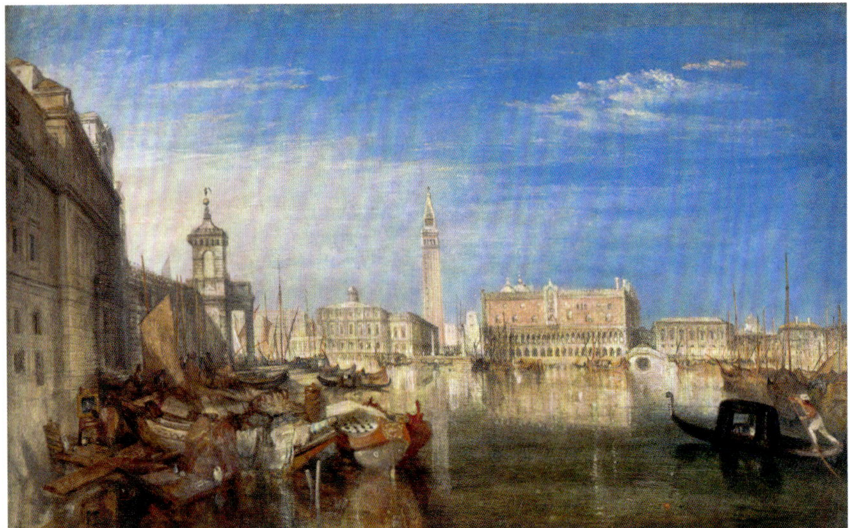

Fig. 26 J.M.W. Turner (1775–1851), *Bridge of Sighs, Ducal Palace and Custom-House, Venice: Canaletti painting*, exhibited 1833. Oil on mahogany. Tate, N00370

100 watercolours, made on the spot or from memory in the painter's room at the Hotel Europa (now the Palazzo Giustinian). Some of these luminous and spontaneous sketches – on 'Whatman' paper brought from England – are now among the artist's most admired works, not least because Ruskin included three from the 'Storm' sketchbook in his gift to Oxford in 1861 (fig. 26), and two more (plus a further Venetian subject) to Cambridge in the same year; and most of the others are also in public collections. In addition, Turner bought sketchbooks and single sheets of mid-toned paper locally – both in Vienna and Venice – which he used for highly atmospheric interiors of St Mark's and the theatre, night scenes and frequent storms. Together, they 'present Venice as a sequence of phantasmagorical visions, where perspective and scale are often ambiguous and topographical features not always in sight'.[53]

Unlike his contemporary studies in Switzerland, which were frequently developed into large finished watercolours, Turner's watercolour sketches of Venice remained private exercises. The city did, however, provide him with 17 further exhibited oil paintings, of which nine were sold. Frequently, Turner appended to the title a quotation, or sometimes merely a reference, to his own poem, 'The Fallacies of Hope', reflecting his Byronic belief that the city was doomed. For example, when shown at the Royal Academy in 1843, *The Sun of Venice Going to Sea*, with its obvious symbolism of decline and eclipse, suggested that 'Fair shines the morn, and soft the zephyrs blow / Venecia's fisher spreads his painted sail so gay / Nor heeds the demon that in grim repose / Expects his evening prey'.[54] By no means all the late Venetian subjects are so despondent; indeed, one critic failed to notice the lines of verse and described the boat as being 'like a thing of life … so gay – so buoyant – so swift'.[55]

Ruskin may have been responsible for the fact that this painting did not sell: he had reserved both *The Sun of Venice* and *San Benedetto Looking towards Faustina* (Tate) at the exhibition, but could not decide which his father should buy. When he saw the former painting again in 1856, he noted that, in spite of the degradations in the colour of the sea and the darkening of the lead white in the sky, 'the marvellous brilliancy of the arrangement of colour in this picture renders it, to my mind, one of Turner's leading works in oil'. He did not acquire a major Venetian oil by Turner until 1847, when his father paid 850 guineas for *The Grand Canal, Venice,* which had been exhibited ten years earlier.[56] Its upright format and jostling crowds on gondolas in the middle of the canal – and on the piers on the edge – give it a mood of exuberance far from the melancholy of the broader views. This painting was perhaps better suited to Ruskin's increasing irritation with Turner's despondent view of the city.

Turner's paintings of Venice owe a great deal to Ruskin's advocacy. As early as 1841, he confided to a friend that Venice was 'quite beyond everybody but Turner'.[57] In the first volume of *Modern Painters* (1843), he repeatedly praised the latest views of Venice, convinced that they were the artist's finest late oils. In 1845, he made a special trip to Venice to obtain 'authority for all that Turner has done for her'.[58] Increasingly in his own drawings, he abandoned the shimmering mirage of Turner's watercolours to make carefully observed studies of architectural fact. When Turner died in 1851, Ruskin was, by coincidence, in Venice gathering material for the later volumes of *The Stones of Venice*. When he heard that his hero had died, he wrote that 'everything in sunshine and the sky so talks of him. Their Great witness lost'.[59]

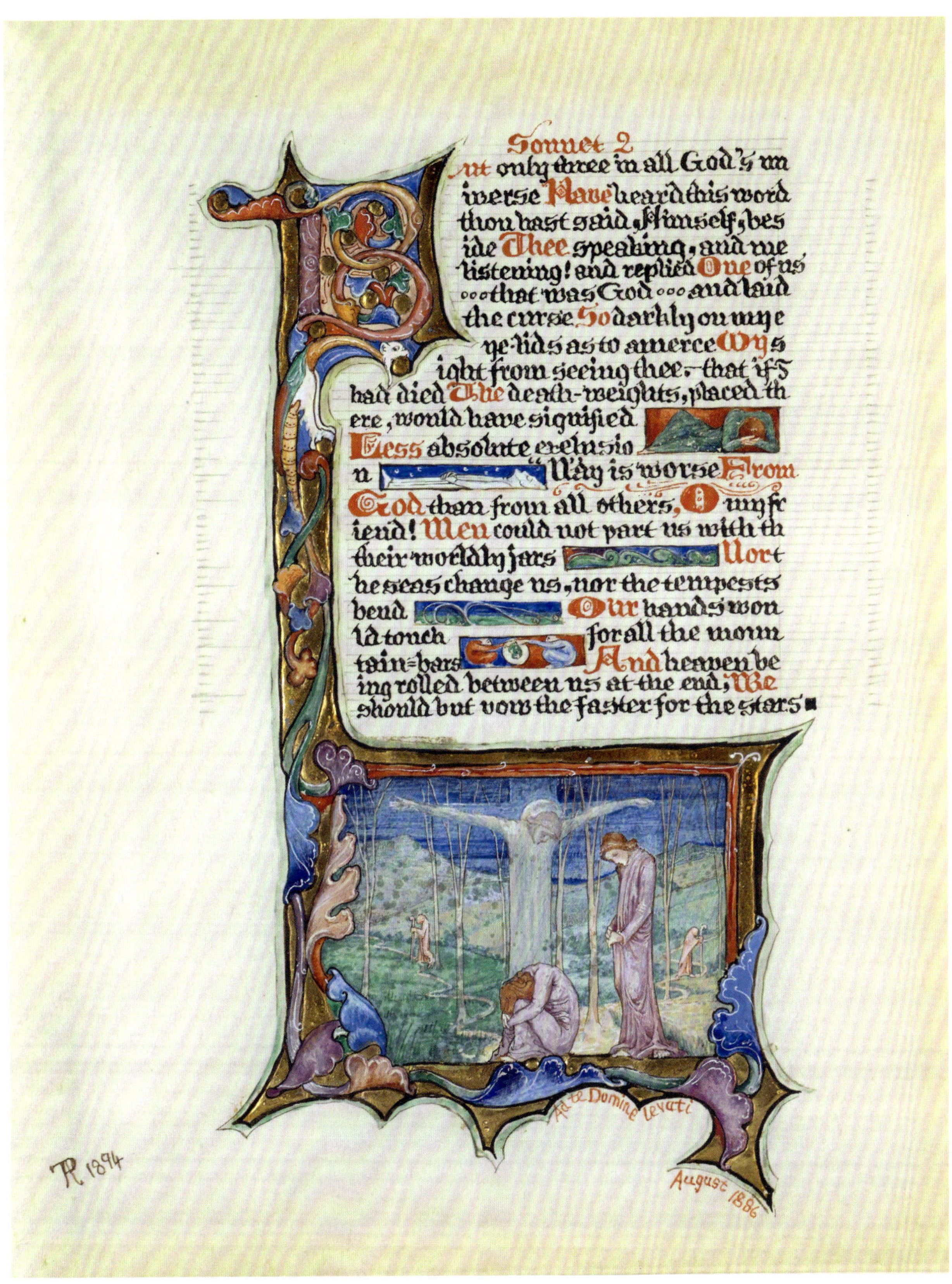

Fig. 27 Phoebe Anna Traquair (1852–1936), illuminated page from *Sonnets from the Portuguese* by Elizabeth Barrett Browning, 1894–6. Pen and ink and bodycolour over pencil on vellum. National Galleries of Scotland, Edinburgh, DNG1870

'The Gothic school of colour': Reviving the Hues of the Middle Ages

Charlotte Ribeyrol

In her memoir of her husband's life, Georgiana Burne-Jones reported that 1854 had been a turning-point for Edward Burne-Jones, then still a student of theology at Exeter College. That year, having walked past the ruins of twelfth-century Godstow Abbey in north Oxford, he embraced a 'passion of enthusiasm' for art and all things medieval[60]:

> I came back in a delirium of joy, the land was so enchanted with bright colours, blue and purple in the sky, shot over with a dust of golden shower, and in the water, a mirror'd counterpart, ruffled by a light west wind – and in my mind pictures of the old days, the abbey, and long processions of the faithful, banners of the cross, copes and crosiers, gay knights and ladies by the river bank, hawking-parties and all the pageantry of the golden age – it made me feel so wild and mad I had to throw stones into the water to break the dream.[61]

The intense, dreamlike vision of 'gay nights and ladies' is, however, soon further dispelled by the appearance of steam from the nearby train station: 'the sound of earthly bells in the distance, and presently the wreathing of steam upon the trees where the railway runs, called me back to the years I cannot convince myself of living in'. [62]

Fig. 28 A.W.N. Pugin (1812–1852), 'Contrasted Residences for the Poor', from *Contrasts, Or, a Parallel between the Noble Edifices of the Fourteenth and Fifteenth Centuries and Similar Buildings of the Present Day, Shewing the Present Decay of Taste*, 1841. Etching

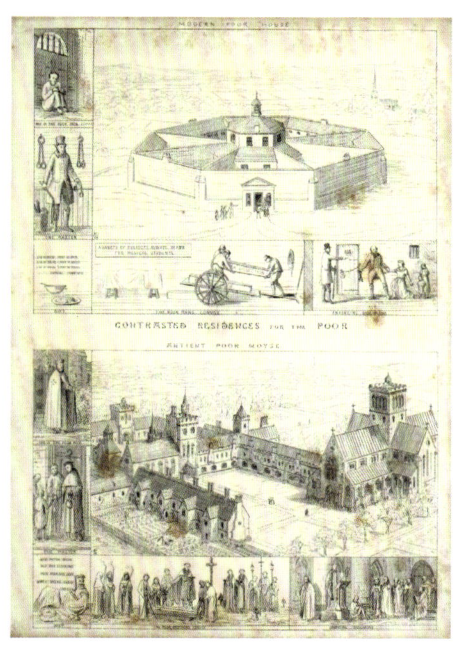

A key figure of the Gothic Revival, the architect and designer Augustus Pugin had already contrasted his own medieval utopias with the bleak industrial present, which seemed increasingly subject to social unrest. But contrary to Pugin's black and white *Contrasts* (fig. 28), Burne-Jones's oneiric evocation of the 'pageantry of the golden age' is particularly colourful, the 'blue and purple in the sky' conjuring up a procession of dazzling banners and vestments. Such idealising 'pictures of the old days' were fuelled as much by the ruins themselves as by the historical romances and poems Burne-Jones and his friend and fellow Exeter student William Morris were reading at the time: from 'the merrie England' of Walter Scott and his colourful tournament scenes, to John Keats and Alfred Tennyson's sensual poetry set in medieval *décors*. Even more influential were John Ruskin's writings on art and architecture, notably *Stones of Venice* (1851–1853) and its 'Nature of the Gothic' chapter, which was a 'revelation' to the young Morris.[63] Breaking away from the Renaissance depiction of the Gothic as the 'dark age' of barbaric Goths, Ruskin drew on the preserved beauty of stained-glass windows and illuminated manuscripts as evidence to claim:

> the title 'Dark Ages', given to the mediæval centuries, is, respecting art, wholly inapplicable … They were the ages of gold: ours are the ages of umber. The Middle Ages had their wars and agonies, but also intense delights … Their gold was dashed with blood; but ours is sprinkled with dust. Their life was interwoven with white and purple; ours is one seamless stuff of brown.[64]

Ruskin celebrated the Gothic as the 'school of colour', at one with nature:[65]

> I cannot, therefore, consider architecture as in anywise perfect without colour … Our building, if it is well composed, is one thing, and is to be coloured as Nature would colour one thing – a shell, a flower, or an animal.[66]

This emphasis on natural colour inspired a new generation of architects like William Butterfield, William Burges and George Edmund Street, to whom Morris became apprenticed in 1856. This led to experimentations with 'structural polychromy', which Butterfield most spectacularly applied to All Saints' Church on Margaret Street in London (1850–59). The use of colour both inside and on the outside of this Anglo-Catholic centre of worship was immediately viewed with great suspicion, as it smacked of the supposedly Pagan ritualism practised in Roman Catholic countries. According to Anglicans, coloured materials distracted the eye rather than saved the soul.

In the early 1870s the controversy was still ongoing when Butterfield was commissioned by Edward Pusey (who had laid the foundation stone of All Saints' a few years earlier) to design a new Oxford college named after John Keble (fig. 29), a leading figure in the Oxford Movement. 'Tractarians', as they were sometimes called, advocated the revival of Catholic heritage and practice within the Church of England.

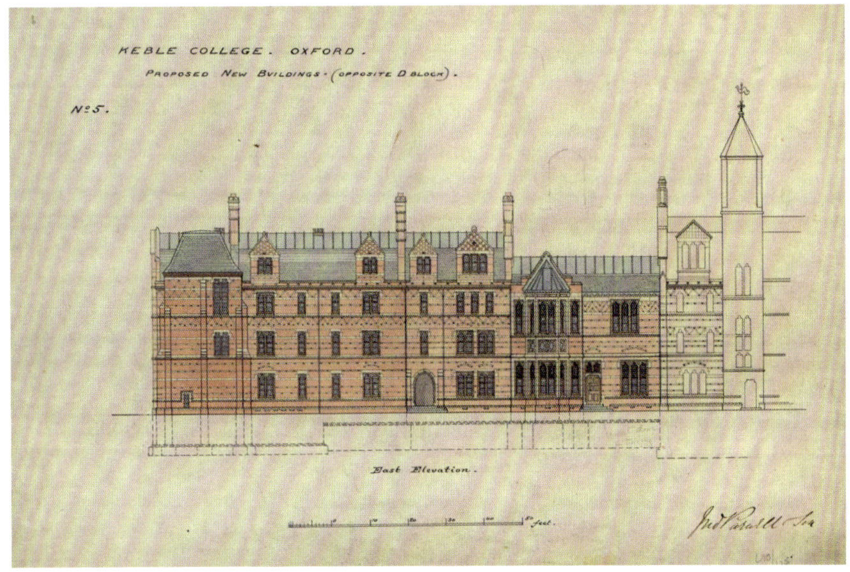

Fig. 29 William Butterfield (1814–1900), *Keble College – Proposed New Buildings opposite block D. No 5. East Elevation*, c.1865–80. Pen and ink and wash. Keble College, Oxford

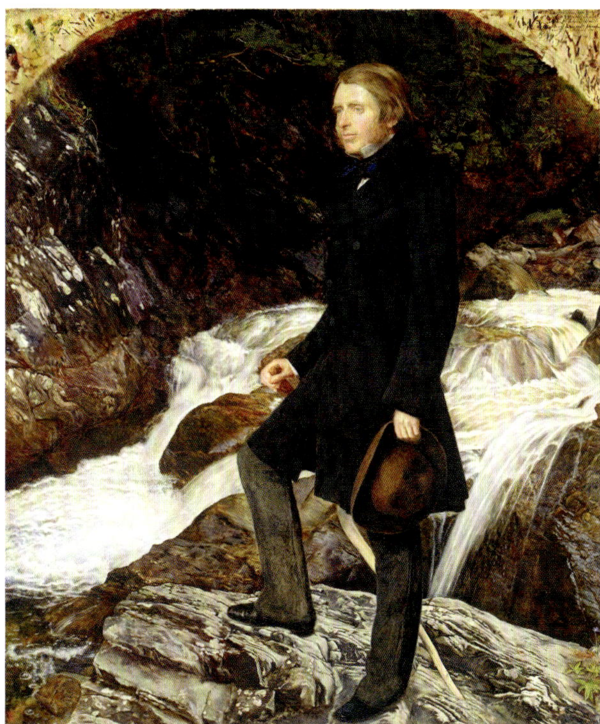

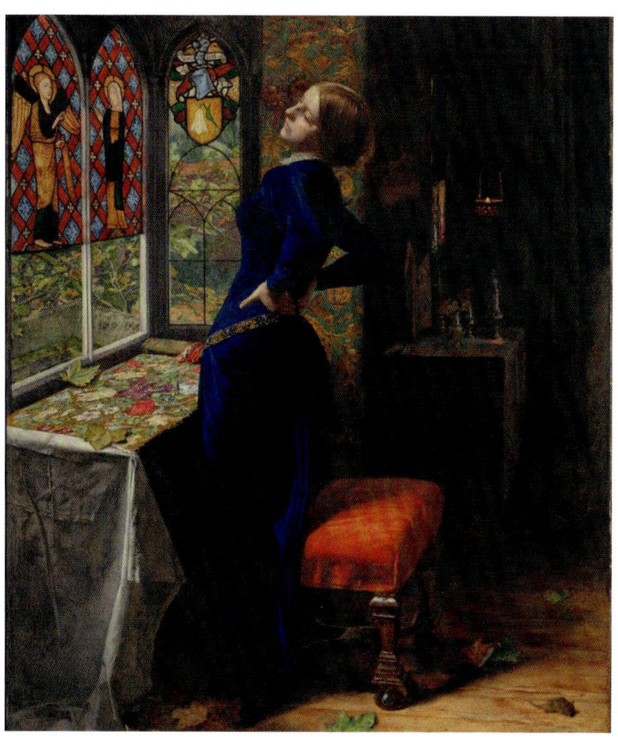

Above left: Fig. 30 John Ruskin (1819–1900) by Sir John Everett Millais (1829–1896), 1853–4. Oil on canvas. Ashmolean Museum, WA2012.67

Above right: Fig. 31 Sir John Everett Millais (1829–1896), *Mariana*, 1851. Oil on canvas. Tate: Accepted by HM Government in lieu of tax and allocated to the Tate Gallery 1999, T07553

Although a staunch Anglican, Ruskin was also drawn to the colours of the pre-Reformation past. In the early 1850s he became a champion of the Pre-Raphaelites, whose dazzling colours emulated the bright palette of early Italian artists. John Everett Millais was one of his protégés: in 1853 Ruskin's father even commissioned the young artist to paint his son during a holiday in Scotland (fig. 30). Despite their subsequent falling out after Millais ran off with his wife Effie, Ruskin claimed in an 1878 lecture aptly entitled 'The Three Colours of Pre-Raphaelitism' that Millais's *Mariana* (fig. 31) was 'the perfectest of his works, and the representative picture of that generation.'[67] The painting is full of literary references such as were dear to the Pre-Raphaelite Brotherhood, of which Millais was a founding member. The female figure is based on Shakespeare's Mariana in the play *Measure for Measure*, who longs to be reunited with her fiancé Angelo after he abandons her when her dowry is lost in a shipwreck. The play, in turn, inspired Alfred Tennyson's 1830 poem 'Mariana', the following lines from which originally accompanied the painting: 'She only said, 'My life is dreary – He cometh not!' she said; She said, 'I am aweary, aweary – I would that I were dead!' Mariana's melancholy is suggested by her contorted posture and half-closed eyes, but as Millais's first biographer Marion Spielmann noted, the jewel-like colours of the painting seem almost too 'brilliant' to express her dejection.[68] The painting also references the rich paraphernalia of medieval faith – from the dazzling stained glass window based on panels in the chapel of Merton College, Oxford, to the triptych and silver casket on the altar, and even the embroidery which Mariana has momentarily set aside so she can stretch her back. When *Mariana* was first exhibited Ruskin was therefore careful to distance himself from Millais's 'high church',

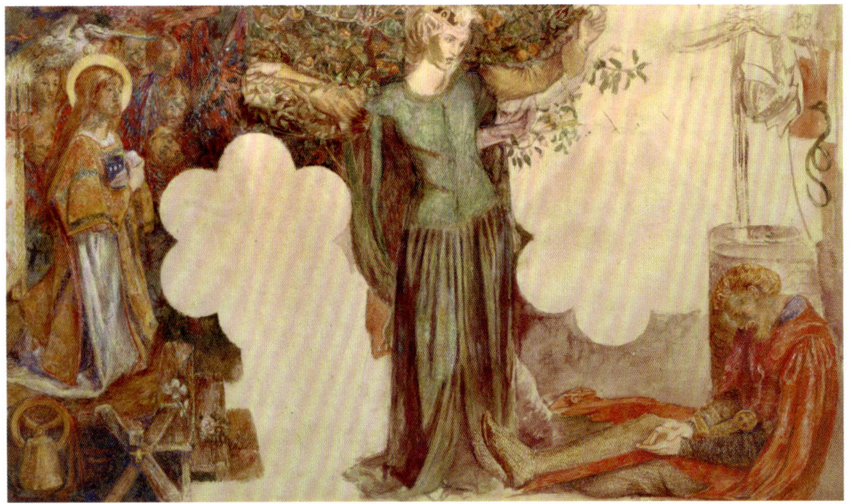

Fig. 32 Dante Gabriel Rossetti (1828–1882), *Sir Launcelot's Vision of the Sanc Grael*, 1857. Watercolour and bodycolour over black chalk. Ashmolean Museum, WA1950.7

Tractarian sympathies. He wrote: 'I am glad to see Mr. Millais's lady in blue is heartily tired of her painted window and idolatrous toilet table.'[69]

After the original Pre-Raphaelite Brotherhood disbanded, a new artistic circle formed at Oxford around Morris and Burne-Jones, extolling the same intense love of colour, medieval art and literature. Like Millais and William Holman Hunt, they admired Keats and Tennyson, but favoured more ancient poetic sources such as Dante, Geoffrey Chaucer, Christine de Pizan and Thomas Malory. The latter's fifteenth-century *Morte d'Arthur* inspired the murals which the young friends painted in the library of the Oxford Union in 1857, under the guidance of Dante Gabriel Rossetti (fig. 32). This first collaborative venture was praised by the poet Coventry Patmore, a friend of both Tennyson and Ruskin, who compared the frescoes to Butterfield's polychrome church on Margaret Street, singling out Rossetti's paintings as particularly glowing:[70]

> Mr. Rossetti, whom Mr. Ruskin has pronounced to be the only modern rival of Turner as a colourist, must at least be allowed, whether we admit that rivalry or not, to equal Turner in one of the noblest and least attainable qualities of harmonious colour – namely, its mysteriousness. The apparition of the 'Damsel of the Sanct Grael', surrounded with angels, on the wall of the Union, is a remarkable example of this mysteriousness. It is no skilful balance, according to academical rules or recipes by Mr. Owen Jones, of a red robe here, with a blue one there – it is 'like a steam of rich, distilled perfumes', and affects the eye much as one of Mendelssohn's most unwordable 'Lieder ohne Wörter' impresses the ear. The colour is as sweet, bright, and pure, as that of the frailest waif of cloud in the sunrise; and yet, if closely looked into, there is scarcely a square inch of half those hundred square feet of colour which has not half-a-dozen different tints in it. The colours, coming thus from points instead of from masses, are positively radiant, at the same time that they are wholly the reverse of glaring.[71]

Patmore distinguished the synaesthetic harmony of the murals from the new chromatic 'rules' advocated by Owen Jones and the French chemist Michel Eugène Chevreul, whose scientific theories of simultaneous colour contrast Jones helped to popularise in England. By contrast, both Patmore and Ruskin believed that 'a man of no talent, a bad colourist, would be ready to give you mathematical reasons for every colour' he uses, and that 'the real man of talent should work entirely by instinct'.[72]

Ruskin and his disciples understood colour not as a science but as something 'sacred'. Hence their praise of the vivid hues of illuminations which inspired the Oxford murals, described by Patmore as 'the adoption of a style of colouring so brilliant as to make the walls look like the margin of a highly illuminated manuscript'.[73] However, the young, inexperienced artists applied their coloured materials directly onto the whitewash without prior preparation of the walls, and the colours soon faded. The painters were evidently more familiar with medieval texts than with the techniques of fresco painting.

During the 1850s Morris and his friends devoted much time to the study of French and English medieval painted manuscripts, which Ruskin praised for their 'bold rejection of all principles of perspective, light and shade, and drawing' and 'the vivid opposition of their bright colours and quaint lines'.[74] Among the medieval volumes that the young artists consulted – either in the Bodleian Library or in the British Museum – were the collected works of the fifteenth-century poet and court writer Christine de Pizan (fig. 33), one of the first women to earn a living from her writing. This finely illuminated manuscript was a gift to Queen Isabeau of Bavaria, wife of Charles VI of France.

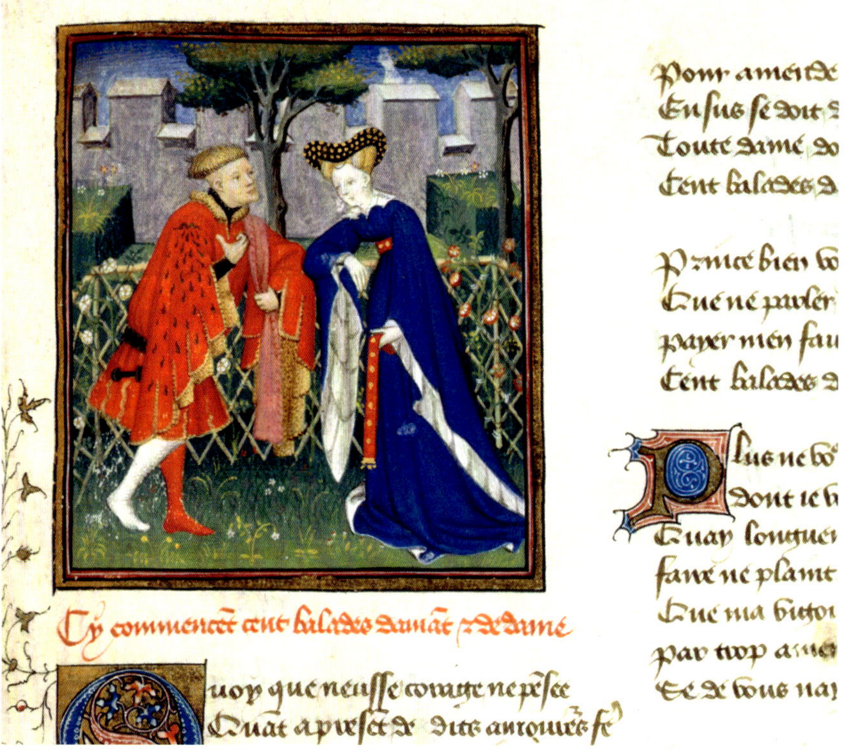

Fig. 33 Christine de Pizan (1364–1430), 'Lovers in conversation', from *Cent ballades d'amant et de dame*, c.1410–14. Illuminated manuscript. The British Library, Harley MS 4431, f. 376r

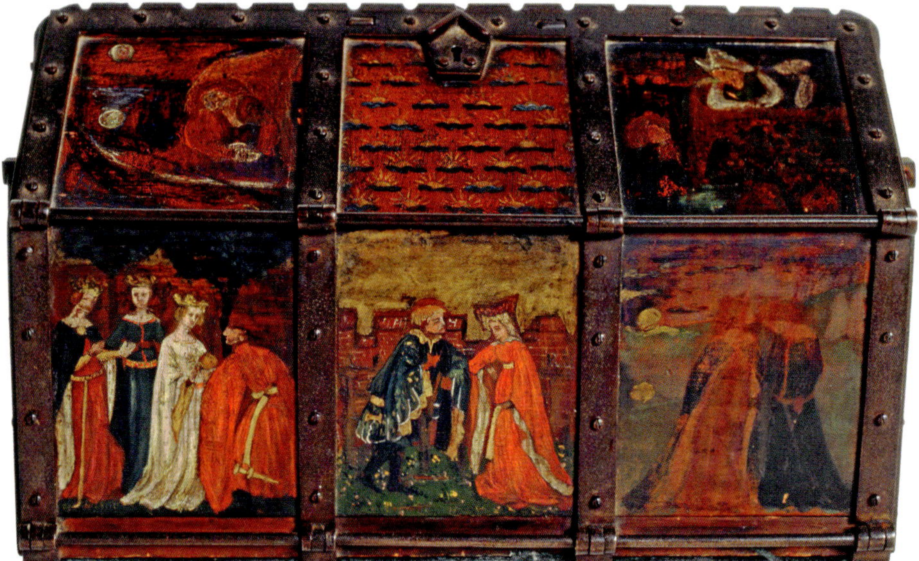

Fig. 34 Jewelled casket by Dante Gabriel Rossetti (1828–1882) and Elizabeth Siddal (1829–1862), *c.*1859. Society of Antiquaries of London (Kelmscott Manor), KM202

It opens with Pizan's first major collection of poems, *Cent Ballades de dame et d'amant* (1402). Rossetti read this volume in the late 1850s; he and his future wife Elizabeth Siddal even copied several of its folios to decorate a jewel casket which they gave to Jane Morris as a wedding gift (fig. 34). Rossetti may have been drawn to Pizan's work because of her Italian origins and professed admiration for Dante. Siddal, on the other hand, an artist and poet herself (fig. 35), most certainly saw the author of the proto-feminist utopia *La Cité des Dames* as a role model.[75] Although Rossetti and Siddal reversed the red and the blue of the original illumination in folio 376, the painted panels of Jane Morris's casket are clearly a tribute to the rich colours of the Middle Ages. Frederick Sandys, who joined Rossetti and Morris's circle around this period, explored similar medieval sources, as his own vivid watercolours based on Pizan's folio testify (fig. 36).

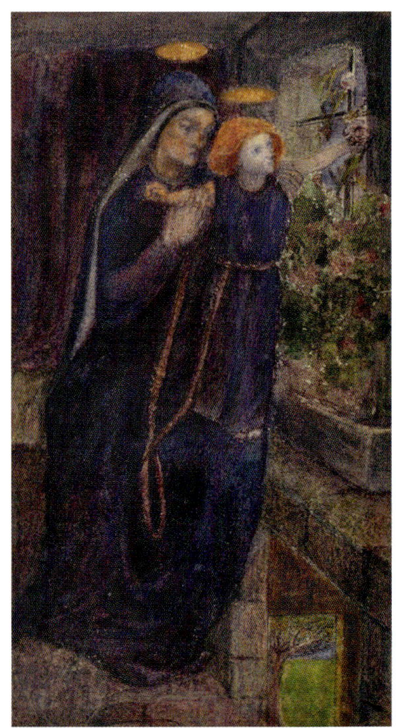

Fig. 35 Elizabeth Siddal (1829–1862), *Madonna and Child, c.*1850–62. Watercolour. Ashmolean Museum, WA1977.95

Not only did these artists all emulate medieval motifs, they also applied them to a wide range of different media – as with the clump of daisies pattern inspired by *Le Bal des Ardents* ('The Dance of the Wodewoses'), an illumination from Jean Froissart's fourteenth-century *Chroniques* (fig. 37). This text had been a key source for Walter Scott, who was one of the first authors to revive the colours of the Middle Ages in his historical novels. Morris and his friends most probably consulted the Froissart manuscript in the mid 1850s. *Le Bal des Ardents* is still one of the best-known illustrations from this volume, showing a group of dancers dressed as wild woodsmen at a masquerade ball given by Queen Isabeau on 28th January 1393. The party turned to tragedy after a torch was thrown into the dancers (including Charles VI, in disguise), setting fire to some of the men. This extremely colourful scene had already been chromolithographed by Henry Noel Humphreys in his *Illuminated Illustrations of Froissart* (1844–49), a copy of which both Morris and Burges owned. But rather than this extraordinary episode, it was the decorative embroideries in the background of *Le Bal des Ardents* that caught the attention of Morris, who

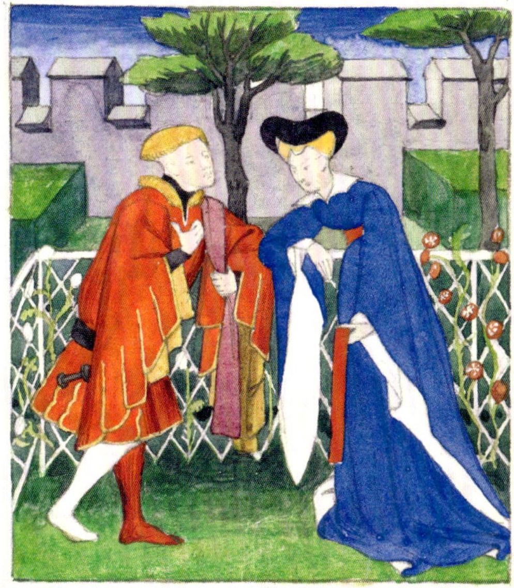

Left: Fig. 36 Frederick Sandys (1829–1904), *Scene from the Oeuvres of Christine de Pizan*, 1850–60. Watercolour. Birmingham Museums Trust on behalf of Birmingham City Council, 1906P906

Below: Fig. 37 Attributed to Philippe de Mazerolles (d. 1479), *Le Bal des Ardents*, from Froissart's *Chroniques*, vol. IV, part 2, *c.*1470–2. Illuminated manuscript. The British Library, Harley MS 4380, f.1

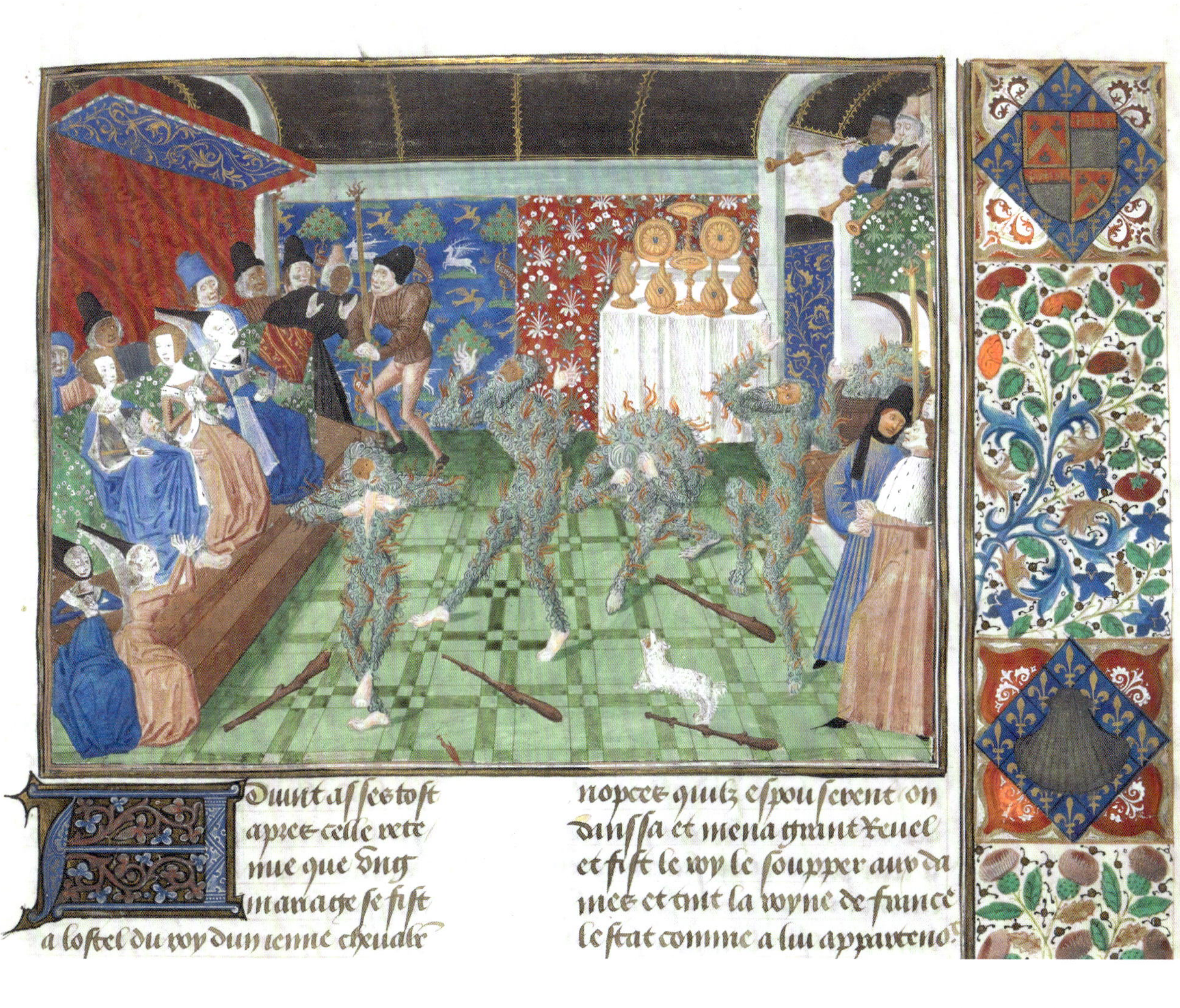

repeated the tree pattern in his first and only painting of his wife Jane in 1858, *La Belle Iseult* (fig. 38). Morris also selected the clump of daisies motif for one of his earliest wallpaper designs, as well as for a series of hand-painted tiles in blue and yellow. Around this time Jane, who played an active role in the decoration of the Morris family's Red House, wove an embroidery based on the same pattern which is now at Kelmscott Manor (fig. 39).[76]

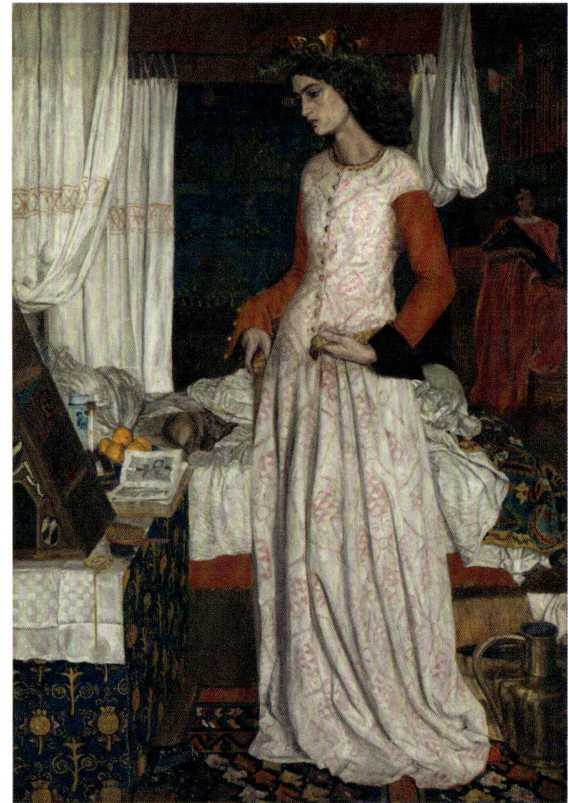

Fig. 38 William Morris (1834–1896), *La Belle Iseult*, 1858. Oil on canvas. Tate, N04999

This love of medieval colour was not, however, confined to artistic circles. By the middle of the century, the art of missal painting had almost become a middle-class hobby. Humphreys's chromolithographs encouraged the craze: his *Illuminated Books of the Middle Ages* (1849), coloured with the help of Owen Jones, allowed the 'refining influence of beautiful combination in art' to reach beyond the limited realm of 'few of the rich and powerful' (fig. 40).[77]

Pugin had also been an early adopter of the new colour printing device which he had discovered in Jones's chromolithographed study of the Alhambra in Granada. Following his conversion to Catholicism in 1834, Pugin used the technique extensively, in particular for the illustrations of his *Glossary of Ecclesiastical Ornament and Costume* (1844, fig. 41), a dazzling plea in favour of more colourful ceremonials. Pugin's *Glossary* reproduces numerous motifs and props associated with pre-Reformation worship, from liturgical vestments to crosses. The same vivid hues highlight the heraldic badges representing Edward the Confessor and Richard II in his wallpaper designs for the new Palace of Westminster (fig. 42). In the text of the *Glossary* itself the colour red, strongly associated with popish Rome, is given a particularly long entry. Although Ruskin denied Pugin's influence, accusing him of having converted for aesthetic rather than religious reasons – 'blown into a change of religion by the whine of an organ pipe; stitched into a new

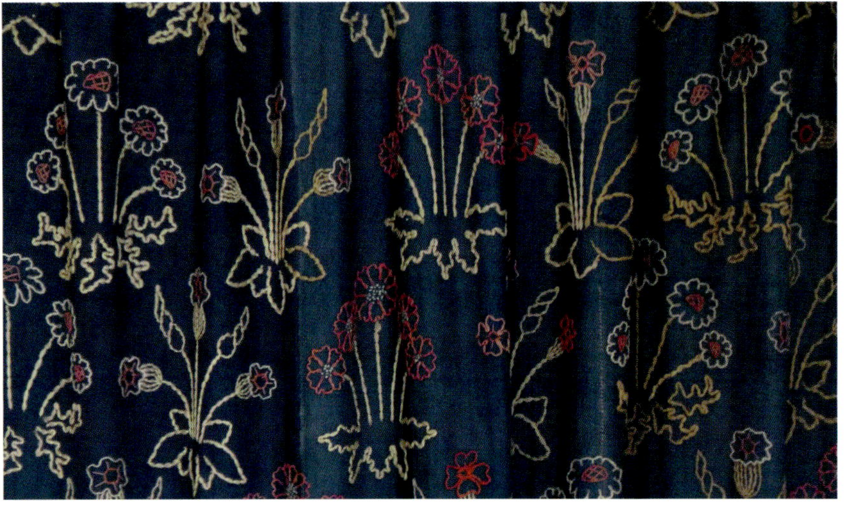

Fig. 39 Daisy wall hanging by Jane Morris (1839–1914), 1862. Embroidered wool. Society of Antiquaries of London (Kelmscott Manor), KM033.3

Right: Fig. 40 Henry Noel Humphreys (1810–1879) and Owen Jones (1809–1874), chromolithographed plate from *The Illuminated Books of the Middle Ages*, 1849. Bodleian Library, University of Oxford, 257735 b.39

Below left: Fig. 41 A.W.N. Pugin (1812–1852), chromolithographed plate from the *Glossary of Ecclesiastical Ornament and Costume*, 1844. Bodleian Library, University of Oxford, 137 c.13

Below right: Fig. 42 A.W.N. Pugin (1812–1852), Design for wallpaper for the Palace of Westminster, 1851. Pencil with blue, red, brown, yellow, green and pink washes on paper. Victoria and Albert Museum, D.733-1908

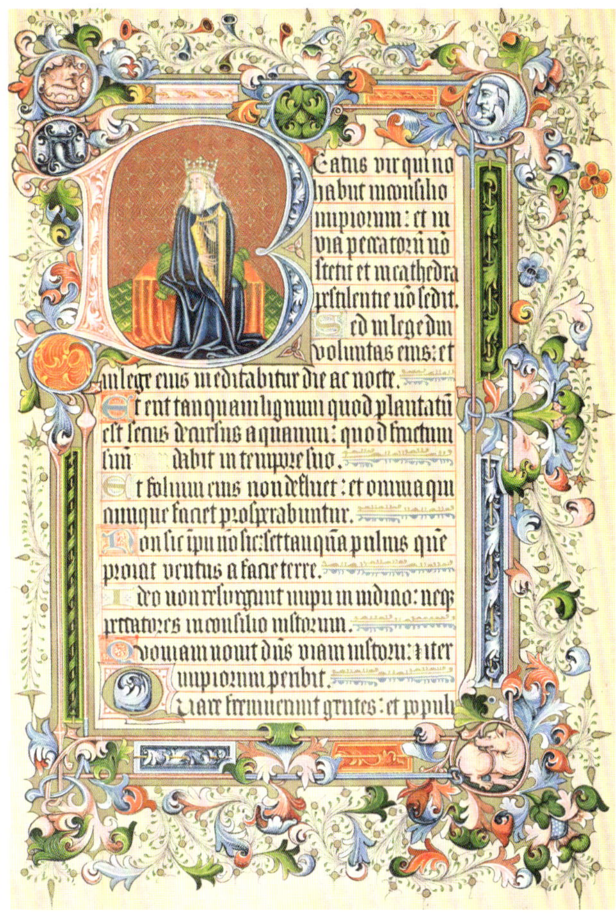

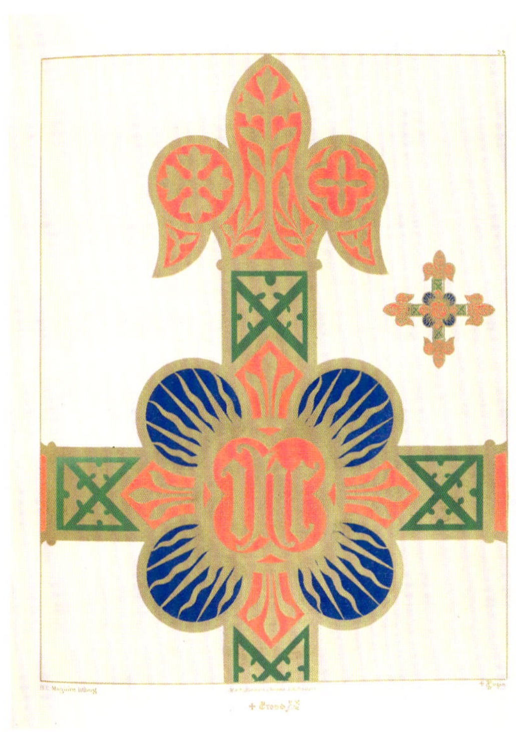

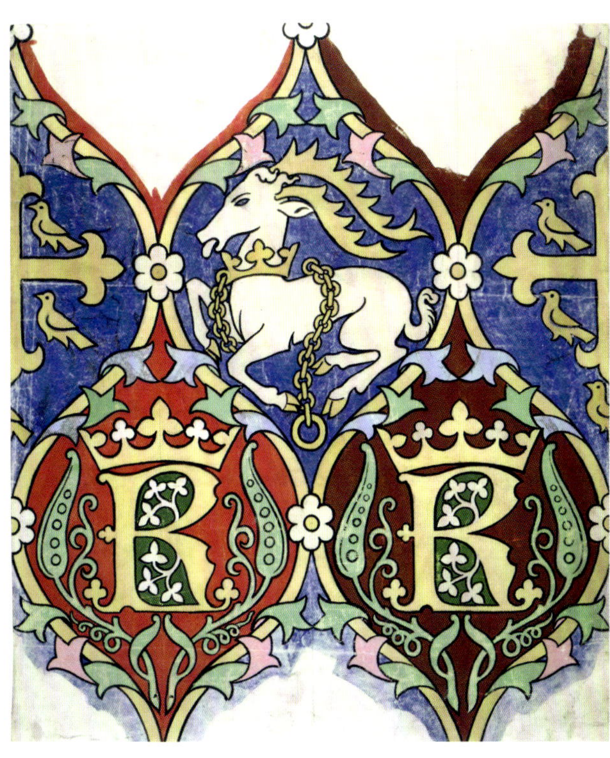

creed by the gold threads on priests' petticoats' – it is evident that the two men shared a common belief in the chromatic superiority of early Christian art over the modern.[78] However divided their theology, their common conception of the Gothic past as a colourful age shaped nineteenth-century religious and artistic practice.

In the wake of the Oxford Movement, colour increasingly featured in liturgical debates. *The Ecclesiologist* was particularly distrustful of the 'grey Protestantism of hue':[79]

> We are surely not called upon to prove that colour is beautiful. If it be not, why employ stained glass at all? We are consistent; we would have every inch glowing. Puritans are consistent; they would have every inch colourless.[80]

A regular contributor to *The Ecclesiologist*, Burges was commissioned by the Ecclesiological Society to design the 'medieval court' at the London International Exhibition of 1862. Burges's version was a tribute to that designed in 1851 for the Great Exhibition (fig. 43), for which Pugin had presented numerous colourful artworks, including Minton majolica tiles made all the more vivid by the use of new, industrially produced glazes (fig.44). Although Pugin only designed a small number of jewels in his lifetime, he also displayed a Gothic parure which he had given to his third wife in 1848. Inscribed with the words 'CHRISTI CRUX EST MEA LUX' ('Christ's cross is my [guiding] light'), the headband of enamelled gold set with a ruby, diamonds, turquoises and pearls (fig. 45) almost seems directly inspired by some of the ecclesiastical motifs chromolithographed in *The Glossary of Ecclesiastical Ornament and Costume*.

Burges's 'court' proved just as diverse and dazzling. Among its strikingly polychrome pieces was a flagon (fig. 46) designed by Pugin's son-in-law John

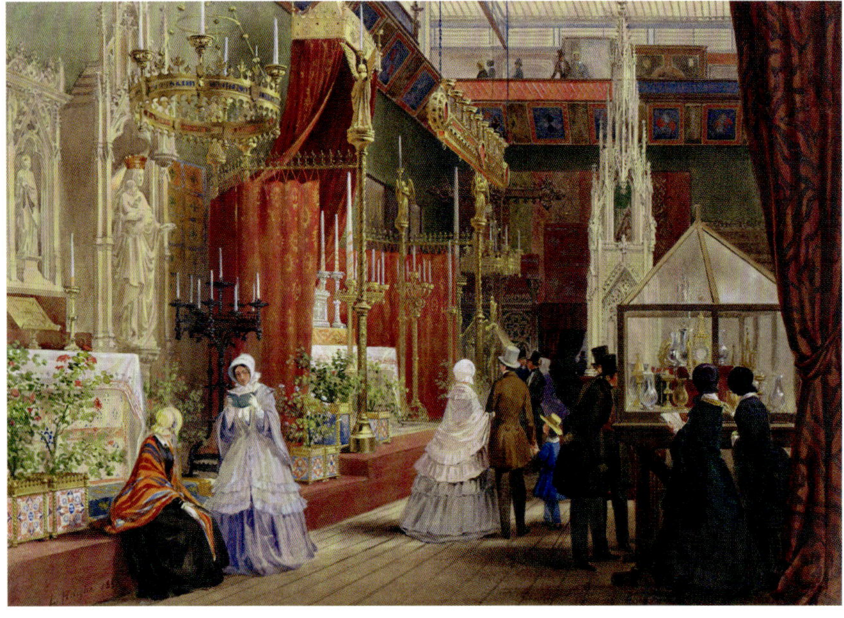

Fig. 43 Louis Haghe (1806–1885), *The Great Exhibition: the Medieval Court*, 1851. Watercolour and bodycolour with gum arabic over pencil. Royal Collection Trust, RCIN 919976

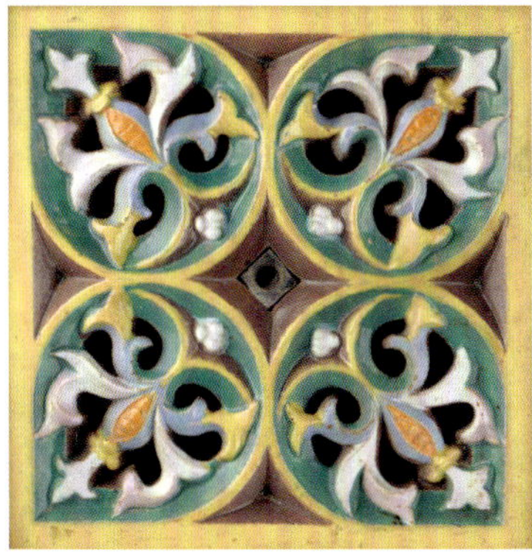

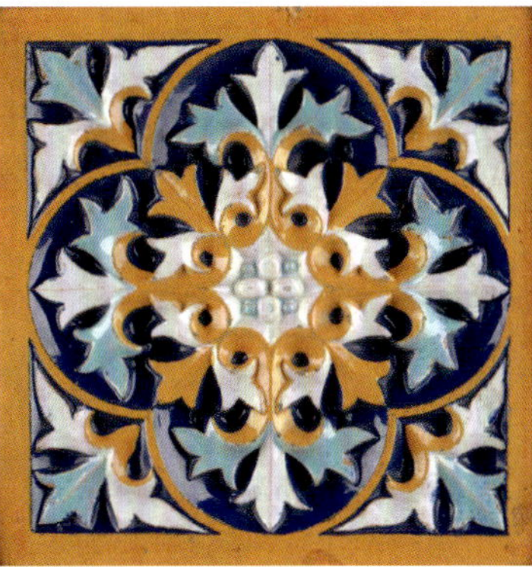

Fig. 44 Tiles from the stove in the Medieval Court by A.W.N. Pugin (1812–1852) for Minton, 1851. Earthenware with majolica glaze. Ashmolean Museum, WA2021.26

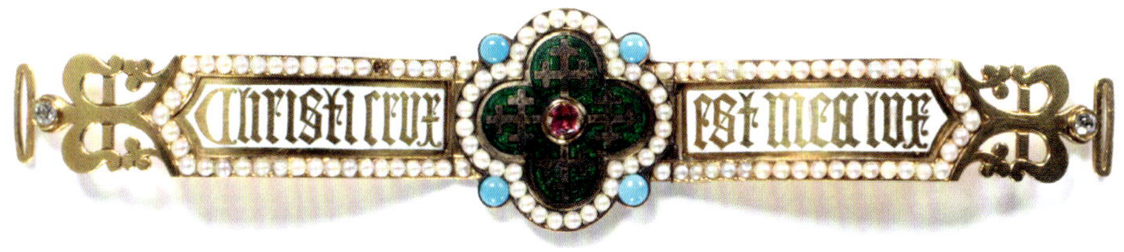

Fig. 45 Headband by A.W.N. Pugin (1812–1852) for Hardman & Co., 1848. Enamelled gold, set with a ruby, brilliant-cut diamonds, turquoises and pearls. Victoria and Albert Museum, M.10-1962

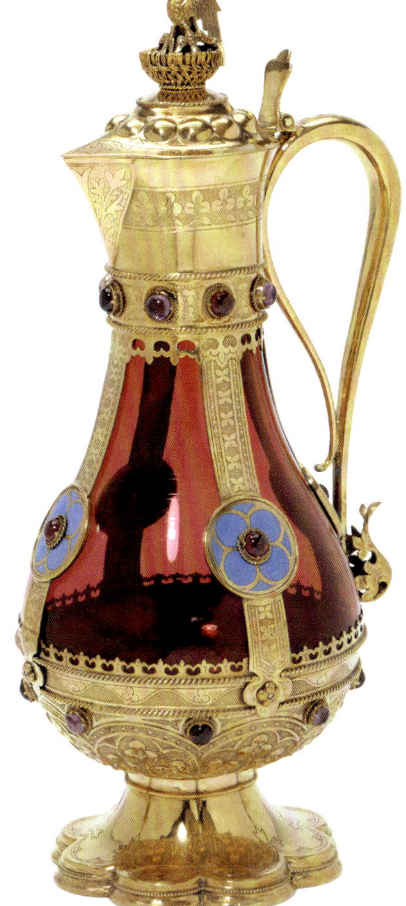

Fig. 46 Flagon by John Hardman Powell (1827–1895) for Hardman & Co., 1858–9. Ruby glass mounted in silver gilt and embellished with cabochons and enamels. Victoria and Albert Museum, formerly in the collection of Charles and Lavinia Handley-Read, M.39–1972

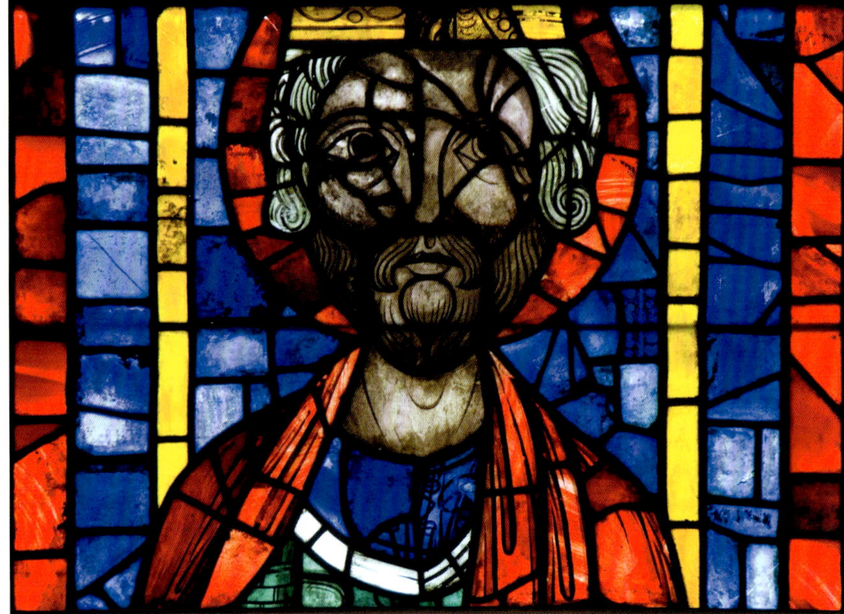

Left: Fig. 47 Side window representing the bust of a King in the clerestory of the choir of Soissons Cathedral, France, c.1210. Stained glass and lead. Stained Glass Museum, Ely, ELYGM:2003.3

Below: Fig. 48 Panel from St James's Church, Marylebone by Edward Burne-Jones (1833–1898) for Morris & Co. Enamelled stained glass and lead. The Whitworth, The University of Manchester, F.1987.1.1

Hardman Powell, made of ruby glass, silver gilt, enamel, and shaped and polished gemstones. It was made in the medieval manner, even if its style appears distinctly Victorian.[81] But contrary to Pugin, Burges was not a religious man. His admiration was for thirteenth-century French Gothic, which he applied to chalice, cathedral and private commissions alike. He was also a great supporter of the new firm Morris, Marshall, Faulkner & Co., whose works were displayed for the first time at the 1862 International Exhibition. The firm's 'fine art workmen' revived medieval stained-glass techniques in which the painting of details of line and shadow in brown or black oxides were fired onto translucent coloured glass (figs 47, 48). This achieved a transparency and luminosity which eighteenth-century windows painted in enamels on large pieces of glass lacked. The second half of the nineteenth century thus became the most active period in the production of stained glass since the Middle Ages.

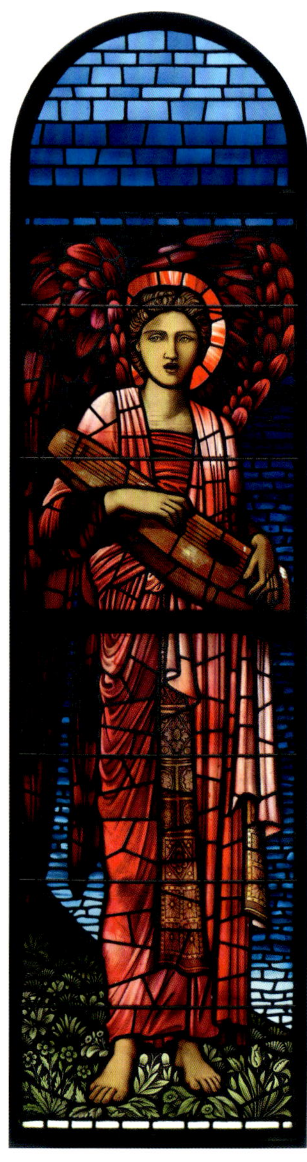

At the 1862 'court', however, the main innovation was painted furniture in the medieval vein, as epitomised by the firm's King René Honeymoon Cabinet and Burges's own Great Bookcase (see pp. 116–21). The structure of this three-meter-high artwork echoes the polychrome porch of a Gothic cathedral, although its style is far more eclectic, blending Byzantine, Pompeiian, Egyptian and Japanese influences (fig. 49). Burges may even have been one of the first *Japonistes* in England. In 1862 he went as far as to claim that the closest to a medieval court was not his own recreation but that of the Japanese, as that country was presenting its artefacts for the first time in the West.[82]

The bookcase was painted by no fewer than 13 promising young artists, including Burne-Jones, Simeon Solomon, Edward Poynter and Albert Moore. In the manner of stained-glass windows, its eight panels reflect the Pagan and Christian origins of the arts of poetry, painting, sculpture and architecture. Not only are these panels extremely colourful, they also shed light on Victorian debates about the colours of the past. For instance, Solomon's New Jerusalem

Right: Fig. 49 Japanese carps, detail from The Great Bookcase, 1873–5. Ashmolean Museum, WA1933.26

Below left: Fig. 50 Simeon Solomon (1840–1905), *St John and the Angel Measuring the Heavenly Jerusalem*, detail from The Great Bookcase, 1873–5. Ashmolean Museum, WA1933.26

Below right: Fig. 51 Edward John Poynter (1836–1919), *Dante's Vision*, detail from The Great Bookcase, 1873–5. Ashmolean Museum, WA1933.26

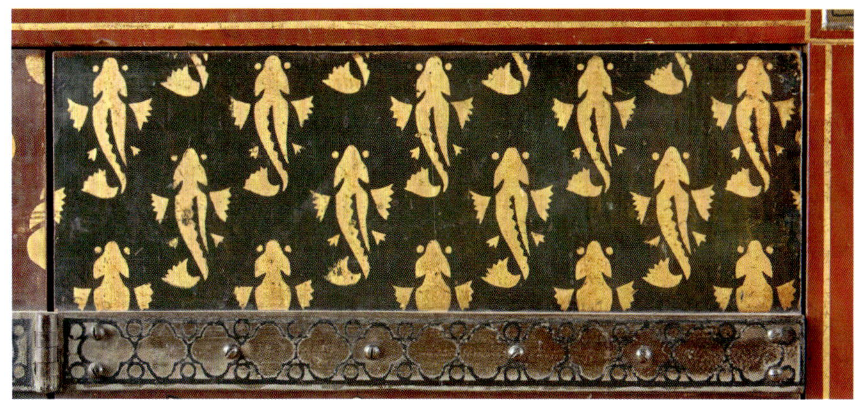

panel (Christian Architecture) (fig. 50) represents the Holy City's 12 jewel-like foundation stones, referring not only to the vision of St. John in Revelation 21:9–23, but also to the original dedication rites of twelfth-century cathedrals, which colour-loving architects like Burges were particularly interested in at the time. Edward Poynter's Dante panel is equally revealing in the context of the revival of medieval colour (fig. 51). It is, however, Rossetti's name which is inscribed next to the panel devoted to Christian poetry, depicting Dante's vision of Beatrice. Rossetti particularly admired Dante: in the 1850s he painted numerous pieces in tribute to the Florentine poet's work, including *Beatrice Meeting Dante at a Marriage Feast, Denies Him Her Salutation* (fig. 52). He also actively encouraged his circle of friends to embrace Dante's works. Interest in

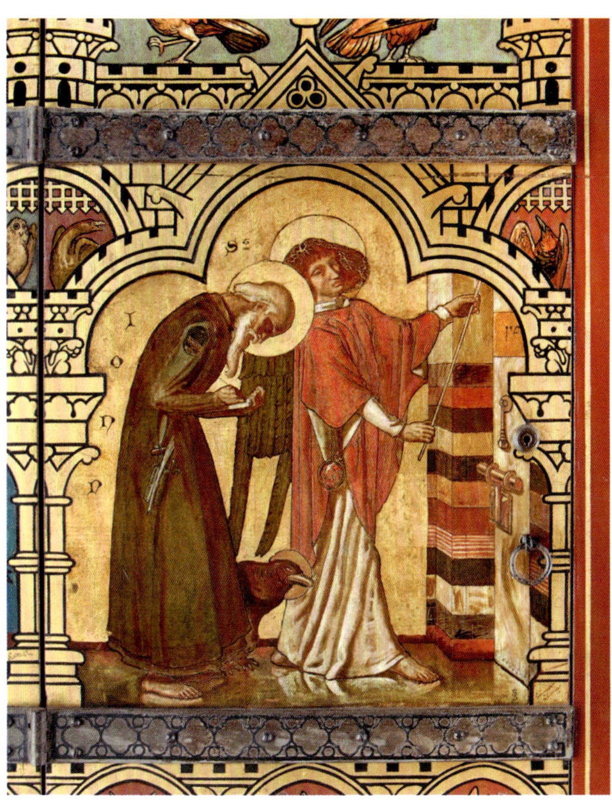

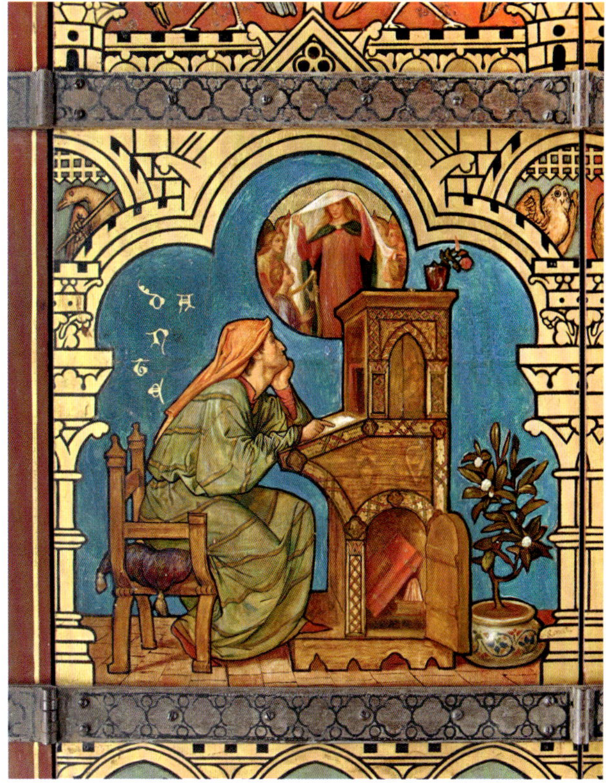

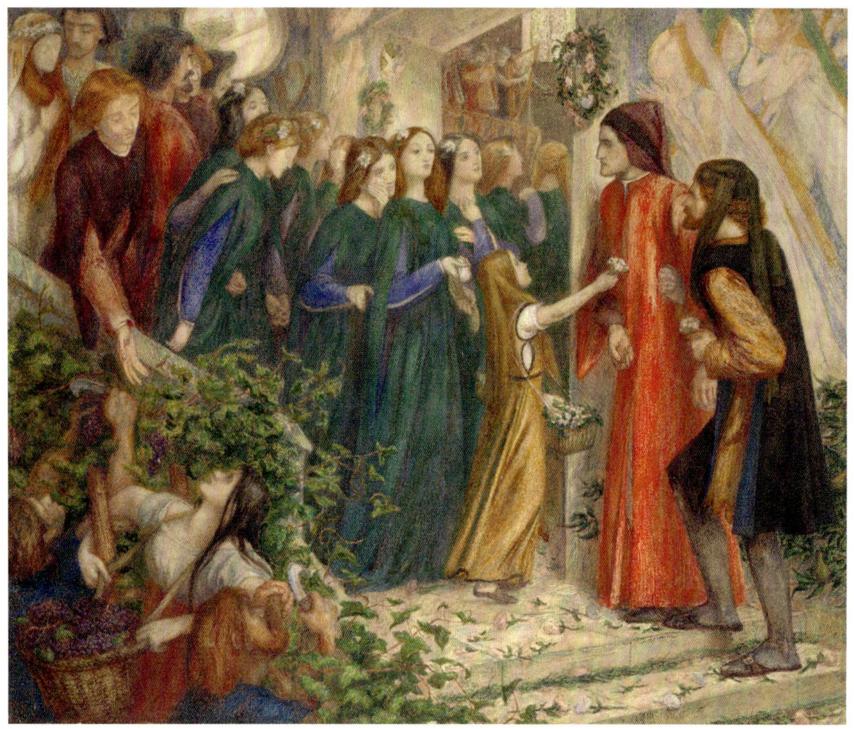

Left: Fig. 52 Dante Gabriel Rossetti (1828–1882), *Beatrice meeting Dante at a Marriage Feast, denies him her Salutation*, 1855. Watercolour. Ashmolean Museum, WA1942.156

Below: Fig. 53 Facsimile after Seymour Kirkup of a portrait of Dante Alighieri by Giotto (d. 1337) discovered in 1840 in the Bargello at Florence, 1859. Chromolithograph. Wellcome Collection

the Florentine poet had been given new impetus following the discovery in 1840 of a fresco depiction of a young Dante by Giotto in the Podestà Chapel of the Palazzo del Bargello in Florence (fig. 53). The Giotto portrait was a revelation for the Anglo-Italian artist and writer Seymour Kirkup, who openly criticised the controversial restoration of its colours in the heated context of the Italian struggle for political unity known as the *Risorgimento*. Kirkup, who was a friend of Rossetti's father, had been particularly outraged by the replacement of the poet's green collar – the colour of the new nation – by a dull brown, as if to thwart any hopes of emancipation. By choosing to depict the poet in this vivid 'forbidden green', Poynter and Burges may have been alluding to these controversies, still ongoing in the late 1850s.[83]

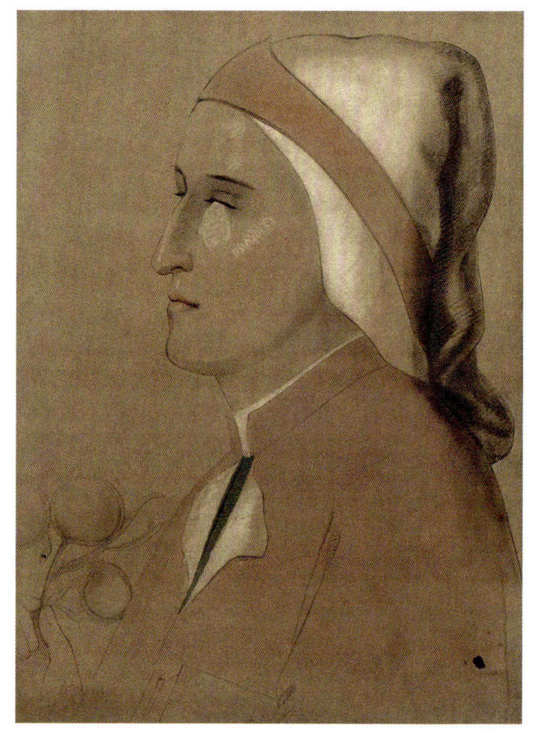

The bookcase, like the artworks produced by Morris, Marshall, Faulkner & Co., was a collaborative venture, created in the spirit of medieval artists and craftsmen who, according to Burges, had worked hand-in-hand, paying no heed to the distinction between fine art and applied art introduced during the Renaissance. The passion for colour – from the dazzling hues of illumination to the fired colours of stained glass – would prove enduring for all the members of this nostalgic avant-garde. In 1894, Morris gave a lecture on twelfth-century manuscripts, celebrating in Ruskinian terms their 'unerring system of beautiful colour … founded on the juxtaposition of pure red and blue modified by delicate but clear bright lines and 'pearlings' of white'.[84] The love of medieval hues was by then also being embraced by the next generation: in

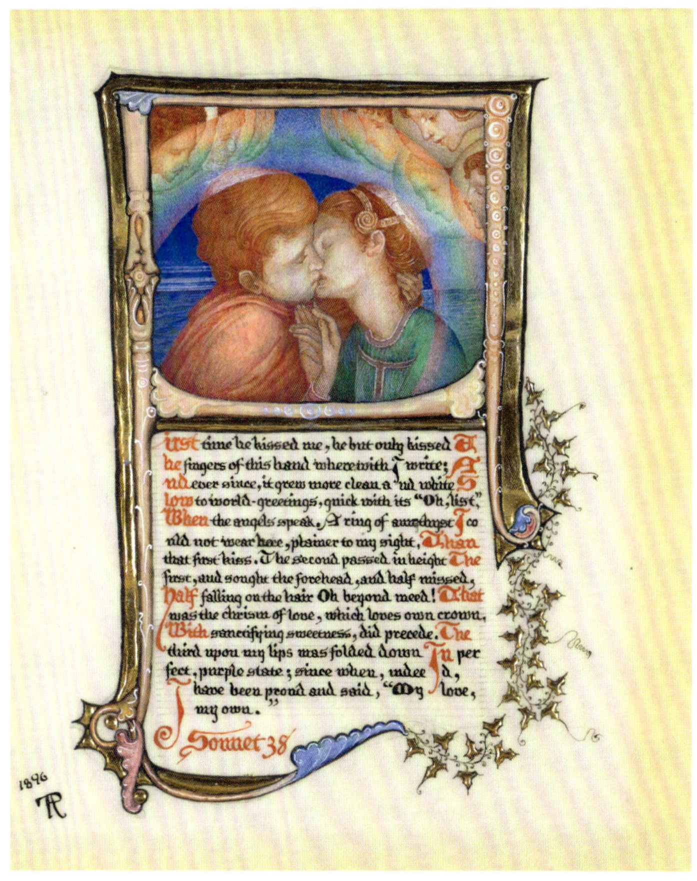

Fig. 54 Phoebe Anna Traquair (1852–1936), illuminated page from *Sonnets from the Portuguese* by Elizabeth Barrett Browning, 1894–6. Pen and ink and bodycolour over pencil on vellum. National Galleries of Scotland. Phoebe Anna Traquair Bequest 1936, DNG1870

the early 1890s Irish artist Phoebe Anna Traquair, a great admirer of Ruskin, Morris and his circle, illuminated the love sonnets of Elizabeth Barrett Browning to her husband. These poems were originally published in 1850 as supposed 'translations from the Portuguese', partly to veil their personal dimension (fig. 54). Sonnet 38 evokes Elizabeth and Robert Browning's first kiss in the sacred language of jewels:

> A ring of amethyst
> I could not wear here plainer to my sight,
> Than that first kiss.

As if to suggest this transmutation of colour into light, Traquair illustrates this sonnet with a rainbow encompassing the two lovers. The image of the glowing rainbow was a favourite of Traquair, as well as of Ruskin, whose advice on illumination she had sought in the late 1880s. Ruskin's lament about the damage caused by the Industrial Revolution and the loss of faith – 'the hues of our cathedrals ha[d] died like the iris out of the cloud' – therefore led generations of artists to embrace and revive the pure colours of a fantasy medieval past, not just as an escapist dream but as an act of resistance against their own Dark Age.[85]

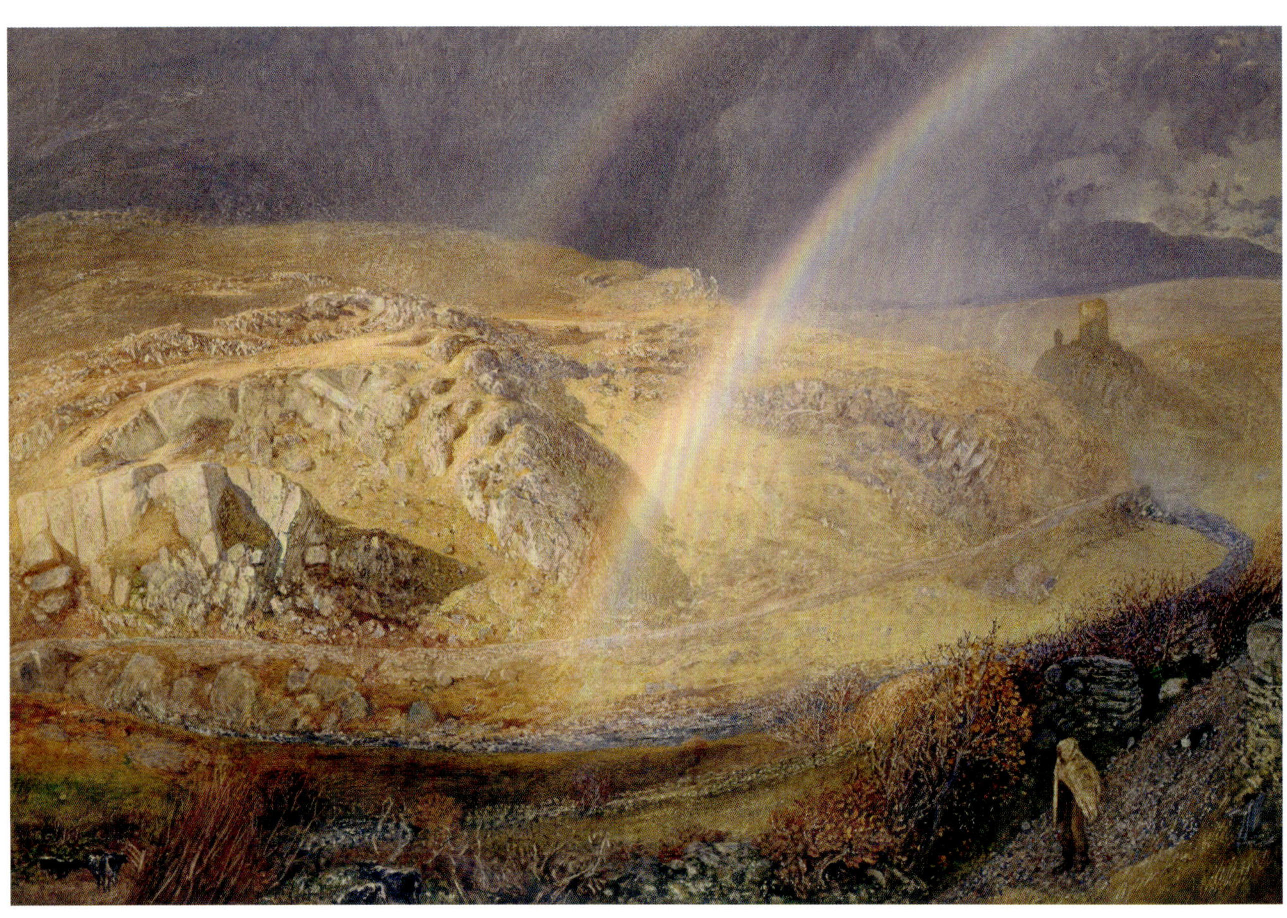

Fig. 55 Alfred William Hunt (1830–1896), *A November Rainbow, Dolwyddelan Valley, November 11, 1866, 1 p.m.*, 1866. Watercolour. Ashmolean Museum, WA1922.1

Unweaving the Rainbow: Nature's Colours in Art, Fashion and Design

Madeline Hewitson

In the nineteenth century, science and art were engaged in a close dialogue, sparked by a cultural revolution that brought scientific discovery together with mass culture for the first time.[86] In 1700, there were just ten scientific journals in Britain. By 1870, there were 10,000 English-language science publications with titles such as *The Entomologist's Weekly Intelligencer, Hardwicke's Science-Gossip* and *Midland Medical Miscellany*, to accommodate the tastes of such a broad new readership.[87] The rapid development of the natural sciences, particularly subjects such as biology, chemistry, zoology and botany, quickly spilled over into popular culture, becoming a source of entertainment as well as education. Scientists used visual tools to help disseminate new knowledge. These visual means of communication included diagrams, charts, drawings and anatomical illustrations to share research with peers as well as general audiences. As a result, artists, many of whom collaborated with scientists to produce these images, began to take note of scientific discourses and the way in which they altered people's perceptions of the world. From oil painting to ceramics to newspaper illustrations, art was indelibly influenced by the culture of science. In 1856, the sculptor John Lucas Tupper declared, using a historical term term generally replaced by the word 'scientist' from the early 1830s, that there had never been 'so broad a road of intercourse between artist and [natural] philosopher as now'.[88] Scientific culture had a powerful impact on the Victorians and shaped the ways artists and designers depicted the natural world.

Colour was one of the shared discourses between art and science and a mutual site for invention and experimentation. At the Royal Academy banquet in 1871, the biologist Thomas Huxley gave the toast to 'Science'. He remarked to the artists gathered around him: 'We both seek truth and we both seek beauty.'[89] However, there had been anxieties about the role of science in dissecting and revealing the secrets of colour, which had a long history of association with poets and writers. In 1820, the Romantic poet John Keats wrote that natural philosophy, 'Will clip an Angel's wings / Conquer all mysteries by rule and line / Empty the haunted air, and gnomed mine / Unweave a rainbow'.[90] Keats was making a specific reference to Sir Isaac Newton, who proposed that there were seven colours of a rainbow visible to the human eye, after he conducted experiments refracting light through prisms. Before this, in 1664, Robert Boyle had identified just five colours in the rainbow: red, yellow, green, blue and purple. Newton added orange and indigo, secondary colours located between red and yellow and blue and purple on the visible spectrum. However, Newton wove poetic rationale into the prism experiments. A rainbow with seven colours conformed to the heptatonic scales of musical composition. Newton believed that this created a harmonious analogy between the two (fig. 55). Despite this, Keats railed that Newton had 'destroyed the poetry of a rainbow by reducing it to a prism'.[91]

Debates about the rainbow's colours continued throughout the nineteenth century and were highly subjective across cultures. In nineteenth-century Japanese woodblock prints, the rainbow was typically represented with just the three primary colours, or sometimes with no colour at all. In *A Fine Evening on the Coast in Tsushima Province* (fig. 56), Hiroshige emphasised the shape of the bow across a vertically presented landscape. This rainbow, one of only three

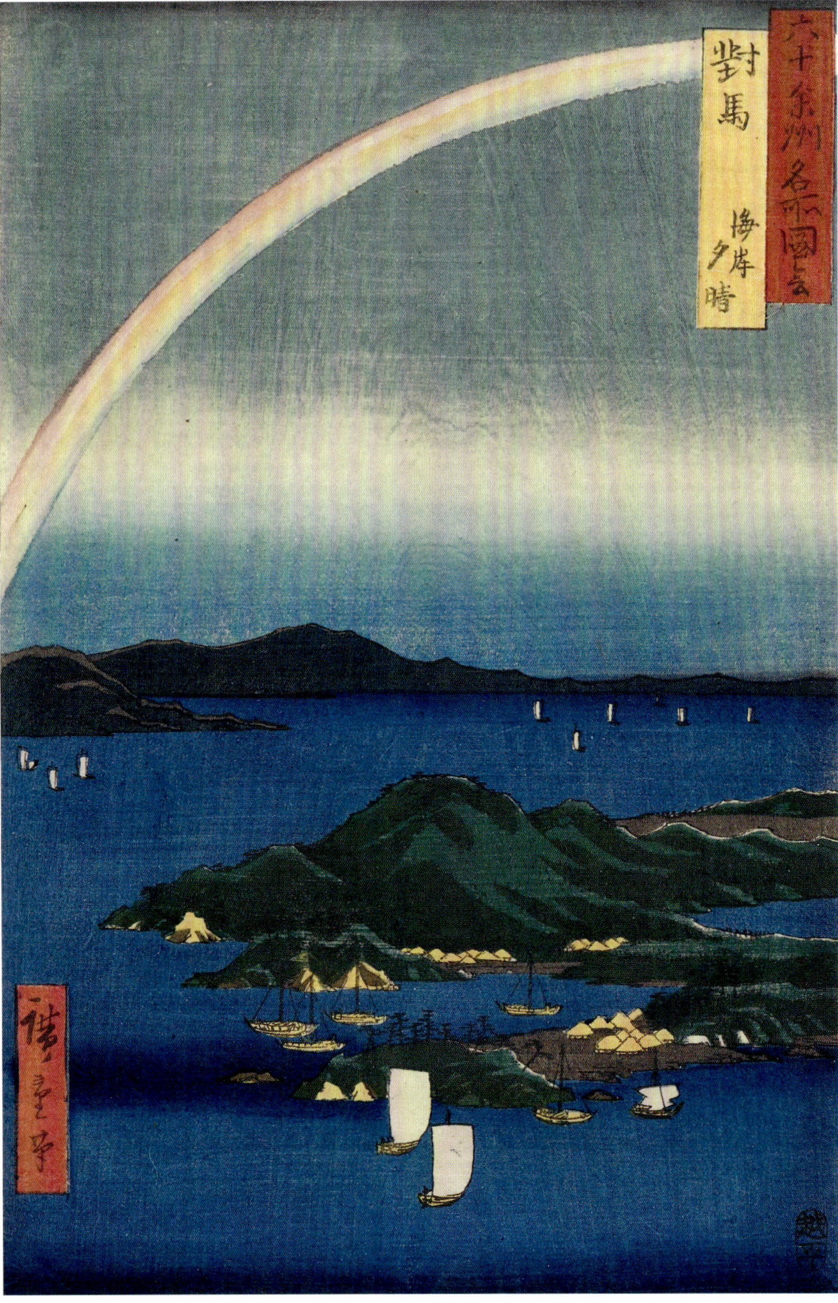

Fig. 56 Utagawa Hiroshige (1797–1858), *A Fine Evening on the Coast in Tsushima Province*, 1856, from *One Hundred Famous Views of Edo*. Woodblock print. Ashmolean Museum, EAX.4346

examples of rainbows in Hiroshige's work, reveals his subtle use of *bokashi*, the technique of shading colours in a woodblock. Despite this, the language of colour in Japanese is intimately tied to nature, seasons and environment.

COLOURFUL DIFFERENCES

No account of Victorian science can fail to mention Charles Darwin, whose singular contribution to the natural sciences marked a paradigm shift in the cultural landscape. Darwin's defining publications *On the Origin of Species* (1859) and *The Descent of Man, and Selection in Relation to Sex* (1871) galvanised public attention to the study of organic nature. Through Darwin, visual representations of plants and animals also became an important way of understanding the purpose of colour in the natural world. Darwin's account of colour as an evolutionary function had a significant impact on Victorian aesthetics by providing a new explanation for beauty. While Darwin's aim was to set out a biological explanation for the purpose of beauty in the context of evolution, he engaged in evocative artistic and poetic constructs to communicate ideas to his audiences.

In *On the Origin of Species*, the word 'colour' is used 133 times, and there are nearly 400 different colour terms. Darwin's interest in colour coalesced while conducting research during the voyage of the HMS Beagle in 1832. In his journal from the five-year trip, he recorded his observations of octopus and cuttlefish in a shallow pool of water:

> These animals also escape detection by a very extraordinary chameleon-like power of changing their colour. They appear to vary their tints according to the nature of the ground over which they pass. When in deep water, their general shade was brownish purple; but when placed on the land, or in shallow water, this dark tint changed into one of a yellowish green. The colour, examined more carefully, was a French gray [sic], with numerous minute spots of bright yellow: the former of these varied in intensity, the latter entirely disappeared and appeared again by turns. These changes were effected in such a manner that clouds, varying in tint between a hyacinth red and a chestnut brown, were continually passing over the body.[92]

The poetic language of colour in this interlude was not Darwin's own invention, but taken from a book he had brought on the journey, *Werner's Nomenclature of Colours*. The text was edited by a Scottish artist, Patrick Syme, and synthesised the work of eighteenth-century German mineralogist Abraham Werner – along with a number of other European naturalists – to create a standardised classification system for naming colours. The system comprised 108 standard colours presented in neat tables and grouped by dominant colour headings. Each colour was identified with a hand-painted swatch, pasted into the book, which could be used for comparative purposes during scientific fieldwork. An example of each colour's presence in the animal, vegetable and mineral kingdoms was given next to the swatch. For example, under the heading 'Yellow (i)', primrose yellow was identified in the feathers of a pale canary bird, the flowers of a wild primrose and the crystalline solid form of pale colour sulphur. The mix of disciplines was intended to make it accessible to the entire scientific community.

In Darwin's journals the poetics of colour language was used to help communicate to the scientific community the variety and ubiquity of colour in the natural world. At the same time, his use of *Werner's Nomenclature* was an attempt to bring scientific rationale to it. Syme's aim had been to resolve the subjectivity of colour. He wrote: 'An object may be described of such a colour by one person, and perhaps mistaken by another for quite a different tint.'[93] In theory, the book solved this problem. One biologist in England and another in North America could read Darwin's writing, consult their copy of the book and picture the same French grey cuttlefish as he had seen first-hand. However, each version contained different, hand-painted squares of colour which inevitably meant no two versions were exactly the same. Nevertheless, *Werner's Nomenclature* expanded researchers' abilities to describe colour using poetic descriptions to engage their readers.

Darwin's most controversial theory argued that sexual dimorphism – differences in the 'structure, colour or ornament' between males and females of the same species – was a consequence of natural selection. It is hard to overstate the extent to which the subjects of colour, beauty and sex were intertwined and seen through a Darwinian prism in the Victorian period. In visual terms, sexual selection was frequently communicated to general audiences using bird feathers. In his main publication on the subject, *The Descent of Man*, Darwin used the eye-spotted tail feathers of the Argus pheasant to explain that colourful male plumage served as a sexual charm to attract female mates. He described the pheasant's primary wing-feathers, once again in Wernerian detail:

> They are of a soft brown tint with numerous dark spots, each of which consists of two or three black dots with a surrounding dark zone. But the chief ornament is a space parallel to the dark-blue shaft, which in outline forms a perfect second feather lying within the true feather. This inner part is coloured of a lighter chestnut, and is thickly dotted with minute white points.[94]

He had shown his drawings of the feathers to several artists who 'expressed their admiration at the perfect shading', declaring them 'more a work of art than of nature'.[95] However, he pushed back at this explanation, convinced that their colour was a powerful tool in the procreative drive of every animal, including humans.

While the Argus pheasant was an adequate illustration for Darwin, Victorians quickly seized upon the feathers of an altogether different bird in debates across popular culture on sexual selection: the peacock. However, the magnificent, shimmering, iridescent feathers of the male bird presented a fundamental challenge to Darwin's theories (fig. 57). Since he believed that natural

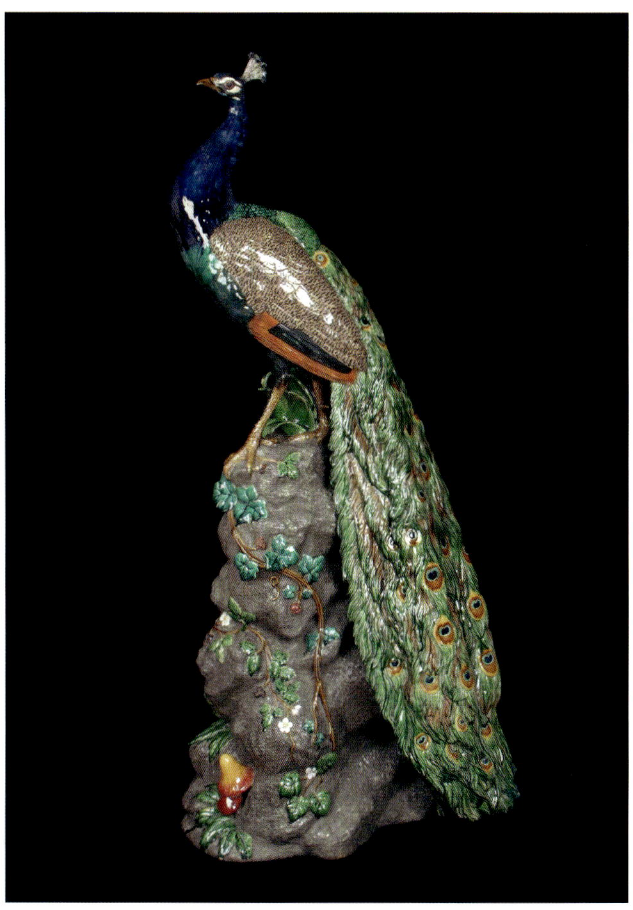

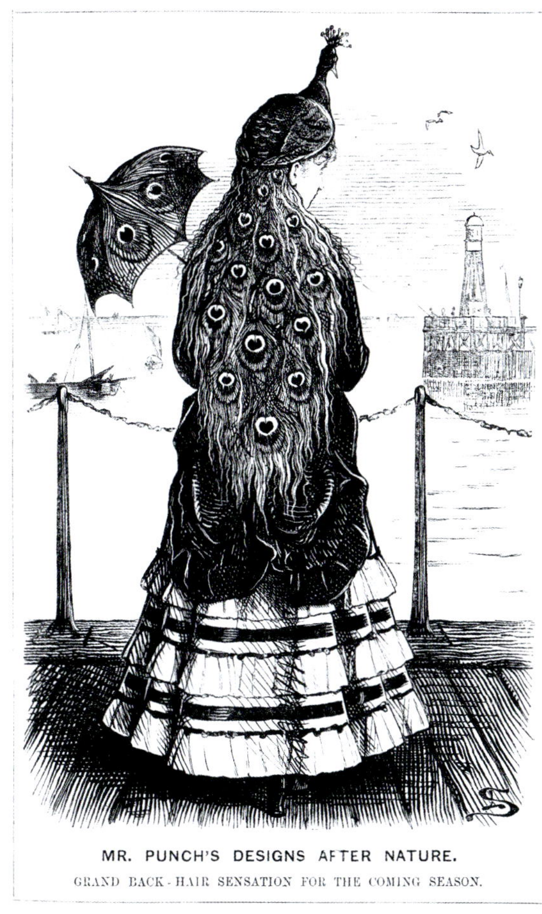

Above left: Fig. 57 Majolica Peacock by Minton & Co., 1873. Potteries Museum & Art Gallery, Stoke on Trent

Above right: Fig. 58 'Mr Punch's Designs after Nature', from *Punch*, 4 June 1870

selection was driven by survival, a heavy, cumbersome tail that would slow a bird's escape from danger made no sense at all. In 1860, he exclaimed: 'The sight of a feather in a peacock's tail, whenever I gaze at it, makes me sick!'[96]

While the theory of sexual selection focused on males possessing bright varieties of colour, in the Victorian satirical press the hypothesis was flipped to show women wearing colourful, enticing plumage (fig. 58). In a series of cartoons by Edward Linley Sambourne, otherwise known as Mr Punch, women promenade in public in a series of ornate costumes which turn them into hybridised human-animals. In one image of a woman dressed in a tall, ostrich-feather headdress and bustle, she expresses the desire: 'I would I were a bird', to which Punch replies: 'Impossible, my dear; but here is a suggestion.'[97] *Punch* satirises themes of vanity and the voracious consumption of bird feathers in women's fashion, discussed elsewhere in this catalogue, but the sexual politics of these images were also being discussed. In another cartoon, 'Miss Swellington' walks through the park with a long train of peacock feathers trailing behind her, in addition to a peacock-feather cap and parasol. She is watched by a man leaning against a railing with his hand resting suggestively in his pocket. Another man on horseback watches from afar, holding his riding crop erect.

This phallo-centric interpretation, where women were the objects of beauty and desire, suited the status quo. The implication of Darwin's theory – that females had the agency to choose sexual partners – were perhaps, at this time, too subversive for prevailing hetero-normative and cisgendered social mores. However, artistic representations of women with peacock feathers echoed the classic gendered role of women as seductresses.

Artists associated with Aestheticism, the movement devoted to the creed of 'Art for Art's Sake', also correlated female sexuality with the peacock feather. Between 1858 and 1859, Frederic Leighton produced four paintings of the Italian model, Nanna Risi, while working in Rome. Her dark Mediterranean features perfectly harmonised with the deep autumnal shades of the ocelli and barbules found in the peacock feather eyelet (fig. 59).[98] One of the Nanna paintings was titled *Pavonia*, the feminised version of the Italian word for peacock (pavone). In the painting, Risi looks directly at the viewer with a provocative gaze framed by a spread peacock feather fan, which suggests she is initiating the mating ritual.

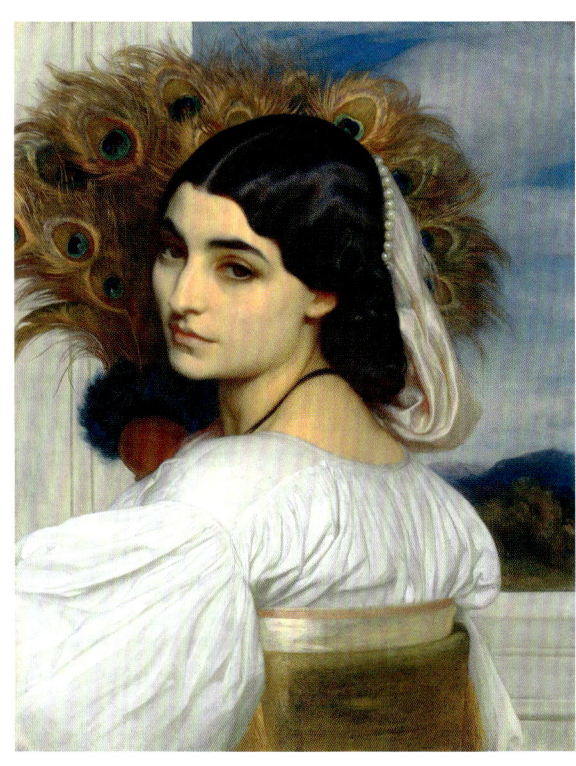

Fig. 59 Frederic Leighton (1830–1896), *Pavonia*, c.1859. Oil on canvas. Private Collection

In Frederick Sandys's *Vivien* (1863; fig. 60), the Arthurian character is also presented in front of a fan of peacock feathers. Sandys based his version on Alfred Tennyson's cycle of narrative poems, *Idylls of the King* (1859–85). *Vivien*, part of the first set of poems, had been published in 1859. In the poem, the 'wily Vivien'[99] seduces Merlin by 'smiling saucily'.[100] In yet another inversion of the peacock's gendered meanings, Tennyson uses the bird as a metaphor for male vanity, describing Gareth as 'peacocked up'[101] when Lancelot notices him.

Opposing views on sexual selection famously came to a head at the Natural History Museum in Oxford in June 1860, when Bishop Samuel Wilberforce debated 'Darwin's bulldog' Thomas Huxley. The venue was eminently suitable for a debate on the purpose of colour in the animal kingdom: the Gothic Revival building, which later influenced William Butterfield's polychromatic Keble College across the road, had been designed with naturalistic decoration by Benjamin Woodward and Thomas Deane. The University Museum, as it was originally known, embraced the collaboration between the arts and sciences which was exemplified by Ruskin and his friend Henry Acland, Oxford University's Regius Professor of Medicine. As John Holmes writes: 'The entire structure was an experiment in using architecture and art to communicate natural history, modern science and natural theology.'[102] As a result of Ruskin's connections to Pre-Raphaelite artists such as Thomas Woolner and Alexander Munro, sculptures of leading scientists were displayed around the central court between columns of coloured marble from quarries across England, Wales and Ireland.

Ruskin is often perceived as Darwin's arch critic and he indeed vehemently disagreed with the theory on sexual selection. He mocked Darwin's ideas that colour's sole purpose was to serve biological functions. He wrote: 'The blush of a girl, when she first perceives the faltering in her lover's step as he draws

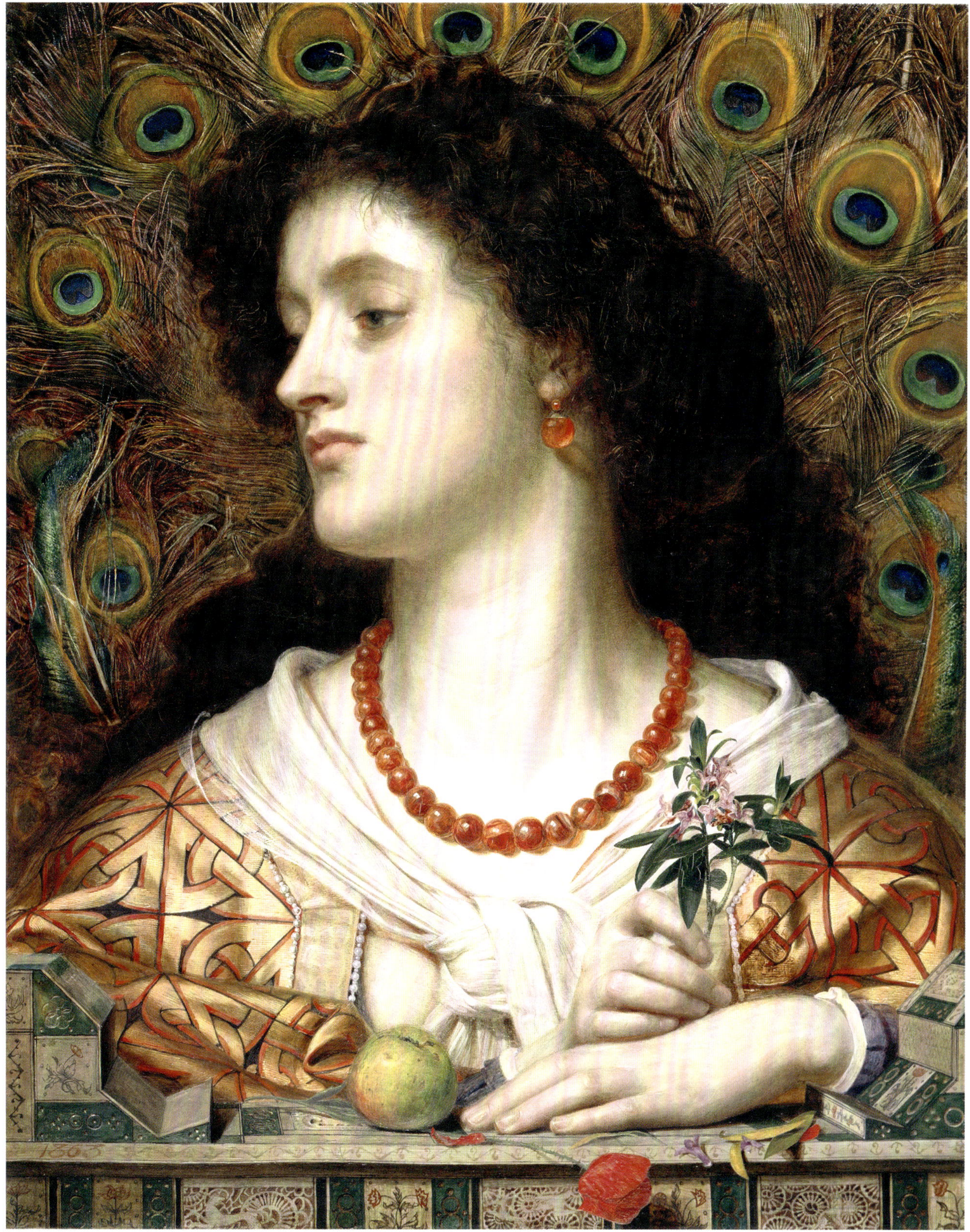

Fig. 60 Frederick Sandys (1829–1904), *Vivien*, 1863. Manchester Art Gallery, 1925.7

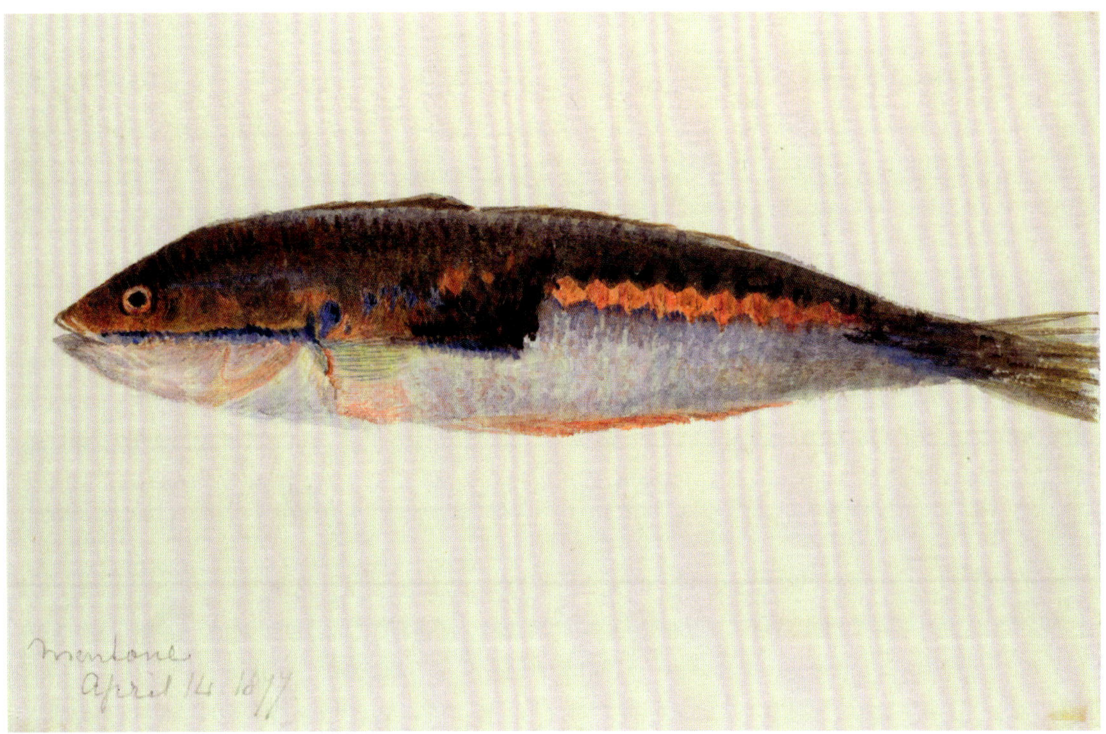

Fig. 61 Sarah Angelina Acland (1849–1930), Study of a Fish, 1877. Watercolour. Ashmolean Museum, WA.RS.UF.44.A

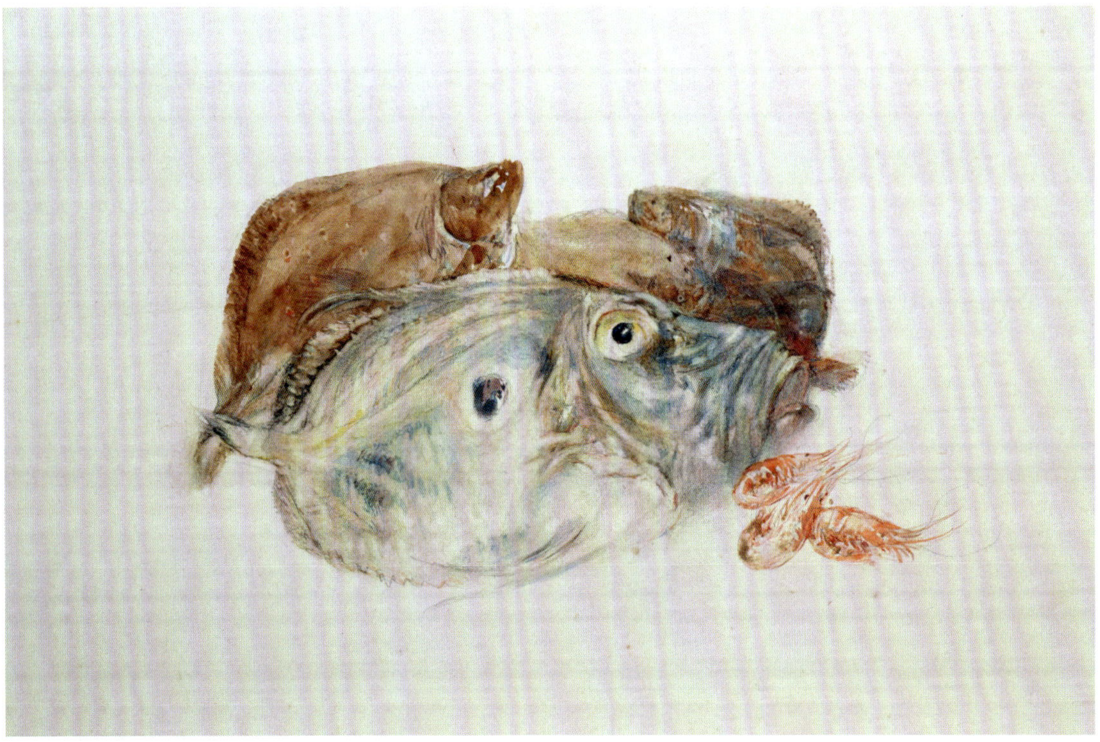

Fig. 62 J.M.W. Turner (1775–1851), Study of Fish, *c.*1835–40. Watercolour over graphite. Ashmolean Museum, WA.RS.ED.181

near, is related essentially to the existing state of her stomach; and to the state of it through all the years of her previous existence. Nevertheless, neither love, chastity, nor blushing, are merely exponents of digestion.'[103] For Ruskin, art and science were inextricably connected in a way that could not be reconciled with Darwin's reductive explanations for the origins and functions of the world.[104] In this sense, colour was too sacred a subject to be minimised by scientific enquiry. Ruskin imparted his beliefs in the spiritual power of colour to his readers in his instructive manual *The Elements of Drawing*, and students such as Henry Acland's daughter Sarah, an artist and, later, a pioneer in colour photography. In the *Elements of Drawing*, he wrote: 'If ever any scientific person tells you that two colours are "discordant", make a note of the two colours, and put them together whenever you can.'[105] Ruskin's riposte is aimed at colour theorists, but Acland's studies of fish reveal the wisdom of these lessons and the young artist's prowess for handling watercolours (fig. 61). We can imagine her peering over her dead subject, a bird's eye view, and studying the variety of tones in the fish scales, a single, round, unlidded eye looking back at her while she worked. Ruskin perhaps also referred her to the work of his favourite artist, J.M.W. Turner. Fishing was Turner's primary hobby, which caused some patrons to complain he spent more time on boats than painting.[106] But it seems he also used his leisure time to make a study of nature, and in his watercolours of fish he draws out the intense tones in a variety of sea life (fig. 62). Ruskin's pedagogy pushed back against a scientific gaze, prioritising the power of nature to instruct artists.

THE COLOURS OF NATURE IN DESIGN REFORM

The debate on the role of colour in nature permeated Victorian culture and was not limited to the popular and fine arts. The design reform movement, which had invigorated the decorative arts in Britain, also looked to nature's colours to inform its own debates on aesthetics. Whereas Ruskin advocated for a realistic, and therefore on principle, imitative, approach to nature, Victorian design reformers attempted to distil the rational laws of modern science and apply them to art and design. Rules and guidelines were a cornerstone of the design reform education programme. At the Government School of Design in South Kensington, which trained this new generation of Victorian designers, a placard on the classroom wall read: 'True Ornament does not consist in the mere imitation of natural objects; but rather in the adaptation of their peculiar beauties of form or colour to decorative purposes controlled by the nature of the material to be decorated, the laws of art, and the necessities of manufacture.'[107]

Their aim was to bring scientific principles such as rationality and replicability to what they perceived as unwieldy naturalistic ornament. For reformists such as Owen Jones and his student Christopher Dresser, the scientific study of colour fit their ideology because it refined colour into a set of rules which they could teach through the use of didactic tools such as colour wheels. Jones and Dresser owned copies of George Field's *Chromotography* (1835) and Chevreul's *The Principles of Harmony and Contrast of Colours* (1839).

Dresser, in particular, was interested in how his designs could refract and reconfigure nature's forms. Whilst a student, in addition to studying with Jones, he attended Art Botany lectures by John Lindley, a botanist who hand painted the flowers in his own scientific publications. Inspired by Lindley's artistic dissections of plants, Dresser later wrote: 'The designer's mind must be like the vital force of the plant, ever developing itself into the forms of beauty, yet while this is free to produce, still in all cases governed by unalterable laws' (fig. 63).[108]

Dresser argued that design should always start from nature – 'nothing can be more important to the ornamentist than the scientific study of art' – and that this applied not only to plant but also insect and animal forms. Dresser's zoomorphic designs play with the shapes and colours of exotic animals. In two ceramics designed for Minton & Co. he dissected the beetle form into its constituent parts of form, colour and line (fig. 64). Although lusterware, popularised at this moment by ceramicist William de Morgan, produced a shimmering, iridescent effect like the wings of a beetle, Dresser prioritised bright, bold colour applied to abstracted form. In these vases, Dresser also draws on Mexican and Aztec colouring and stylisation, which exemplified his belief in incorporating non-Western and historical ornament into new designs.

Dresser's strong polemic brought him commercial success and influenced future generations of Government School of Design students. One of these pupils was Kate Greenaway, who began her studies in 1858. Her coursework shows the impact of Dresser's botanical designs on arts education (fig. 65). Her naturalistic, Ruskinian renderings of flowers transform on the same page into Dresserian heptagonal ornament. This shape, and the schematic rendering, is also reminiscent of viewing a plant specimen under a microscope.[109] While attending evening classes at the Hatherley School of Fine Art, Greenaway met the artist Edward John Poynter. He encouraged Greenaway to break her allegiance to Dresser's strict principles and move towards a more artistic style.

Below left: Fig. 63 Christopher Dresser (1834–1904), *Studies in Design*, 1875. Bodleian Library, University of Oxford, Arts b.110

Below right: Fig. 64 Vase with beetle on the side by Christopher Dresser (1834–1904) for Minton & Co., 1872. Porcelain. Ashmolean Museum, WA2021.22; bequeathed by Peter Rose and Albert Gallichan, 2021

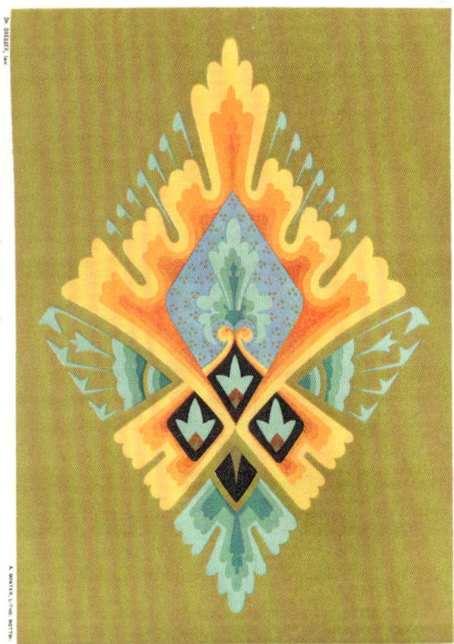

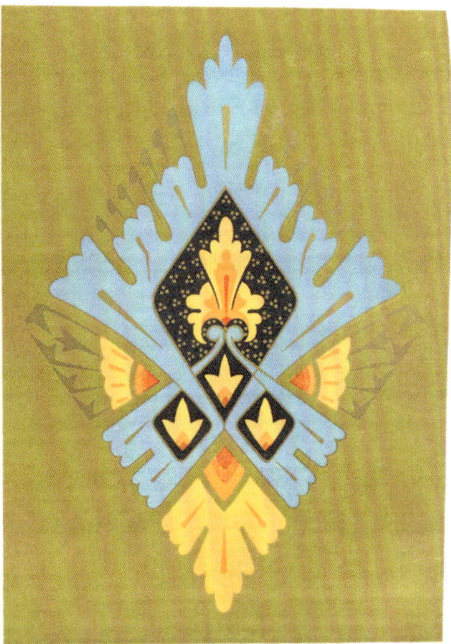

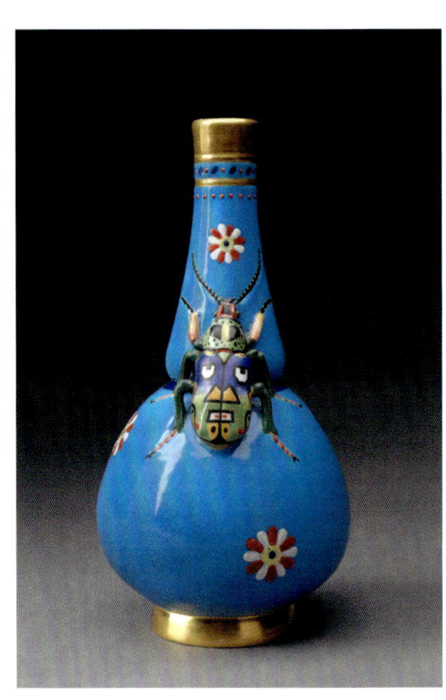

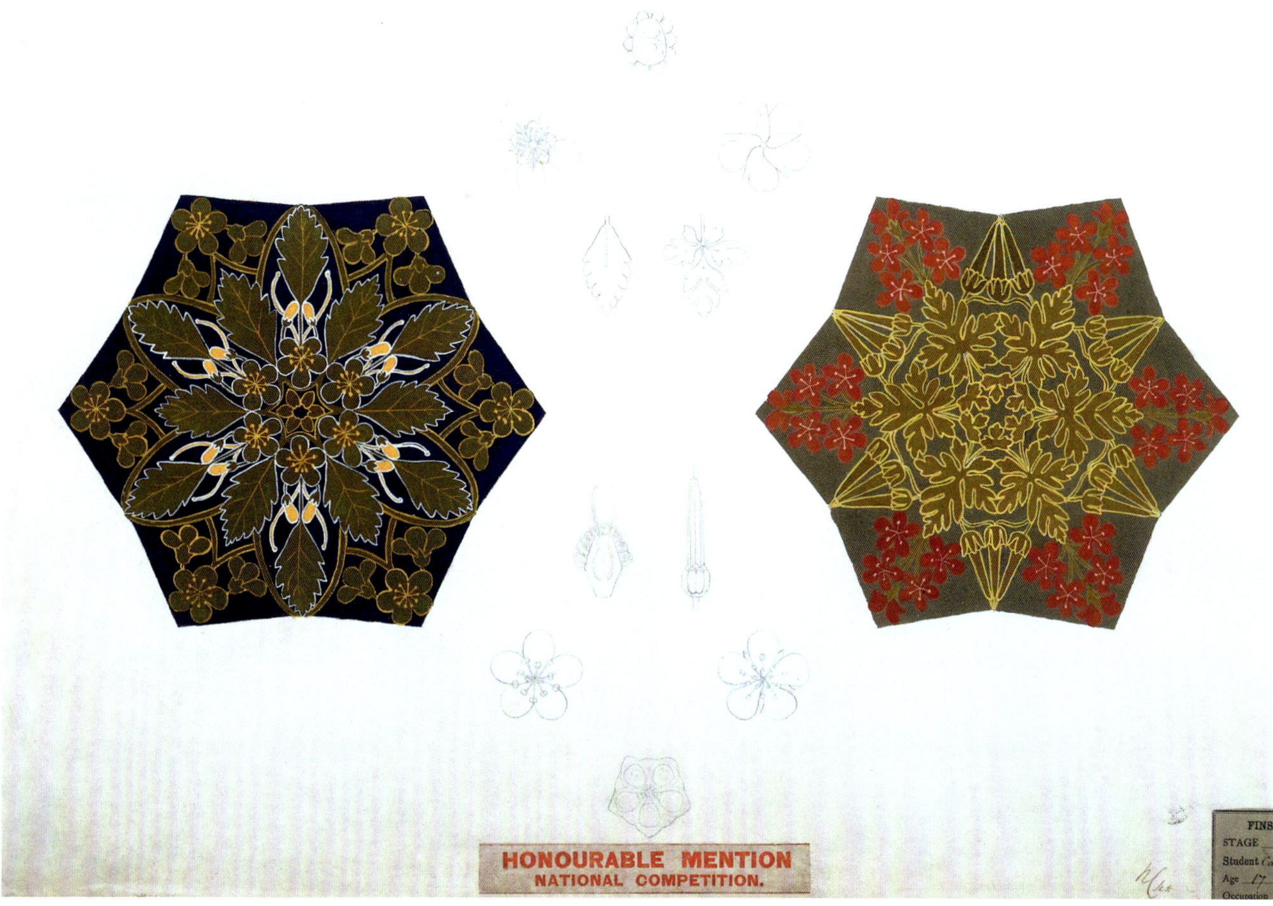

Fig. 65 Kate Greenaway (1846–1901), Two dodecagonal ornamental designs in watercolour, with pencil drawings of flowers and leaves, 1864. Watercolour and pencil. Victoria and Albert Museum, E.3614:2-2004

She soon moved into the field of illustration, which launched her career as an author of children's books. However, many of her characters, often young girls, are depicted in natural surroundings such as gardens and woods. Perhaps she kept in mind some of her first teacher's lessons on the importance of nature.

Art and the scientific study of nature were intimately intertwined during the nineteenth century. They were bound together by a mutual, inexhaustible interest in colour and a quest to discover its meaning and purpose. Victorian science renewed the importance of – and brought a newfound relevance to – depictions of the natural world. At the same time, artists harnessed the colours of plants, animals and insects in their work, as a means of reconciling the plethora of new scientific information about their natural surroundings and man's place within it.

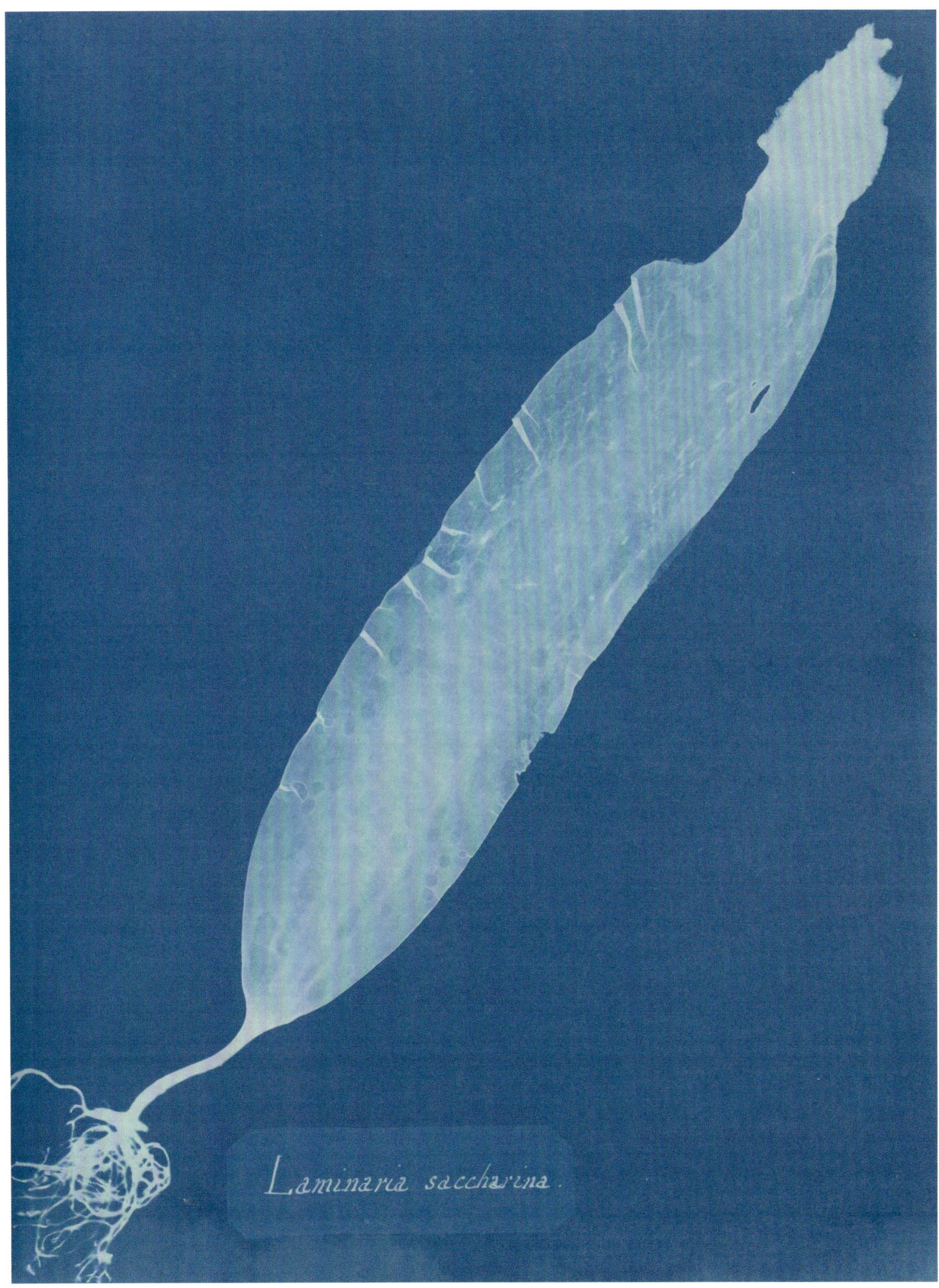

Fig. 66 Anna Atkins (1799–1871), *Laminaria saccharina*, c.1853, from *Photographs of British Algae: Cyanotype Impressions Part I*. Spencer Collection, The New York Public Library (Spencer Coll. Eng. 1843 93-440)

Pretty Plant Photographers or Pioneers? Anna Atkins and Sarah Angelina Acland

Lena Fritsch

Below left: Fig. 67 Anna Atkins (1799–1871), *Ulva Latissima*, 1853, from *Photographs of British Algae: Cyanotype Impressions*. Spencer Collection, The New York Public Library (Spencer Coll. Eng. 1843 93-440)

Below right: Fig. 68 Anna Atkins (1799–1871), *Dictyota dichotoma, in the young state, and in fruit*, 1848–49, from *Photographs of British Algae: Cyanotype Impressions Part XI*. Spencer Collection, The New York Public Library (Spencer Coll. Eng. 1843 93-440)

Translucent white elements with delicate veins glide calmly through abstract compositions; endlessly intertwined lines grow into all directions underwater; fine fronds float suspended atop an intensely Prussian Blue background; opaque white fields contrast with hazy patches that light blue bleeds through. The dynamic interplay of shapes, textures and blue colour convey a unique atmosphere of surreal beauty, oscillating between the concrete and abstract, the micro and macro, the worldly and the cosmic. That is, until small handwritten Latin names and brief descriptions at the bottom inform us what these images actually document: '*Laminaria saccharina*', '*Ulva Latissima*', '*Giogartina purpurascens*', '*Dictyota dichotoma, in the young state, and in fruit*' (figs 66–68) – in other words, algae, seaweed and marine plants native to England.

These atmospheric and yet documentary photograms (photographic images made without a camera) can be found in Anna Atkins's *Photographs of British Algae: Cyanotype Impressions*, which was self-published in multiple

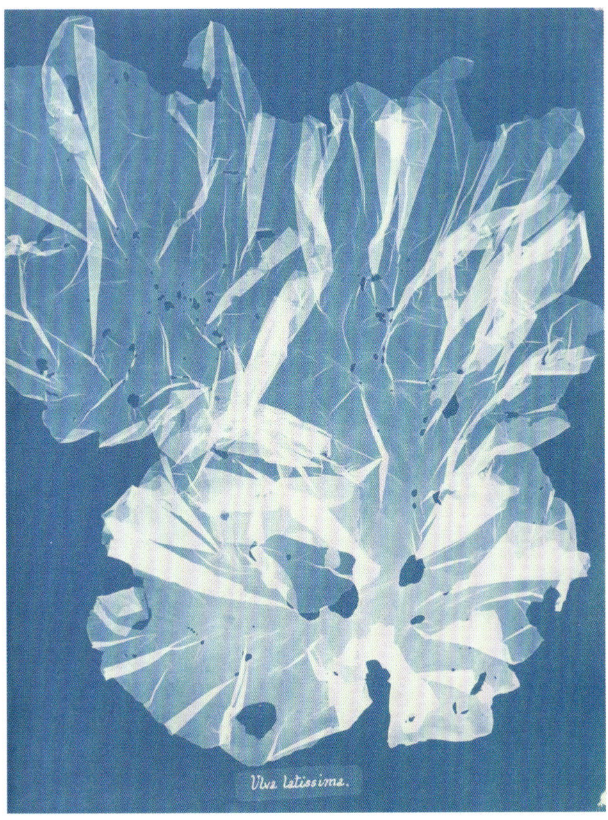

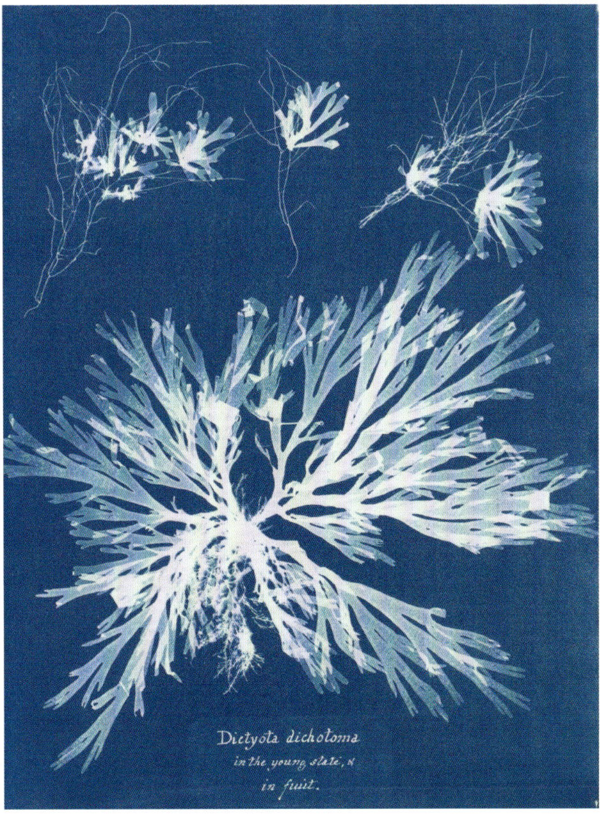

instalments over a period of ten years from 1843. The prints were originally intended to accompany William Harvey's exhaustive *Manual of the British Marine Algae* (1841).

Born in Kent, Anna Atkins (1799–1871) lost her mother very early in life and was raised by her father, renowned British Museum scientist and Royal Society member John George Children. She had access to a scientific education from an early age and, working at her father's side, became an accomplished illustrator of animal and plant motifs. A well-connected photography enthusiast, Children introduced his daughter to Royal Society members William Henry Fox Talbot (1800–1877) and the astronomer and chemist Sir John Herschel (1792–1871), who were both pioneering photographers. Atkins attended their lectures and befriended them. In 1825 she married John Pelly Atkins, a wealthy West India merchant and owner of Jamaican sugar and coffee plantations. In nineteenth-century Victorian England, women were restricted from professionally practising science. Botany, however, was considered an elegant and feminine hobby – as philanthropist Priscilla Wakefield argued in 1796 in her *Introduction to Botany*, its 'ornamental' nature made botany suitable also for 'ladies and effeminate men.'[110] Atkins assembled a collection of dried plants, supplied specimens to botanists at Kew Gardens and was elected a member of the London Botanical Society in 1839.

Shortly after Herschel developed the cyanotype process in 1842, Atkins used this new blueprint technology for her *Photographs of British Algae* project. Hand-printing thousands of photograms and adding hundreds of new motifs over the course of ten years, she refined the chemical solutions and exposure times. After coating the paper with light-sensitive chemicals (ferric ammonium citrate and potassium ferricyanide), Atkins placed the marine plants on the treated surface. The paper was then exposed to the sun, which made it turn a vivid cyan-blue, contrasting with the white shadow impressions of the plants. Atkins fixed the images by washing them in cold water. Her cyanotypes had a botanical purpose – to 'record' systematically extensive varieties of marine specimens as accurately as possible and in real size, benefiting from the indexical nature of photograms. Atkins outlines in the introduction to her book that, unlike human drawings of objects, cyanotypes enabled botanists 'to obtain impressions of plants themselves.'[111] At the same time, the cyanotypes are visually arresting images that convey a striking underwater atmosphere. Atkins arranges the marine plants carefully, considering their shapes, textures and the overall composition, and she presents some of them as liquid, abstract and fantastical. The images are scientific as well as artistic – they reflect Atkins's technological skills and her passion for experimentation, as much as her aesthetic sensorium.

After completing *Photographs of British Algae* in 1853, Atkins turned to cyanotypes of terrestrial plants such as ferns and flowers, often collaborating with her close friend Anne Dixon. She also began to incorporate feathers and even lace in intricate compositions. A print titled *Peacock* features six peacock feathers in different sizes, partly overlapping, in different shades of white and blue (fig. 69). Washed white shadows and fine fibres on the blue background

Fig. 69 Anna Atkins (1799–1871) and Anne Dixon (1799–1864), *Peacock*, *c.*1851–6. From the presentation album of 74 cyanotypes of algae, ferns, flowers, feathers and lace, *c.*1845–56

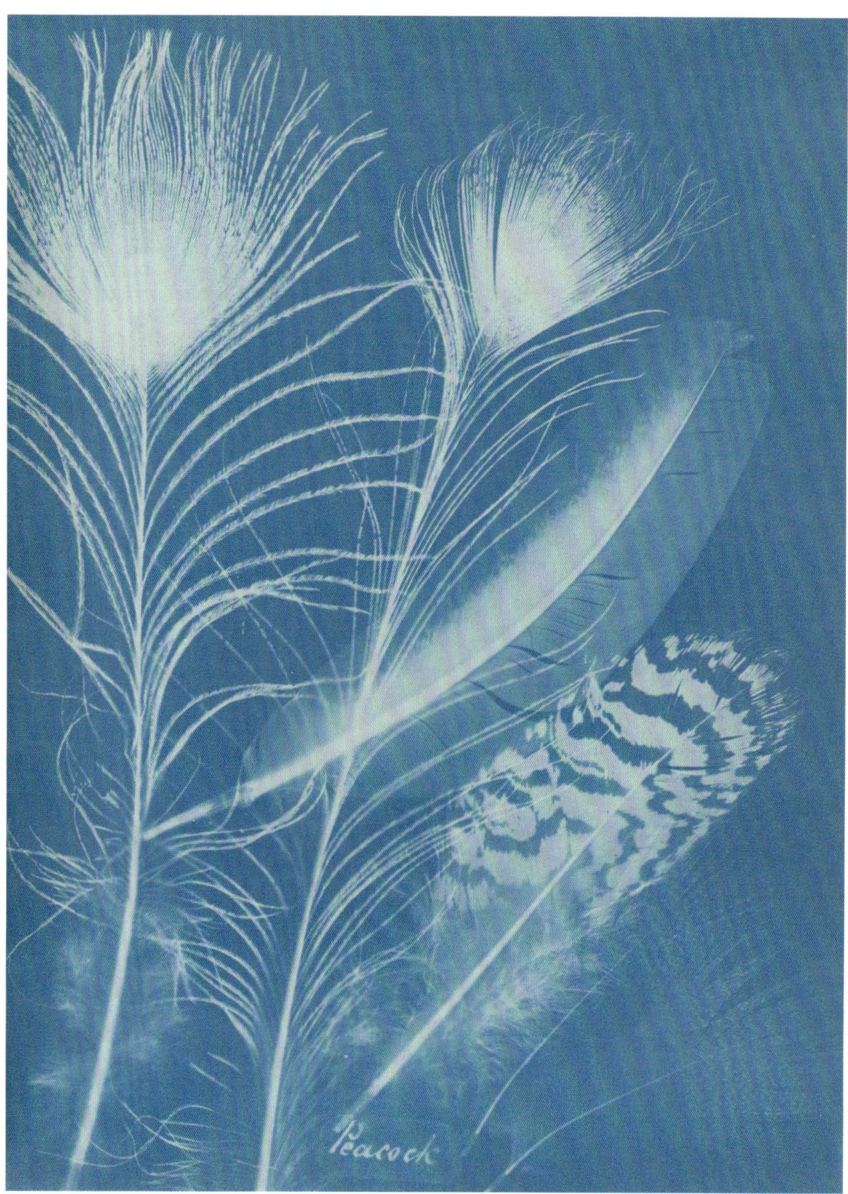

convey a softness that reflects the delicate texture of the feathers. Round lines and a curved feather partly overlapping two larger feathers result in a balanced, dynamic composition, evoking a sense of light movement. It is evident that instead of focusing on accurate scientific documentation, Atkins allowed herself to become absorbed in visual properties: blue hues and composition, line and form, transparency and opacity.

Atkins's cyanotypes are amongst the earliest examples of a photographic process in a single colour. The first part of *Photographs of British Algae* was published in October 1843 – eight months before Talbot released the first instalment of his famed *The Pencil of Nature*. Unlike Talbot's, Atkins's book was not publicly marketed or commercially distributed. Instead, the author published it privately and presented copies with handwritten dedications to

Fig. 70 Sarah Angelina Acland (1849–1930), Colour Photograph (Autochrome) of a Rainbow over Park Town, Oxford, *c.*1908

'botanical friends' and family acquaintances, including Talbot and Herschel. By the late nineteenth century, Atkins's achievements were nearly forgotten. It was not until the late 1970s, when American photography historian Larry J. Schaaf researched her work in depth and published his essay *The First Photographically Printed and Illustrated Book*, that scholars and artists began to rediscover the cyanotypes.[112] Schaaf's 1985 book *Sun Gardens: Victorian Photograms by Anna Atkins* is the first fully illustrated monograph on Atkins's work; with a revised 2018 edition, it remains a benchmark publication.

Born 50 years after Atkins, Sarah Angelina Acland (1849–1930) was also a practitioner of early colour photography with a passion for science and art. She lived in Oxford, the daughter of physician Henry Wentworth Acland, Regius Professor of Medicine at the University of Oxford, and philanthropist Sarah Acland. Like Atkins, Acland developed an interest in drawing, including botanical and animal motifs, before taking up photography. After studying at the Oxford School of Science and Art (now Oxford Brookes University), Acland took private lessons from writer, art critic and educator John Ruskin, who lodged with the wealthy family during his first two years as Slade Professor of Fine Art at the University of Oxford. They maintained a close friendship for many years. Acland also met Pre-Raphaelite artists including Dante Gabriel Rossetti. Her watercolours painted in Mentone on the French Riviera in 1877 are typical of her work at the time: fish are carefully drawn in vibrant colours, focusing on the pattern of the scales (fig. 61, p. 66). The drawings were probably presented by John Ruskin to the Ruskin Drawing School in 1906, before they entered the Ashmolean's collections.

Acland took up monochrome photography in 1891, first specialising in portraiture. Well-balanced light and shadow contrasts and a soft focus in portraits of Ruskin, Prime Minister William Gladstone and many others reflect the influence of photographer Julia Margaret Cameron (1815–1879) on her practice. In 1894 Acland joined the new Oxford Camera Club as its first female member, becoming vice-president. She was elected a member of the Royal Photographic Society in 1900 and remained so until her death. Her most important contribution to the field of photography, however, was her work using the Sanger Shepherd method in 1900, shortly after it was invented.[113] This complicated colour technique involved taking three separate exposures on one plate – each through a different chromatic filter – before printing the red negative onto glass, and the green and blue negatives onto transparent celluloid that was then stained yellow and pink. These were combined in one lantern slide which could either be shown through a projector or printed on paper. Acland's photograph of Oxford's New College garden from 1900 and of a rainbow over Park Town, taken around 1908, convey the photographer's joy in having mastered this new technology to capture successfully the bright colours of nature (figs 70, 71). She also experimented with colour photography indoors, as an autochrome featuring Millais's celebrated portrait of Ruskin shows (fig. 72). The portrait had been given to Acland's father by his close friend Ruskin; Acland tried to capture its colours as accurately as possible, in accordance with Ruskin's belief that 'the truth of nature is a part of the truth of God'.

Four slides of a peacock feather from 1899 (fig. 73) – divided into the colour layers of yellow, magenta and blue, and one of full colour – are Sanger Shepherd sample slides. Acland owned such slides and used them in one of her lectures in 1900 to demonstrate the technology.[114] The Sanger Shepherd process set a pathway for future colour photography, followed notably by Kodak's dye-transfer process of the 1940s. Art and photography historian Kate Flint wrote that Acland was 'endlessly experimental with cameras, lenses,

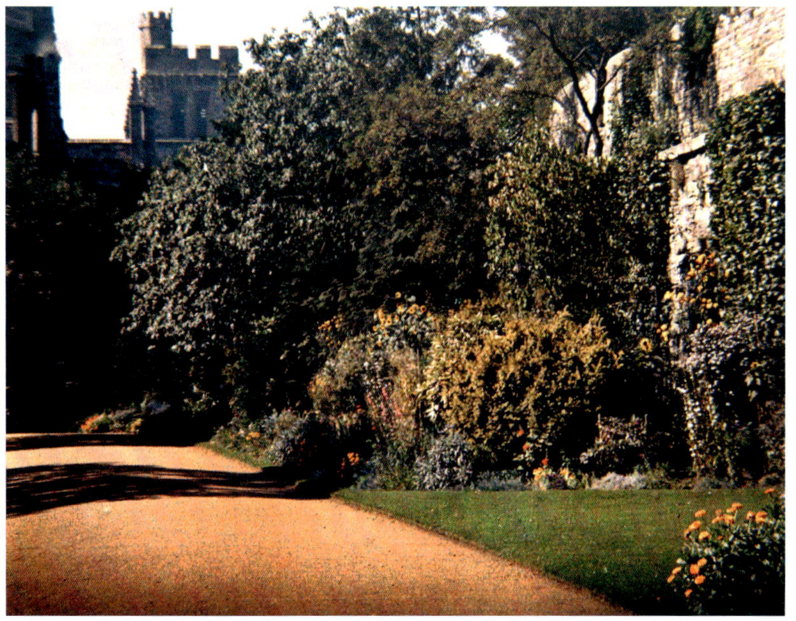

Below left: Fig. 71 Sarah Angelina Acland (1849–1930), *Autumn Colours in New College Gardens*, September 1907

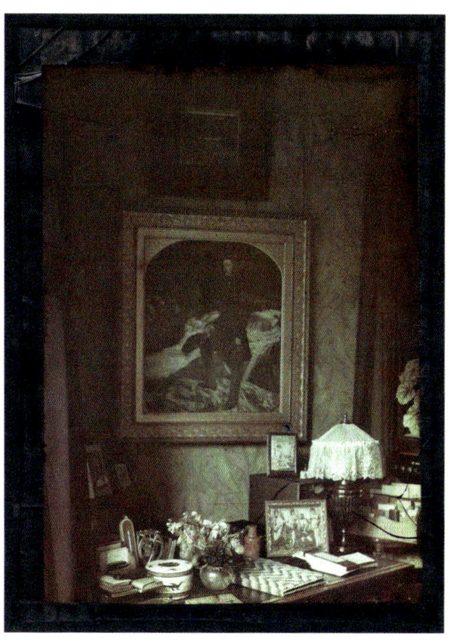

Below right: Fig. 72 Sarah Angelina Acland (1849–1930), colour Photograph (Autochrome) of the Millais Portrait of John Ruskin, hanging in Sarah Acland's House at Park Town, Oxford, 1913–17

and methods'[115] and produced a variety of colour photographs in Oxford and further afield, including in Gibraltar and Madeira (fig. 74). She also used the French Autochrome process when this was introduced in 1907, and gave popular lectures on her use of colour photography at the Royal Photographic Society. After Acland passed away, her work was stored in archives in Oxford[116] but was soon forgotten by the wider photography community.

Anna Atkins and Sarah Acland were pioneers of early colour photography, using colour as scientific and artistic material rather than just 'sensual' matter. Their legacies go beyond what is ironically described as 'pretty plant photographers' in this essay title: Atkins was at the forefront of cyanotype printing in 1840s Britain, linking serious technological achievement with botanical cataloguing and evocative art. Of even more consequence, she published the world's first 'photobook': *Photographs of British Algae*. Acland's Sanger Shepherd photographs were taken seven years before the brothers Auguste and Louis Lumière launched their Autochrome process in Paris, but it is the latter which was given credit as the first (commercial) colour photography technology.

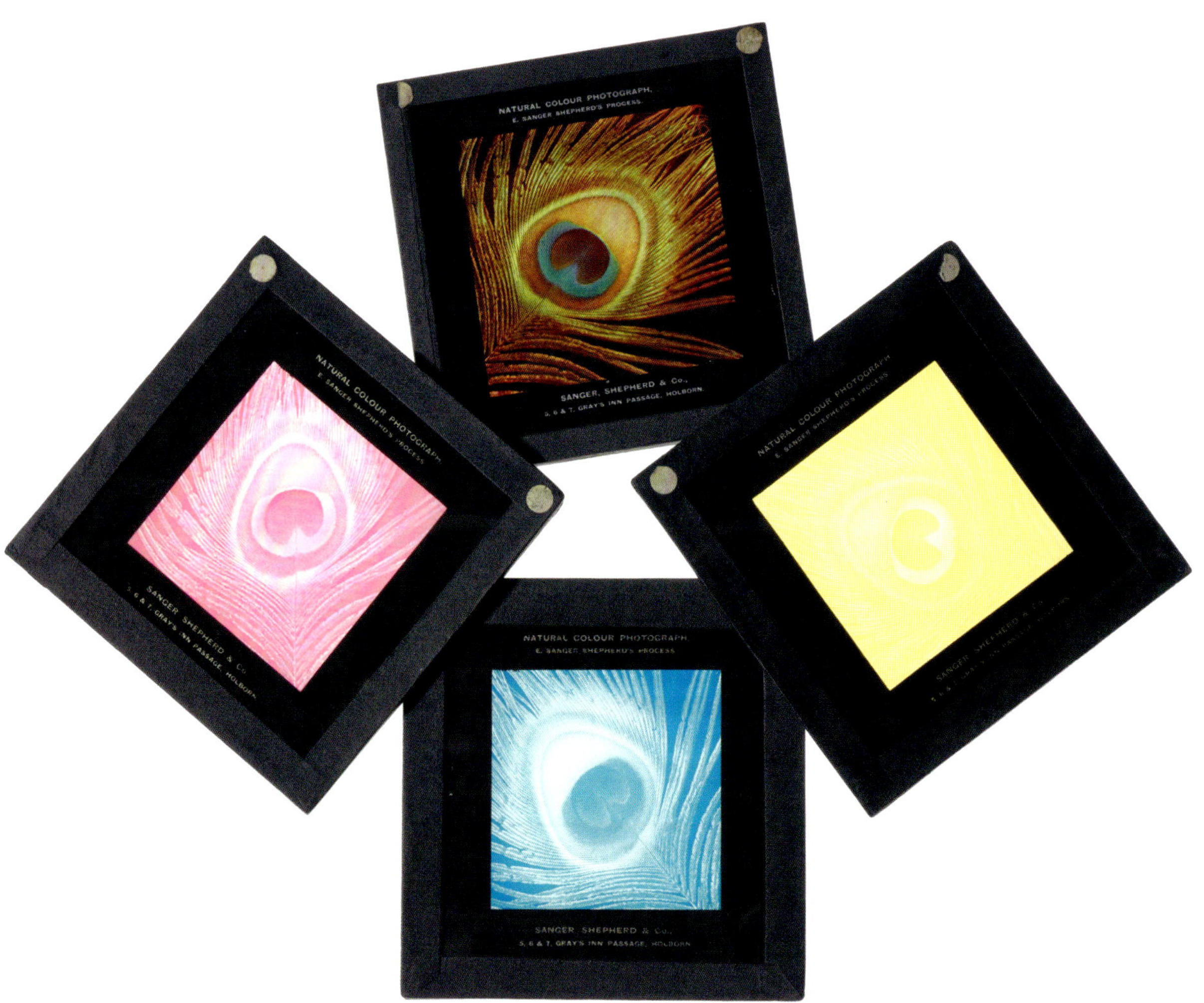

Fig. 73 Colour photograph (Sanger Shepherd Lantern Slide) of a Peacock Feather by E. Sanger Shepherd & Co., London, 1899, used by Sarah Angelina Acland in 1900

Fig. 74 Sarah Angelina Acland (1849–1930), *Funchal Bay, Madeira*, c.1910

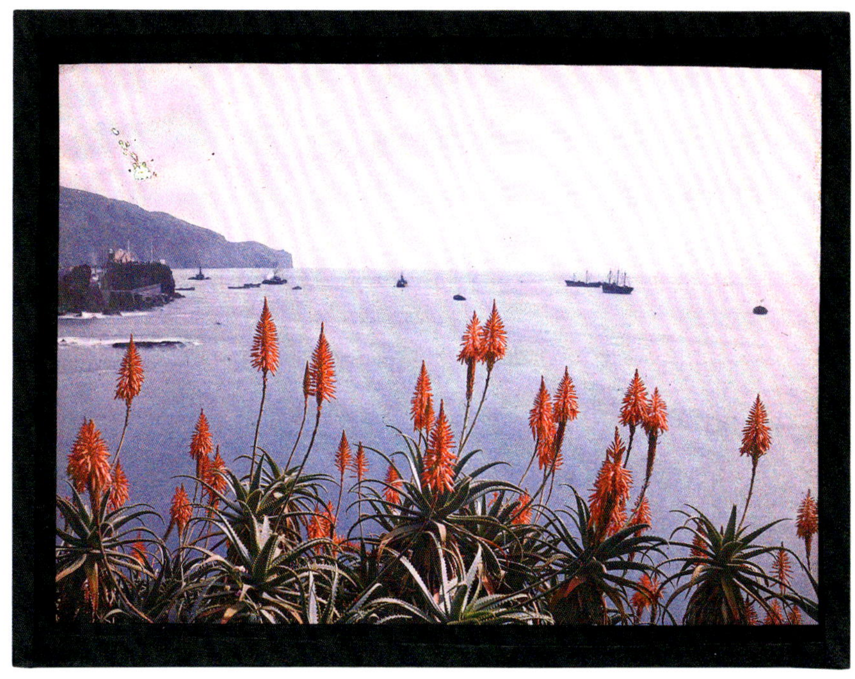

The way both women's work was overlooked is now being corrected: in the last decade, literature, symposia and exhibitions have rediscovered both Atkins and Acland. In 2018, the New York Public Library staged an exhibition on Atkins's life and work, and Schaaf published a revised edition of his seminal book on her cyanotypes.[117] Giles Hudson explored Acland's work in his monograph *Sarah Angelina Acland: First Lady of Colour Photography*, published by the Bodleian Library in 2012.[118] Four years later a blue plaque was installed at 10 Park Town, Oxford, where she lived, acknowledging her role as a 'pioneer of colour photography'. Researchers are exploring the traces of women's accomplishments in early colour photography.[119] Let us continue to re-write the history of photography by paying more attention to the contributions of its female practitioners, and by carefully disentangling its complex web of technology, art, gender and imperialism.

Object in Focus

Harry Emanuel, 'Hummingbird Necklace' (1865)

Hummingbirds stood little chance in the face of relentless demand from Victorian Britain. In their natural habitat, throughout the Americas, poachers laid nets in the rainforests and woodlands where the birds built their nests and peacefully fed on nectar-filled flowers. Once a great number were captured in the same net, they soon suffocated under the weight of so many other birds. Or they were killed by other methods such as 'sand being blown at them by means of a tube'.[120] Thousands were transported on ships to London every week. They arrived in paper- or tin-lined wooden trunks – no longer birds but a commodity referred to as 'skins'. These skins went to auction houses and were usually sold to the capital's dressmakers and milliners, who bought them to service an insatiable market which, since the early 1870s, called for colourful hummingbird skins to adorn fashionable hats, dresses and accessories (fig. 75). During one week in 1888, 400,000 skins came under the hammer.[121] The following week it was a mere 370,000.[122]

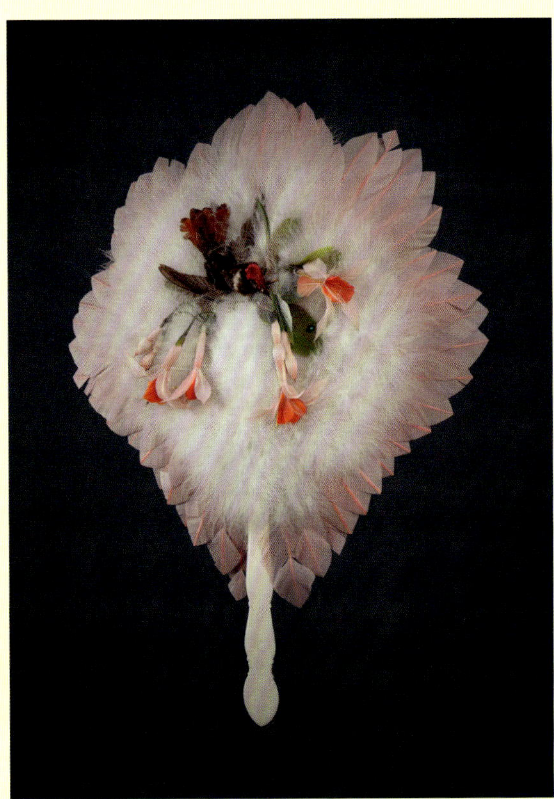

Fig. 75 Hummingbird fan and handscreen, Rio de Janeiro, c.1875. Manchester Art Gallery, 1958.68

What was it about these small creatures – from such distant parts of the world – that so beguiled Victorian women and the designers who dressed them? It wasn't the distinctive hum made by their wings, which can flap up to 80 times per second, because most Europeans had only ever seen dead birds due to the difficulty of transporting them alive and breeding them. The true reason was that hummingbirds were revered by Victorians as nature's most colourful animal. Compared to other birds, hummingbirds have the most colour differentiation of any avian species. Between 1758 and 1849, nearly 300 species were identified and named by ornithologists to highlight the brilliant variety of their coloured feathers. Species were defined by colour, with names such as the 'amethyst-throated sunangel', the 'green-breasted mango' and the 'rainbow-bearded thornbill'.

Ornithological texts such as *A Monograph of the Trochilidæ, or Family of Humming-birds* (1849–61) were another facet of the hummingbird craze. This six-volume series was compiled by the ornithologist John Gould (fig. 77) and illustrated with hand-coloured lithographs. Gould used gold leaf to replicate the iridescence of their feathers and painted in oil rather than watercolour, which had been used in earlier bird books, to produce a more brilliant effect. In his introduction Gould wrote: 'Where is this person, I ask, who, observing

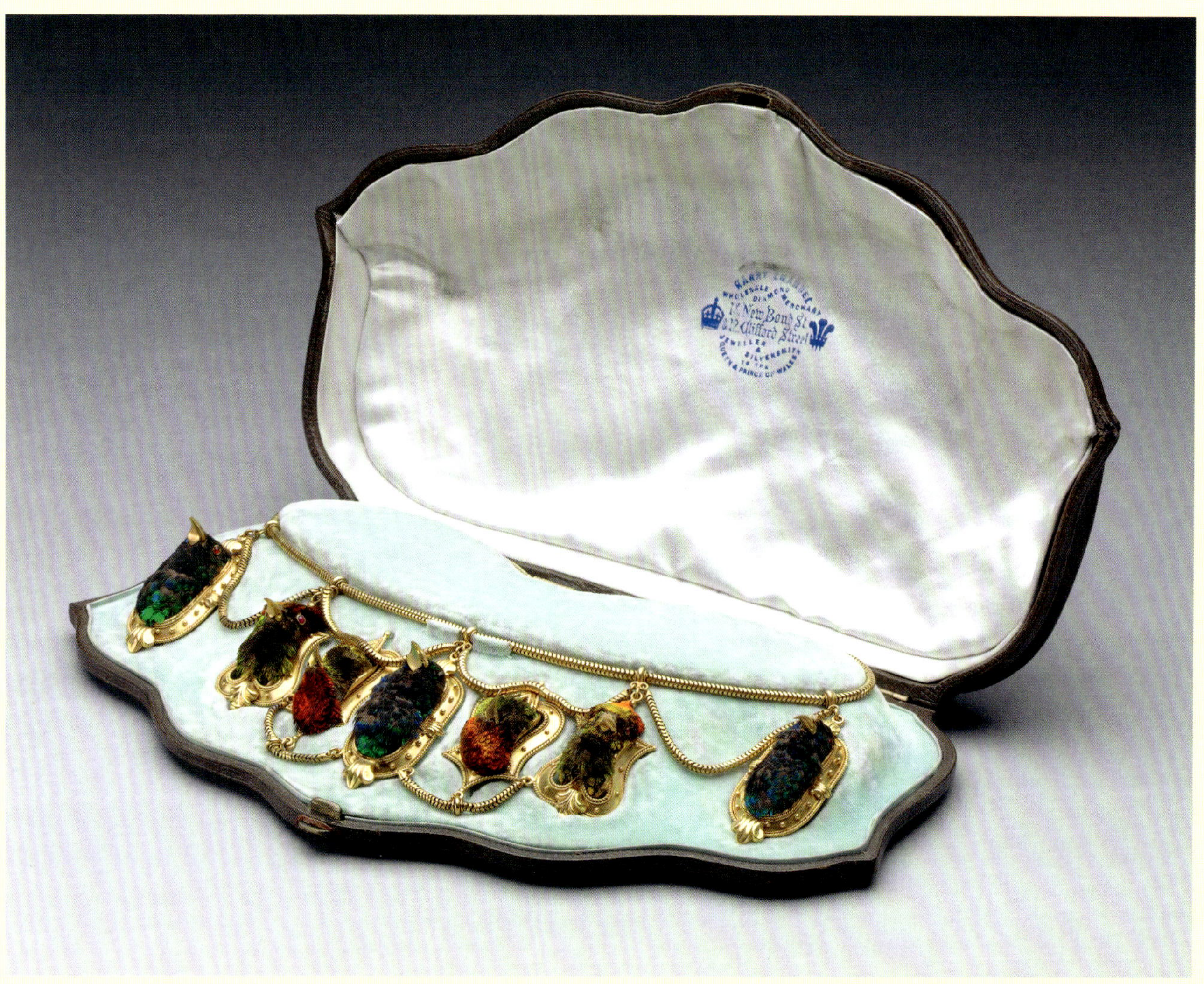

Fig. 76 Harry Emanuel (1831–1898), Humming bird necklace and case, 1865. British Museum, 1993,0205.1. Purchased from Roger Garlick

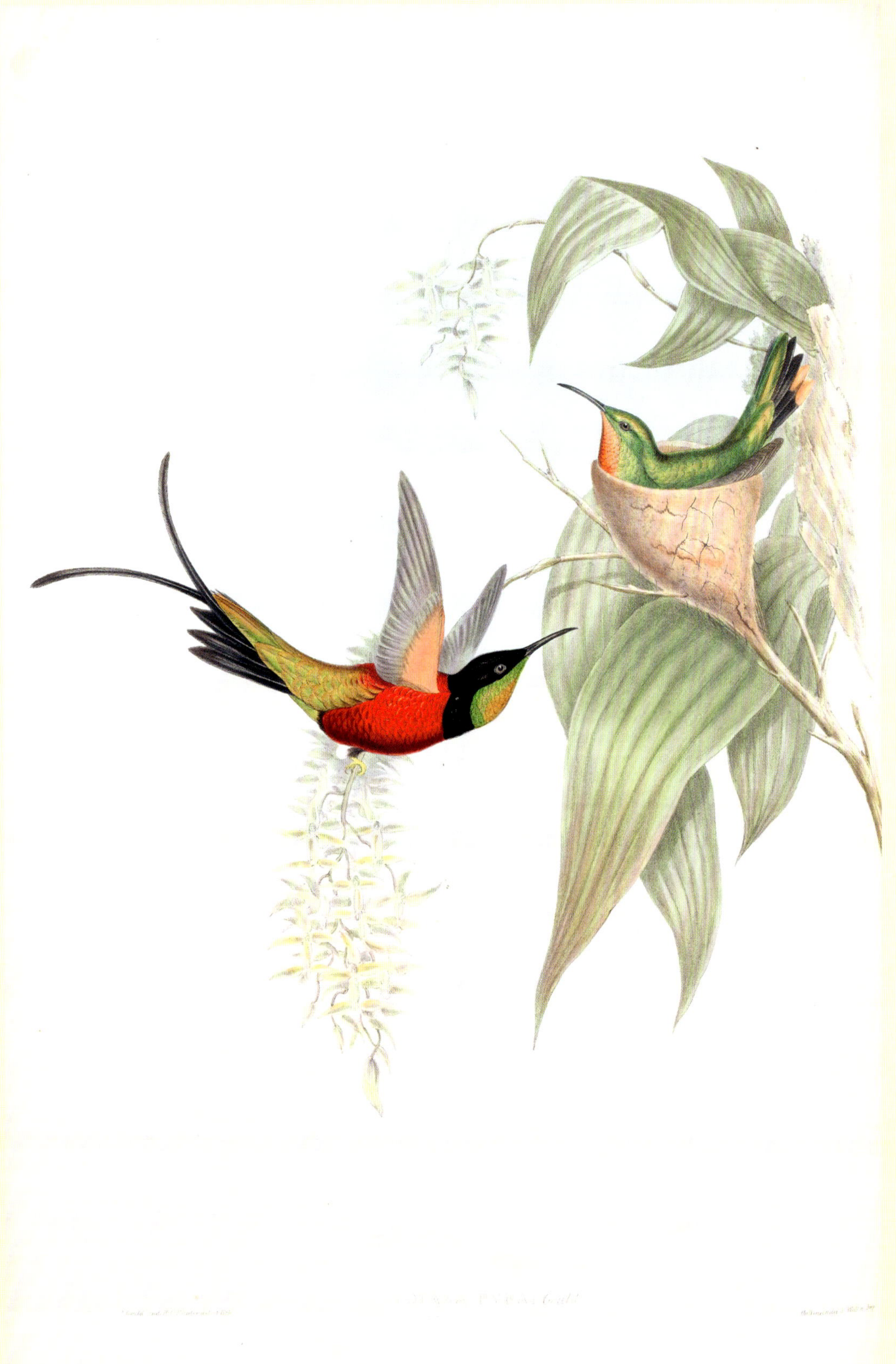

Fig. 77 John Gould (1804–1881), 'Topaza Pyra' from *A Monograph of the Trochilidæ, or Family of Humming-birds*, 1861–87. Bodleian Library, University of Oxford, CR.D.14/4

this glittering fragment of the rainbow, would not pause, admire and turn his mind with reverence towards the Almighty Creator, the wonders of whose hand we at every step discover?'[123] At the Great Exhibition of 1851, Gould displayed his personal collection of 3,800 mounted hummingbirds in 24 specially lit revolving cases. Queen Victoria, along with 75,000 others, saw the display and wrote in her diary: 'It is impossible to imagine anything so lovely as these little hummingbirds, their variety, and the extraordinary brilliance of their colours.'[124] For Gould, the queen and other observers including John Ruskin, the hummingbird was a sacred gift. Ruskin told an interviewer: 'If I could only have seen a humming-bird fly, it would have been an epoch in my life.'[125]

While peacocks conjured a vision of orientalised decadence, it was their detached feathers that were valued as ornaments to be placed in Chinese blue-and-white vases, affixed to the wooden frame of a fan or sewn into clothes, as was the case for the Duchess of Devonshire's fancy ball dress (fig. 7, p. 22). With hummingbirds, Victorians generally used the whole body - which was often no more than five grams in weight - to decorate their fashion items. However Harry Emanuel, a wholesale diamond merchant and jeweller, was an innovator. In 1865, Emanuel received a delivery of hummingbird skins, likely from his contacts in the Dominican Republic, at his premises on New Bond Street. He selected three short-tailed emerald and four ruby-topaz birds and decapitated them. He covered their beaks with gold leaf and replaced their eyes with tiny red gemstones before mounting the heads on gold backings and stringing all seven pendants on two sturdy gold foxtail chains to create a necklace (fig. 76). Two of the ruby-topaz heads were set upside down so that, upon opening the necklace's leather case, made from the skin of another animal, a cow, the bright ruby heads would immediately draw the eye. Ruby and topaz hummingbirds were extremely popular amongst naturalists and fashionistas, and Gould noted: 'Were it not for the extreme abundance of the species it would have been long ago exterminated.'[126] As Judy Rudoe and Charlotte Gere note, the necklace's careful arrangement in its case creates the impression of a specimen box.[127] The ornate mounted heads are also suggestive of taxidermied hunting trophies. Its presentation in the case simultaneously suggests the violence of hunting and the gentility of fine jewellery and craftsmanship (fig. 78).

This necklace was part of a series of hummingbird creations using Emanuel's patented mounting technique. It is unsurprising that hummingbirds eventually caught the attention of a jeweller as they were so often described as the 'jewels' and 'living gems' of the natural world.[128] William Bullock, owner of the Piccadilly Egyptian Hall, who had originally trained as a goldsmith and jeweller in Birmingham, declared that all the 'precious stones and metals polished by our art, cannot be compared to this jewel of nature'.[129] Using a hummingbird in place of a jewel offered something even the brightest ruby or richest sapphire could not: as the wearer of Emanuel's necklace walked or turned, their motions reanimated the dead birds' heads and their ruby, emerald and scarlet feathers shimmered and changed colours in the varying light. This effect, known as iridescence, is caused by the structural colour in the birds' feathers , which refracts sunlight. Against the opaque flesh of the wearer, the iridescent feathered heads transformed from red to orange, green to blue and back again, creating a dynamic piece of jewellery akin to the new kaleidoscopic technologies of the early nineteenth century. These allowed the viewer to imagine the piece as a series of dancing jewels rather than dead heads. Emanuel's invention blurred the lines between scientific naturalism and fantasy.[130]

The German philosopher Friedrich Nietzsche came up with a term to describe society's obsession with beauty at the expense of all else: 'creative destruction that was creatively destructive'.[131] The hummingbird fashion craze captures the essence of this idea: a fashion trend for beautiful, coveted items that nearly caused the extinction of a species. While hummingbird populations eventually recovered, many other

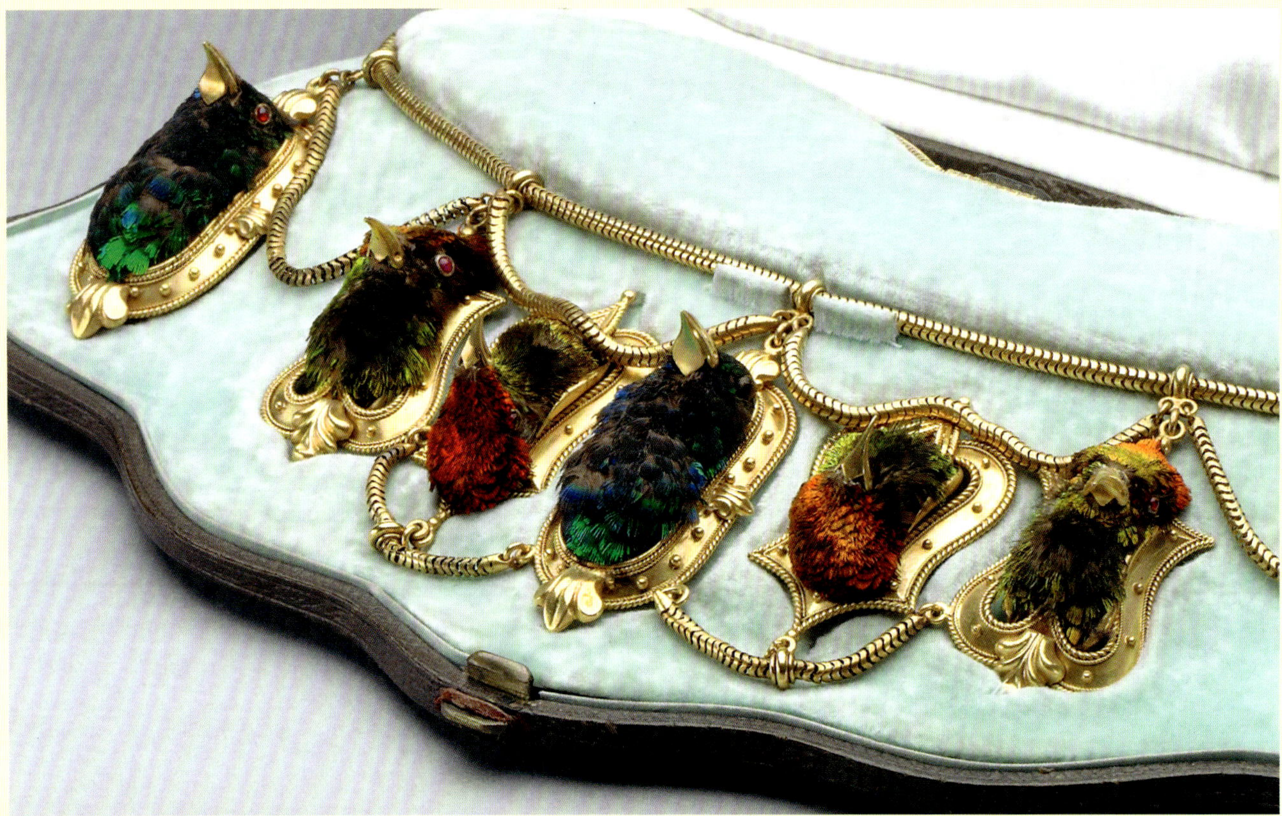

Fig. 78 Harry Emanuel (1831–1898), close-up of Hummingbird necklace and case. British Museum, 1993,0205.1. Purchased from Roger Garlick

birds whose feathers were also prized did not. For example the snowy egret, with its fine white buff plumage, was extinct in several North American regions for decades, until new breeds were introduced by conservationists in the early twentieth century.

After a generation of 'murderous millinery', women decided to save the hummingbird (fig. 79).[132] In 1891, two groups – the Plumage League, founded by Emily Williamson, and the Fur, Fin and Feather Folk, founded by Eliza Phillips and Etta Lemon – merged to form The Society for the Protection of Birds (SPB).[133] After several failed attempts and the disruption of the First World War, the Importation of Plumage (Prohibition) Act was passed in 1921. By this time, the craze for hummingbirds had faded thanks to campaigning efforts which convinced women to stop buying the feathers, but the fight to protect many other species carried on (and continues). For many of these women, the fight to save endangered birds was their first taste of political activism. Several prominent members of the SPB went on to join Emmeline Pankhurst's Women's Social and Political Union to advocate for women's suffrage. Suffragettes had popularly worn plumed hats until Lemon distributed a pamphlet amongst members which included the following warning: 'if women are so empty-headed and stupid that they cannot be made to understand the cruelty of which they are guilty in that matter, they certainly prove themselves to be unfit voters'.[134]

Today, Harry Emanuel's hummingbird necklace is a colourful oddity – a relic of a particularly cruel cult of beauty that came at the expense of living beings. But above all, it is evidence of the lengths Victorians went to to capture and creatively wear colour.

Madeline Hewitson

THE ILLUSTRATED LONDON NEWS, FEB. 14, 1903.—227

"MURDEROUS MILLINERY": FEATHERS FOR THE EUROPEAN MARKET.

DRAWN BY P. FRENZENY.

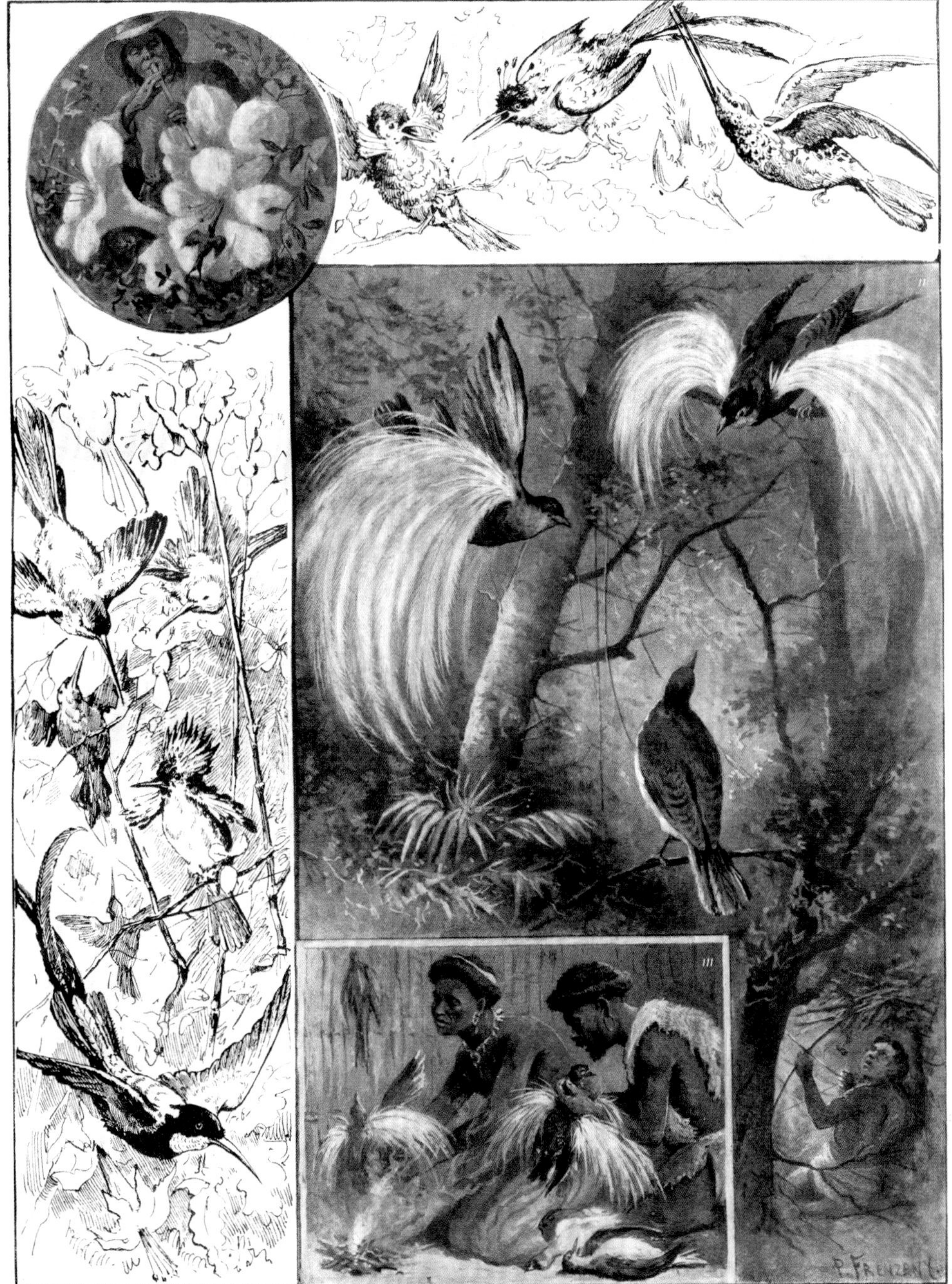

1. SHOOTING HUMMING-BIRDS WITH THE BLOW-GUN. 2. THE BIRD-OF-PARADISE: COURTSHIP AND DEATH. 3. SMOKING THE SKINS. 4. HUMMING-BIRDS AT HOME.

When the male birds-of-paradise assemble to woo the female by displaying their wonderful plumage, the fowler builds a screen in the lower branches and shoots the male with blunt arrows, so as not to draw blood. The feet, wings, and skull are then removed, and the skin smoked over a slow fire. Humming-birds are usually shot with a blow-tube loaded with fine sand. The skins are smoked and packed in crates for transport. At a meeting of the Society for the Protection of Birds, held on February 10, mention was made of the new Act of 1902 for protecting birds at home, and the Indian order limiting the exportation of feathers. The Duke of Bedford spoke in condemnation of "murderous millinery."

Fig. 79 Paul Frenzeny (1840–1902), '"Murderous Millinery": Feathers for the European Market', from *The Illustrated London News*, 18 Feb 1905

2

COLOUR FOR ALL

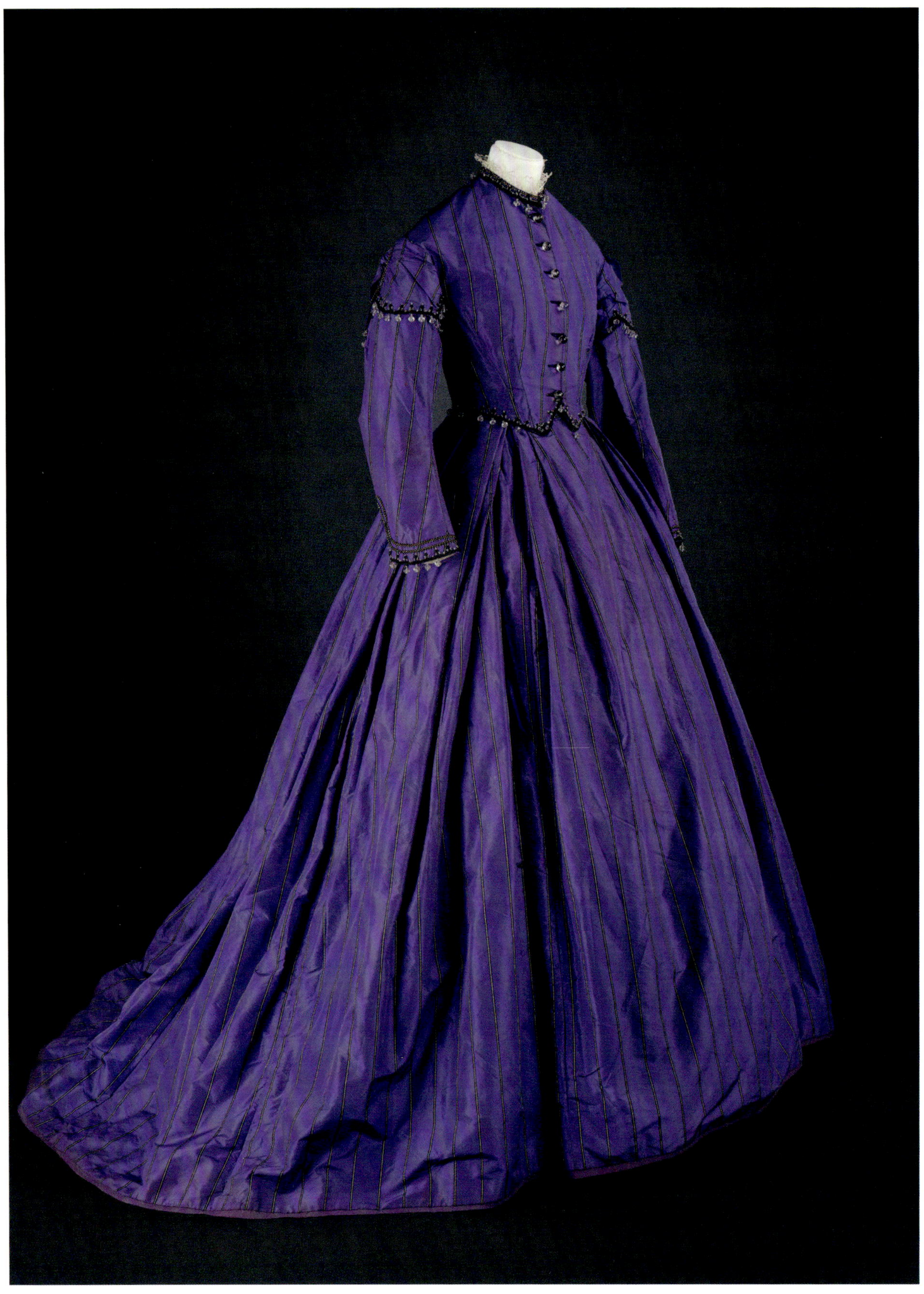

'The Triumph of Colour': the Synthetic Colour Revolution

Matthew Winterbottom

> The violet mauve led the way, followed by the red magenta, the blue azuline, the yellow phosphine, the green emeraldine, the orange aurine, by purple, and brown, and black … The world rubbed its eyes with astonishment; and truly it seemed almost as wonderful to produce the colours of the rainbow from a lump of coal, as to extract sunshine from cucumbers.[1]

An 1860s day dress worn by Mary Eleanor Cunliffe (1846–1896), daughter of a Leicester Baptist minister, still astonishes the modern viewer with the intensity of its vivid purple colour (fig. 80). One can imagine the impact it would have had on her contemporaries. That a respectable, middle-class young woman in an English regional town could wear such an extraordinarily coloured dress was down to a seismic revolution in the dye industry that had started in the previous decade. This 'Second Industrial Revolution'[2] would transform the modern world and lead to the democratisation of colour for the masses.

For thousands of years, textiles had been coloured using traditional natural dyes made from plants and some insects and animals. Many of these, such as madder, indigo and cochineal, were produced in faraway lands in Asia and the Americas. Traditional dyes were often expensive and difficult to work with and their supply could be precarious. Imperial expansion had helped guarantee the supply of some key dyes, such as Indian indigo, for British textile manufacturers.

'COLOURS FROM COAL'

Brightly coloured textiles and clothes were the preserve of the wealthy and powerful, and were key markers of status and taste. This all changed in 1856 when William Henry Perkin (1838–1907) (fig. 81), an 18-year-old student and assistant of German chemist August Wilhelm von Hofmann (1818–1892), the brilliant head of the Royal College of Chemistry in London, produced aniline purple, a vivid violet dye, from coal tar. This was the first of the so-called aniline dyes and it is considered the world's first commercial synthetic dye. Coal tar was a thick, sticky black effluent – the material that remained when coal was converted into the gas that, since the 1820s, had been used for lighting. As the demand for gas lighting increased, so too did the problem of disposing of this hazardous industrial waste. Considered of no commercial use, it was dumped, often into rivers, poisoning the water. Some chemists, including Hofmann, were intrigued by the chemical possibilities of this noxious 'gas liquor'. Incredibly chemically complex and rich in elements that form the basic building blocks of organic chemistry, Hofmann believed it was

Opposite: Fig. 80 Day dress worn by Mary Eleanor Cunliffe (1846–1896), English, late 1860s. Aniline dyed silk, glass beads. Manchester Art Gallery, 1951.207

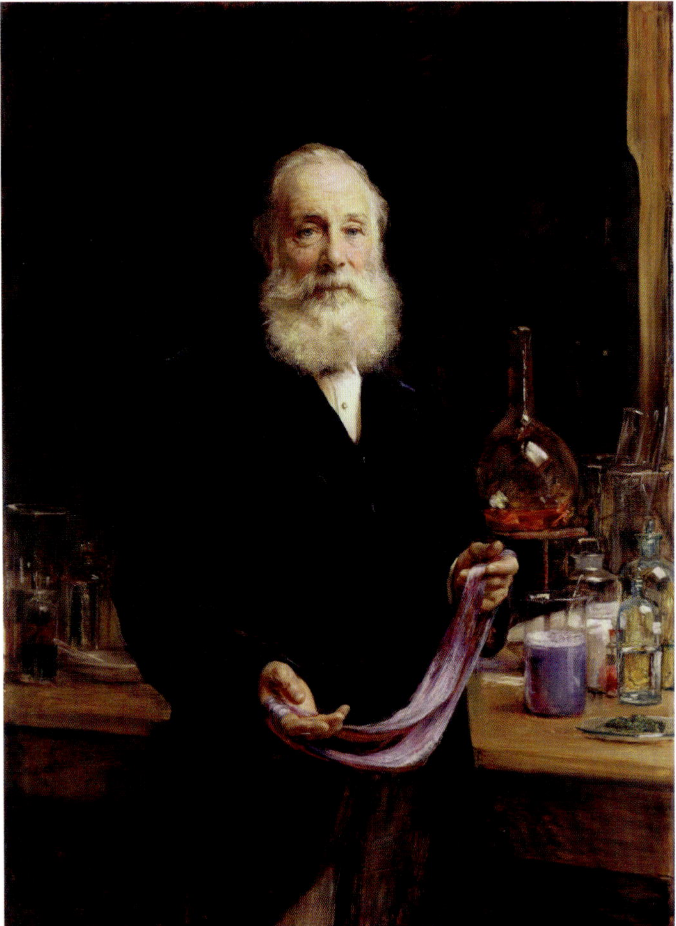

Fig. 81 Sir William Henry Perkin (1838–1907) by Sir Arthur Stockdale Cope (1857–1940), 1906. Oil on canvas. This portrait, showing Perkin with samples of mauvine, was painted 50 years after his initial discovery. National Potrait Gallery, NPG 1892

possible artificially to create natural substances from coal tar derivatives. In 1856, he charged Perkin with creating artificial quinine from coal tar chemicals. Quinine, made from the bark of the South American cinchona tree, was the main treatment for malaria but its production was jealously guarded. Britain, with its rapidly expanding Empire, imported vast quantities of quinine to treat its troops and civil servants abroad. One of coal tar's derivatives is aniline, a colourless organic compound first isolated from natural indigo dye by chemists in the 1820s. Named after the Arabic name for indigo, *anil*, aniline was subsequently created from benzene that had been distilled from coal tar. Perkin was unsuccessful – quinine was not successfully synthesised until many years later – but during one of his experiments on aniline he accidentally created an intense purple stain. Others, including Hofmann, had noticed this before, but it was Perkin who recognised its commercial potential as a synthetic textile dye. Without Hofmann's knowledge Perkin continued his experiments, with the aim of turning the experimental purple stain into a commercial dye. He was able to patent the process later that year and, at the tender age of 19, open the world's first synthetic dye works at Greenhill, near London.[3]

The fact that the new colour was a brilliant purple was significant. In 1856, purple and mauve were already the height of fashion. These were the favourite colours of the trend-setting Empress Eugenie of France. Purple and mauve vegetable dyes were traditionally made from lichen, but in the 1850s this process was improved and perfected by French chemists to create a new brilliant dye known as French Purple. At the same time another bright purple dye – murexide – was brought to market. Named after the murex snail, this semi-synthetic dye was originally made by German chemists from snake excrement in the 1820s. It was thought close in colour to the fabled Tyrian Purple of the ancient world, a shade reserved for Roman Emperors and the sails of Cleopatra's barge. Genuine Tyrian Purple was made from the mucus glands of thousands of murex sea snails (fig. 82). It was produced via a smelly, difficult process that yielded only tiny amounts of dye. Tyrian Purple production ceased in the thirteenth century and the method of making it was forgotten. Murexide remained a curiosity until the early 1850s, when scientists discovered it could be made commercially from bird guano, a fertilizer that was imported in huge quantities from South America and Africa. French Purple and murexide purple clothes and accessories were the height of women's fashion from 1856

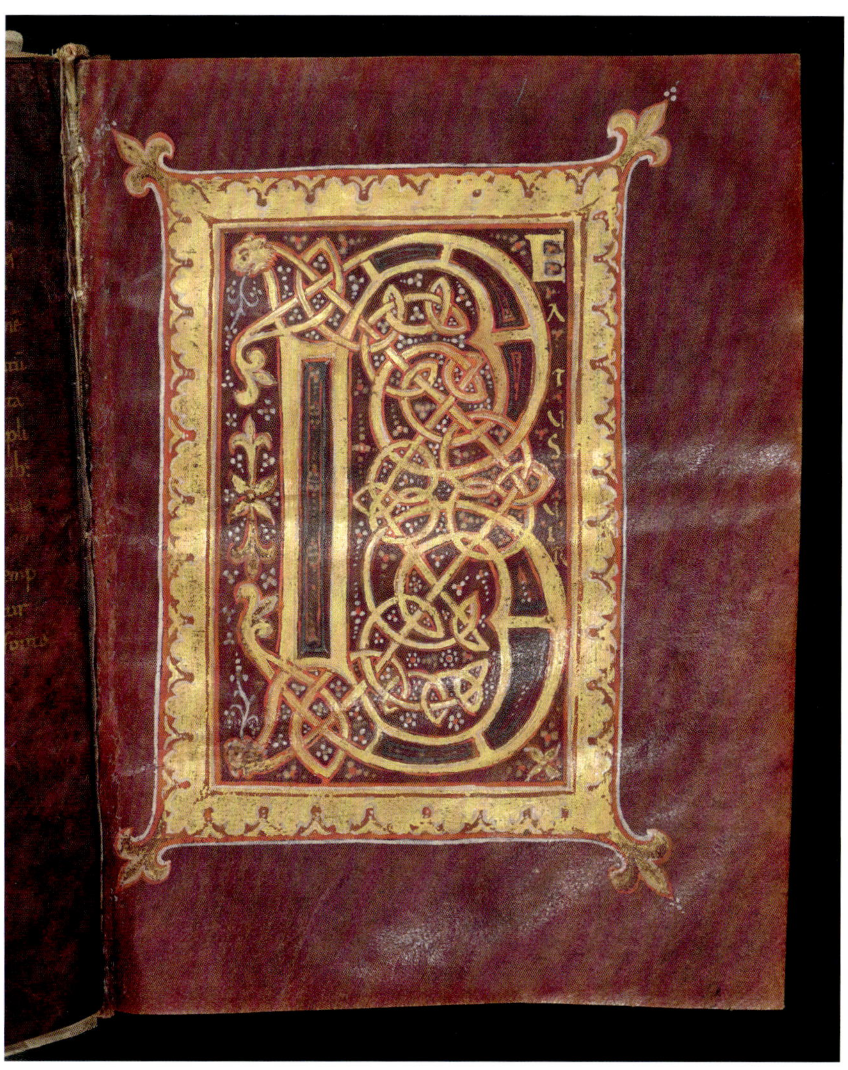

Fig. 82 Psalter from the Rheims area of France, ninth century. Purple parchment with gold inscriptions. Although long believed to have been dyed using Tyrian Purple from murex snails, recent analysis on medieval purple codices suggests that the dyes were probably from lichens. Bodeian Library, University of Oxford, MS. Douce 59, fol. 4r

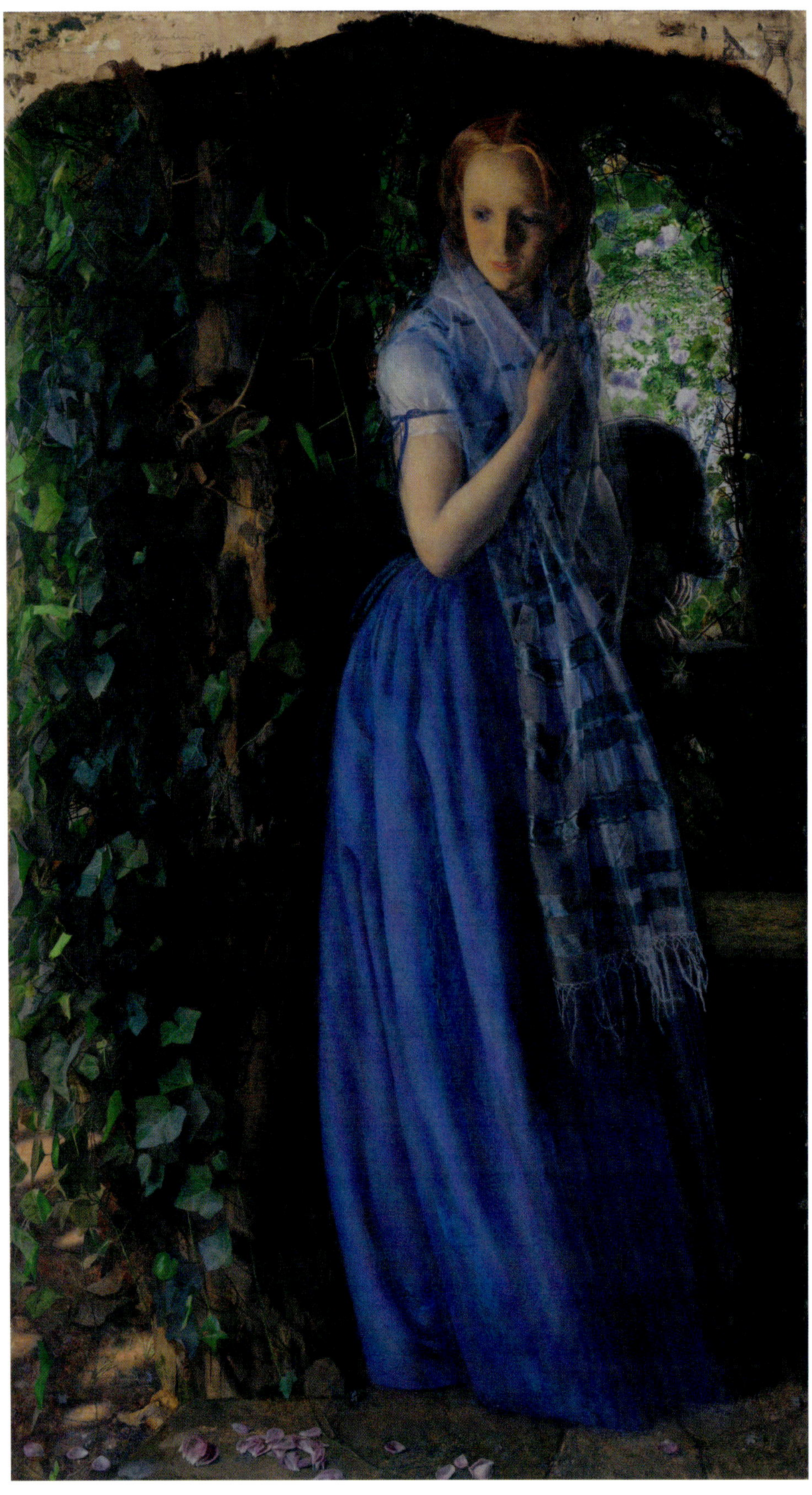

Fig. 83 Arthur Hughes (1832–1915), *April Love*, 1855–6. Oil on canvas, Tate, N02476

until 1858. The French called paler purple shades 'mauve' after the French name for the mallow flower, and the name soon spread to Britain. Soon, even the more vivid purples and violets were being referred to as 'mauve'.

April Love, painted by Arthur Hughes in 1856 (fig. 83), the year of Perkin's discovery, shows a young woman wearing a fashionable, intense violet-blue dress that contrasts beautifully with the surrounding green foliage. Hughes revisited this pairing of purple and green in many of his subsequent paintings. If, as seems likely, *April Love* depicts a real dress, it cannot have been dyed using Perkin's aniline purple. Perkin spent two years perfecting his dye and consulting with textile manufactures before it became commercially available in late 1858. Hughes's dress must therefore have been coloured using expensive, imported French Purple, made from lichen or murexide. So too must Queen Victoria's 'mauve' dress, worn at the wedding of her eldest daughter, the Princess Royal, at St James's Palace in January 1858.[4] However, both these dyes were prone to fading, and murexide had the disadvantage of discolouring when exposed to sulphur. This was a major problem in towns and cities, where the air was filthy with coal smoke and gas fumes. In contrast, Perkin's purple, as it was first known, had no such problems. It was a brilliant violet-purple colour, believed to be non-toxic, relatively easy to work with, stable and not prone to fading. Charles Dickens described its permanence as having a 'moral superiority over other purples'.[5] Perkin had initially wanted to call his new dye Tyrian Purple, after the ancient dye, but newspapers were soon calling it mauve. In 1863, Perkin officially renamed his discovery Mauvine, a portmanteau of mauve and aniline. Traditional mauve, like the mallow flower after which it is named, is a pale pinkish-purple and this is the colour now most associated with the name.

'MAUVE MEASLES'

Following its introduction in 1858, Perkin's mauve became wildly popular. While praising the dye as 'rich and pure, and fit for anything; be it fan, slipper, gown, ribbon, handkerchief, tie, or glove', Dickens gently mocked the 'fashionable insanity for Perkin's purple': 'One would think that London was suffering from an election, and that those purple ribbons were synonymous with "Perkins [sic] for hever!" and "Perkins and the English Constitootion!" The Oxford-street windows are tapestried with running rolls of that luminous extract from coal tar ... As I look out of my window now, the apotheosis of Perkins's purple seems at hand – purple hands wave from open carriages – purple hands shake each other at street doors – purple hands threaten each other from opposite sides of the street; purple striped gowns cram barouches, jam up cabs, throng steamers, fill railway stations: all flying countryward, like so many purple birds of migrating Paradise; purple ribbons fill the windows, purple gowns circle out at shop entrances, purple feather fans beckon to you in windows. We shall soon have purple omnibuses and purple houses.'[6]

In September 1859 *Punch* denounced the 'Mauve measles' that had gripped the nation: 'One of the first symptoms by which the malady declares itself consists in the eruption of a measly rash of ribbons, about the head and neck of the person who has caught it. The eruption, which is of a mauve colour, soon spreads, until in some cases the sufferer becomes completely covered with it ... Confinement to the house is a most excellent corrective.'[7]

Yet this was just the beginning of the aniline colour revolution. Perkin's discovery encouraged chemists across Britain, France, Germany and Switzerland to search for new synthetic colours from coal tar. Heinrich Caro, one of the founders of the modern dye chemistry, described how 'the beauty, the fastness, and the brilliant success' of the first aniline colours acted like 'sparks on tinder': 'A new world was disclosed full of magic promise, and all joined eagerly in the search, the manufacturer and the professor, the business man and the adventurer; for the one a new gold-mine, for the other new opportunity.'[8] In 1858 the second aniline dye – an intense crimson-red – was created simultaneously in England and France. Officially named Fuchsine, after both the fuchsia flower and the German name for fox, it was renamed Magenta by the French in 1859 in honour of their victory over the Austrians at the Battle of Magenta in Piedmont. Solferino – an intense pink, named after another French victory – soon followed. By the early 1860s an entire rainbow of synthetic dyes – 'the most superb and brilliant that ever delighted the human eye'[9] – had been created from coal tar (fig. 84). An 1861 newspaper article entitled 'The Triumph of Colour' noted: 'never were the ladies of England dressed in such brilliant hues as in the present day'.[10] There were even aniline blacks, which provided a better, more stable colour for menswear and mourning dress than traditional black dyes.

Although initially expensive to produce – weight-for-weight Mauvine cost the same as platinum – aniline dyes were extremely potent. A block of pure Mauvine measuring only 20 inches by 9 inches (51 centimetres by 23 centimetres), exhibited by Perkin at the 1862 International Exhibition, was said to be sufficient to dye 300 miles of silk fabric. This block was the 'product of no less than 2,000 tons of coal'.[11] As production increased the price of the new dyes rapidly reduced, making bright, fashionable colours available to the masses for the first time.

Writing in 1862, Hofmann captured the true global significance of the aniline revolution, which he believed would 'influence in a remarkable manner the industrial fortunes of Great Britain': 'For, if coal be destined sooner or later to supersede, as the primary source of colour, all the costly dyewoods hitherto consumed in the ornamentation of textile fabrics ... are we not on the eve of profound modifications in the commercial relations between the great colour-consuming nations and colour-producing regions of the globe? ... England will beyond question, at no distant day become herself the greatest colour-producing country in the world ... by the strangest of revolutions, she may ere long send her coal-derived blues to indigo-growing India, her tar-distilled crimson to cochineal-producing Mexico, and her fossil substitutes for quercitron and safflower to China, Japan, and the other countries whence these articles are now derived.'[12]

While Hofmann was correct to predict the devastating impact the new artificial dyes would have on traditional dye-producing countries in Asia and the

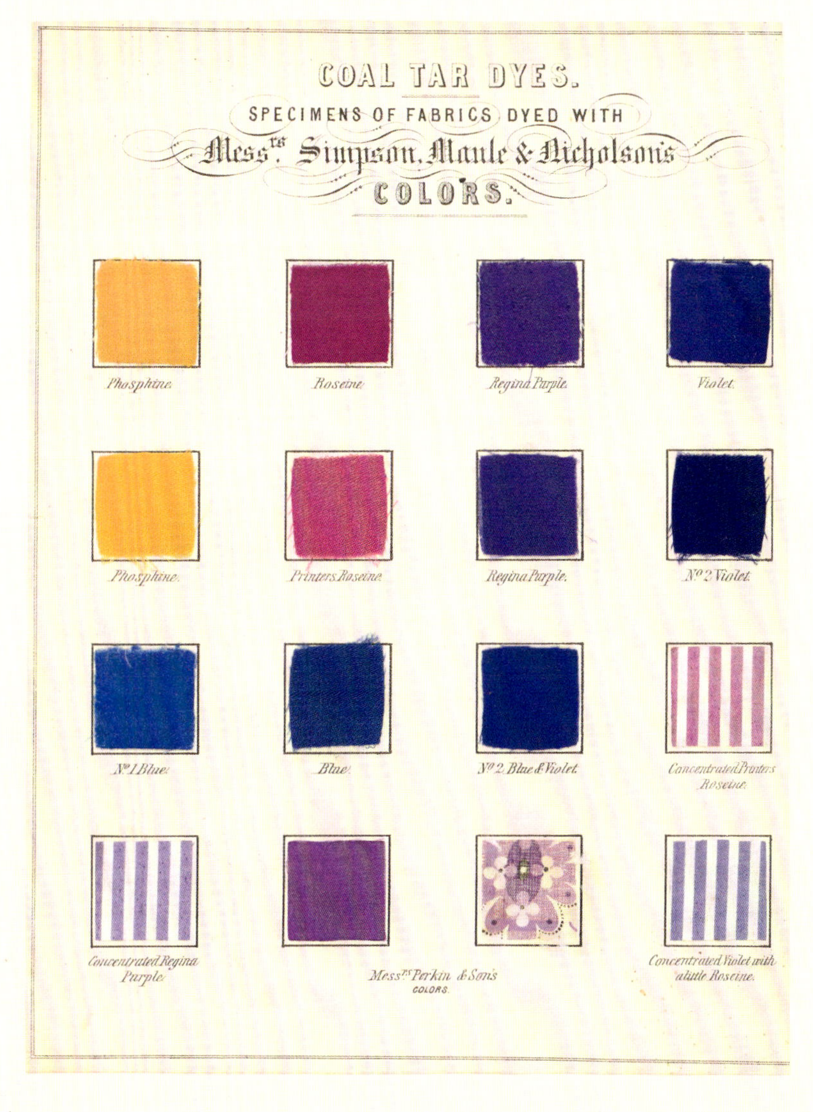

Fig. 84 *Coal Tar Dyes. Specimens of Fabrics Dyed with Messrs. Simpson, Maule & Nicholson's Colors*, c.1865. Cotton on card. Bodleian Library, University of Oxford, John Johnson Collection, Soap 1 (41) subsect. Dyes (Coal Tar Dyes, 1860–1880)

Americas, he was wrong about Britain becoming the greatest colour-producing nation in the world. Despite Britain and France's pioneering roles, it was Germany and Switzerland who rapidly came to lead and then dominate the new synthetic dye industry. By the 1880s Britain, like much of the world, relied on Germany for her synthetic dyes. This work laid the foundation of Germany and Switzerland's modern pharmaceutical and chemical industries. IG Farben, for example, was founded in 1925 from a conglomeration of German chemical companies that had all started as synthetic dye manufacturers. Hofmann himself was to encourage this by returning to his native Germany in 1864. German scientists were better trained and funded to work on developing new synthetic dyes and other related products. And unlike Britain and France, Germany lacked a far-reaching empire to supply its manufacturing industries with traditional dyestuffs. The sample card of the Aktien-Gesellschaft für

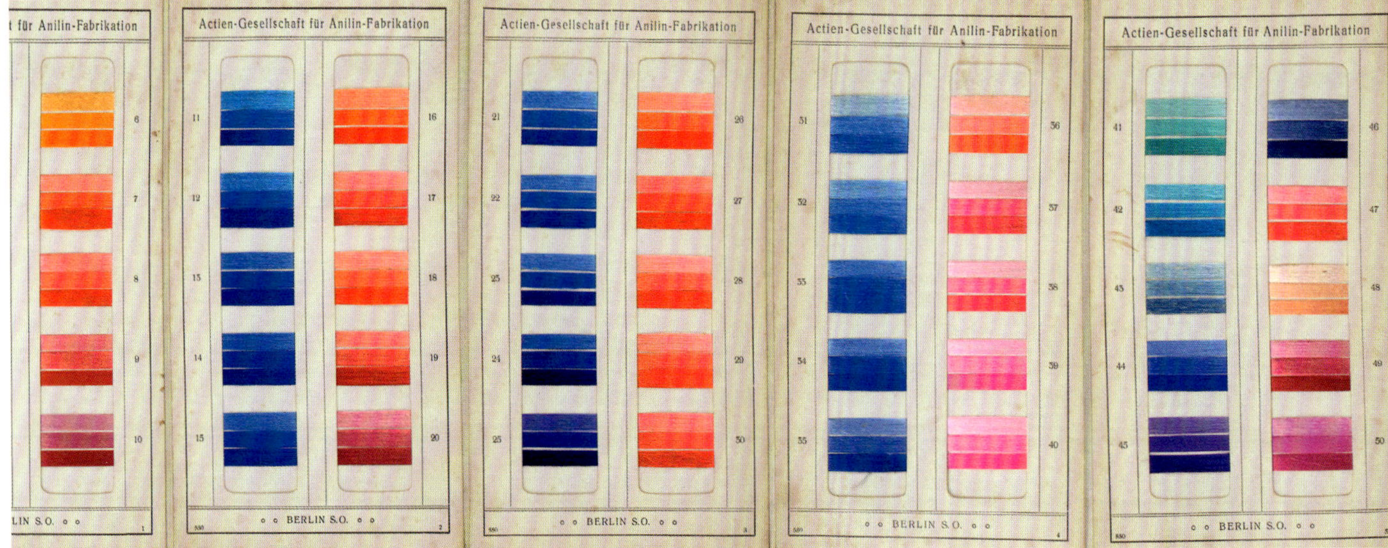

Fig. 85 Dyed Textile Samples, Aktien-Gesellschaft für Anilin-Fabrikation (Corporation for Aniline Production), Germany, *c.*1900. Synthetic dyed silks on card. © Museum of the History of Science, Oxford, inv.76705

Anilin-fabrikation (Corporation for Aniline Production), known as Agfa, shows the extraordinary range of German synthetic colours available by 1900 (fig. 85). By 1914 the range of basic synthetic colours ran into the hundreds, and was said to be 'sufficiently comprehensive for all purposes'.[13]

The trade in tropical dyewoods, indigo, madder and other natural dyes was hugely important to many Asian, African and Latin American economies. The progressive discovery of synthetic colours caused a devastating collapse in this trade. In 1867 Perkin discovered how to make synthetic alizarin, the active colorant of madder root, a traditional vegetable dye for reds, pinks and browns. Before this discovery Britain imported around 70,000 tons of madder a year, at a price of around £50 per ton. Within ten years the cost of synthetic alizarin had dropped to £18 per ton and imports of natural madder had fallen by 90%.[14] Perkin, worried that madder faced extinction, even planted some on his estate.[15]

Synthesising indigo, the main vegetable source of blue colours, proved more problematic – it was not until 1897 that artificial indigo was launched by German company Badische Anilin- & Sodafabrik (BASF). For the British economy this was a disaster, as Indian indigo had been a highly profitable colonial product. By 1914, indigo production had all but ceased in most of India and its price had fallen by 60%.[16]

As predicted by Hofmann in 1862, synthetic dyes were soon being exported to the very countries that had previously exported traditional dyestuffs to the West. Brightly coloured aniline dyes were used on traditional Asian textiles, carpets and clothing. Early tinted photographs of Japan show how these dyes began to replace vegetable colours from the 1860s. In 1904, the Shah of Persia even banned the importation of synthetic dyes in an attempt to preserve his country's traditional carpet industry.

These changes were not just limited to textiles. The introduction of new dyes coincided with the Cotton Famine of the 1860s, when supplies of

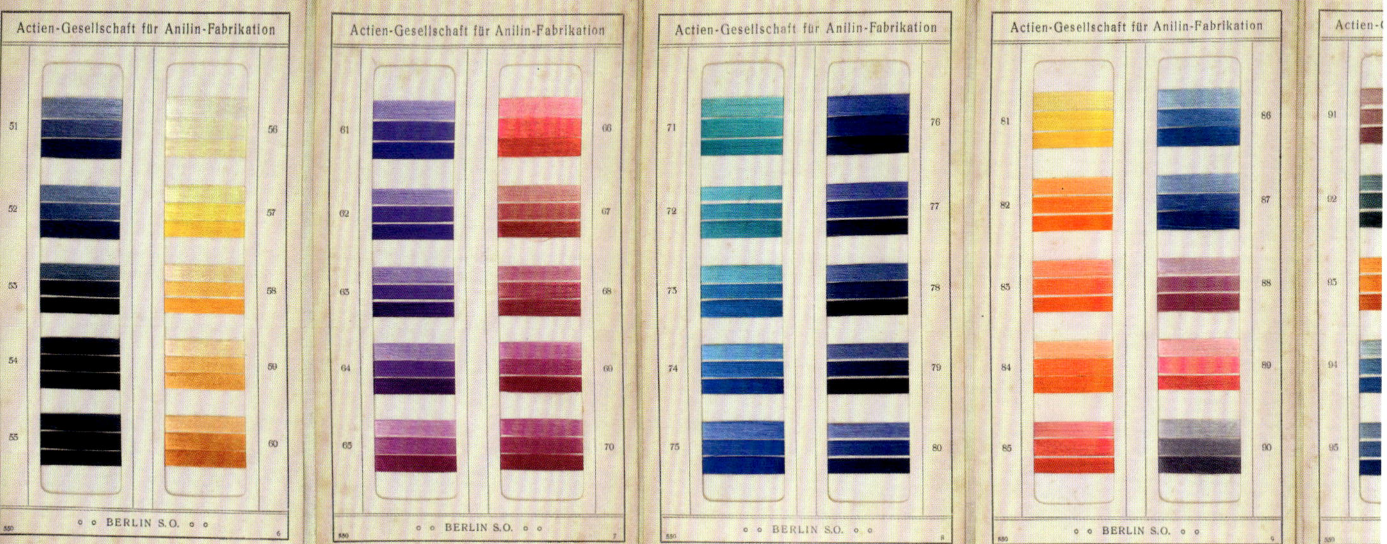

American cotton were disrupted by the Civil War. Aniline manufacturers – starved of cotton – looked for alternative uses for their dyes. Soon they were being used to print postage stamps, and to colour paper, inks, pigments, paints, scientific specimens and even food. Less than ten years after the opening up of Japan to the West in the 1850s, Japanese woodblock prints were using vivid aniline purples and reds (see pp. 212–15).[17]

Unlike many traditional dyes, aniline dyes are transparent. This made them popular for tinting monochrome photographs. They were also used extensively to colour early silent films (see pp. 217–21).

Not everyone welcomed this synthetic colour revolution. John Ruskin despised the new anilines: 'we moderns, who have preferred to rule over coal-mines … have actually got our purple out of coal instead of the sea … and have completed the shadow, and the fear of it, by giving it a name from battle, "Magenta".'[18]

A French visitor to England in the 1860s found the colours of women's dresses 'outrageously crude … gaudy and overdone', particularly among 'shopkeepers' wives', where 'the absurdity was at its height'. He complained of dresses 'of a really ferocious violet, purple or poppy red silks, grass-green dresses decorated with flowers, azure blue scarves and dresses of purple silk, very shiny so that they reflect the light dazzlingly … The glare and glitter is brutal'. He described one violet dress as so garish that it 'would have made a painter cry out!'[19]

'CHROMATIC TORPEDOES'

The new dyes were soon being used to colour underwear, which had traditionally been white or indigo blue. One writer complained: 'In the matter of colour the ladies are becoming rather too "loud". Not that we would diminish the colour, if tastefully employed, which is spent on hats, bonnets, cloaks, shawls, dresses. Let them be as brilliant as the children of tar can make them. But the

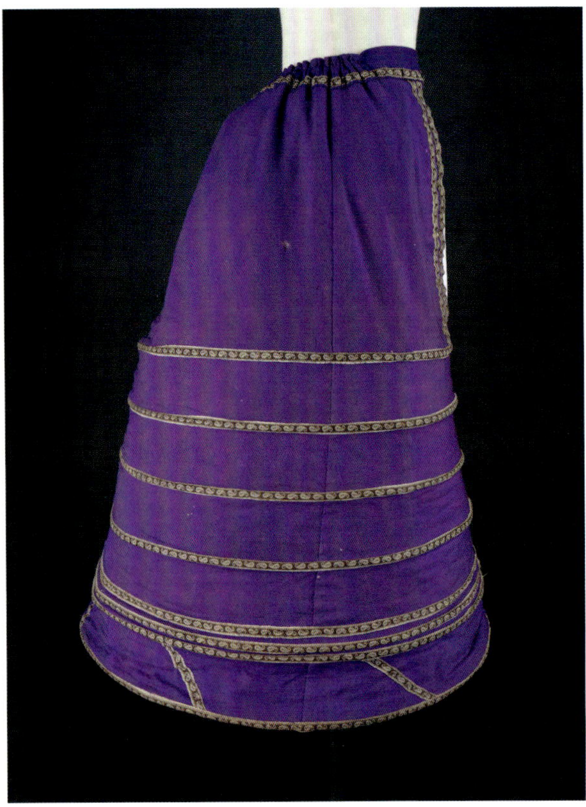

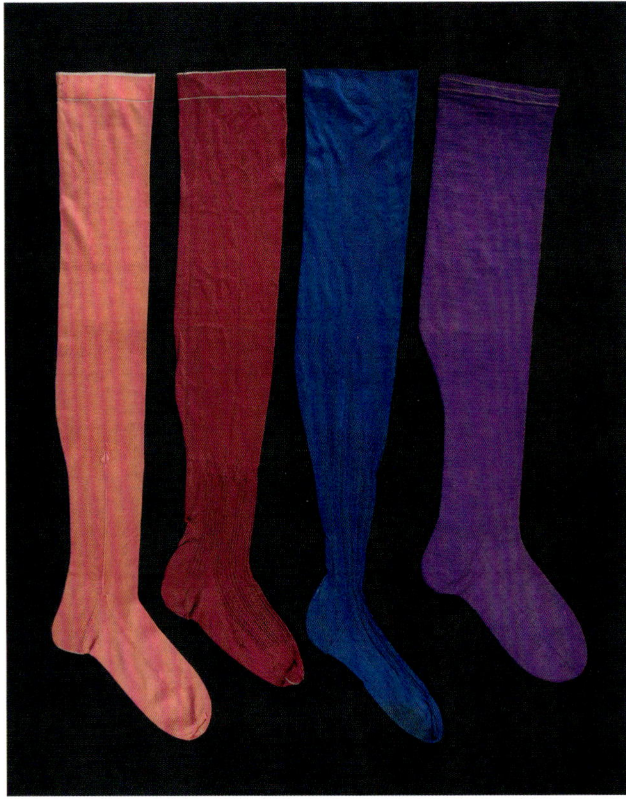

Above left: Fig. 86 Crinoline, English, mid-1860s. Aniline dyed cotton. Manchester Art Gallery, 1961.8

Above right: Fig. 87 Ladies' stockings, 1860s–1880s. Aniline dyed silk. Fashion Museum Bath, BATMC1.22.166 & A, BATMC1.22.5.2A BATMC1.22.160 & A

intense hues which lately have descended to the stocking and petticoat appear to us more suitable to the *demi-monde*. Multitudinous colours and patterns have been invented for the "tempestuous-petticoat".'[20]

Colourfully striped stockings were particularly popular. In 1861 a writer for *The Lady's Newspaper & Pictorial Times* described the effect of the bright array: 'the sudden apparition of particoloured and diversified stockings, the tints of which were so bright and glaringly contrasted, that at first sight one supposed that the wearers must be going to take part in some fancy ball … dance before one's astonished eyes in all the shop windows and beneath all those ample flouncings that sweep so gracefully along the pavement; positively one's attention is directed to the rainbow-spanned ankle.'[21]

The enormous, swaying, steel-framed crinolines of the early 1860s, together with slightly shorter skirts popularised by Empress Eugenie, gave ample opportunities to show off these colourful petticoats, stockings and footwear (figs 86–88). Moreover, this was not limited to women's clothing. Men's fashions had become increasingly sombre since the 1840s, but their socks could be just as colourful as women's stockings. In the privacy of home, men might also wear brightly coloured Berlin woolwork slippers, braces or smoking hats embroidered for them by their wives or daughters (fig. 89).

Reports of severe rashes caused by the new dyes when worn next to the skin sparked concerns that they were toxic. *Punch* was quick to satirise:

Fig. 88 Lady's boots, probably English, 1870s. Silk. Manchester Art Gallery, 1935.271

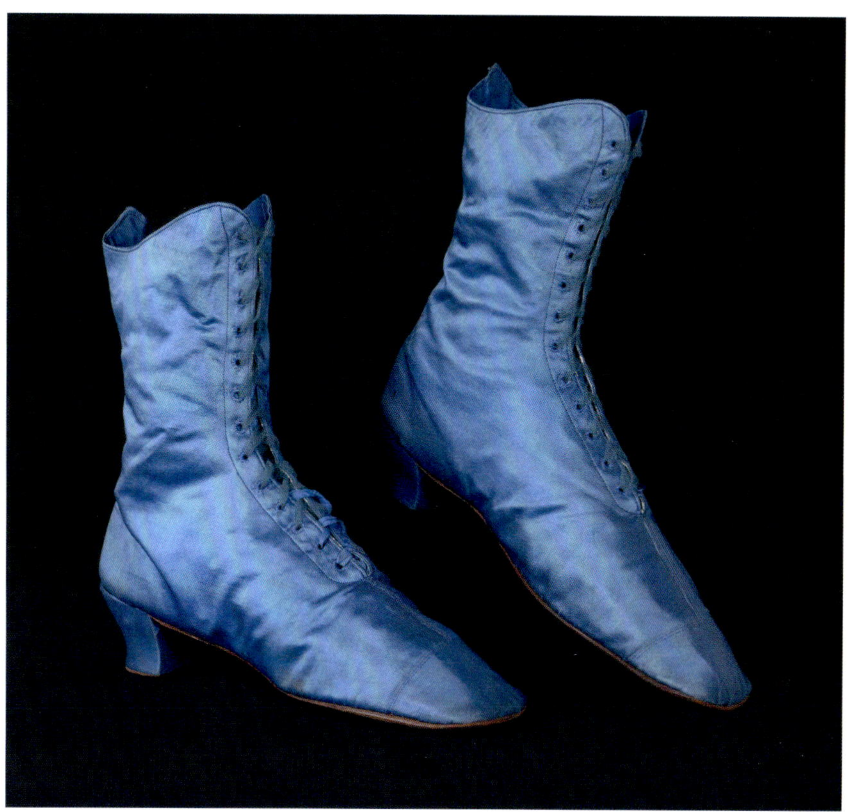

Fig. 89 Men's slippers, English, early 1860s. Berlin wool work on canvas. Manchester Art Gallery, 1960.181

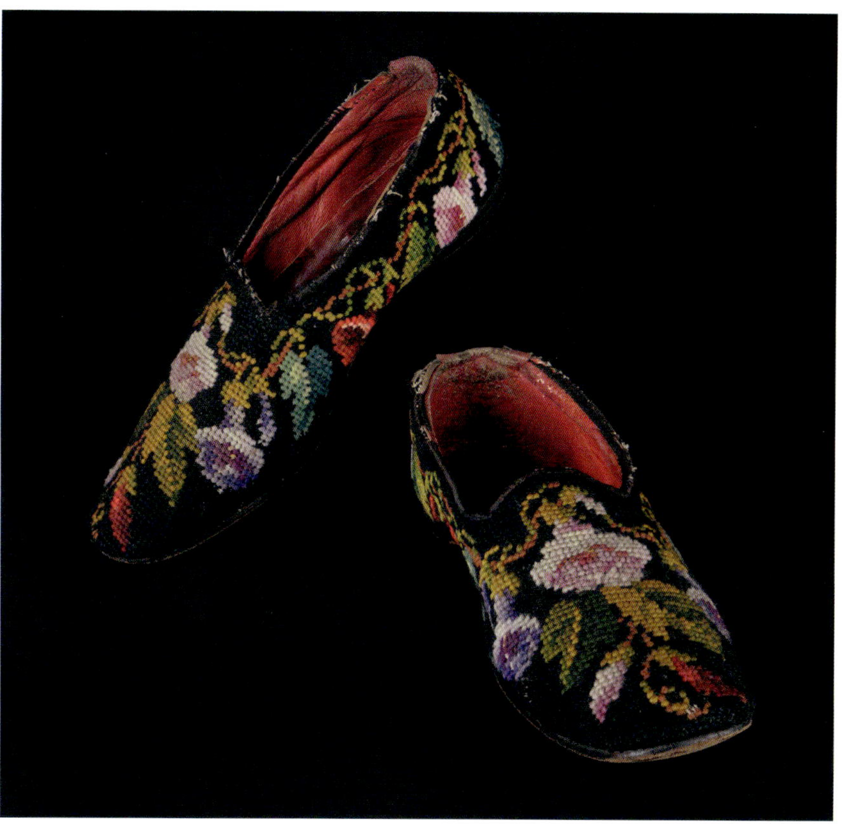

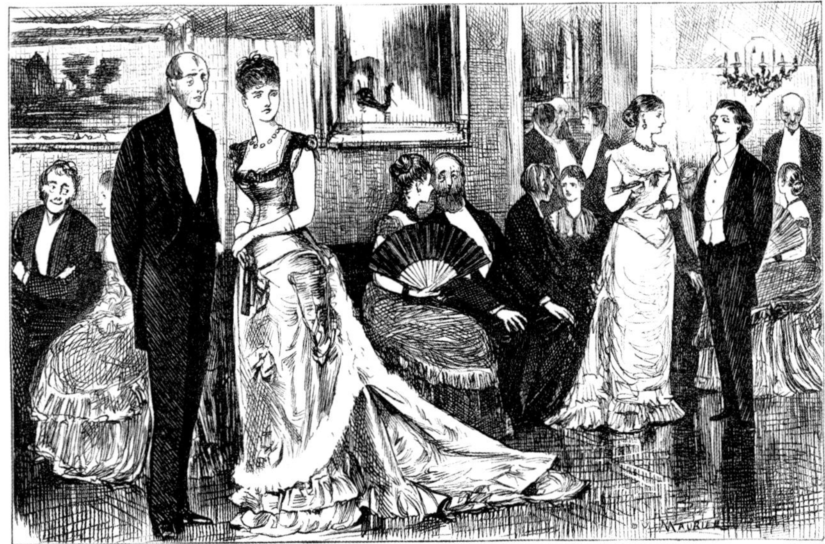

Fig. 90 George du Maurier (1834–1896) 'True Artistic Refinement', from *Punch*, 17 February 1876

'We've heard of socks that poisoned feet,
Hats 'gainst heads are now combining.
With poison in the four-and-nine,
Lined with the dye of aniline –
Death may haunt any linin!'[22]

William Crooke, an assistant of Professor Hofmann, tried to reassure the public in an article on 'Poisonous Dyes' for the *Huddersfield Chronicle*: 'it would appear that the taste for gaudy hose is general throughout the country and, as I am informed that there are several hundred dozen pairs of these chromatic torpedoes already let loose upon society, may I ask you to kindly give me space for a few words which may help to allay the panic which has seized upon manufacturers and the public, and to assure them that there is no reason why our young men and maidens should not continue, as heretofore, to indulge in attire of as startling and varied a colour as their good taste may permit.'[23]

'MALIGNANT MAGENTA'

Inevitably, there was a backlash. The new colours began to be viewed as gaudy, cheap and vulgar. By 1872, one fashion magazine opined that 'unmixed colours and all high colours, such as bright crimson, scarlet, clear blue and green have disappeared from choice goods and are only found in cheap materials made for the million.'[24] Writer and artist Mary Eliza Haweis explained: 'of late our manufacturers, urged on by the vulgar craving for gaudiness, have so much advanced in colour distilling and dyeing that our modern colours are hideous through their extreme purity.'[25] By the late 1870s, Mrs Haweis was warning that mauve could turn the wearer's complexion 'a ghastly orange' and was advising fashionable women to wear 'toned down', 'artistic' colours of 'indescribable tints'.[26]

A cartoon entitled 'True Artistic Refinement', published in *Punch* in February 1877, mocked the aesthetes' rejection of bright aniline colours (fig. 90). Subtitled 'Died of a colour, in aesthetic pain', it shows an aesthetic man caustically remarking that a young woman 'affects aniline dyes, don't you know? I wreally [sic] couldn't go down to suppah [sic] with a young lady who wears mauve twimmings [sic] in her skirt, and magenta wibbons [sic] in her hair!'[27] In 1899 garden designer Gertude Jekyll, who was greatly influenced by the writing of both Ruskin and William Morris, even warned against including 'malignant magenta' in the flower border.[28]

In his 1889 lecture 'The Art of Dyeing', Morris complained that the discovery of the new aniline dyes – 'while conferring the greatest honour on the abstract science of chemistry, and while doing great service to capitalists in their hunt after profits' – had 'terribly injured the art of dyeing'. He wrote: 'Henceforward

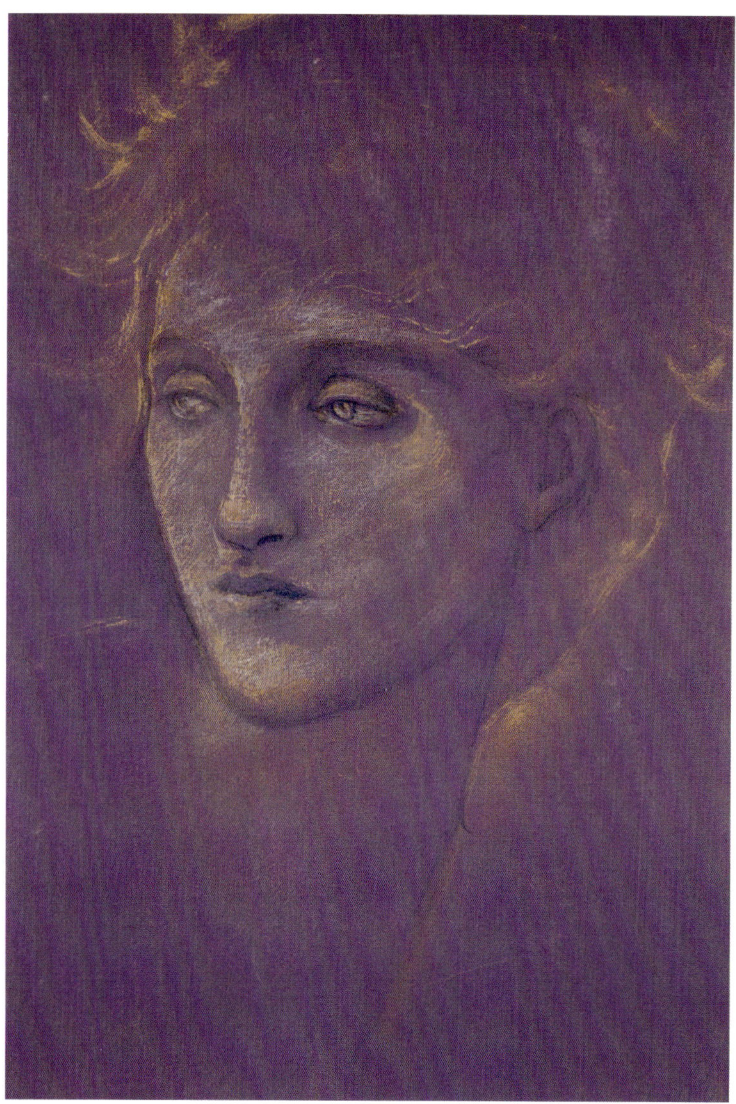

Fig. 91 Edward Burne-Jones (1833–1898), *Head of a Woman*, c.1890. Gold paint on synthetic purple prepared ground. Ashmolean Museum, WA1939.12

there is an absolute divorce between the *commercial process* and the *art* of dyeing.'[29] Morris sought to revive the use of traditional vegetable dyes and techniques at a time when they were fast disappearing. He believed traditional dyes remained beautiful even 'in fading', unlike the 'livid ugliness' of faded anilines which he believed had a 'short and by no means merry life'.[30] In fact most of the commercially available sage greens, dull ambers, pale apricots and other 'artistic' colours of the 1870s and 1880s were still derived from coal tar: Morris's vegetable-dyed textiles were simply too expensive for most.

At a Royal Society of Arts lecture in 1880, William Holman Hunt, one of the founding members of the Pre-Raphaelite Brotherhood, complained about the adulteration or replacement of traditional artists' pigments with 'pestilential' aniline colours (fig. 91): 'I know it is said that the aniline dye carmine is absolutely in all its elements the same thing as the madder carmine; but ... the character of the unmitigated carmine, as it presents itself to the eye, proves a difference of nature of a very fatal kind; and I am quite sure that the sooner the madder root is again cultivated as before, and this aniline dye is discarded for all high purposes, the better it will be for good taste.'[31] Writing to his wife from Paris in 1891, artist James McNeill Whistler complained similarly about the use of 'Impressionist' aniline colours, including mauve, on paintings that he had seen there. He even deliberately misspelled the word – 'analine' – to emphasise his distaste.[32]

Yet, despite these complaints, there was no going back. Perkin's discovery had brought colour in all the glorious shades of the rainbow into the lives of the masses. From parasols to postage stamps, tinted photographs to early films, wine to sweets, the new colours – inexpensive and readily available – were everywhere. The anilines heralded a wider synthetic revolution – in artificial medicines, cosmetics, food sweeteners and flavourings, pesticides, fertilisers and chemical weapons – that has shaped the modern world.

In 1888 *Punch* used verse to satirise the many ways in which the world was now in thrall to the aniline revolution:

BEAUTIFUL TAR. Song of an Enthusiastic Scientist.

Beautiful Tar, the outcome bright
Of the black coal and the yellow gas-light,
Of modern products most wondrous far,
Tar of the gas-works, beautiful Tar!

In fancy's ear thou seem'st to say,
'Follow me close, I am bound to pay.
On me experiments freely try;
For if there's a *multum in parvo*, 'tis I.'

Men told us once, with a cheek quite calm,
Of the things that the Arabs could get from the palm;
But that fraud botanic is distanced far
By the modern marvel, the black Coal-tar.

House and garments, victuals and drink,
The nomad got from the palm, I think;
But as source of beauty, and bliss, and balm,
Coal-tar from the palm-tree must bear the palm.

Protoplasm? Oh, that' s played out;
The true protoplasm is Tar, no doubt.
As 'promise and potency,'
Tar must take
What vulgar scientists call 'the cake:'

There's hardly a thing that a man may name
Of use or beauty in life's small game,
But you can extract in alembic or jar
From the 'physical basis' of black Coal-tar.

Oil, and ointment, and wax, and wine,
And the lovely colours called aniline:
You can make anything, from a salve to a star,
If you only know how to, from black Coal tar.

'Tis found the basis of all things sweet;
Sugar is settled, and beet is beat;
The western root and the eastern cane
With ubiquitous Coal-tar contend in vain.

You can carry the stuff in your pocket or hat,
And it will not hurt you, or make you fat;
Of saccharine matters the wholesomest far
Is the stuff extracted from black Coal-tar,

The very bees mistake it for honey!
'Tis a fount of pleasure, a mine of money;
And the Bounty question without a jar
Will soon be settled by black Coal-tar,

Triumph, o Tar! Stuff half divine!
The world's whole interests soon will twine
Around thine essence the subtlest far,
Tar of the Gas-works, black Coal-tar![33]

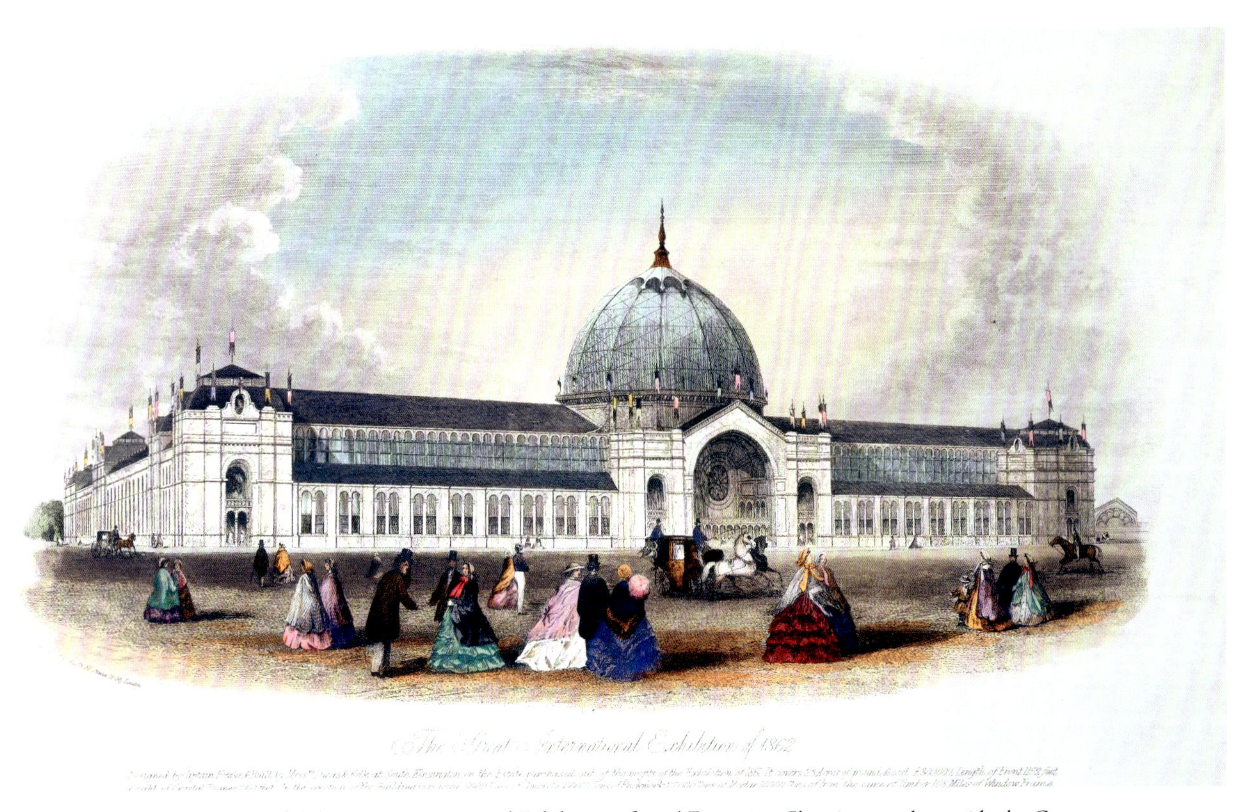

Fig. 92 Robert Ellis (dates unknown), 'The Great International Exhibition of 1862'. Engraving. Showing people outside the Great International Exhibition building in Cromwell Road, London

'More brilliant tints than fancy could conceive' – Exhibiting Colour: The 1862 International Exhibition

Matthew Winterbottom

Long overshadowed by the Great Exhibition of 1851, the 1862 International Exhibition has never received the popular or scholarly attention given its predecessor. Yet in many ways, this ambitious exhibition was the highpoint of the Victorian Colour Revolution. Visiting it was an extraordinarily colourful experience: colour was everywhere, from the exhibition building itself to the thousands of objects displayed inside by more than 29,000 international exhibitors, which was double that of the Great Exhibition. Even the clothes worn by many of the six million exhibition visitors were brightly coloured thanks to the newly invented coal-tar dyes (fig. 92).

One of the reasons the exhibition faded so quickly from public consciousness was the building itself, which failed to recapture the magic of Joseph Paxton's 1851 Crystal Palace in Hyde Park. Designed by Captain Francis Fowke, a military engineer, and built on the sites of the present Natural History Museum, Science Museum and Imperial College in South Kensington, it was a massive building that was widely criticised. In contrast to Paxton's glass 'Palace', the 1862 'Building' had brick walls which were described by Charles Dickens as 'halfway between a factory and a cathedral'.[34] And unlike the Crystal Palace, which was moved to a permanent site in Sydenham in south London, the unloved 1862 building was entirely demolished within two years.

Contemporary criticism of the building was perhaps unfair. The decision to include top-lit Fine Art Galleries on the first floor precluded the kind of glass walls Paxton had employed. It had been intended that the massive brick facades of the building would be beautifully decorated with sculptural terracotta and a series of colourful mosaic pictures designed by leading artists including Frederic Leighton, George Frederic Watts, John Everett Millais and Dante Gabriel Rossetti. Sadly these were never completed and visitors therefore saw only the 'monotonous' brick of the unfinished exterior.[35]

However, if the outside of the building was a disappointment, its vast and colourful interior was widely admired. *Punch* depicted John Bull urging Mrs Britannia – who didn't think the building 'quite so pretty' as the Crystal Palace – to 'see inside'.[36] The interior decorative scheme had been designed remarkably quickly by John Gregory Crace using stencilled patterns in accordance with the colour theories of Michel Eugène Chevreul. Chevreul's *The Principles of Harmony and Contrast of Colours* had been translated into English in 1854. Defending his colourful scheme, which some thought too garish, Crace explained: 'Many rich and valuable stuffs were seriously injured at the

Exhibition of 1851, by injudicious arrangement of them ... It is necessary to bear in mind that all colours have their complementaries, which add or detract from the beauty of the adjoining colours, according to what they may be.'[37] He added: 'Nothing is so charming and so refreshing to the eye as an harmonious arrangement of colours; they are like a sweet chord of music to the senses.'[38]

Owen Jones had designed the interior colour scheme for the Crystal Palace controversially using a primary colour combination of red, blue and yellow that was meant to appear neutral when viewed from a distance. In contrast, Crace's 1862 interior scheme was a wealth of colour and pattern. Visitors entering from the main entrance on Exhibition Road would have surveyed the massive expanse of the 800ft (244m)-long central nave linking the Eastern Dome

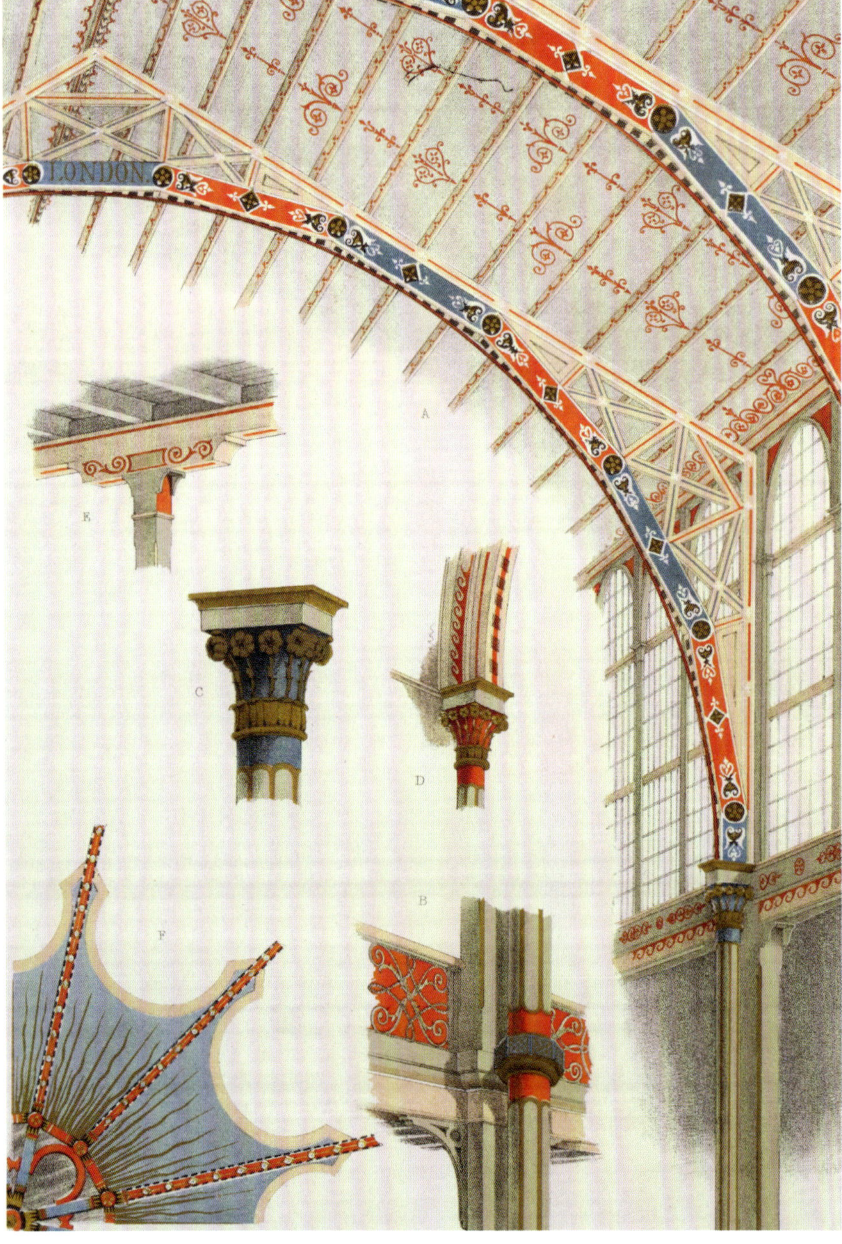

Fig. 93 Robert Dudley (1826–1909), Details of stencilled decorations designed by John Gregory Crace for the interior of the Exhibition building. Chromolithograph. Victoria and Albert Museum, E.6868-1900

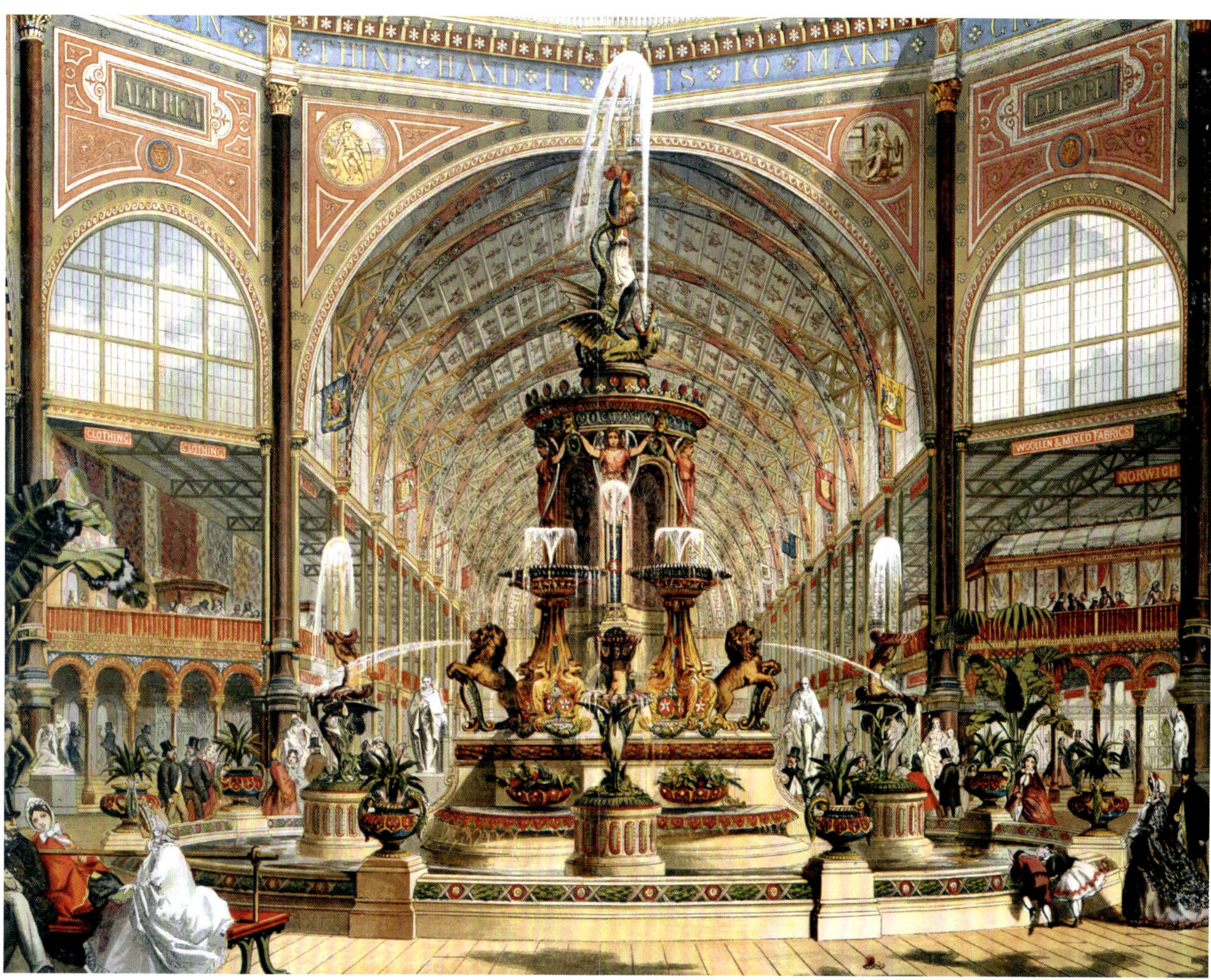

Fig. 94 Robert Dudley (1826–1909), 'The Majolica Fountain in the International Exhibition' from *The Illustrated London News*, 30 August, 1862. Chromolithograph

with the Western one, its colourful ceiling and supports painted with Crace's stencilled patterns (fig. 93). The enormous glass domes each had a diameter of 160ft (49m) and were, at that time, the largest span domes ever to have been constructed.[39]

Directly below the centre of the Eastern Dome was Minton's colourful St George Fountain (fig. 94). Standing 36ft (11m) high and made of brightly coloured majolica ceramic, this was one of the most spectacular exhibits of the exhibition. Designed by sculptor John Thomas, the fountain was surmounted by a life-sized figure of St George and the Dragon. Its water was regularly scented by London perfumier Eugène Rimmel, adding to the range of sensory delights for visitors. It was one of the most popular exhibits in the exhibition and, if Osler's colourless Crystal Fountain came to symbolise the 1851 Great Exhibition, Minton's colourful Majolica Fountain was the embodiment of its successor. *Chamber's Journal* recorded: 'There was a great inarticulate cry of admiration and delight, as the fountain dancing in the sunshine, and the long rainbow-roof of the Nave, shone out upon us, as though a gate had opened in Paradise.'[40] Adding to this colourful spectacle were two gigantic stained glass

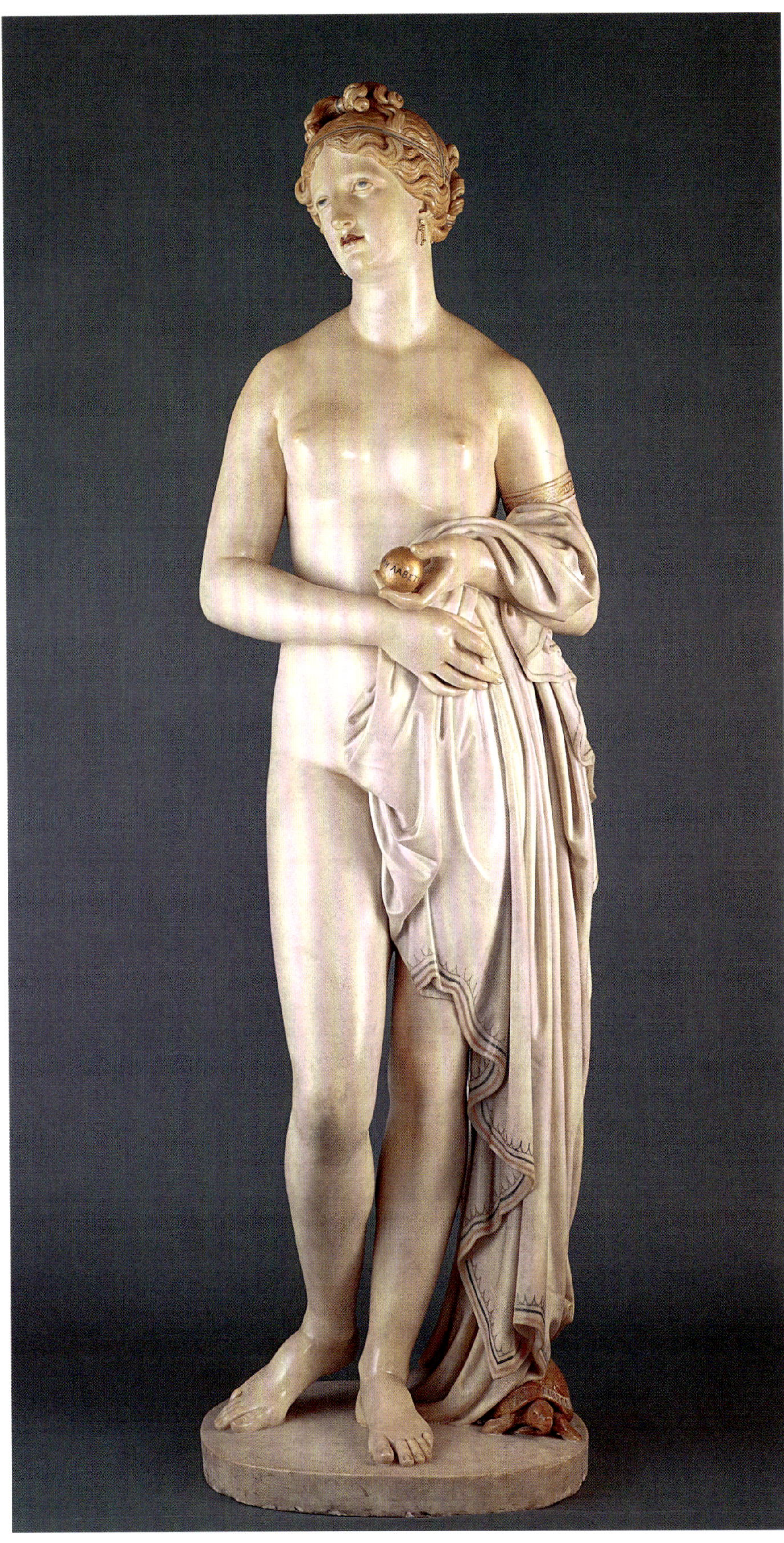

Fig. 95 John Gibson (1790–1866), *Tinted Venus*, 1851–6. Carrara marble with pigments and gilding. National Museums Liverpool, Walker Art Gallery, WAG7808

rose windows at either end of the nave. Minton & Co. displayed a smaller ceramic fountain on their exhibition stand. A surviving version shows the same vibrant colours that were achieved by the firm's lead-rich majolica glazes.

The hundreds of thousands of exhibits displayed within the building formed a kaleidoscopic array of colours from all over the globe. One key exhibit that attracted much comment and debate was sculptor John Gibson's *Tinted Venus*, a life-sized marble statue that Gibson had delicately coloured with tinted waxes in an attempt to recreate the original polychromy of ancient Greek and Roman sculpture (fig. 95). During the mid-nineteenth century there was fierce debate over whether ancient marble sculpture and architecture had originally been brightly painted. This had both fascinated and horrified critics, who were accustomed to the whiteness of surviving pieces. Gibson's *Tinted Venus* and his other coloured sculptures helped galvanise the debate and bring it to a wider public audience. *The Sculptor's Magazine* considered it 'one of the most beautiful and elaborate figures undertaken in modern times', while the *Athenaeum* denounced it as 'a naked impudent English woman'.[41] The sculpture had actually been made some years earlier. Elizabeth Barrett Browning saw it in Gibson's Rome studio in 1854 and wrote that she had 'seldom, if ever, seen so indecent a statue. The colouring with an approximation to flesh tints produces that effect, to my apprehention [sic]. I don't like this statue-colouring – no, not at all'.[42] She felt the statue had 'come out of cloud of the ideal'.[43] For Browning and others, the statue was just too realistic, too sensual. In fact, Gibson's colouring of the body was intended to evoke tinted ivory rather than human flesh, but the blond hair, blue eyes, painted eyelashes and pink lips were too much for many. The evocation of ivory was in reference to the ancient myth of Pygmalion, the Greek sculptor who fell in love with his own ivory sculpture that magically came to life. Like Pygmalion, Gibson claimed he too had fallen for his own creation: 'she seems an ethereal being with her blue eyes fixed on me! At moments I forgot that I was gazing at my own production; there I sat before her, long and often. How was I ever to part with her!'[44]

The *Tinted Venus* was shown publicly for the first time at the 1862 Exhibition. It was prominently displayed in a specially designed, polychrome 'Pompeiian' temple situated in the central avenue, just south of the nave (fig. 96). The temple, designed by Owen Jones, had the *Tinted Venus* in the centre and, at each side, two more sculptures designed and tinted by Gibson: *Pandora* and *Cupid Tormenting the Soul*. Around the cornice above the statues ran gilded Latin inscriptions taken from ancient sources: *Nec vita nec sanitas nec pulchritudo, nec sine colore juventus* (Without colour no life, nor health, nor beauty, nor youth); *Formas rerum obscuras illustrat confusas distinguit omnes ornat colorum diversitas suavis* (The gentle variety of colours illuminates the dark form of things, distinguishes the confused and decorates everything); *In tempio Jovis coloribus ardet lux ipsa diversis* (In the temple of Jupiter light itself burns with diverse colours); and *Formae dignitas bonitate coloris tuenda est* (The dignity of form is protected by the goodness of colour).[45]

The temple was therefore 'designed as a material argument for polychromy, both its aesthetic effect and its historical accuracy'.[46] It prompted much

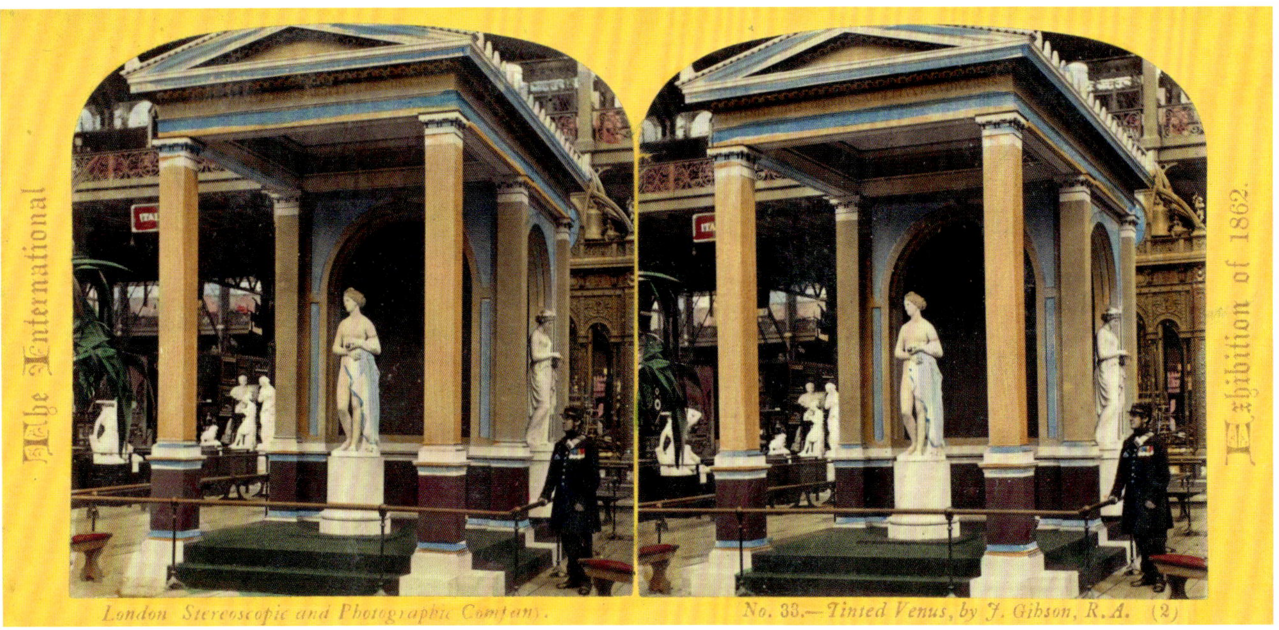

Fig. 96 William England for the London Stereoscopic and Photographic Company, *The International Exhibition of 1862: No. 33 – Tinted Venus by J. Gibson, R.A.*, 1862. Albumen silver print from glass negative with applied colour. The Metropolitan Museum of Art, New York, Gilman Collection, 2005.100.1066.1–.86

controversy: one writer noted: 'Approach the statue any hour of the day and you will hear a merciless running fire of remarks against it.'[47]

Owen Jones had been responsible for the colourful and hugely influential – although much criticised – Fine Art Courts installed in the relocated Crystal Palace in Sydenham in 1853.[48] Made of polychromed plaster, these included ancient Assyrian, Egyptian, Greek, Roman and Alhambra Courts (fig. 97). In the Greek Court, Jones had installed a cast of a section of the Parthenon frieze, painted as he believed it would originally have been. This probably inspired the Dutch artist Sir Lawrence Alma-Tadema, who first visited London in 1862, to paint *Phidias Showing the Frieze of the Parthenon to his Friends* (fig. 98), in which he imagines the ancient Athenian sculptor showing off his recently finished frieze.[49]

The polychrome debate was not confined to elite artistic and intellectual circles. Sir James Duke and Nephews, of the Hill Pottery in Burslem, Stoke-on-Trent, was one of several manufacturers at the exhibition who showed classical revival ceramics decorated with colourful scenes derived from ancient sculptures and ceramics.[50] These mass-produced ceramics propelled the debate about ancient polychromy into middle-class drawing rooms around the country. The firm of Coalport even produced miniature Parian porcelain copies of the *Tinted Venus* that had been delicately tinted like the original.[51]

Displayed just a few metres away from the *Tinted Venus* was another remarkable sculpture that further expanded the debate around 'colour'. A life-sized version of John Bell's *A Daughter of Eve: A Scene on the Shore of the Atlantic* formed part of Elkington and Co.'s enormous 'Galvano-plastic' Trophy. Surmounted by *Boadicea and her Daughters*, by John Thomas, and consisting of several tiers of electrotyped sculptures, the Trophy stood close to 'Precious Metals', in the British section of the nave (fig. 99).[52] Made of bronzed, electroformed copper

Right: Fig. 97 Henry Vaughan Lanchester, Alhambra Court in the Crystal Palace, Sydenham, London: perspective view of the reconstructed Court of the Lions seen through Moorish archways, 1900. Drawing. RIBA Collections

Below: Fig. 98 Sir Lawrence Alma-Tadema (1836–1912), *Phidias Showing the Frieze of the Parthenon to his Friends*, 1868–9. Oil on mahogany panel. Birmingham Museums Trust on behalf of Birmingham City Council, 1923P118

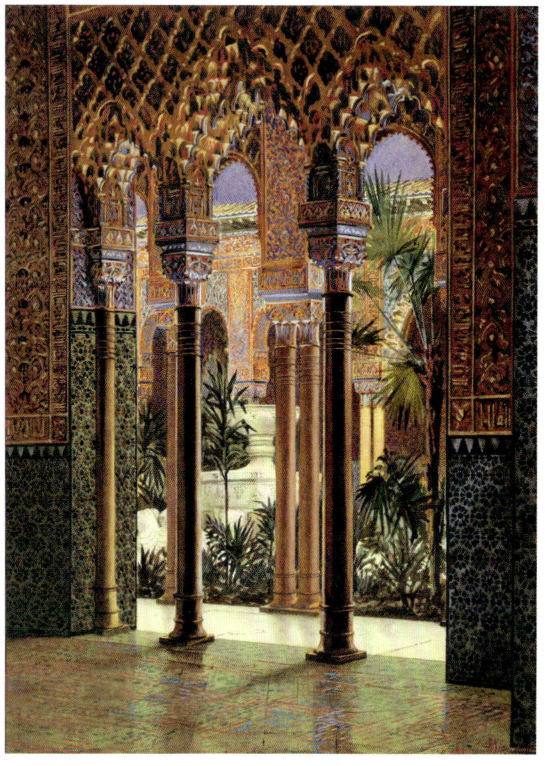

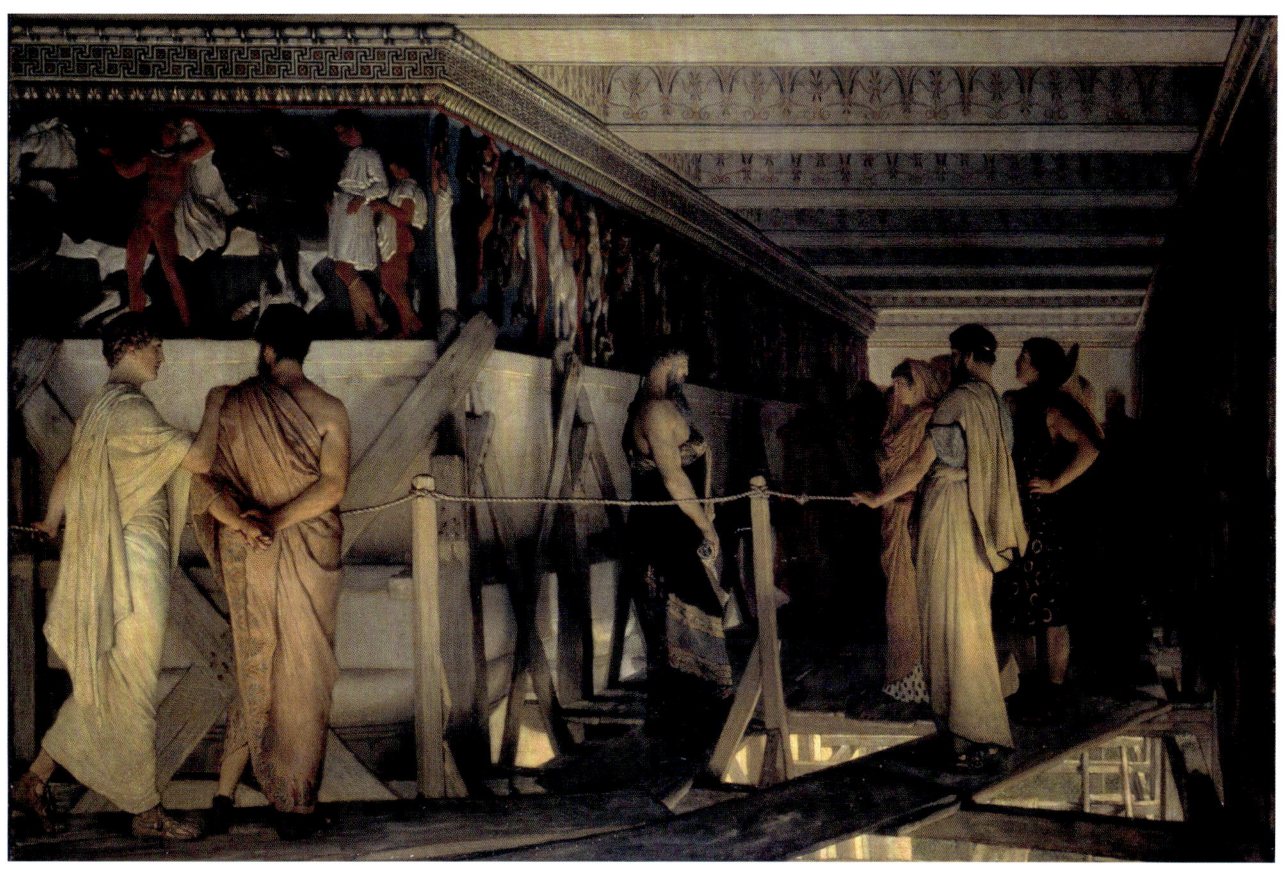

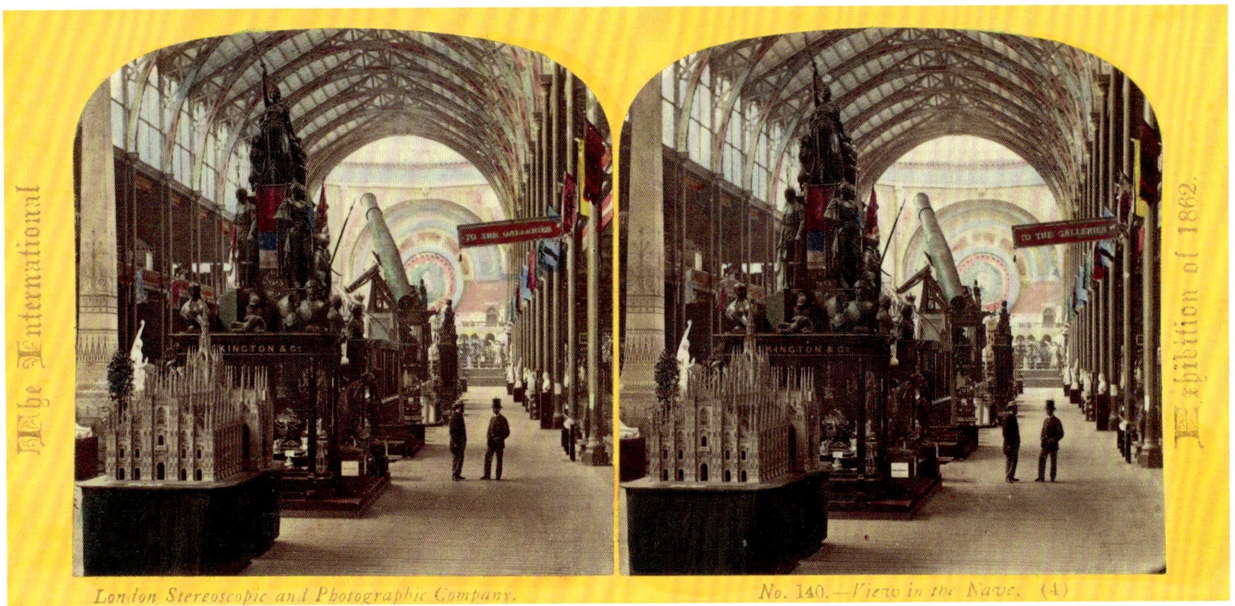

Fig. 99 William England for the London Stereoscopic and Photographic Company, *The International Exhibition of 1862: No. 140 – View of the Nave*, 1862. Albumen silver print from glass negative with applied colour. Showing the Elkington Trophy

– a revolutionary industrial process invented by Elkington and Co. in the 1840s – *A Daughter of Eve* was a figure of a young enslaved African woman waiting in chains to be transported to America (fig. 113; p. 127). The South Kensington Museum curator George Wallis described it as 'touching an appeal against the blasphemous hypocrisy which attempts to justify human bondage on the ground of external physical differences – a happy thought, happily embodied in a singularly suitable material'.[53] Although not polychrome in the same sense as Gibson's *Tinted Venus*, the bronze patination evokes the colour and sheen of the woman's skin – the very reason for her enslavement. She wears gold earrings and her chains are silvered to contrast with her bronze 'flesh'.[54]

First shown at the Royal Academy in 1853, *A Daughter of Eve* aroused much sympathy at a time when slavery in the United States was still legal. The American Civil War, caused in large part by differences in attitudes towards slavery, had been raging for a year when the exhibition opened in May 1862. The American display was much reduced as a result. Despite official British opposition to slavery, its textile industries were heavily dependent on slave-produced cotton grown in the southern US. Cotton textiles were among Britain's most important and lucrative exports at this time. 460,000 British textile workers, about 16 percent of the workforce, were directly dependent on cotton grown by 3 million American slaves.[55] The disruption to the supply of cotton due to the Civil War, known as the Cotton Famine, had a devastating impact on British textile manufacturers and their workers. At the 1862 Exhibition, the British textile manufacturers' displays were shown in open first-floor galleries that ran around the nave and surrounding courts. The cotton displays were in a gallery above the Elkington Trophy, and visitors looking at *A Daughter of Eve* would almost certainly have been distracted by the large 'Cotton' sign hanging directly overhead. Although probably a coincidence, some would have noted the connection.

A half-sized version of the sculpture was also displayed on the Elkington Trophy, perhaps to encourage visitors to purchase copies. Miniature versions in white Parian porcelain were also shown by Minton & Co. These were given the less subtle title *'American Slave'*, a moniker sometimes also used for Bell's original model, although there is no evidence that he ever called it by this name.[56] *A Daughter of Eve* was purchased by William, 1st Baron Armstrong, whose controversial Trophy of Armstrong artillery guns was displayed in the neighbouring Naval Court of the exhibition. The 1851 Great Exhibition had been dedicated to international peace and trade. In the intervening 11 years, increasing nationalism and wars in the Crimea, Italy and the United States had changed attitudes.

The Elkington Trophy was surrounded by the stands of London's leading jewellers and goldsmiths. Crowds gathered to see the magnificent gems and jewels on display, including the famed Koh-i-noor Diamond. One of the most spectacular – and colourful – exhibits was the monumental Devonshire Parure, on the stand of C.F. Hancock & Co. (fig. 100). This seven-piece suite of jewellery was made for the Duke of Devonshire's niece, the Countess of Granville, to wear at the Tsar of Russia's coronation in 1856. The Countess had been there to represent Queen Victoria, only a few months after fighting in the Crimea between the two countries had ceased. Made of gold 'richly enamelled in the renaissance style',[57] the parure is set with diamonds and 88 engraved gems and cameos in semi-precious stones from the Devonshire collection.[58] The lavish use of coloured gems and enamels, and the sheer size of the parure, were clearly intended to impress the Russian Court and convey British prestige.

Although first discovered in 1856 and in commercial production since 1858, it was not until the 1862 Exhibition that the new synthetic aniline dyes were exhibited to an international audience. These 'remarkable and beautiful colours' were said to have created 'a new era in the tinctorial art',[59] and their discovery was hailed as one of the most important inventions in the eleven years since the 1851 Great Exhibition. By 1862 annual production of aniline dyes was valued at a staggering £400,000 (£62 million in current terms) and many exhibition visitors were already wearing clothes coloured with them (fig. 101). Two of the most fashionable aniline colours, Magenta and Solferino, were named after French victories over the Austrian army during the Second Italian War of Independence. This war, between two major European powers – and exhibitors – had delayed the opening of the exhibition by a year.

Visitors could see the new dyes in profusion in the silk, cotton and woollen fabrics and accessories in the British and French textile displays on the first floor galleries. However, it was the didactic displays by the dye manufactures and chemists that really captured visitors' imaginations. A writer for *The Ladies Treasury* waxed lyrical: 'Even the sunbeams of ages past are here reproduced in more brilliant tints than fancy could conceive. Rose, magenta, green, violet, all the colours of the rainbow, are palpable to the touch, as visible to the eye.'[60] These displays were in the 'Colours' section – within 'Chemicals', in the south-eastern corner of the exhibition's Eastern Annex. William Perkin, inventor of the first aniline dye in 1856, 'exhibited a valuable and interesting series of

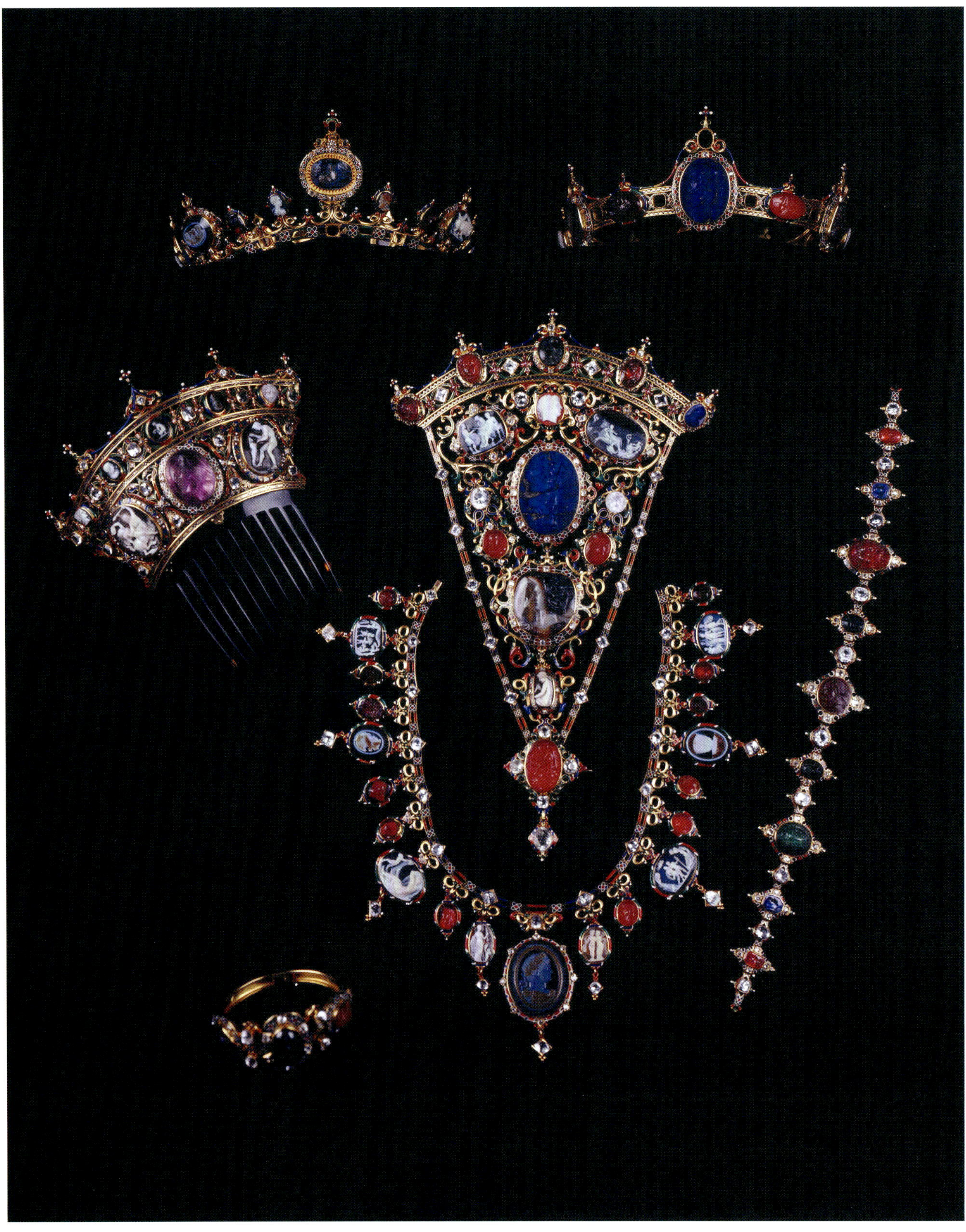

Fig. 100 The Devonshire Parure by C.F. Hancock & Co., 1856. Enamelled gold, diamonds and semi-precious gems. The Devonshire Collections, Chatsworth

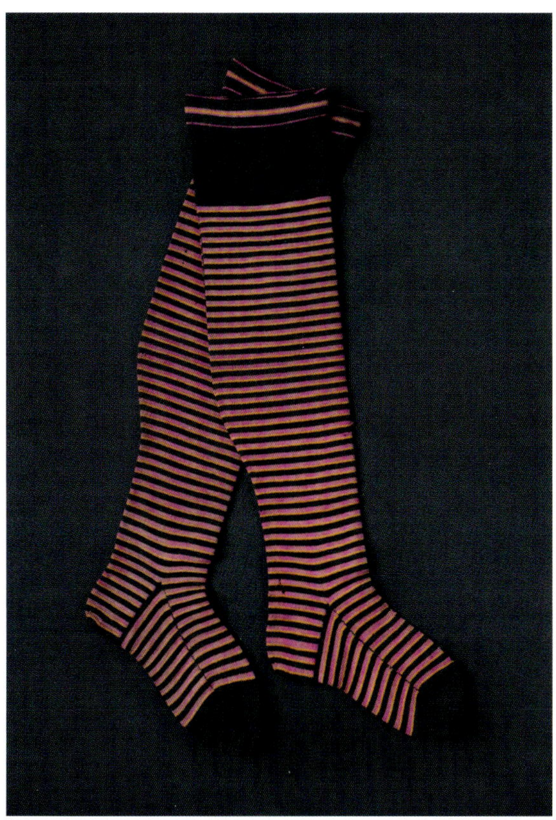

Fig. 101 Pair of stockings exhibited at the 1862 International Exhibition, English. Aniline dyed wool. Manchester Art Gallery, 1955.324

specimens illustrating every stage of the process from coal to dyed silk'.[61] During one visit into the 'chemical labyrinth' of the Eastern Annex, Charles Dickens described 'glass cups holding various coloured anilines: green and blue, and yellow, and dull red, and purple, and dirty looking mauve ... magenta powder, a beautiful mass of rainbow-coloured grains like crushed peacock ore ... and then there are aniline orange, and aniline deep purple, and cyanine blue from aniline, and opaline blue'.[62]

Like many visitors, Dickens was particularly struck by the 'magnificent' and 'very curious and very lovely' gold-green crowns made by Messrs. Simpson, Maule & Nicholson, from pure magenta (fuchsine) crystals that had been grown onto wire frames in huge vats. Described as 'as lustrous as the wing of the diamond beetle',[63] each crown was valued at £400 and was said to contain enough aniline crystals to 'dye the Thames magenta from the sea to its source'.[64] According to one account these displays represented 'a new power for manufacturing England. No longer compelled to import our dyes, we draw in great variety some of the most beautiful of known colours out of the darkness of our own inexhaustible coal mines'.[65] Dickens also admired the pigment and paint displays of the artists' suppliers: 'the artist's colour-cases are still the most beautiful! Has anyone ever seen anything like Winsor and Newton's cups of chromes and carnations and scarlet lakes and royal blues, and paler azures and insolent oranges, and purples, and greens, and snowy knubbles of flake white, and primrose daintiness, and crimsons loud and fierce as a war-cry, and pinks tender and loving as a young girl?'[66]

One of the most successful and popular British displays in the 1851 Great Exhibition had been the Medieval Court. The 'strikingly-harmonious combination of its stained glass, hardware, wood-carving, hangings, encaustic tiles – all successful repetitions of Gothic models'[67] had been fastidiously arranged by A.W.N. Pugin to promote his messianic belief that Gothic was the true Christian style. Therefore another was planned for 1862. However much had happened in the intervening 11 years. Pugin had died in 1852, exhausted from overwork, but the popularity of the Gothic Revival continued to grow and develop. The Ecclesiastical Society asked architects William Slater and William Burges to organise and arrange the displays. Burges was one of a small group of London architects in the late 1850s that had designed painted furniture based on surviving medieval cabinets and woodwork. He believed that medieval furniture had been 'covered with paintings, both ornaments and subjects; it not only did its duty as furniture, but spoke and told a story'. Other exhibitors of medieval-style painted furniture included Morris, Marshall, Faulkner & Co. – 'Fine Art Workmen in Painting, Carving, Furniture and the Metals' –founded in 1861 by William Morris, Philip Webb and others including Ford Madox Brown, Edward Burne-Jones and Dante Gabriel Rossetti. Burges ensured that 'all the principal and rising architects, and a very large proportion of the best manufacturers' were represented.[68] He was content, however, that there was 'no mediaeval court properly speaking, for mediaevalism has ceased to be a sort of curiosity penned up in one little court, but has become a national style, and is to be found more or less in every part of the building.'[69] Although Pugin had embraced the vibrant colours of the Middle Ages in many of his designs, most of his Gothic wooden furniture had been unadorned. By contrast, the defining feature of the 1862 Medieval Court was 18 pieces of Gothic furniture painted with colourful scenes and ornament. These included five 'picant painted'[70] pieces by Burges himself (fig. 102).

Dominating the Medieval Court was Burges's massive Great Bookcase, designed for his own use (fig. 104, p. 117). Painted by 14 different artists depicting Pagan and Christian scenes, it was loosely based on surviving thirteenth-century French painted cabinets. The Great Bookcase also included ancient Egyptian, Greek and Roman scenes, and incorporated Indian and Florentine inlaid marbles, along with Japanese 'katagami'-style stencilling of sea creatures and insects.[71]

Burges considered the arts and crafts of contemporary pre-industrialised countries in the Middle East and Asia to be close in spirit to those of medieval Europe. He regularly incorporated Islamic and Asian designs, and even objects,

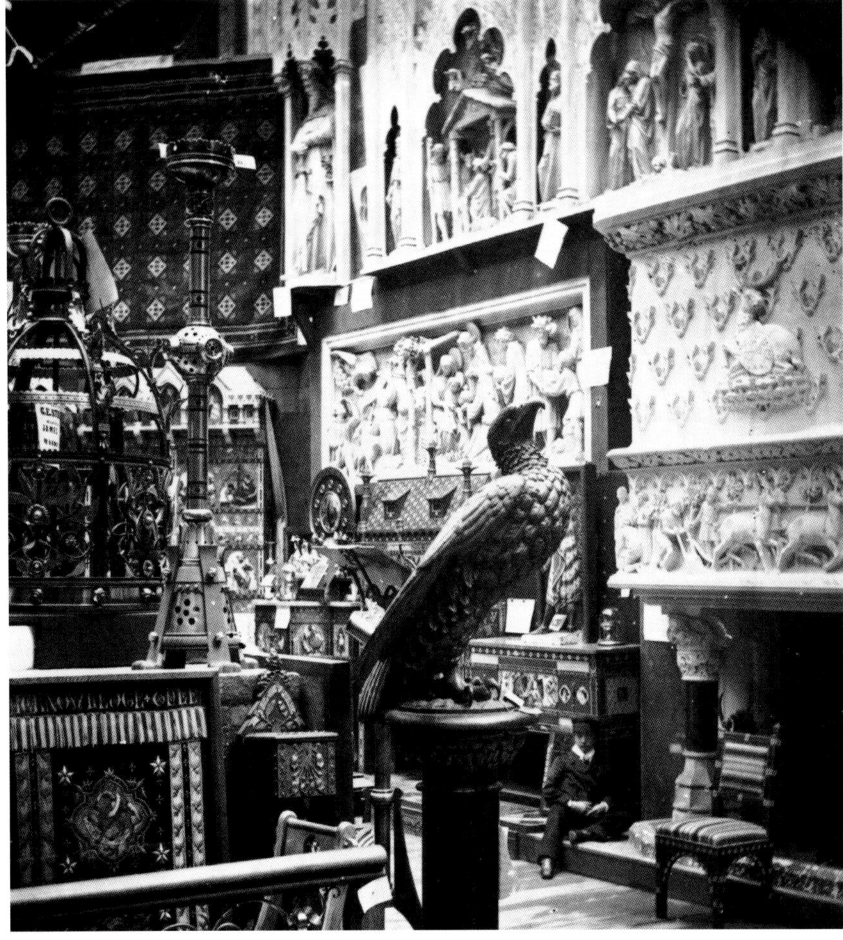

Fig. 102 View of The International Exhibition of 1862: the Medieval Court showcased painted furniture designed by William Burges. The Great Bookcase is just visible at the back left

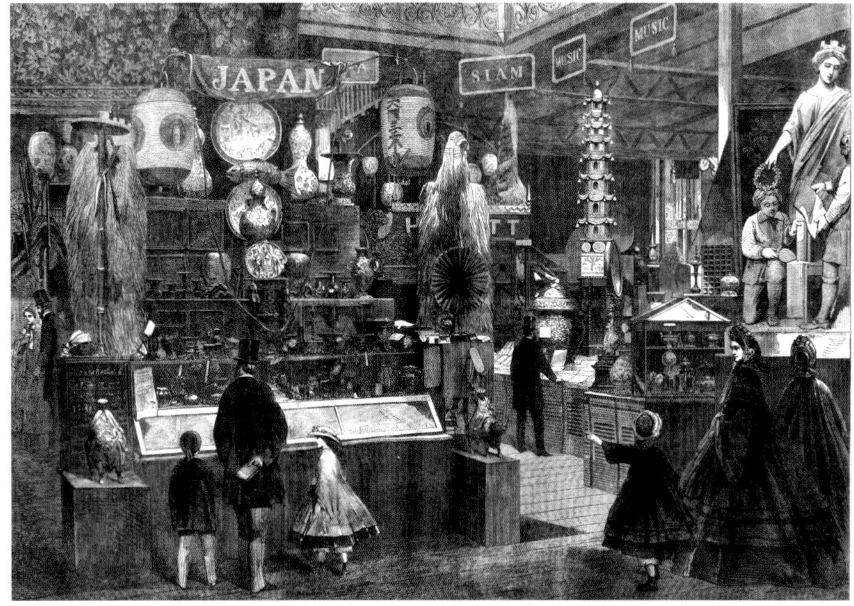

Fig. 103 'The International Exhibition: The Japanese Court. From a Photograph by the London Stereoscopic Company' from *The Illustrated London News*, 20 September 1862

into his own work. Burges was one of the earliest collectors of colourful Japanese woodblock prints, which started to arrive in the West in the 1850s.[72] One of the revelations of the 1862 International Exhibition had been the Japan Court, situated at the opposite end of the 'Furniture' section from the Medieval Court (fig. 103). Japan had essentially been closed to the West since the early eighteenth century, so the 1862 Exhibition was the first time most visitors had seen contemporary Japanese arts and crafts. Burges wrote: 'If the visitor wishes to see the real Middle Ages, he must visit the Japanese Court, for at the present day the arts of the Middle Ages have deserted Europe, and are only to be found in the East.'[73] He told students interested in reviving the arts of the thirteenth century that 'an hour, or even a day or two, spent in the Japanese department will by no means be lost time, for these hitherto unknown barbarians appear not only to know all that the Middle Ages knew, but in some respects are beyond them and us as well.'[74] Both designer Christopher Dresser and artist James McNeill Whistler visited the Japan Court in 1862, which sparked a lifelong fascination with the country for both men. The distinctive colours of Japanese art, especially the blues found in woodblock prints and indigo-dyed textiles, had an important impact on the Aesthetic Movement in the later 1860s and 1870s.

The death of Prince Albert, one of the key figures behind the 1851 Great Exhibition in December 1861, five months before the opening of the 1862 Exhibition, cast a pall over the entire project. While the Great Exhibition remains one of the most famous and extraordinary events of the nineteenth century, the 1862 Exhibition, although more ambitious, is largely forgotten. Yet its colourful legacy – from the innovative use of complementary colour theories for its interior decoration, to its colourful exhibits, was of profound and lasting importance.

Object in Focus

The Great Bookcase: Between Medieval and Victorian Colour

Colour is often the protagonist in art, but in a few rare cases the materials used for painting are so many and so diverse that they result in an intense spectacle for the eye. Because of its monumental size (317.5 x 173.9 x 49.5 cm) and outstanding chromatic variety, the Great Bookcase is one of these rare works (fig. 104).

Covering a surface of more than six square metres, the complex intertwining of colours was achieved by its architect, William Burges, and 13 young artists he gathered to paint the bookcase between 1859 and 1862. Burges designed this rare example of Gothic Revival painted furniture to hold his own book collection. Because of its neo-medieval iconography and design, the Bookcase was displayed as the centrepiece of the Medieval Court at the International Exhibition in 1862.[75]

During the Middle Ages, pigments were mostly prepared by processing natural sources. For instance, an intense red colour was extracted from the root of the plant *Rubia tinctorum*, and a precious, deep blue pigment known as ultramarine blue was obtained from the stone lapis lazuli. Furthermore, synthetic pigments – or man-made compounds obtained via different chemical reactions – were sometimes prepared to obtain colours that were not readily available in nature. The oldest of them all, Egyptian Blue, has been manufactured since at least the third millennium BCE by fusing limestone, sand and a copper compound.[76] Lead White, a popular pigment in use since Antiquity, could be either foraged in nature or artificially manufactured, as reported by author Pliny the Elder.[77] In spite of this long history of artificially manufactured pigments, however, the term 'synthetic' remains closely linked to the nineteenth century because of the rapid development of synthetic industrial colour manufacture.

At the dawn of the Industrial Revolution, scientific and technological progress led to the discovery and mass production of the pigment Prussian Blue, which started the first wave of industrially produced synthetic colours. From the nineteenth century onwards, dozens of new pigments were introduced every decade. Cobalt Blue, Chrome Yellow, Emerald Green, Iodine Scarlet and synthetic Ultramarine Blue had all been introduced by the 1820s.[78] Therefore, the choices available to artists multiplied rapidly as these new colours presented fresh possibilities for chromatic expression. In his treatise *Chromatography*, the chemist and artists' colourman[79] George Field pointed out the prospects introduced by the novel rose colours prepared from madder, describing them as 'the most valuable acquisition of the palette in modern times, since perfectly permanent transparent reds and rose colours were previously unknown to the art of painting'.[80]

Therefore, when Burges and the artists started working on the bookcase in 1859, the artists' palette had considerably expanded compared to the Middle Ages. During those years, a growing enthusiasm for the new possibilities introduced by scientific and technological innovation pervaded England, triggered by William Henry Perkin's discovery of Mauvine in 1856.[81] The pavilions of the 1862 Exhibition buzzed with excitement while an array of international manufacturers proudly displayed fabrics dyed with the most vibrant new colours.

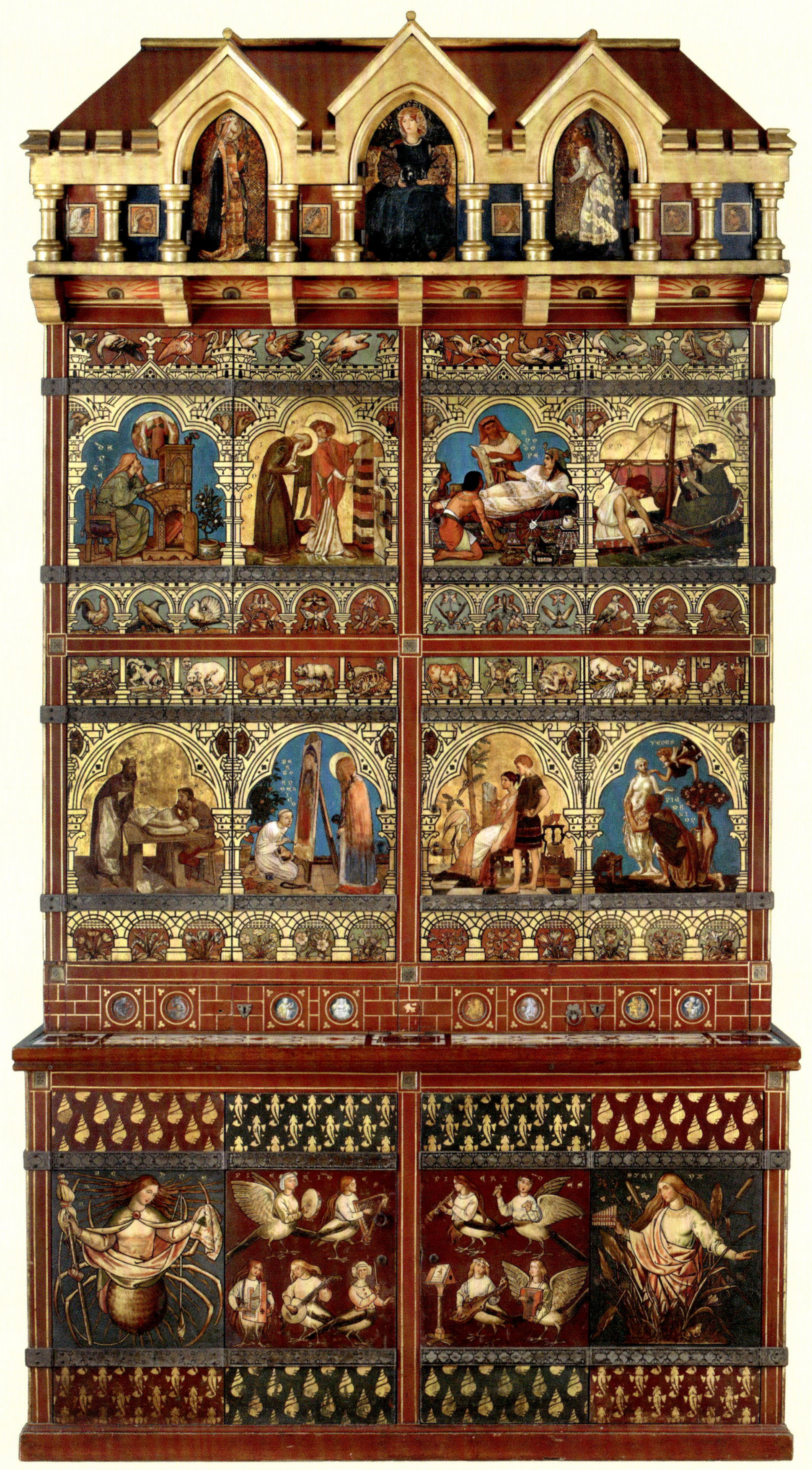

Fig. 104 William Burges (1827–1881) and others, The Great Bookcase, 1859–62. Painted and gilded wood, *pietra dura* panels. Ashmolean Museum, WA1933.26

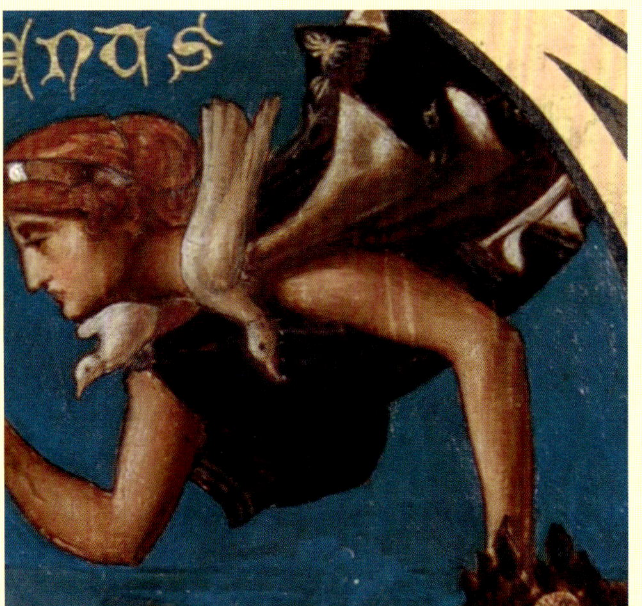

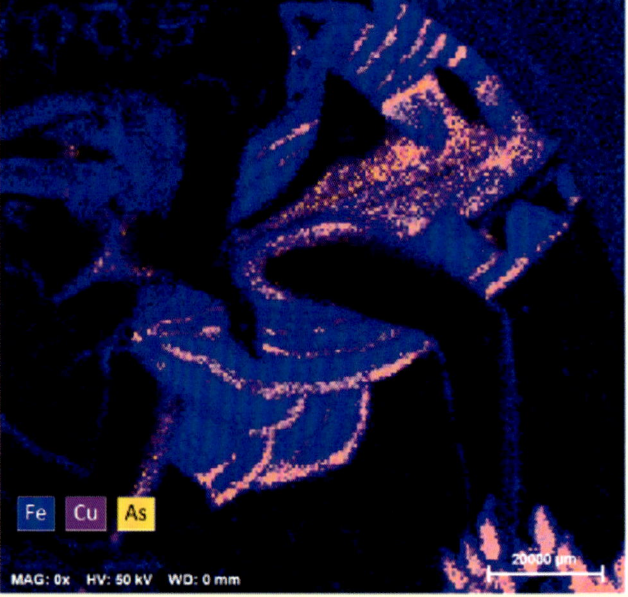

Fig. 105 Visible image (left) and XRF elemental map (right) of the Venus in Simeon Solomon's Pygmalion panel. The gown, now dull and two-dimensional, was originally painted with different colours: an iron-based pigment (shown in blue) and a pigment containing arsenic and copper (shown in pink)

But the nineteenth-century cultural environment was not all about eagerness for progress: developments in science were accompanied by a keen interest in the past, as the iconography depicted on the bookcase reminds us. Not only were medieval iconographical models reintroduced across art and architecture, but the material culture of historic arts and crafts was also systematically investigated. In the 1840s, Sir Charles Eastlake published his *Materials for a History of Oil Painting*, and Mary Merrifield translated into English a series of historic treatises on the arts of painting, gilding and dyeing.[82] Burges was very engaged with medieval material culture, owning copies of technical manuals by Theophilus and Cennino Cennini.[83] Therefore, inspired by the medieval world yet dealing with an increasing number of new colours that expanded and transformed the artistic palette,[84] Burges and his artists must have faced quite a conundrum when creating their Gothic Revival bookcase: would they have limited themselves to recreate the Middle Ages stylistically? Or, could they have attempted to use historically inspired colours?

The composition of the pigments used on the Bookcase was recently determined, primarily using X-ray fluorescence (XRF), a non-invasive method. To complement the XRF, a few samples were analysed using visible and electron microscopy. Finally, the results were compared with compositional information on nineteenth-century pigments, available thanks to prior archival and material investigations.[85] The analyses showed that Burges and the artists largely resorted to contemporary materials in painting the Bookcase. Emerald green, a toxic compound containing copper and arsenic (and a favourite of the Pre-Raphaelites), dominated the surface of the Bookcase.[86] In addition, chromium-based greens, Prussian and cobalt blues, lemon and chrome yellow were used to paint the Bookcase's neo-medieval scenes.

Since industrial pigments were often heavily adulterated and sold with labels that barely described their content, we cannot be entirely sure the artists knew the precise material composition of the pigments they used. However, such extensive use of new synthetic industrial pigments, as observed on the Bookcase, could not have been entirely unintentional. Clearly, the availability of new colours and their appealing, vibrant hues greatly influenced Burges and the artists. In fact, analyses revealed that the colours of the Bookcase were originally even more vibrant than now, as some areas have dulled through ageing (fig. 105).

Further analyses added nuance to this story and revealed the continuous and articulate decision-making process that resulted in the Bookcase as we see it nowadays. A microscopic examination of the surface of the eight central painted panels showed an elaborate overlapping of different colours resulting from several repaintings – evidence that the design of each panel was a fluid process. Furthermore, it revealed that the golden and blue that now alternately cover the background of the painted scenes were not initially part of the composition. Infrared photography has uncovered the underdrawings beneath these paint layers, revealing that the original settings featured both outdoor landscapes and indoor scenes (fig. 106).

One of the pigments found in the blue background, lithopone, marketed from the 1870s onwards, indicates that the Bookcase was reworked at a later period. It seems that when it collapsed in 1878, Burges took the opportunity to repaint some of its decoration, including adding blue and golden backgrounds.[87] The in-depth investigation with electron microscopy of a small blue paint flake revealed that, together with lithopone, the pigments making up this colour are Prussian Blue and a few tiny particles of ultramarine blue. From his studies, Burges would have certainly been aware that ultramarine blue was the most precious medieval pigment, worth more than gold at that time.[88] Since it is reported that lithophone and Prussian Blue were used

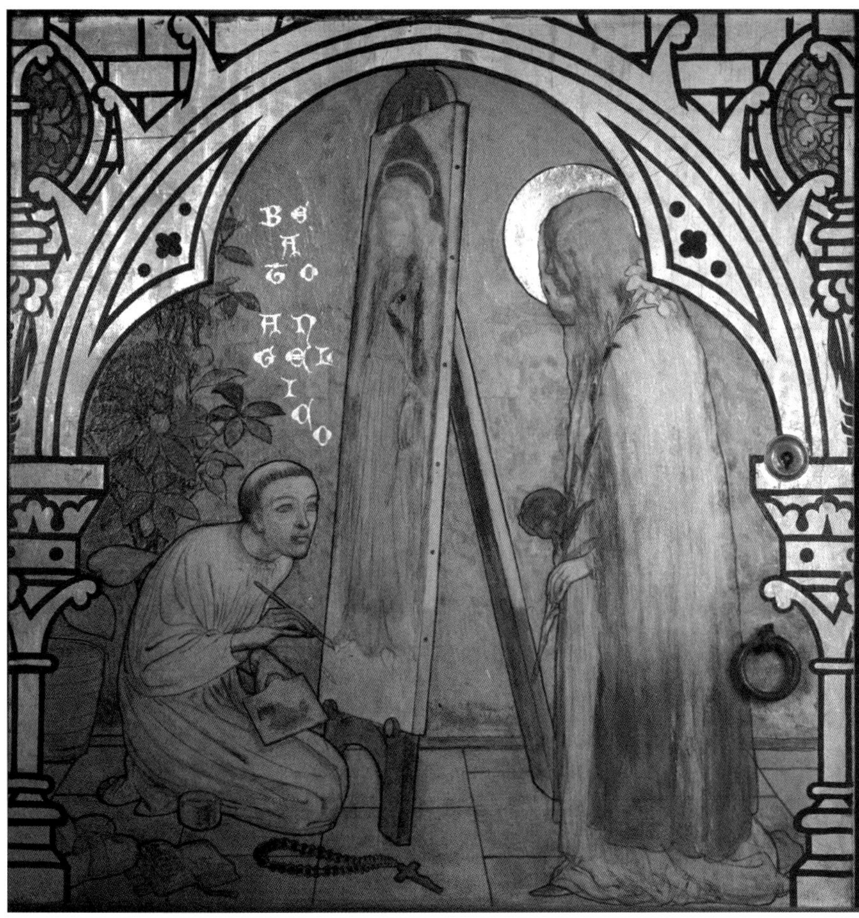

Fig. 106 Infrared image of the original setting of Thomas Morten's Beato Angelico panel. A stone wall with ivy is visible between the easel and the Virgin

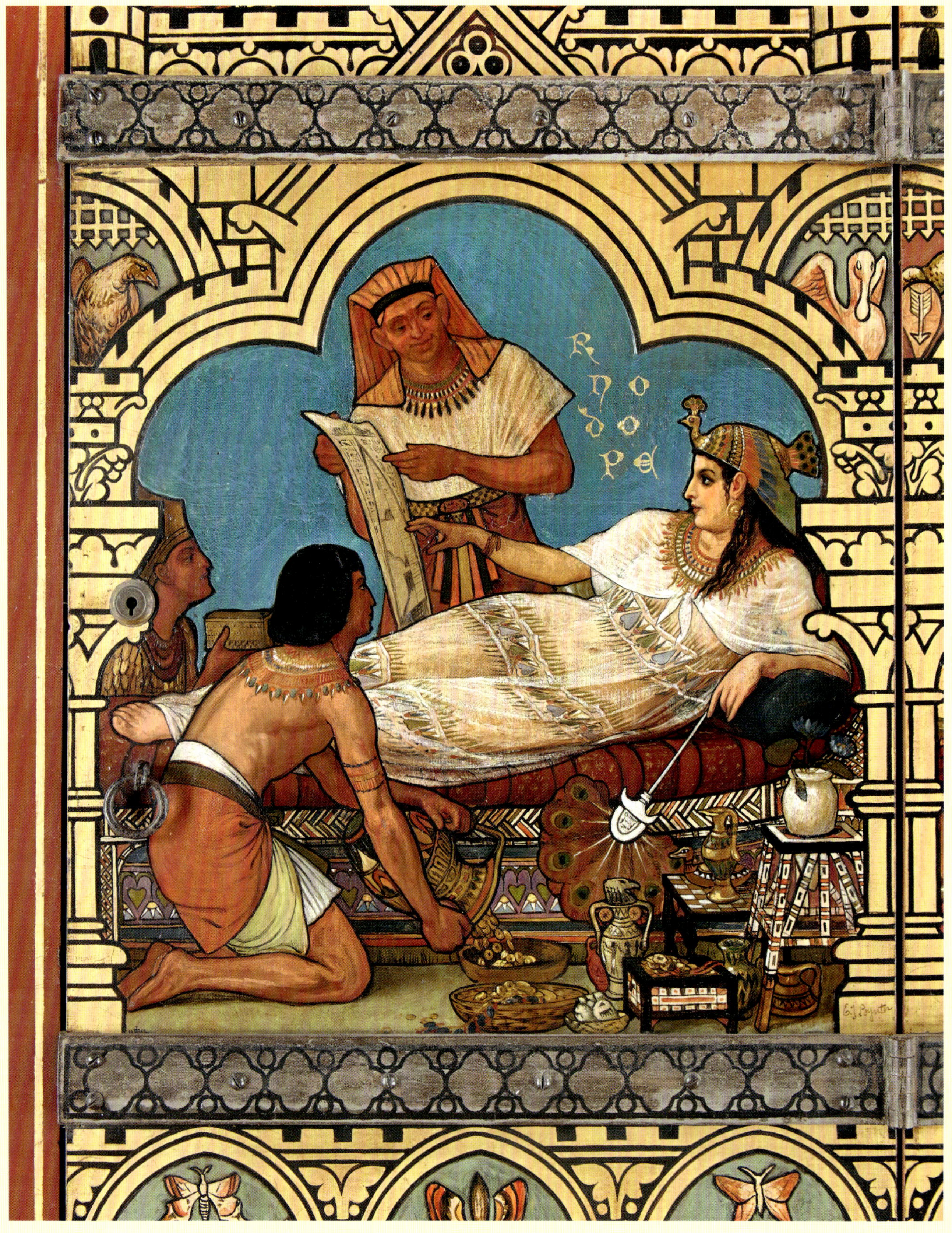

Fig. 107 Edward John Poynter (1836–1919), *Rhodopis*, detail from The Great Bookcase. Ashmolean Museum, WA1933.26

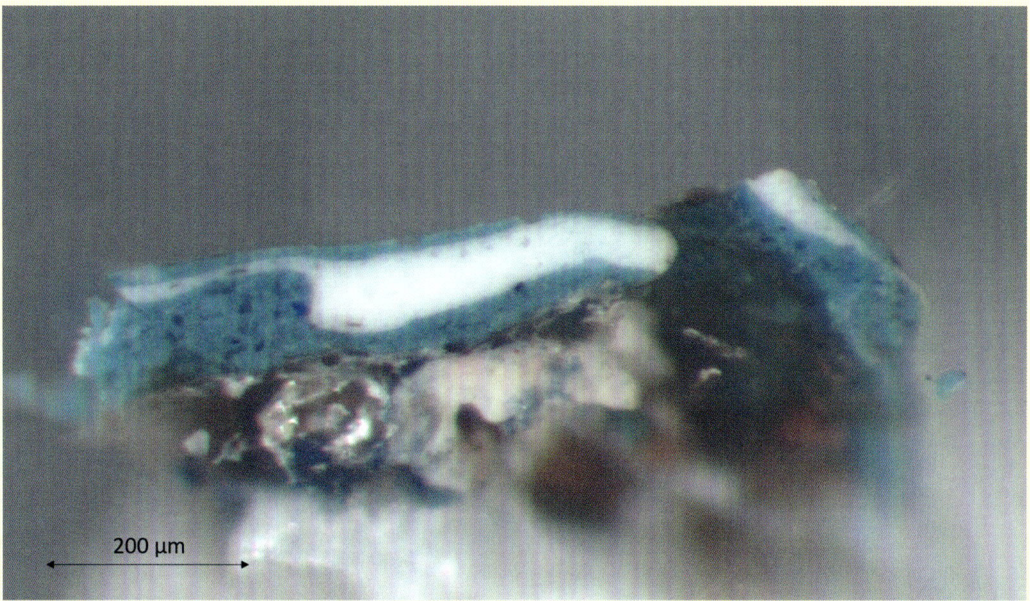

Fig. 108 Blue paint flake from the background of Edward Poynter's *Dante's Vision* panel, with few tiny bright blue particles of ultramarine pigment

in industrial formulations to adulterate colours marketed as 'ultramarine blue',[89] it is likely that Burges intentionally attempted to use a medieval-inspired pigment when reworking the Bookcase. Ultramarine blue and golden monochrome backgrounds would have also stylistically recalled the abstract setting of religious icons (fig. 108).

The materials of the Great Bookcase wonderfully represent a synthesis of past and present, mainly echoing the scientific and technological breakthroughs achieved during the nineteenth century, yet partially recalling medieval colours. Since its materiality and iconography are a tribute to Victorian and medieval times, the Bookcase rightfully belonged at the 1862 Exhibition, where interest in the medieval past and enthusiasm for Victorian progress were equally celebrated. Standing tall in the middle of the Medieval Court, the Bookcase transported the observer back to 'the ages of [ultramarine blue and] gold',[90] while also acknowledging the new pigments that vividly illuminated the neighbouring pavilions.[91] Although inspired by the Middle Ages, the pigments used on the Bookcase prove that it was never meant to be an exact historic replica. In fact, it appears the artists were unconcerned about using modern pigments to reproduce medieval iconography. Rather, they aimed to create something entirely new, merging interest in the past and enthusiasm for innovation – two paramount cultural aspects of nineteenth-century Europe.

Tea Ghigo

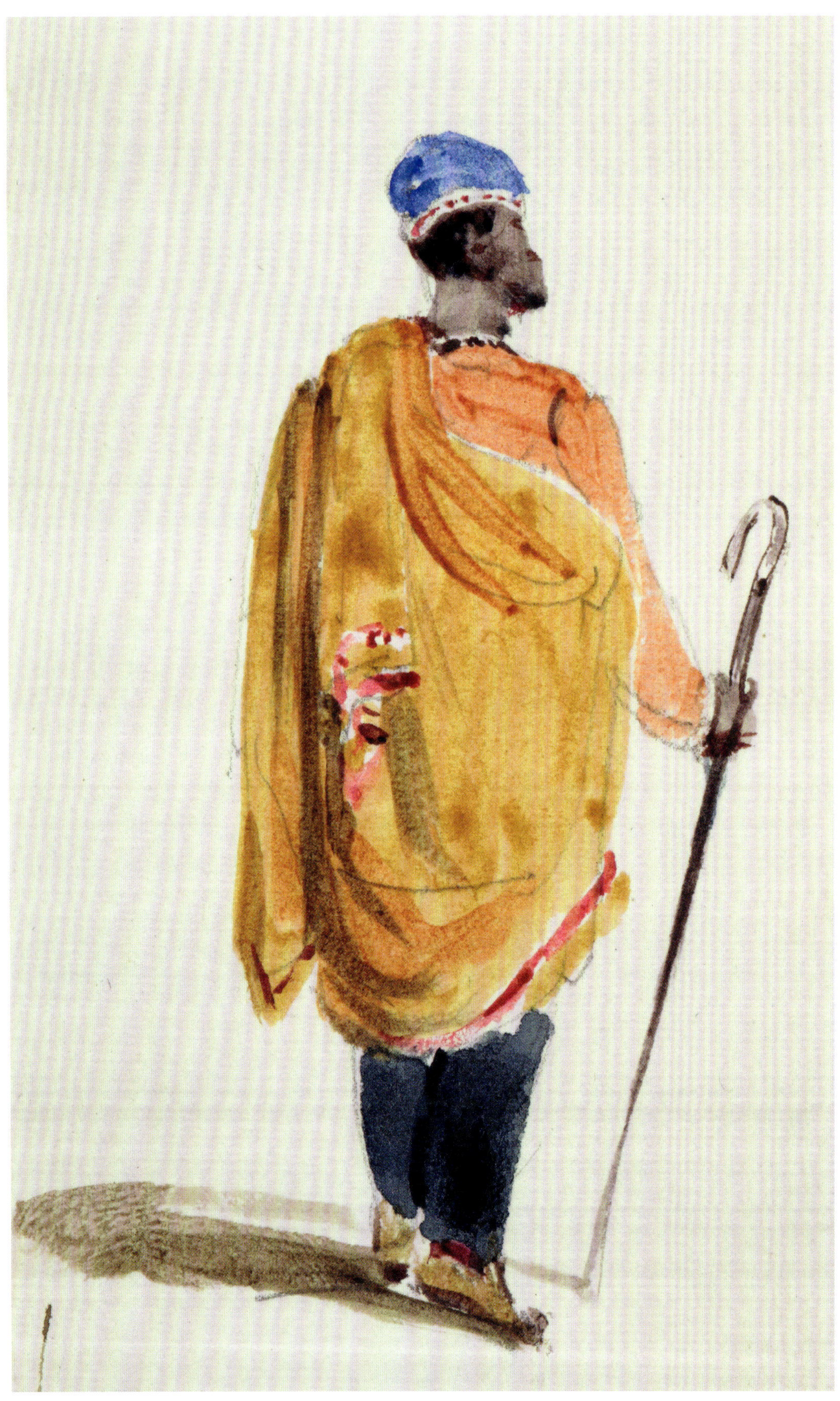

Surface Matters: Skin Colour, Race and Materiality

Madeline Hewitson

This chapter discusses historical racism which some readers may find distressing.

An account of colour in the nineteenth century cannot omit the subject of skin colour, which dominated racial discourses during the period and whose potent legacies still shape our thinking about the visual markers of social difference. The idea that someone's race can be described using the language of colour is manipulative and has a flattening effect. It reduces the infinite diversity of human beings to simplistic and, ultimately, symbolic shades: black, white, red, yellow. As the cultural historian Roger Bastide summarised: 'Colours are not important in themselves as optical phenomena, but as bearers of a message.'[92]

The way artists portray skin colour is foundational to the history of figurative art. However, in the nineteenth century, the idea that race could be defined visually in colour terms took on a new significance with developments in the emerging field of anthropology. By the middle of the century, Victorian anthropologists were moving away from previous racial categorisation methods – developed during the Enlightenment in the eighteenth century – which were known as 'types' and based on physical features such as bone structure, hair texture or even cultural signifiers such as ethnic costume (fig. 109).

In 1873, the French anatomist Charles-Philippe Robin discovered melanin as the source of skin pigmentation in the human body. As a result of this discovery, anthropologists soon devised new methodologies to separate the races by quantifying the amount of pigment found in skin. In 1879, Paul Broca published the 'Broca chart for determining eye colour and skin tone' (fig. 110). The chart measured skin tone, from lightest to darkest, using a structure which mirrored the neat tables found in publications on colour theory, or naturalist texts such as *Werner's Nomenclature of Colours*. These developments were concurrent with the invention of new synthetic pigments and dyes and, as such, realigned ideas of 'natural' colour away from vegetables and minerals and towards the human body.

Darwin's revelations in *The Descent of Man* (1871) played a significant role in new racial discourses. Although he proposed that all men came from a single, common ancestor, he also believed that differences in skin colour were caused by sexual selection and that females expressed a preference for lighter-skinned males. The 'survival of the fittest' narrative was also misappropriated by Victorian eugenicists, including his nephew Thomas Galton, to argue that racial tensions were a natural part of human evolution. These ideas quickly filtered into popular culture through exhibition displays such the 'Ethnographic Courts' at the Crystal Palace in Sydenham (fig. 111). Visitors encountered plaster

Opposite: Fig. 109 George Jones (1786–1869), *African Man in Costume*. Watercolour. Ashmolean Museum, WA1881.353.1

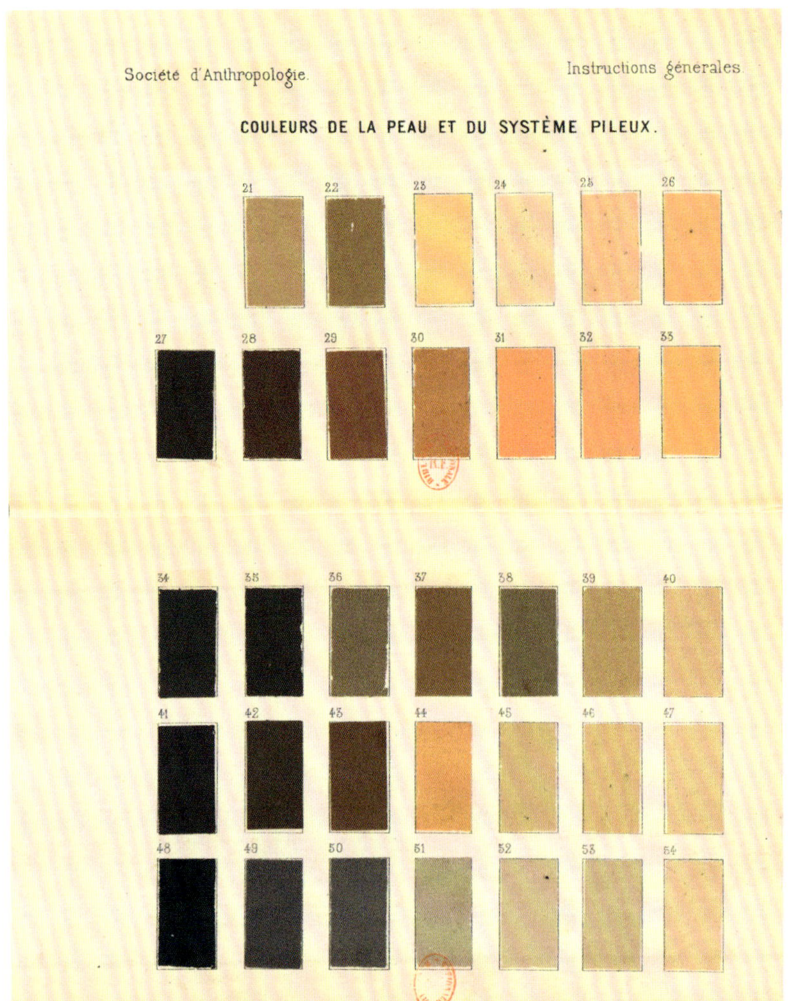

Fig. 110 Paul Broca's 'Broca chart for determining eye colour and skin tone'

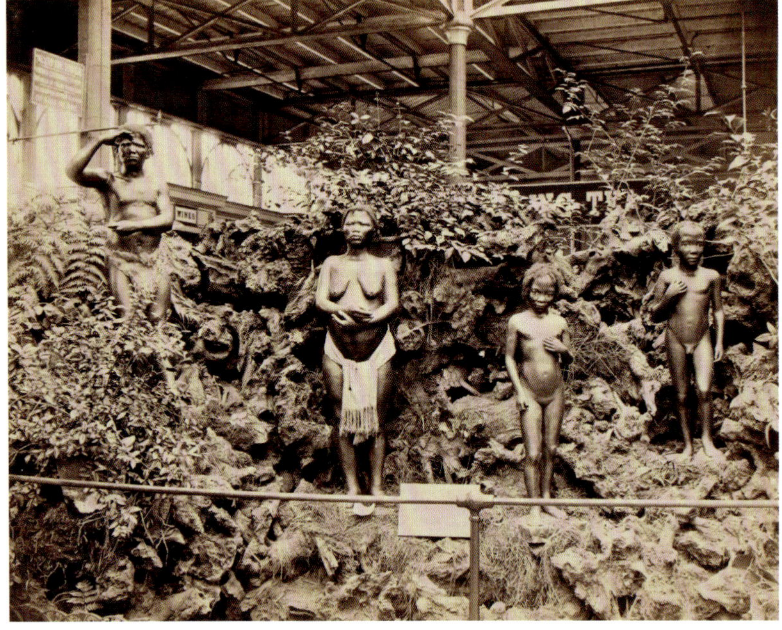

Fig. 111 Ethnographic Courts at the Crystal Palace, Sydenham. Pitt Rivers Museum, University of Oxford, prm1998.211.9

models of various non-European ethnic groups considered 'uncivilised' by the court's ethnographer-curator, Robert Gordon Latham. They would then move on to the 'Fine Arts Courts', where there were no human models but instead recreations of classical and European art and architecture were exhibited, mirroring the supposed progress of civilisations from 'savagery' to high culture.

The Crystal Palace at Sydenham also claimed to tell the complete history of empires – from the Assyrians to the Romans – a narrative which framed the Victorians as inheritors and stewards of empire. Colourism formed a cornerstone of this narrative. The relief carvings in the Assyrian Court, the first Empire profiled in the Fine Art Courts, were copied in plaster from archaeological fragments in the British Museum. They depicted Assyrians kings and soldiers, who were described as 'Semitic', 'dark haired' and 'dark in complexion' by Victorian philologists and Orientalists in the Crystal Palace guidebook. On the other hand, the 'Pompeiian Court', a recreation of the 'House of the Tragic Poet' which existed during the late Roman Empire, was originally envisioned as a 'domestic space' where English ladies could take refreshments during their visit, play-acting the domestic rituals of ancient Roman women.[93] This fantasy, enacting scenes of antiquity through domestic spaces, was also visualised in the paintings of Lawrence Alma-Tadema.[94] He also extended this beyond the domestic sphere and in another example, *Phidias Showing the Frieze of the Parthenon to His Friends* (fig. 98, p. 109), we can see a fantasy of antiquity totally inhabited by white Europeans.

There were other areas of entertainment where Victorians could enact fantasies about skin colour. In 1897, at the Devonshire fancy dress ball several ladies including the Duchess of Devonshire came dressed as 'Oriental' queens. The Duchess was Zenobia, the ancient Queen of Palmyra, while the others came dressed as Cleopatra and the Queen of Sheba (fig. 8, p. 23). All three queens brought 'Black' attendants, whose blackness served as an extension of their costumes.[95] The Duchess of Devonshire appeared at the party with a retinue that included, as one newspaper reported, 'Egyptian footmen, some negroes themselves, in their own quaint and barbaric Eastern dress.'[96] Some of these men were hired from a troupe of African actors, while others were their European servants whose skin they had darkened to appear African.

Amongst the British elite at the ball, racialised 'fancy dress' was just another facet of the evening's entertainments. However, there were clear class hierarchies where, once again, colourism was an important marker of difference. The aristocratic women, who did not darken their skin, could play exoticised light-skinned 'Oriental' – but ultimately acceptable – queens, whereas male servants were relegated to play 'negroes' by virtue of their race or having their skin darkened.

In 1898, the Cambridge anthropologist Alfred Cort Haddon examined the idea of race as colour from a different perspective. He travelled to the Torres Strait and Papua New Guinea to compare the colour perception of the islanders against Englishmen. He conducted his experiments using a 'tintometer', a machine developed by an English brewer which tested subjects' ability to distinguish between different shades of red, yellow and blue using 88 coloured slides.[97] Haddon wanted to test whether race played a role in how different people perceived colour, and his work went on to influence field perception studies until the 1960s.

In the nineteenth century skin colour was used to anchor theories of race and enshrine them in the visual realm.[98] As recent exhibitions have attested, materiality played an important role in this endeavour.[99] Consequently, sculpture, which as we have seen played a significant role in Victorian debates on colour in fine art, became a key medium that engaged with ideas on race and skin colour.

As an all-white team of curators and art historians at the Ashmolean, we are acutely aware of our personal subject positions in relation to this discussion. More importantly, perhaps, we also recognise the power of the institution we represent and the entangled history of colonialism and race at the University of Oxford. While we have sought to remove ourselves from the centre of this debate and instead listen and incorporate the voices of curators, scholars, students and local Oxfordians of colour, we also recognise that these actions only go so far to mitigate our positions of privilege in the context of the Museum.

There is a topical anecdote to illustrate this point. In August 2022 we took a group of sixth form students, who were visiting Oxford on a widening participation scheme, on a tour of the Museum. Standing in the Randolph Sculpture Gallery, a pantheon of Greek and Roman antique sculpture full of Western beauty ideals, we asked a simple question: 'Do you feel this museum is for you?' Most of the group shook their heads. One girl raised her hand and said: 'Why would I want to bring my family to a place that either never talks about Black people or only talks about Black pain?' We were taken aback – our plan that day had been to proudly tell them all about our efforts to decolonise our research and collections. In other words, projects about 'Black pain'. Her perceptive question also challenged our thinking about this exhibition – particularly the inclusion of *A Daughter of Eve: A Scene on the Shore of the Atlantic* (1862) by John Bell (fig. 112).

This sculpture is an important example of Victorian industrial art – a polychrome electrotyped bronze exhibited at the International Exhibition of 1862, a key chromatic event of the nineteenth century. On the other hand, it depicts a shackled and half-naked anonymous Guinean woman about to be trafficked across the Atlantic and used as enslaved labour in the American cotton trade. Where does this object fit into the story of the Victorian colour revolution? Is it an example of the new colour technologies and social consciousness, widely cited in Victorian newspapers and exhibition reviews as an abolitionist artwork? Or is it an exploitative image and a fetishising presentation of a bare-breasted Black woman whose eyes are cast downwards in subjugation as the (probably white) viewer gazes upon her? It is both.[100] Because of this, it is not an easy object to curate. But, as is evident from its extensive exhibition history, there is an opportunity to think about race and gender and its expression in Victorian art.

A Daughter of Eve: A Scene on the Shore of the Atlantic was first exhibited in white plaster at the Royal Academy summer exhibition in 1853.[101] Bell was

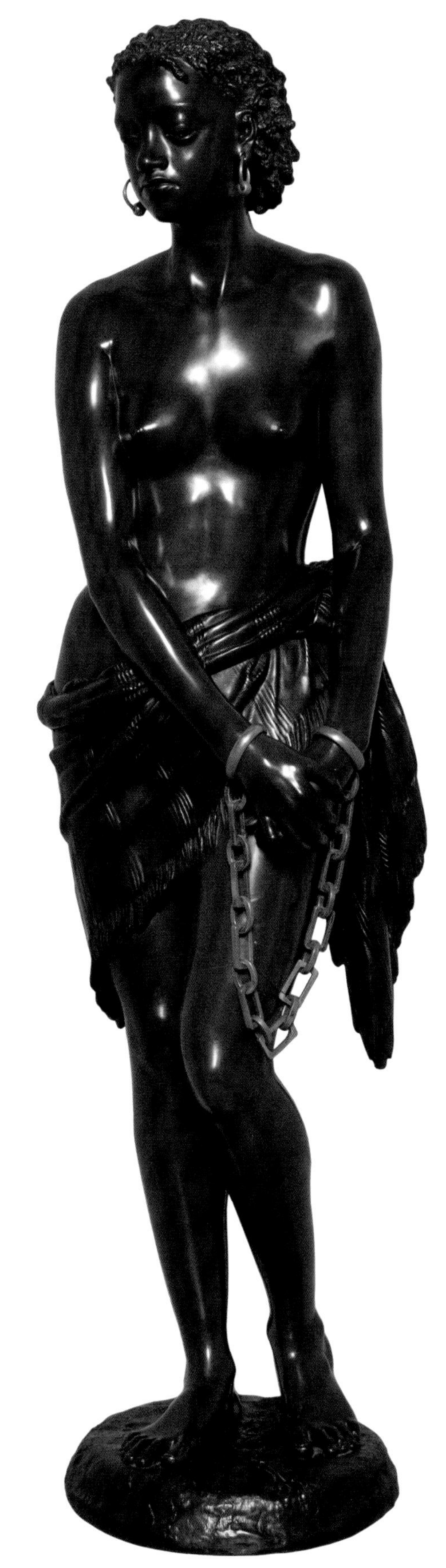

Fig. 112 John Bell (1811–1895), *A Daughter of Eve: A Scene on the Shore of the Atlantic (The American Slave)*, 1853. Bronze or bronze-patinated electrotype, silver and gold plate. Cragside, Northumberland, National Trust, NT 1228372

best-known for his neoclassical subject *The Eagle Slayer* (1837), the first sculpture ever to be produced in cast iron, which was a highlight of the Fine Arts display at the Great Exhibition of 1851. However, the sculptural show-stopper of the Great Exhibition had been Hiram Powers's *The Greek Slave*, a full-size marble statue which depicted a Caucasian girl captured by Ottomans during the Greek War of Independence.[102] This sculpture was an instant icon and was quickly circulated through monochrome photographs and newspaper illustrations.

A Daughter of Eve was a direct response to *The Greek Slave*. It tackled the subject of contemporary African slavery in America head on, in contrast to Powers's demurring approach to the subject, which highlighted white, Christian slavery as the great ill of modern society – rather than the vastly larger and more impactful transatlantic slave trade. Bell's title was a direct reference to the language of the abolitionist movement, which was closely associated with Christianity and members of the Church of England. Its subtitle – 'A Scene on the Shore of the Atlantic' – staked it as a political object that spoke directly to the present moment. The title 'The American Slave' was not used until Minton created a white Parian version in 1862, a marketing ploy which coincided with the start of the Civil War. Various other titles used, including *The Negress Slave* and *The Slave Girl*, have kept the woman and model at the centre of this object anonymous and inextricably connected to her bondage. Similar sculptures depicting naturalistic yet anonymous African women in bondage were also created at the time, perhaps most famously Jean-Baptiste Carpeaux's *Why Born Enslaved!* (1868), but also ethnographic works by the French sculptor Charles Cordier.[103] The fact that there was a burgeoning 'genre' for this subject calls attention to the uncomfortable tension between abolitionist messages and the erotic obsession with bound, Black female bodies.

Although it was originally exhibited in white plaster, Bell had always intended to execute the sculpture in bronze. This specific instruction highlights the importance of materiality and colour in putting across Bell's message. As Michael Hatt persuasively writes: 'In the racialised representational schemas of the nineteenth century (and beyond), white skin is transparent, and black skin is opaque. A white person represented in bronze retains his or her white identity, while the material becomes literalised when the black body is represented, as if that blackness provides the definitive meaning of the person. This curious asymmetry whereby skin colour becomes the defining feature of, say, an African person, but not of a white American, is rooted in an implicit idea that whiteness can be metaphysical, while blackness is irredeemably physical.'[104]

Two electrotyped versions were eventually created by the Birmingham firm Elkington & Co. for the International Exhibition of 1862. Electrotyping was a technical process whereby bronze patina was applied to a copper object, making a much cheaper and lighter object. Once again, however, Bell was overshadowed at the exhibition. Gibson's *Tinted Venus* was the subject of equal amounts of praise and derision as it galvanised debates on polychromy. *A Daughter of Eve* sits chronologically and metaphorically between *The Greek Slave* and *Tinted Venus*, and embodies the different ways colour was used as a racialised, gendered and sexual construct, as Charlotte Ribeyrol discussed earlier in this catalogue. However, colour was also a central concern of *A Daughter of Eve*: it reflected debates on the subject of skin colour in a more direct and political way than the *Tinted Venus*, which, ultimately, was a white, idealised and classical subject. Bell wrote a statement to accompany his work: ' The poor slave girl, represented in bronze, does not struggle with her fate; but that very resignation should plead the more against the injustice and degradation of that position to which the colour of her skin condemns her.' Bell acknowledges the arbitrary category of skin colour which has condemned his figure to such an awful fate. However, in his representation he plays up her passivity, showing her bare-breasted, revealing the colour of her skin, in chains and looking towards the ground, a trope which revictimises her as somehow complicit in her enslavement.

This contradiction persisted beyond the exhibition, when the sculpture was acquired by the industrialist and arms manufacturer Thomas Armstrong for his home at Cragside in Northumberland. The extent of Armstrong's own involvement with the transatlantic slave trade and the American Civil War are still contested by historians today, but it is generally accepted that his purchase of the sculpture was a statement of his support for the abolitionist cause. Today, *A Daughter of Eve* is part of the collections of the National Trust, an institution undergoing its own reckoning with the legacies of colonialism and racial injustice. The thinking behind *A Daughter of Eve* remains complicated and contested; now, once again, it serves as an exhibition object to spark debate. We hope that, this time, there are some differences in the context in which it is displayed. More diverse voices actively guided the thinking about why this object was included in an exhibition on colour, and how and where to do so. Perhaps most importantly, those voices showed us that this exhibition is not just for White edification and 'Black pain', but to create a space to share everyone's stories.

The histories of colour are central to understanding nineteenth-century discourses around race and the symbolic power of 'skin colour' for white and non-white peoples. Colour was never a static category: in the nineteenth century the establishment – scientists, government officials, colonial administrators, artists – used colour as a powerful ideological tool to define difference. This was a 'colour revolution' of a different sort, but one no less transformative and consequential, even into the present day.

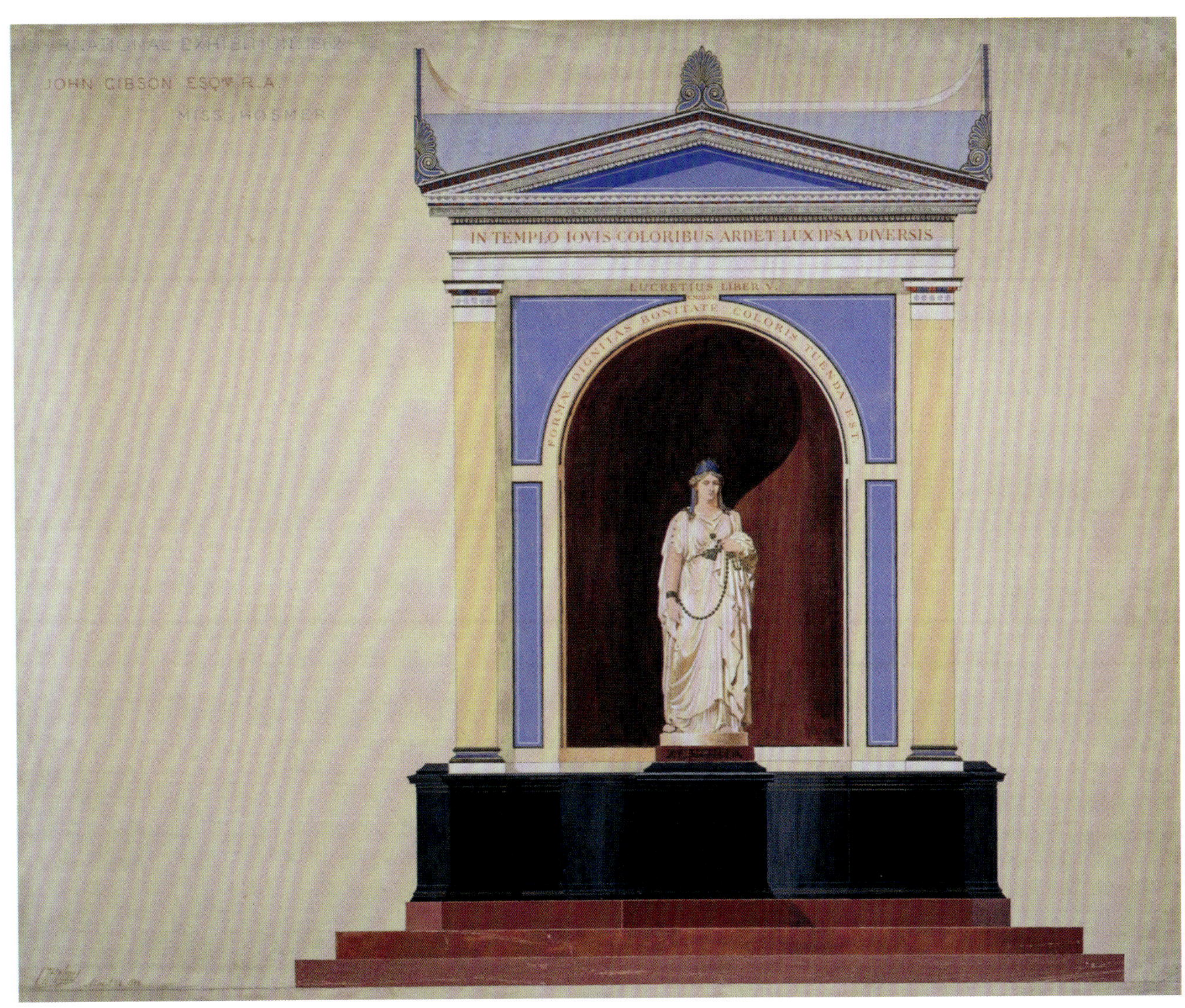

Fig. 113 Owen Jones (1809–1874), *Design for the Greek temple erected in the Great Exhibition, 1862, to house various statues*, 1862. Watercolour. Victoria and Albert Museum, E.1712-1912

'Wedding archaeology with art': the Rediscovery of Ancient Polychromy

Charlotte Ribeyrol

When John Gibson's *Tinted Venus* was displayed at the 1862 International Exhibition (fig. 95, p. 106), it was presented in a polychrome temple specially designed by Owen Jones. The statue was set against a deep porphyry-coloured background, surrounded by ochre columns and surmounted by a blue pediment to match the tints used by the sculptor to highlight the hair, breast, lips and drapery of his sculpture (fig. 113).

In 1862, Jones's reputation as one of the most active chromophiles of his time was already firmly established. A key figure in the design reform movement and celebrated author of *The Grammar of Ornament* (1856), the architect had repeatedly given colour pride of place in his designs and publications. The breakthrough in his public career as a colourist came with his decoration of the 1851 Crystal Palace. In an enthusiastic article entitled 'The Harmony of Colours as Exemplified in the Exhibition', Mary Philadelphia Merrifield, an expert who had made a name for herself by translating medieval treatises on colour, described Jones's chromatic scheme in glowing terms. It reflected, she wrote, the new laws of colour contrast devised in 1839 by the director of the Gobelins Dye Works, French chemist Michel Eugène Chevreul.[105] Although John Gregory Crace also referred to Chevreul's work when defending the colours used to decorate the 1862 exhibition building, his own arrangement was unfavourably compared to that of Jones:

> Compare the colouring of the 1851 building, or the Crystal Palace at Sydenham, with this, and we see that ... [the] blues and yellows are not of that violent kind that Mr. Crace's artist, as he calls him, has been allowed to throw in 'quite promiscuously' as to tint.[106]

Contrary to Crace's, Jones's chromatic arrangements were directly inspired by his painstaking studies of the polychromy of the past, which the architect spent his life trying to revive as a means to help contemporary artists find their own style.

Jones's first pivotal chromatic revelation was triggered by his study of the Alhambra in 1832 with the architect Jules Goury, former assistant to the German chromophile Gottfried Semper. When *Plans, Elevations, Sections and Details of the Alhambra* were published in 12 parts over a period of almost ten years, from 1836 to 1845, they were lavishly illustrated with dazzling chromolithographs, a new technique which Jones helped to pioneer. To highlight the key role the Alhambra played in Jones's career, Henry Wyndham Phillips painted the architect in a typically Victorian black suit, but standing in a room

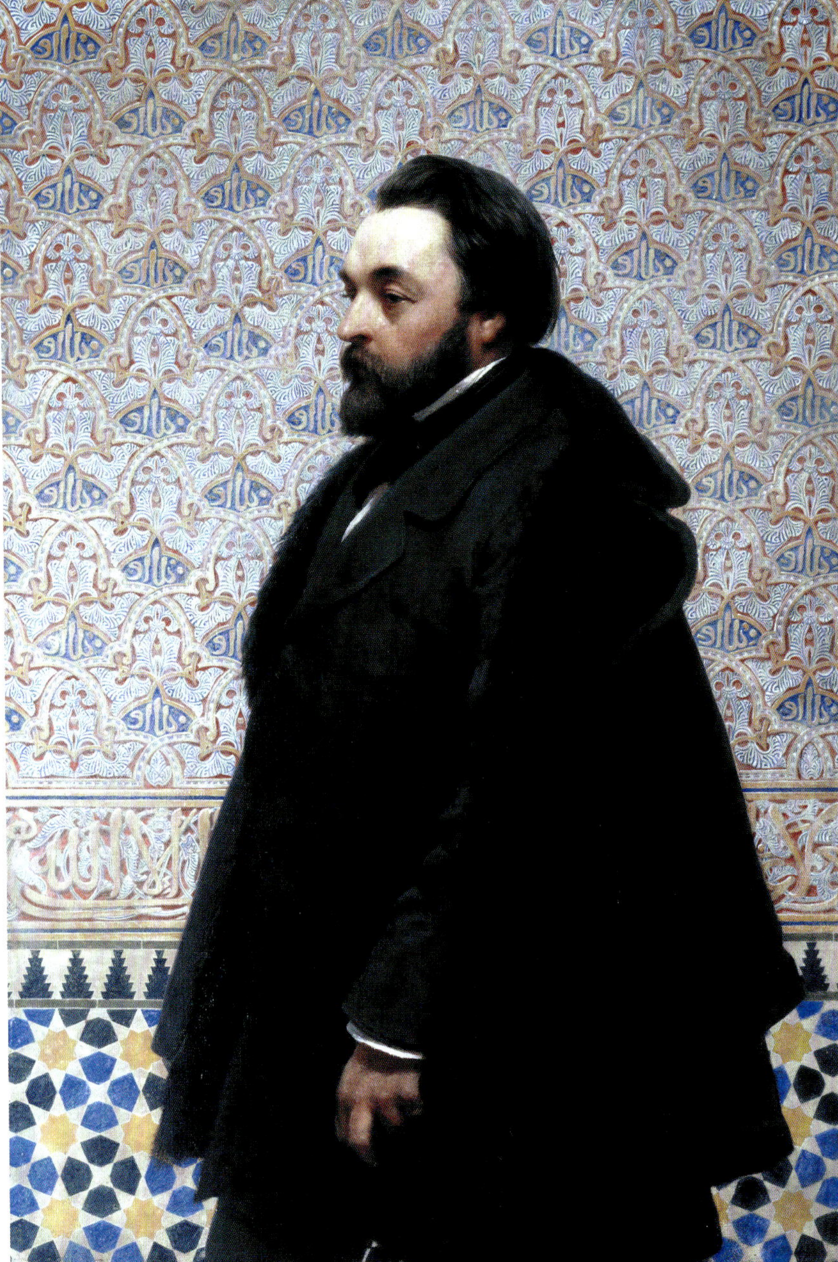

Fig. 114 Owen Jones (1809–1874) by Henry Wyndham Phillips (1820–1878), 1856. Oil on canvas. RIBA Collections, PCF56

decorated in Moorish style, most probably inspired by Jones's own polychrome reconstitutions for the Alhambra Court at Sydenham (fig. 114). Two years earlier the Crystal Palace had been moved to Sydenham under the supervision of Jones himself and Matthew Digby Wyatt, who imagined a series of 'Fine Arts Courts', or period rooms, to introduce visitors to the history of art and design. Jones was responsible for designing the Alhambra Court as well as the Egyptian and Greek Courts, all of which were full of colour. Although these reconstitutions were based on archaeological evidence, their generalised polychromy was much criticised at the time, in particular by author and critic Lady Elizabeth Eastlake:

> Under the high-sounding, but now ever ridiculous, name of Polychromy they have introduced an element which may be familiar to the sailor in his figure-head, to the mechanic in his tea-garden, and to the child of five years old in the picture-book he has polychromed for himself, but which is simply a puzzle to the ignorant and a torture to the enlightened. We shall be told perhaps that no such view to the accommodation of all tastes presided over the application of the paint-pot; but this would invalidate their only excuse; for if the investing Egypt and Nineveh in the gaudiest hues of Manchester cottons, if the colouring Anglo-Saxon effigies with a coarseness of illusion Madame Tussaud would disdain, and if the transformation of the glorious Panathenaic Procession into a bad Pilgrimage to Canterbury – derogatory alike to Stothard and Phidias – were not intended to please the ignorant, for whom could it have been designed?[107]

Casting herself as a refined *connoisseur,* Lady Eastlake compared the colours of the past – whether Greek, Egyptian, Assyrian or Greek – with the 'gaudiest hues' of her own industrial age, turning colour into a 'class-based issue' which apparently appealed only to the 'ignorant' and supposedly primitive 'sailor[s]' and 'mechanic[s]'.[108] The colours of the Greek Court, featuring Jones's reconstitution of the Parthenon frieze in its original polychromy, were deemed the most shocking of all. If the Gothic hues of 'Anglo-Saxon effigies' dangerously smacked of Catholicism, the colouring of antique statues and temples was seen as barbaric, directly challenging the prevailing idea that the ancient Hellenes had been the glorious ancestors of the modern West.[109] The backlash was so fierce that Jones felt the need to publish an *Apology for the Colouring of the Greek Court in the Crystal Palace* in 1855, with contributions from Semper (who had just spent four years in London working on *The Four Elements of Architecture*), the classical and Shakespearean scholar W. Watkiss Lloyd and the philosopher G.H. Lewes. While most of the *Apology* focused on 'material evidence' of ancient polychromy, Watkiss Lloyd and Lewes discussed classical texts referencing ancient colouring practices, in particular a much-quoted passage from Pliny's *Natural History* in which the author mentions the painter Nicias's mysterious *circumlitio* ('finishing') in his collaboration with the sculptor Praxiteles:

> The meaning of this passage hangs on the word *circumlitio*. Winckelmann follows the mass of commentators in understanding this as referring to some mode of polishing the statues; but Quatremère de Quincey, in his magnificent work 'Le Jupiter Olympien', satisfactorily shows this to be untenable, not only because no sculptor could think of preferring such of his statues as had been better polished, but also because Nicias being a painter, not a sculptor, his services must have been those of a painter … Even Winckelmann … after noting how the ancients were accustomed to dress their statues, adds, 'This gave rise to the painting of those parts of the marble statues which represented the clothes, as may be seen in the Diana found at Herculanæum in 1760. The hair is blonde; the draperies white,

with a triple border, one of gold, the other of purple, with festoons of flowers, the third plain purple.[110]

It is rather surprising to find the name of J.J. Winckelmann mentioned in this discussion, given that the eighteenth-century German art historian had encouraged the Neoclassical taste for immaculate statues with the following claim: 'Since white is the colour that reflects the most rays of light, and thus is most easily perceived, a beautiful body will be all the more beautiful the whiter it is.'[111] And yet Lewes describes Winckelmann as a pioneering commentator on ancient colour and a key witness to the first excavations at Pompeii and Herculanæum, two former Greek colonies. There the German historian had befriended the English diplomat and collector Sir William Hamilton, whose fascination with Greek and Etruscan vases he embraced as an illustration of the union of sculpture and painting. Some of these red figure vases offered a glimpse of antique colour. In his *History of the Art of Antiquity* (1764), Winckelmann notably singled out Hamilton's large hydria by the so-called 'Meidias' Athenian red-figure vase painter (fifth century BCE), which was the diplomat's favourite (fig. 115).[112] Josiah Wedgwood also admired Hamilton's collection, which largely inspired his own iconic blue and white Jasperware. However, as Philippe Jockey notes, the cameo style of most of these ceramics paradoxically contributed to reinforcing the myth of the whiteness of ancient sculpture.[113] One of Wedgwood's best-known designs was his copy of the Portland Vase in the British Museum (fig. 116). It remained an extremely popular piece throughout the Victorian age – numerous copies and variations were still being produced in the 1850s and 1860s. But more colourful versions had by then become available, reflecting the tastes of the day and a soaring interest in ancient polychromy.

A reference to Winckelmann's discussion of antique colour may also be found in John Gibson's own defence of his *Tinted Venus* (fig. 95, p. 106).[114] The controversial cleaning of the Parthenon Marbles in 1858 and the display of Gibson's statue at the 1862 Exhibition certainly gave new impetus to Victorian debates about Pliny's *circumlitio* and the morality of art, whether antique or modern. The keeper of the British Museum Richard Westmacott Jr thus described polychromy as a 'meretricious accessory' and a 'means of corruption'.[115] Derived from the Latin *meretrix*, signifying 'harlot, prostitute', the adjective 'meretricious' implicitly aligned polychromy with a form of dangerously alluring make-up. The term was also used by a critic from the *Athenaeum* journal to describe Gibson's Venus, although the statue was only 'tinted', a term certainly used by the sculptor to make the 'delicate' colouring of his creation more acceptable.[116] But for *The Art Journal*'s editorial, Gibson had crossed the line between high and low art:

> We consider the adjunct of colour ... as a departure from the original high purpose of sculpture, which never aimed at more than an abstract type of the subject represented in form and expression; its end being to idealise rather than to realise.[117]

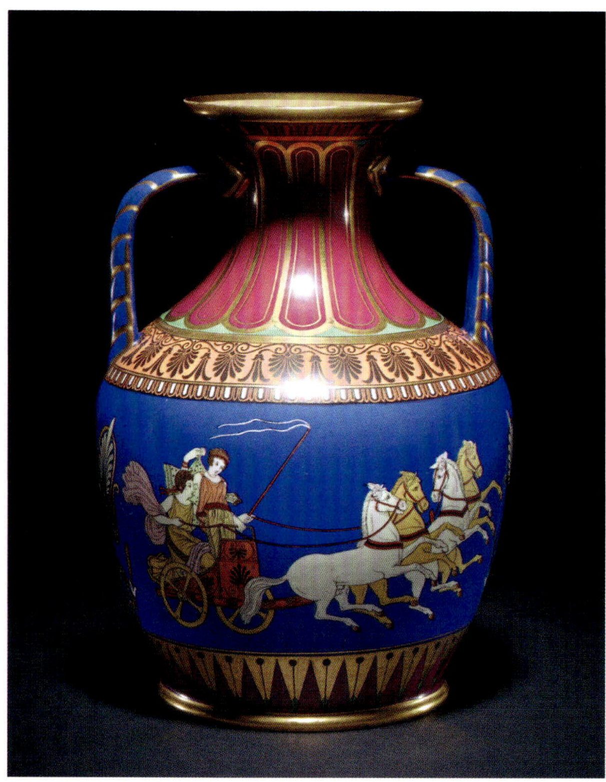

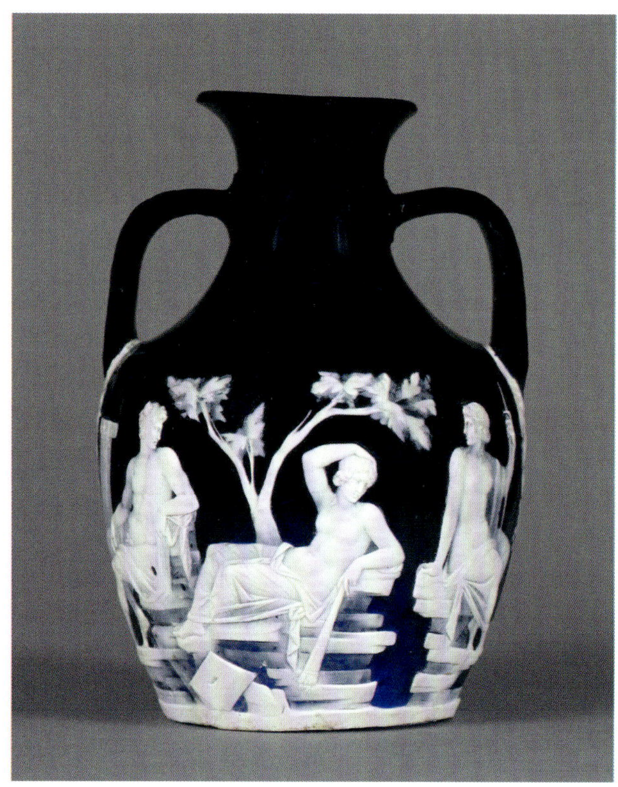

Above left: Fig. 115 Vase from the Hill Pottery, Stoke-on-Trent, in the form of the Portland vase, painted with a scene from the Meidias Hydria in several colours, c.1860–70. Bone china. British Museum, 2021,8005.1. Given in memory of Ian Jenkins OBE (1953–2020), British Museum curator, by his colleagues: Andrew Burnett, Frances Carey, Jill Cook, Lesley Fitton, Antony Griffiths, Judy Rudoe and Kim Sloan

Above right: Fig. 116 The Portland Vase, 1st century CE. Amphora in translucent dark cobalt blue and opaque white cameo glass. The Trustees of the British Museum, 1945,0927.1

After all, Gibson himself had succumbed to the charm of his *Venus*, as reported by Lady Eastlake in her 1870 book *Life of John Gibson, R.A.*:

> When all my labour was complete I often sat down quietly and alone before my work, meditating upon it and consulting my own simple feelings. I endeavoured to keep myself free from self-delusion as to the effect of the colouring. I said to myself 'Here is a little nearer approach to life – it is therefore more impressive – yes – yes indeed she seems an ethereal being with her blue eyes fixed upon me!' At moments I forgot that I was gazing at my own production; there I sat before her, long and often. How was I ever to part with her![118]

Here the shift to the present tense blurs the boundary between reality and art, as in the myth of Pygmalion, which Lady Eastlake explicitly refers to in one of the chapter headings of her biography.[119] But for the sculptor, the parallel went beyond the simply literary; he refused to part with his beloved creation for more than four years, to the great dismay of his patron Mrs. Preston:

> I retained the Venus in my studio for four years after she was completed – a proceeding on my part which put Mrs. Preston's patience to a severe trial. I received several angry letters from that amiable lady. At last she asked me, point blank, whether I did not think I was using her very ill. I immediately

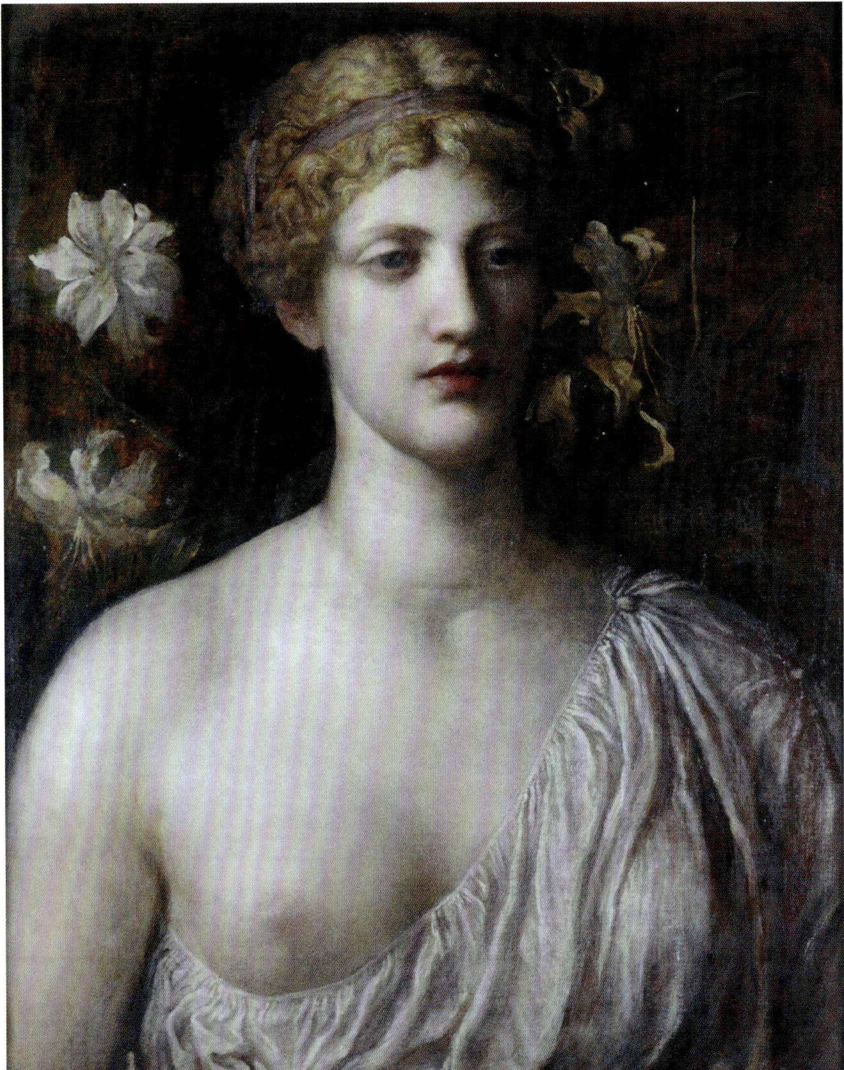

Fig. 117 George Frederic Watts (1817–1904), *The Wife of Pygmalion, A Translation from the Greek*, 1868. Oil on canvas. The Faringdon Collection Trust, Buscot Park

> confessed my sin and replied, 'There is no doubt that I am using you abominably ill – yes – but the truth is I cannot screw up my courage to send away my Goddess. It is almost as difficult for me to part with her as it would be for Mr. Preston to part with you.'[120]

By confessing his 'sin' of idolatry, Gibson partly confirmed Westmacott's accusations as to the 'corruption' of the 'Polychromists': 'My eyes have now become so depraved that I cannot bear to see a statue without colouring.'[121]

The Pygmalion myth was a Victorian favourite which artists and poets alike actively revisited, notably Edward Burne-Jones and William Morris. In the context of the rediscovery of the colouring of ancient statues, the Ovidian story was also increasingly read as a foundation myth of sculptural polychromy – colour being the key sign that the sculpture has come to life and fulfilled the mimetic dream of its creator. This is exemplified by G.F. Watts's *Wife of Pygmalion*, a portrayal of Pygmalion's statue turned into a fleshly nude (fig. 117).

Watts's painting was subtitled 'A translation from the Greek', a misleading title as no surviving Hellenic text relates the story of the Cyprian sculptor. The translation is, in fact, a modern pictorial translation of an antique sculptural model – the so-called 'Oxford bust' supposedly representing the poetess Sappho (fig. 118). The bust, of which Watts had acquired a cast, was part of the Arundel Marbles collection, which the painter had discovered when visiting the Ashmolean Museum with Sir Charles Newton. Watts associated this Roman sculpture with the perfection of the art of the Greek sculptor Phidias (fifth century BCE). Drawing on this model, he painted *The Wife of Pygmalion* for the same Royal Academy exhibition at which his own marble bust, entitled *Clytie*, was presented. Watts never saw any contradiction in associating

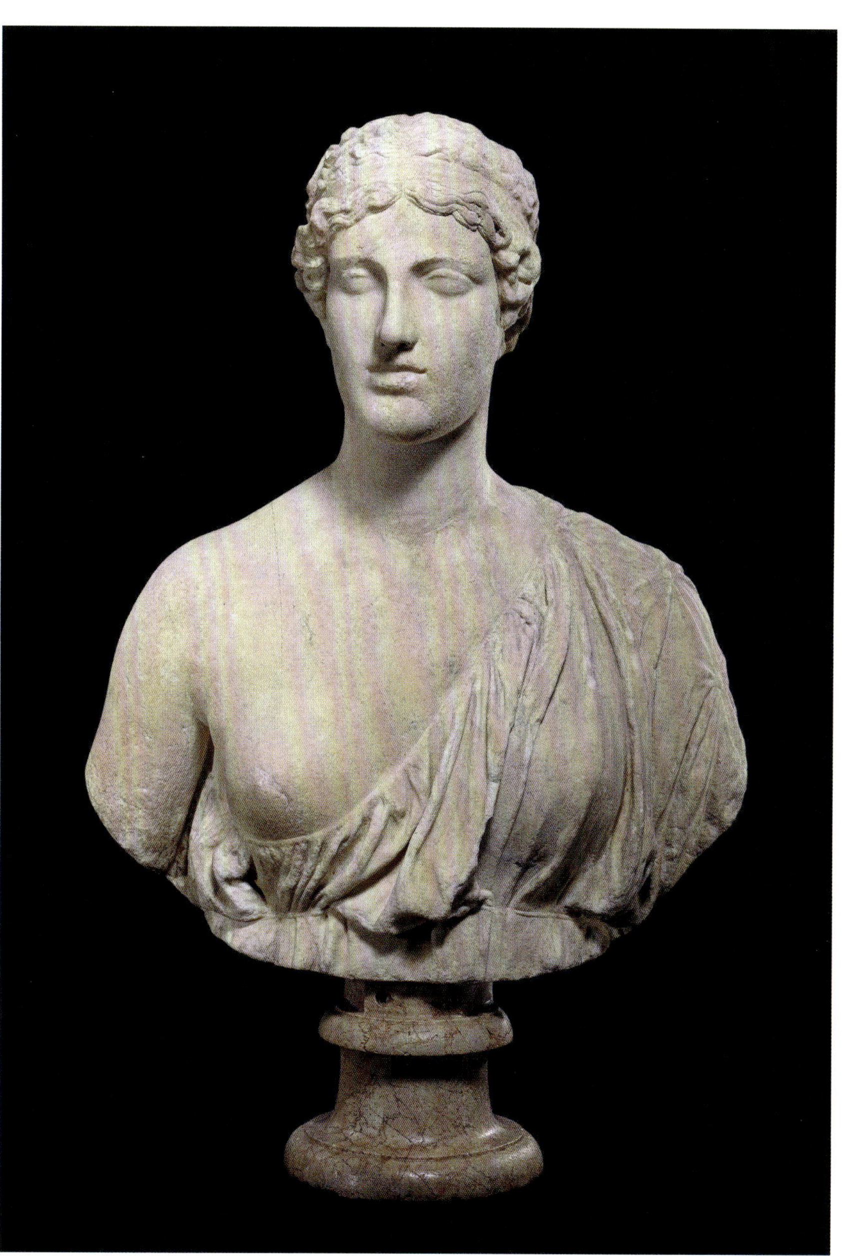

Fig. 118 Female bust of Sappho, known as the 'Oxford Bust', 1st–3rd century CE. Marble. Ashmolean Museum, Oxford, ANMichaelis.59

painting and sculpture, since he believed Phidias to be 'eminently pictorial'.[122] Contrary to most of his contemporaries, Watts surprisingly praised the Greek sculptor as a colourist rather than as a designer, finding affinities for Phidias's style in the glowing works of the Venetian painters Giorgione and Titian.[123] A half-length portrait, *The Wife of Pygmalion* is also reminiscent of the sensual colours of Dante Gabriel Rossetti's Venetian beauties such as *Bocca Baciata* (1859) or *Venus Verticordia* (1864–1868).

According to Ian Jenkins, Watts had been drawn into 'the polychromy issue' when he joined Newton's excavation of the Halicarnassus Mausoleum in 1856.[124] With the assistance of Robert P. Pullan, Newton then reproduced some of the traces of colour found on the reliefs (fig. 119). Watts also believed that Phidias had his own sculptures coloured, but that 'his method of suggesting difference of texture and colour (by means of his chisel alone) would certainly go far to render colour unnecessary'.[125] His own 'translation from the Greek' reveals that Watts was willing to move away from a purely philological approach to the classical canon, towards a more material understanding of Hellenic artistic culture. Brushing aside the ideal of Hellenic 'sweetness and light' which Matthew Arnold had championed that same year in his essay *Culture and Anarchy*, Watts embraced the sensuality of colour that others then believed to be incompatible with such a pristine Greek ideal. It therefore comes as no surprise that the painting attracted the attention of the subversive poet Algernon Charles Swinburne:

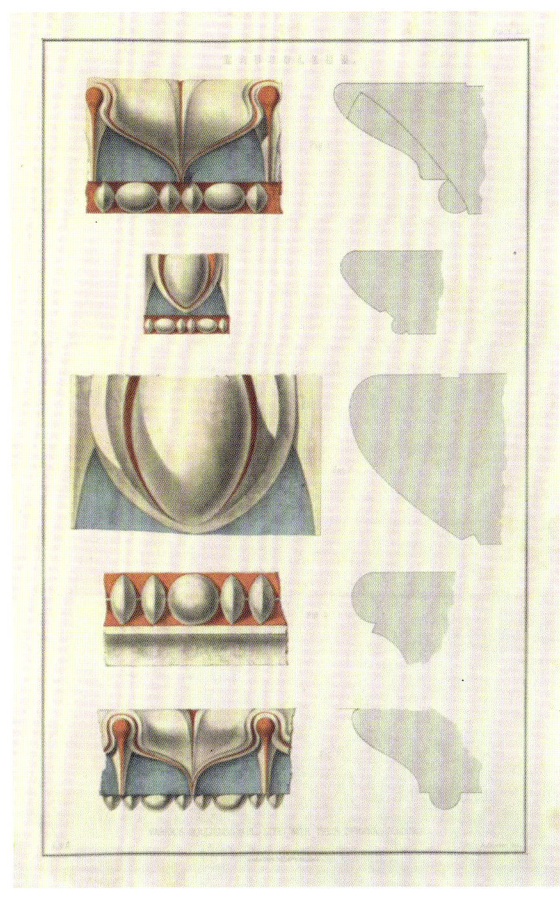

Fig. 119 R.P. Pullan, 'Various mouldings (full size) with their original colours', from C.T. Newton, *A History of Discoveries at Halicarnassus, Cnidus & Branchidae*, 1862. Chromolithograph. Bodleian Library, University of Oxford, (OC) 203 h.107

> The soft severity of perfect beauty might serve alike for woman or statue, flesh or marble; but the eyes have opened already upon love, with a tender and grave wonder; her curving ripples of hair seem just warm from the touch and breath of the goddess, moulded and quickened by hands diviner than her sculptor's. So it seems a Greek painter must have painted women, when Greece had mortal pictures fit to match her imperishable statues ... In this 'translation' of a Greek statue into an English picture, no less than in the bust of Clytie, we see how in the hands of a great artist painting and sculpture may become as sister arts indeed, yet without invasion or confusion; how, without any forced alliance of form and colour, a picture may share the gracious grandeur of a statue, a statue may catch something of the subtle bloom proper to a picture.[126]

Lawrence Alma-Tadema similarly explored the artistic potential of allying sculpture and painting in his own colourful reconstitution of the Parthenon frieze. Painted the same year as Watts's *Wife of Pygmalion*, *Phidias Showing the Parthenon Frieze to his Friends* is yet another controversial 'translation from the Greek' which restored the frieze to its formerly bold polychromy and original

Athenian location from which it had been 'removed' by Lord Elgin – a much debated issue from 1816 to this day.[127] The painting was possibly inspired by Jones's own reconstitution at Sydenham, which Alma-Tadema may have seen during his first visit to London in 1862. There, Jones's frieze was shown at eye level. Similarly, the viewing depicted by Alma-Tadema takes place on a scaffolding from which Phidias's guests could better admire the painted reliefs. The sculptor is given pride of place in front of his *oeuvre*. In the foreground, in an intimate gesture, a young man rests his hand on the shoulder of his male friend. This may be an allusion to so-called 'Greek' love – a topic as repressed as colour at the time. Writers like Walter Pater, J.A. Symonds and later Oscar Wilde also drew on ancient polychromy to evoke homoerotic desire, to the point that the Greek word *poikilia* (meaning 'varied' or 'multi-coloured') soon became a 'homosexual code' in Hellenist circles: it suggested the possibility of different types of love.[128]

Growing fascination with the Pygmalion myth in the context of the controversial rediscovery of antique polychromy may explain why William Burges and Simeon Solomon selected this story to illustrate the Pagan origins of sculpture on the Great Bookcase, a key piece of painted furniture presented at the Medieval Court of the 1862 Exhibition (see pp. 116–21). Conflating references to the *Venus of Milo* with Botticelli's *Birth of Venus* and her flying zephyrs, Solomon depicts the goddess of love applying rouge to the cheeks of Pygmalion's statue, whose drapery is delicately tinted like that of Gibson's *Venus*, which Burges had most probably seen in Rome before it was moved to London. Throughout the eight panels of the Bookcase, Burges indeed explored ancient polychromy in all its forms, whether Egyptian, Greek or Pompeiian. Frederick Smallfield's panel, for instance, references frescoes from Pompeii as well as specific artefacts from the Museo Borbonico in Naples.

Equally colourful, Edward Poynter's panel on the Pagan origins of architecture – allegorically symbolised by the figure of the courtesan Rhodopis, who supposedly commissioned the first pyramid – is an archaeologically accurate (and yet fictional and anachronistic) assemblage of domestic objects on display at the British Museum (fig. 107, p. 120). The panel is a tribute to the dazzling colours of the Egyptian past from Rhodopis's rainbow-like headdress to the blue lotus motifs that Poynter probably copied from Jones's *Grammar of Ornament* (fig. 18, p. 29). According to Stephanie Moser, the Rhodopis panel might well have been Poynter's first incursion into Egyptian art, a topic he also explored in his monumental *Israel in Egypt* (fig. 121). This grand biblical painting launched his career as an archaeological painter.[129] Drawing on Exodus 1:7-11, it depicts enslaved Israelites pulling a gigantic sculpture of a lion. The narrative elements are, however, secondary to the goal of archaeological accuracy. Like Alma-Tadema, Poynter played a key role in 'shifting the popular image of Egypt from the Bible to the excitement of archaeological discovery'.[130] The level of detail in the decorative scheme attests to Poynter's attempt to recreate the grandeur of ancient Egypt, despite the anachronistic arrangement of monuments (the temples of Thebes and Philae, the Obelisk from Heliopolis, the Great Pyramid at Giza). This bears comparison with the

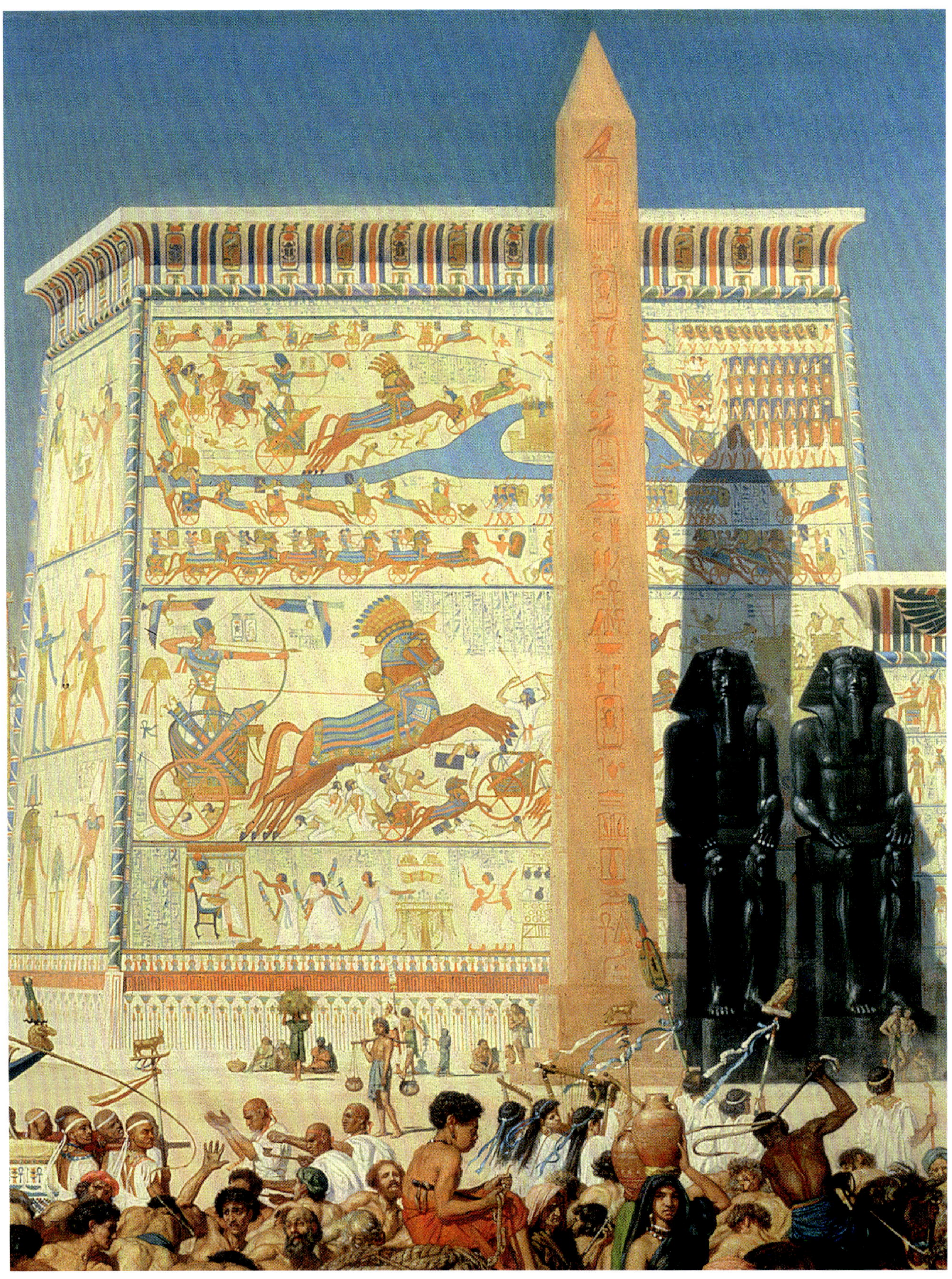

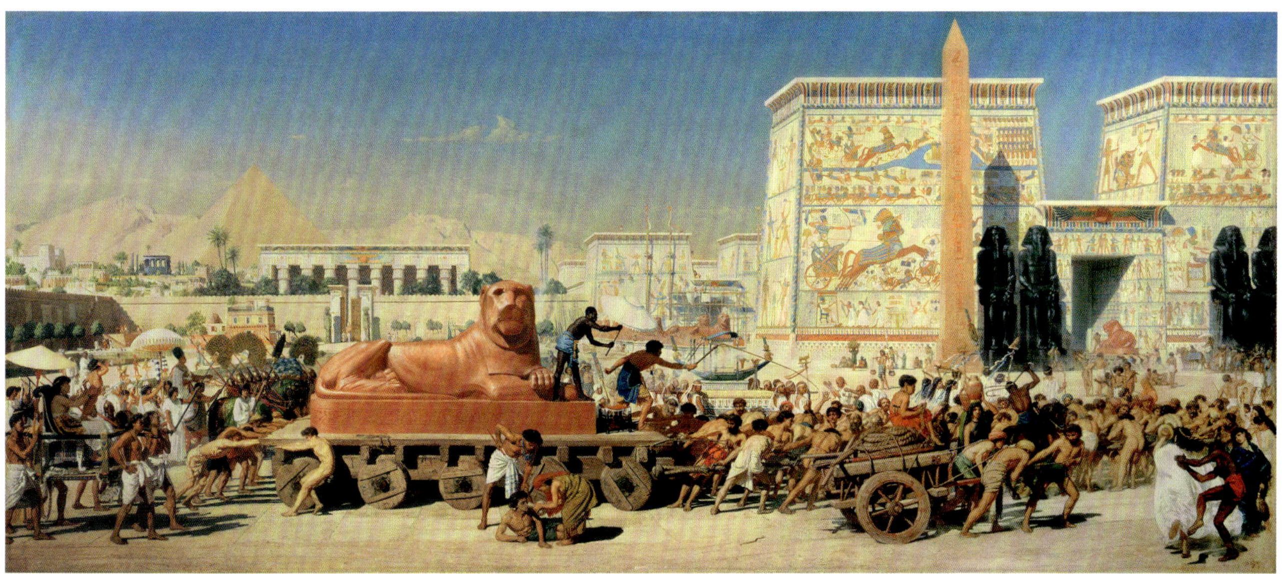

Opposite: Fig. 120 Detail of fig. 121

Above: Fig. 121 Edward J. Poynter (1836–1919), *Israel in Egypt*, 1867. Oil on canvas. Guildhall Art Gallery, City of London Corporation

eclectic ensemble displayed in the Egyptian Court at Sydenham, where similar red granite lions featured (see pp. 158–9). For *The Illustrated London News*, Poynter gave 'every evidence of having fully profited by recent Egyptological research … [it is] a typical example of the successful application of the modern principle of wedding archaeology with art'.[131] Poynter achieved this successful alliance of archeological evidence and pictorial practice by using bold colour extensively: from the vividly painted figures and ornaments on the gateway and Pharaonic carriages, to the red and black granite lions, statues and hieroglyphic inscriptions on the ochre obelisk matching the Pyramid in the background. Poynter also introduced subtle nuances of skin colour to depict the Pharaoh, the Egyptians and the Israelite slaves pulling the monumental lion. At the time slavery was still indeed a much-debated issue, as British newspapers reported on both the American Civil War and evidence of forced labour during the construction of the Suez Canal.[132]

By unveiling a wide range of polychrome ornaments from the ancient past, Jones's chromophilia proved particularly influential, not only with architects and designers but also with painters such as Alma-Tadema and Poynter, whose archaeological fictions were brought to life through colour.

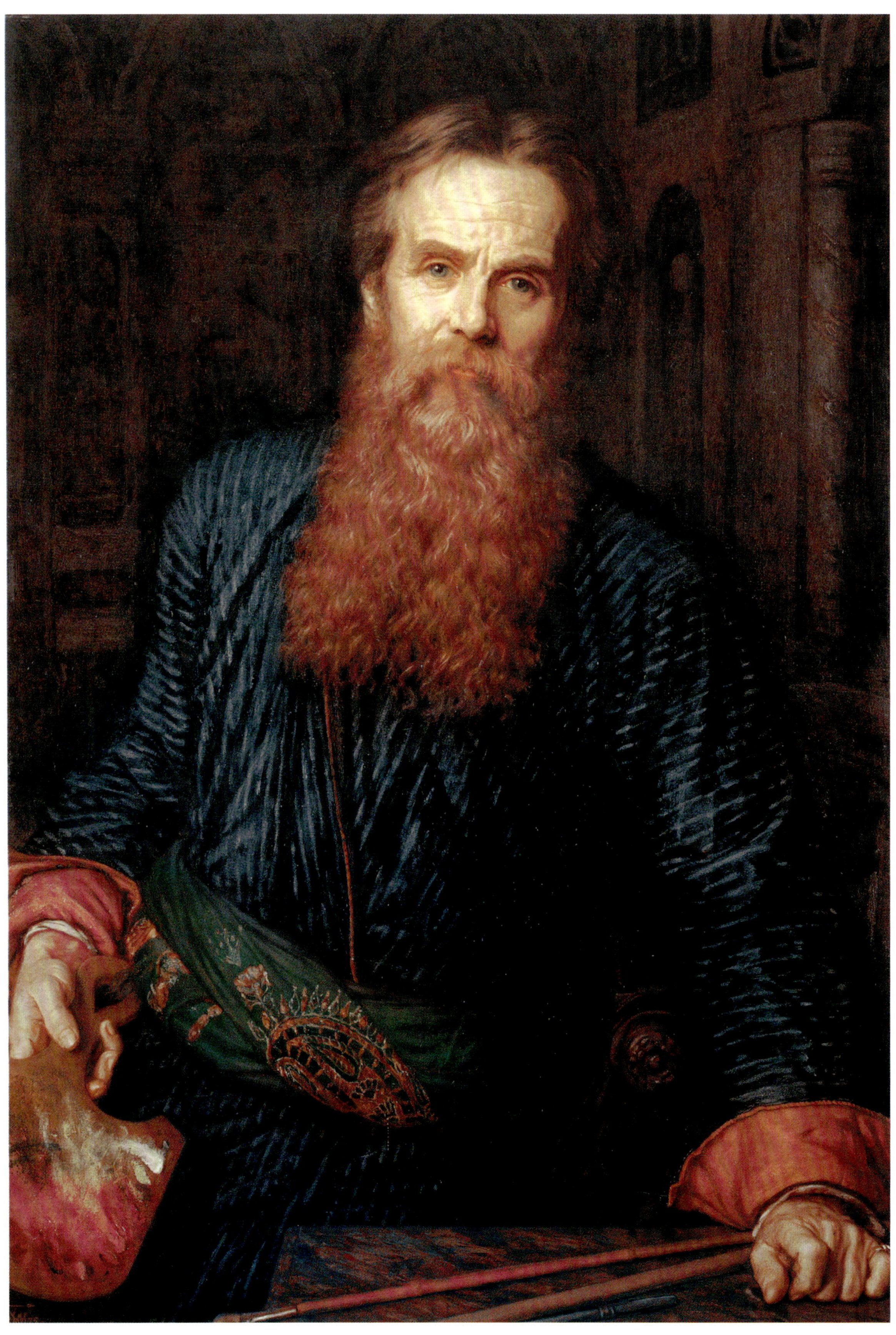

Journeys for Colour: Artist-Travellers and British Orientalism

Madeline Hewitson

In February 1869, Thomas Cook and his son John Mason offered the world's first package holiday: a 70-day tour of Egypt, Palestine and Syria. In his guidebook, Cook described Egypt as a place of 'brilliant' and 'dazzling' colour.'[133] His chromolithograph advertisements depicted ancient monuments, sweeping desert vistas and the crystalline blue waters of the Nile in intense primary colours intended to lure customers. One month into Cook's expedition, one passenger, Miss Riggs, noted in her diary as their boat steamed towards Aswan: 'On the return [there was the] most gorgeous sunset – sands deep gold and mountains deep violet-red – it was a colouring I had never seen before – suppose tropical in tint.'[134]

The Cook excursion sailed in the wake – quite literally some days – of the Prince and Princess of Wales, who were on their own Nile journey as guests of Khedive Isma'il, who had ruled Egypt since 1863. Sir William Howard Russell, a veteran journalist with *The Times*, accompanied the royal party and as they sailed from Cairo wrote that the city was 'a rainbow of transcendent brightness and beauty'.[135] For British travellers from the highest echelons of society to the burgeoning 'mass tourists', the Middle East was an exciting new destination to experience colour.

In the eighteenth century, British tourism had centred on the Grand Tour. This was the journey young, wealthy European bachelors made through the Alps, Switzerland and Italy, where they gained a classical and cultural education. A century later this new, extended 'Grand Tour' now departed from the southernmost tip of Italy and traversed the Mediterranean with destinations in many countries under the dominion of the Ottoman Empire. Strong diplomatic and cultural ties between the two Empires during the mid-nineteenth century exposed British travellers to the material and artistic culture of the Islamic world.

Although Egypt was the most popular destination for Victorian travellers, it was not the only option to experience Middle Eastern colour. When horse breeder Anne Blunt crossed into the Nefud Desert in present-day Saudi Arabia in 1865 she wrote: 'What surprised us was its colour, that of rhubarb and magnesia, nothing at all like the sand we had hitherto seen, and nothing at all like we have expected.'[136] In the caravan on his pilgrimage to Mecca in 1853 the explorer Richard Burton observed: 'every slight modification of form or colour rivets observation; the senses are sharpened, and perceptive faculties ... act vigorously when excited by the capability of embracing each detail'.[137] And as the author William Makepeace Thackeray passed the coast of Lebanon by boat he wrote that the water was 'magnificently and unexpectedly blue ...

Fig. 122 William Holman Hunt (1827–1910), *Self-Portrait*, 1907. Oil on canvas. Uffizi Gallery, Florence and [it] sparkled like quicksilver'.[138] The panoply of unique colour experiences delighted these travellers.

Much like the authors of these ekphrastic passages, artists were also at the forefront of this wave of travel and discovery. For some Victorian artists, travelling became central to their careers and formed a crucial part of their identities. Subsequently, the 'artist-traveller' as a distinct identity emerged. These globe-trotters actively set out in search of new subjects and experiences to use in their work.

This persona is perhaps best encapsulated by two images of the Pre-Raphaelite William Holman Hunt. Hunt travelled extensively, making trips to Egypt, Syria and Palestine in 1854–6, 1869, 1875–8 and 1892. The first image is a self-portrait for the Uffizi Gallery (1875, fig. 122). Hunt presents himself in local costume: an indigo striped gown fastened with a green patterned scarf. Amongst European travellers, the practice of 'going native', or dressing like the local population, was a popular part of the experience. Despite his long red beard and hair, he presents himself attempting to blend in with the local culture.[139] The second image is a photograph taken in 1894, in which Hunt re-enacts painting *The Scapegoat* (1854), one of his most popular biblically themed paintings, four decades earlier at Mount Sodom in the Judean Desert (fig. 123). He exudes masculine bravado by simultaneously holding a rifle and palette. His military-like outfit and sturdy boots are practical for painting outdoors in the desert and for fighting against possible foreign enemies.

Both images reveal Hunt's desire to be strongly associated with his travels, and the masculine yet artistic traits associated with those trips. However, the presence of a palette in both images also indicates the importance of the act of painting in the Middle East for Hunt. In the photograph, the artist re-enacts

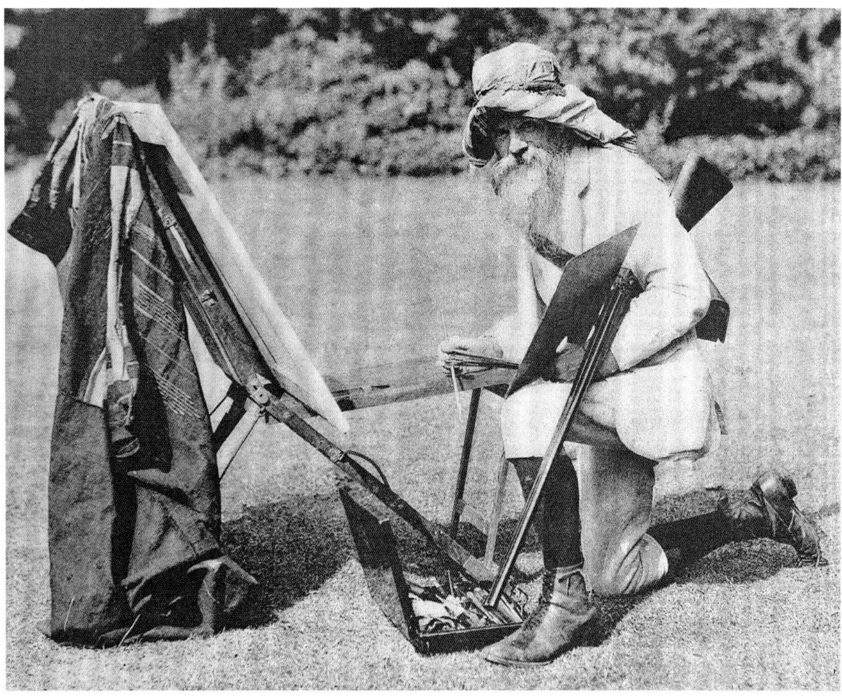

Fig. 123 William Holman Hunt re-enacting the conditions under which he painted *The Scapegoat*. Bodleian Library, University of Oxford, Per. 170 c.9

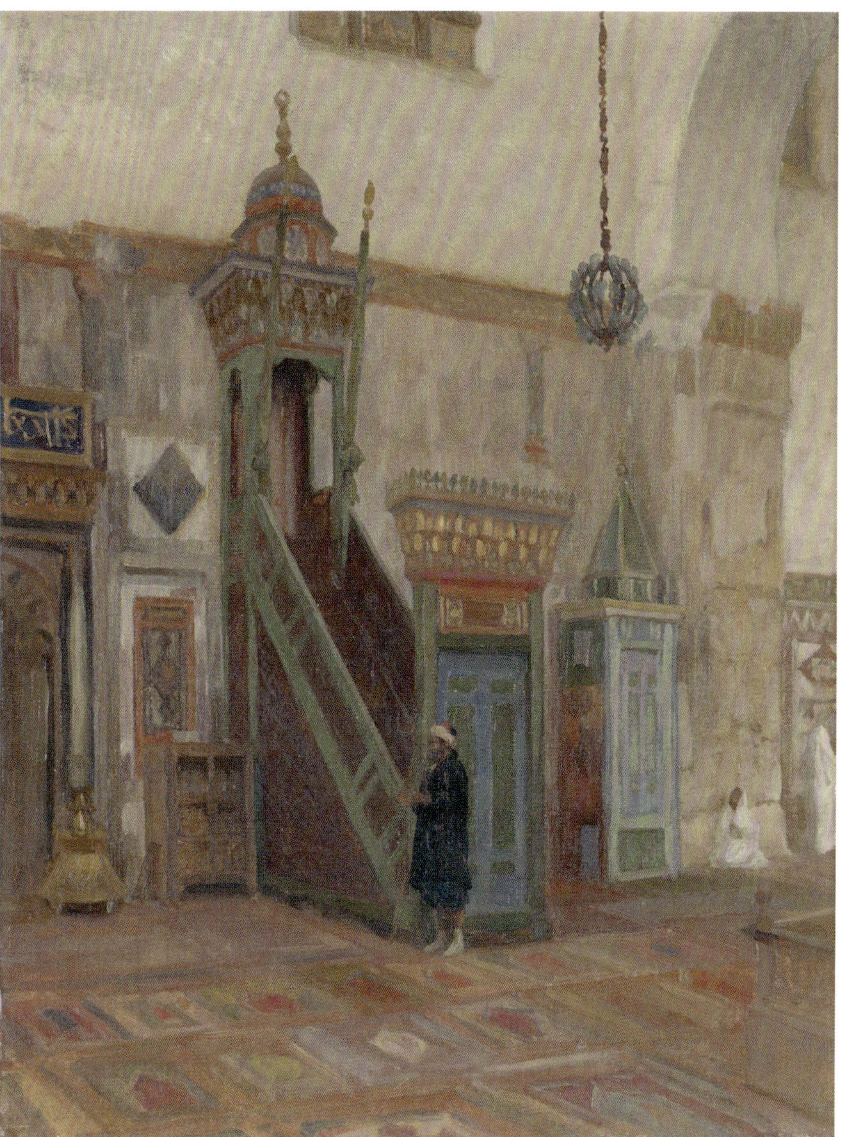

Fig. 124 Frederic Leighton (1830–1896), *Interior of a Mosque or the Mimbar of the Great Mosque at Damascus*. Oil on canvas. Government Art Collection, 17815

painting on the supposed spot of the biblical city of Sodom. His paint box is full of tubes of pigment and he holds his brush towards to the canvas ready to make a mark. In the Uffizi portrait, his palette is covered with diverse combinations of colours. For Hunt and many other artist-travellers, colour was an essential motivation for visiting the Middle East.

They saw the region as a training ground to improve their colour sense, a place with hues, according to Richard Dadd, 'to drink in, with greedy enjoyment'.[140] Colour became a key motivation for artist-travellers – an opportunity to discern a new understanding of the relationship between colour and the intense light, which they regularly cited in letters, travel diaries and interviews.

Hunt and many of the artist-travellers who made their careers in the Middle East were, and are still, referred to as Orientalists and the style of their work as Orientalism. In the nineteenth century, the terms had neutral connotations. They were derived from Latin, *oriens*, meaning 'East'. The iconography of

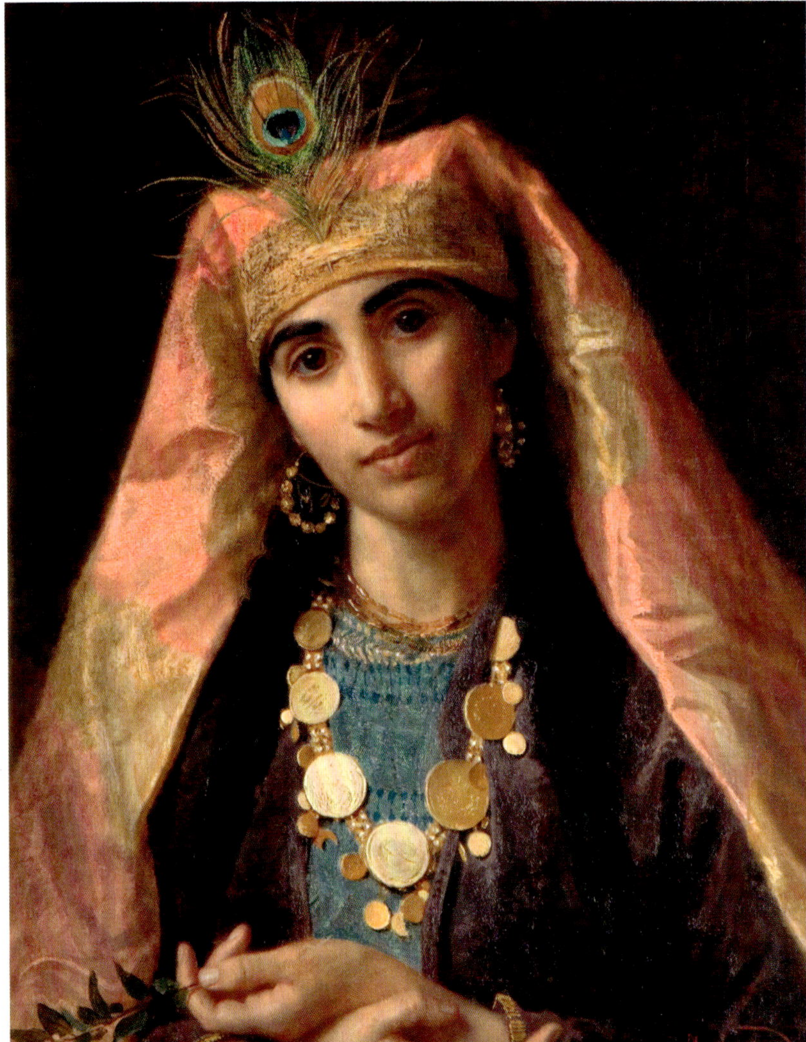

Fig. 125 Sophie Anderson (1823–1903), *Scheherazade*. Oil on canvas. The New Art Gallery Walsall Permanent Collection, P69/76

Orientalism was predicated on Western depictions of predominantly Islamic peoples and places (fig. 124). Today, we understand that these images were a biased European view of the 'East', and in many cases, pure fantasy and invention.

In the twentieth century, the literary theorist Edward Said and the art historian Linda Nochlin opened up the myth of the Orient as an 'imaginative geography' and revealed how Europeans created a binary whereby the West was a place of modernity, enlightenment and progress, while the East was aligned with ancient custom and an inherently 'backwards' exoticism.[141] Texts such as *The Arabian Nights*, translated into English in 1701, cemented this viewpoint and quickly became one of the main cultural conduits of Orientalist visual culture (fig. 125). Between 1800 and 1890, nearly a dozen illustrated editions of the text were published, with illustrations by leading artists such as John Everett Millais, Walter Crane and Gustav Doré.

Victorian artists approached the colours of the so-called Orient with reverence and the receptiveness of a student willing to be taught. However, the alterity of Eastern colour – the idea that it was somehow different to the colours of the West – implies a similarly divisive hierarchy whereby colour is consumed like a resource in the East and sold as a commodity in the West. But colour also offers, to use Mary Louise Pratt's term, a contact zone, 'a social space where disparate cultures meet, clash, and grapple with each other'.[142] Similarly, Natasha Eaton describes 'chromo zones' as spaces where colour presents an opportunity to push beyond European colonial and Orientalist boundaries.[143]

In these senses, colour was an active agent that confronted and clung to British artists in transformative ways, shaping their art, and sometimes their entire careers. As Frederic Leighton wrote, in response to a sunset in Damascus: 'It has dyed our spirits in colours that can never be washed out.'[144]

Landscape painting emerged as an important focal point for translating and describing the colours of the Near East. The desert took centre stage: a sand-coloured panoramic vista mirroring the appearance of a blank canvas and waiting to be filled with colour. It was a challenging outdoor environment and most artists chose to work at dawn or twilight. They attempted to capture the way light and heat transformed the appearance of the landscape throughout the day. Thomas Seddon first travelled to Egypt with Hunt and Edward Lear in 1854. He found success as a 'painter of Eastern subjects' and returned

Fig. 126 Thomas Seddon (1821–1856), *Giza and the Sphinx*, 1854. Watercolour. Ashmolean Museum, WA1944.30

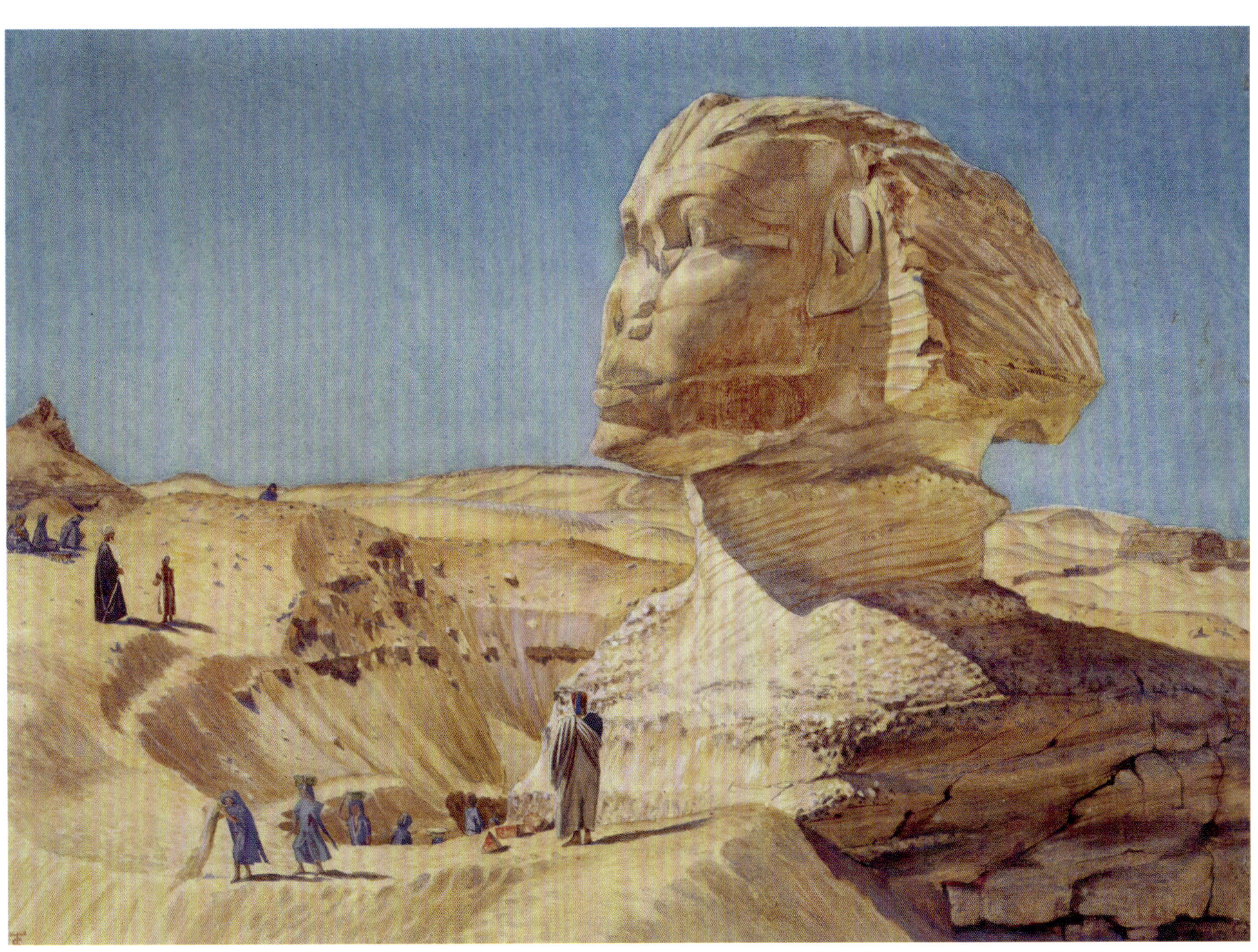

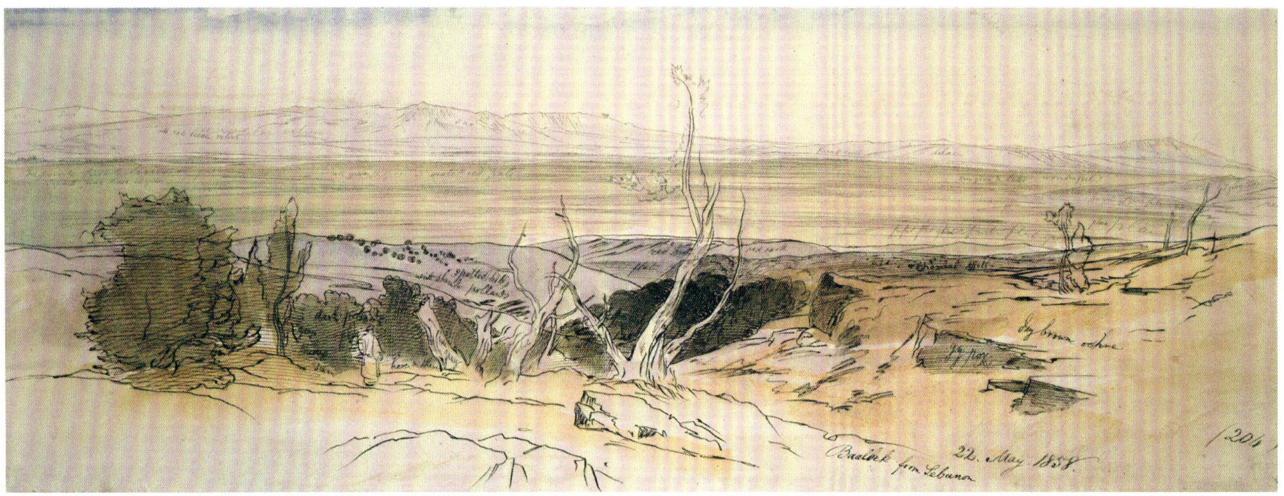

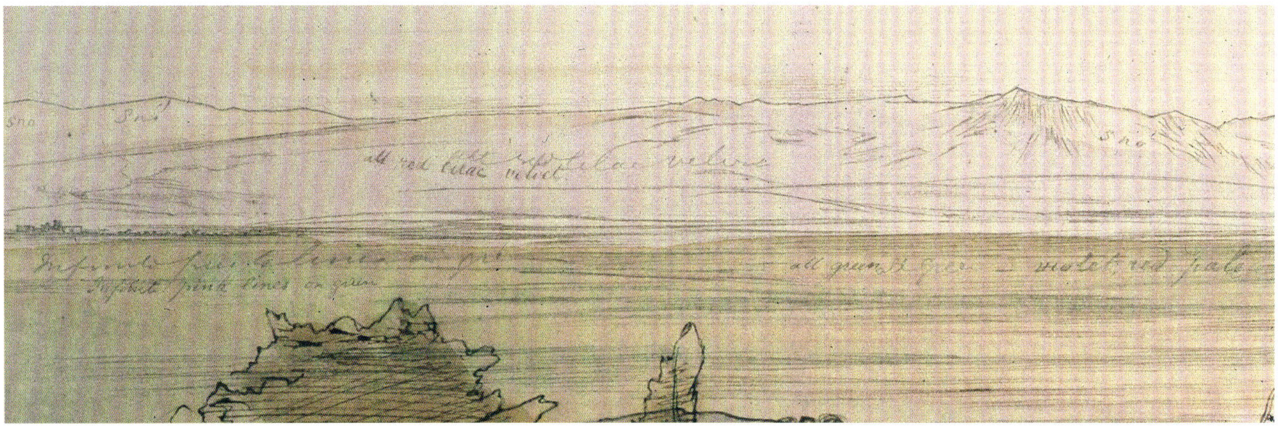

in 1856 to gather new scenes (fig. 126). Upon his arrival in Cairo, however, he was struck by his inadequacy as a translator of colour, writing to Hunt: 'I find that my impressions of atmospheric effects had lost the wonderful delicacy, and glory of colour at the same time, of the reality.'[145] Tragically, it was not a professional weakness he had time to improve: a month after he sent the letter he died of cholera in Cairo – a stark reminder to his friends that such journeys were not without risk.

Top: Fig. 127 Edward Lear (1812–1888), *Baalbek from Lebanon*, 1858. Watercolour and bodycolour. Ashmolean Museum, WA1936.10.9

Bottom: Fig. 128 Detail of fig. 127 showing Lear's annotations

Seddon's anxiety that Middle Eastern colour was somehow untranslatable was felt by many artists. As Lear crossed into Baalbek in Lebanon in 1858, he annotated his sketchbook with written descriptions of his colour experience (fig. 127). After travelling with Hunt and Seddon, Lear spent most of the rest of his life abroad travelling across Europe, the Ottoman Empire and India. His sketches were *aide-memoires* to prompt his memory back in the studio. His other career as a nonsense poet influenced the annotations and he even referred to his art as 'poetical-topographical'.[146] Some of the notes read: 'All red, lilac, velvet', 'Grey and brown here and there', 'Green w/ lines of pink', 'dry brown ochre' and, across the mountains, simply 'Wonderful!' (fig. 128). Lear deliberately turned away from the famous classical landmarks of Baalbek such as the

Roman-era temples of Jupiter and Bacchus and instead prioritised the mountainous landscape. These annotations use language to direct his future palette and attempt to combat memory loss and the distorting effect of time on colour experience.

The pursuit of colour was conducted on water as well as land. The Nile became one of the most important bodies of water in the Victorian cultural psyche. In 1858, armchair adventurers had read about John Hanning Speke's expedition to discover the river's source. Later, Nile river cruises, on sailing boats known as *dahabeahs*, became the most popular mode of travel for Victorian tourists including George Frederic Watts and his new wife Mary, who honeymooned on such a boat in 1886.

On his trip down the river in 1868, Leighton wrote enthusiastically about how colour motivated and transformed his already well-established interest in landscape painting:[147]

> The keynote of this landscape is a soft, variant fawn-coloured brown, than which nothing could take more gratefully the warm glow of sunlight or the cool purple mystery of shadow ... the broad coffee-coloured sweep of the river is bordered on either side by a fillet of green of the most extraordinary vivacity.[148]

This beautifully written description, which uses terminology from the reference book *Werner's Nomenclature of Colours*, is then matched by his oil paintings, of which he painted nearly 40 during his eight-week trip. In many of these paintings, description dissolves into Whistlerian colour harmonies such as pink, purple and brown.

Hunt also picked up on this soft mixture of pink, purple and brown in his Nile imagery. Although *The Afterglow in Egypt* (1861, fig. 129) is a narrow, vertical canvas, Hunt includes a significant portion of the landscape including the near and far banks of the river as well as the fields and palm trees in the distance. The afterglow in the painting's title is not a reference to the sunset but, according to Hunt, an allusion to the 'the meridian glory of ancient Egypt [that] has passed away'.[149] Hunt's Orientalist view was that Egypt did not have a place in the modern world. However, at this very moment, the Nile gained a newfound importance in the context of the modern, industrialised world.

The model, a young woman Hunt found in Memphis, adopts a similar to pose to ancient depictions of the Roman harvest goddess Ceres. She represents Egypt's vital agrarian economy, seen in the stacked bales of hay behind her, which had recently taken on a new importance in the context of British textile production. After the outbreak of the American Civil War in 1862, Egypt's cotton along the Nile Delta became the British Empire's largest source of the raw material which saved the Lancashire textile mills as well as the aniline dye industry. Between 1861 and 1863, Egypt tripled its cotton exports, with England receiving the lion's share of nearly 200,000 bales.[150]

The woman's indigo dress – a rich, saturated colour made using cobalt blue pigment – serves as the focal point of the painting. The dress is an accurate

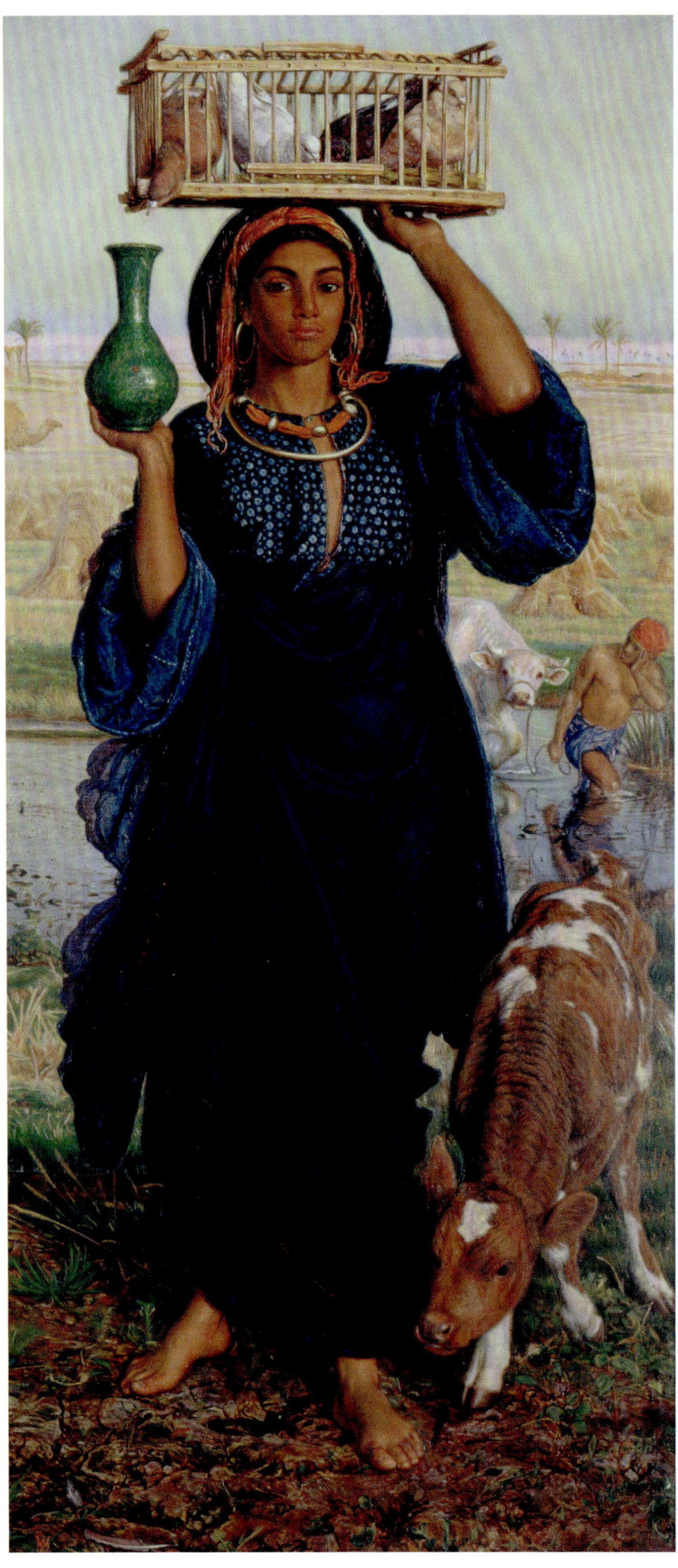

Fig. 129 William Holman Hunt (1827–1910), *The Afterglow in Egypt*, 1861. Oil on canvas. Ashmolean Museum, WA1894.3

depiction of the type of work garments worn by the *fellahin* peasant class in Egypt.[151] While many Orientalist paintings, like Leighton and Lear's landscapes, depict a seemingly depopulated country, examples like *The Afterglow in Egypt*, which show ordinary people, provide a more nuanced picture. The *fellahin* woman's vivid dress and her notably un-anglicised beauty, including a face tattoo, draw attention to modern Egyptians who were impacted by British artists and industrialists alike.

This fascination with the social fabric of Middle Eastern life is one of the hallmarks of Orientalism. Paintings that depicted bustling bazaars and fabled *hammams* and *harems*, off limits to prying Western eyes, were incredibly popular. While landscape painting was an important site for experimentation with colour, these genre scenes were equally important subjects. These images often engaged with elements of Islamic material culture such as costume, architecture and objects which were often highly decorated and richly coloured. They also revealed the dynamics of British encounters with Islamic culture.

The British painter John Frederick Lewis lived in Cairo between 1841 and 1851 and, as an outsider in Ottoman Cairene society, was particularly interested in social dynamics. Thackeray famously described Lewis as a 'languid Lotus eater' living 'a dreamy, hazy, lazy tobaccofied [sic] life', but once again, orientalising stereotypes hid a more compelling subject.[152] In the same account, Thackeray describes Lewis dressed in 'a very handsome grave costume of dark blue, consisting of an embroidered jacket and gaiters, and a pair of trousers, which would make a set of dresses for an English family'. In his painting of 1856, *The Pipe Bearer*, Lewis presents two men dressed in similarly ornate outfits. The older man wears a green sleeveless kaftan while the young man wears a white jacket and trousers with a patterned, red-buttoned shirt and a yellow sash (fig. 130). Green was a significant colour in Islamic tradition, associated with paradise and spiritual purity. The Ashmolean also holds a green Turkish-style jacket and trousers once worn by Edward William Lane, the author of *Manners and Customs of the Modern Egyptians* (1836), which he wore when he lived in Cairo in the 1820s. Lewis played on the stereotype of the *bey* – or wealthy Ottoman – with his clothing. On his honeymoon in 1847, Selina Bracebridge reported that he wore 'Turkish dress – a blue gubbeh, white kaftan, red turban, and a long white beard'.[153]

Lewis never acknowledged that the white-faced, narrow-nosed, bearded man that appears in *The Pipe Bearer* and several other paintings made during his extended residency were self-portraits, but photographs of Lewis reveal a striking likeness (fig. 131).[154] Unlike Hunt's self-portrait, Lewis had a more complicated relationship with the 'languid Lotus eater' persona.

In front of the *bey* figure is the titular character, a servant holding a *nargile* (a water pipe for smoking) and looking over his left shoulder, possibly to a third person beyond the picture space. Thackeray also referenced a 'black face' that watched him arrive from a balcony. This person was later revealed to be Lewis's female cook. The presence of black servants in Lewis's household added yet another layer of exoticism to the writer's visit. Little is known about Lewis's

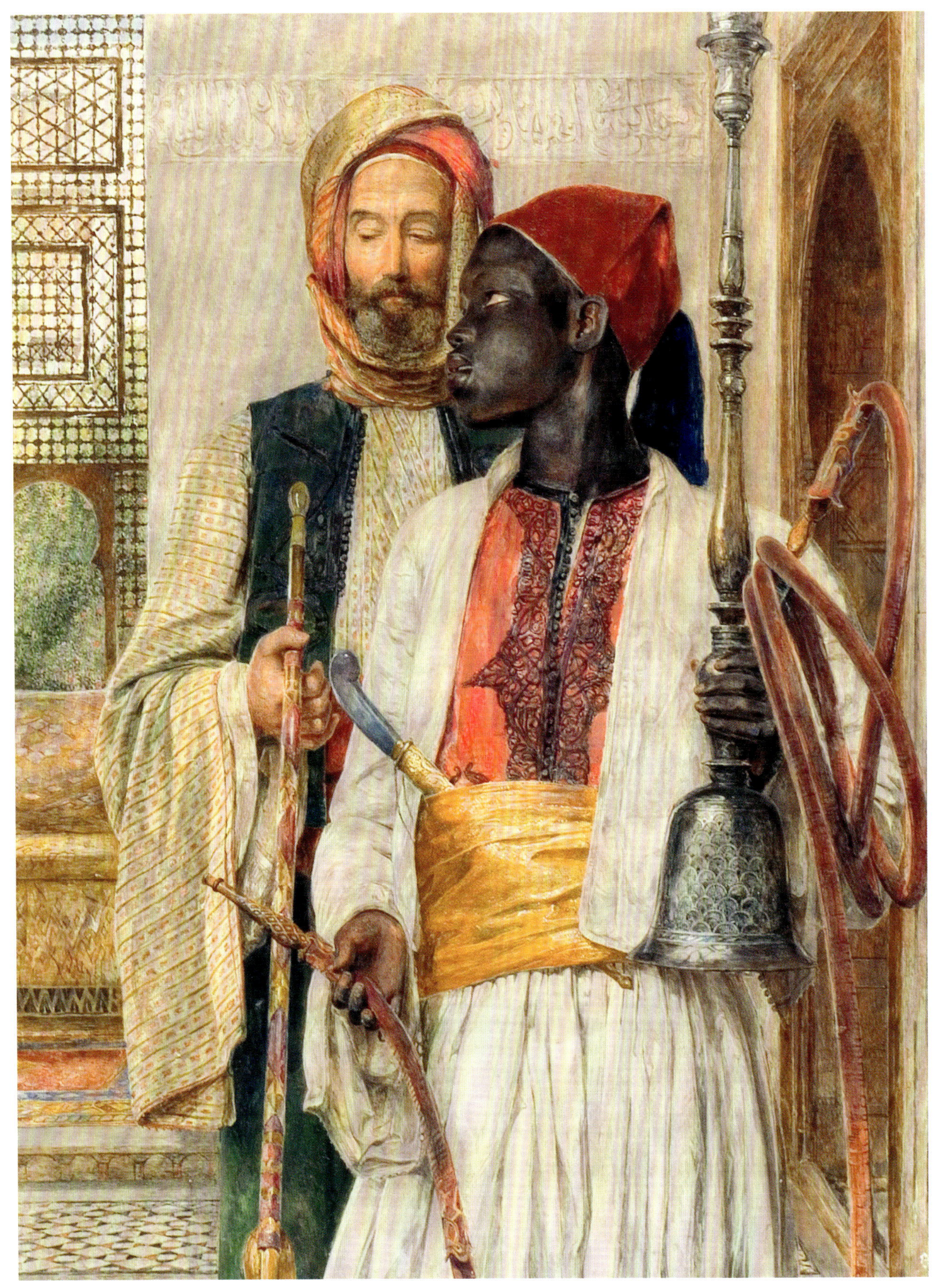

Opposite: Fig. 130 John Frederick Lewis (1804–1876), *The Pipe Bearer*, 1856. Oil on panel. Birmingham Museums Trust on behalf of Birmingham City Council, 1954P11

Right: Fig. 131 Caricature of John Frederick Lewis by Caleb Scholefield Mann (1822–1882). Ashmolean Museum, WA1967.6.3.184

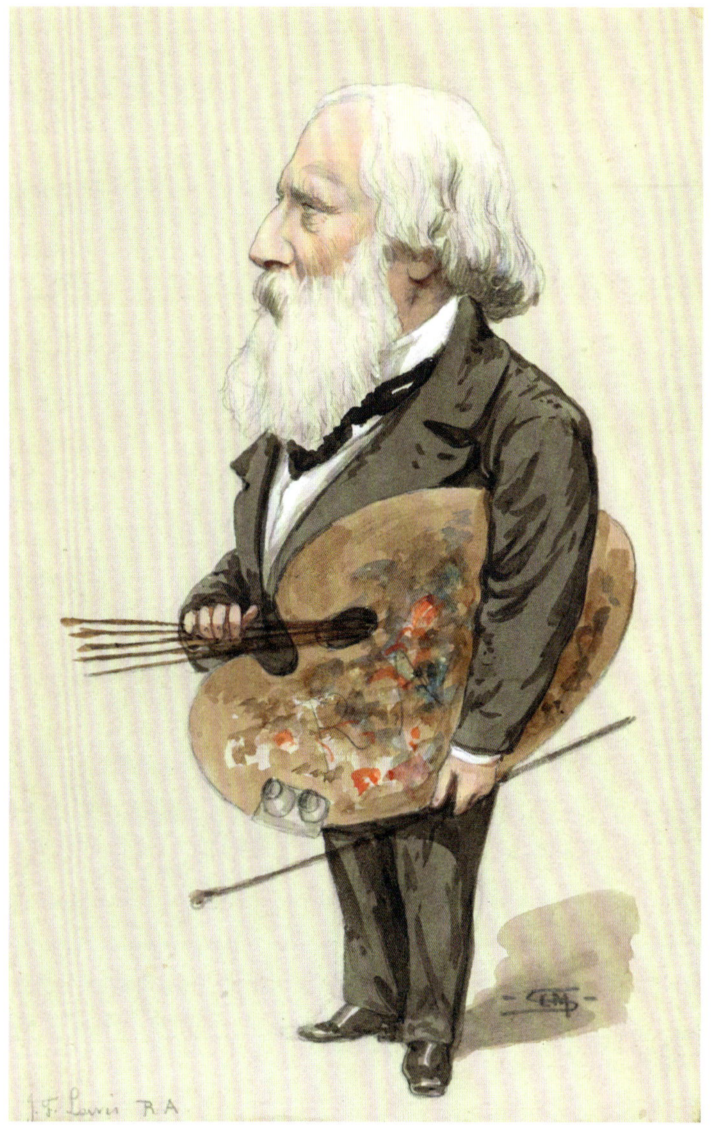

pursuit of local models, but several of his paintings attest to the fact his household servants featured in his art works. This young man features in another painting by Lewis as the attendant of Iskander Bey, the son of a French-born soldier who converted to Islam and worked for the Egyptian ruler Muhammed Ali (fig. 132). This suggests he was a member of Lewis's household, or another household Lewis was familiar with, although we do not have further details about him, such as his name (fig. 133). The men's clothing are brightly coloured, patterned and textured to represent different fabrics. Artist John Lewis Roget reported that Lewis would drape fabrics in his courtyard to see the effect of intense light on coloured materials.[155] Although *The Pipe Bearer* is an oil painting, Lewis honed the intensity of his colours through his frequent use of watercolour. In watercolour, he achieved particularly bright effects by using bodycolour on level white ground.[156] Lewis revelled in these types of small details, while refusing to offer more apparent social commentaries on race and gender.

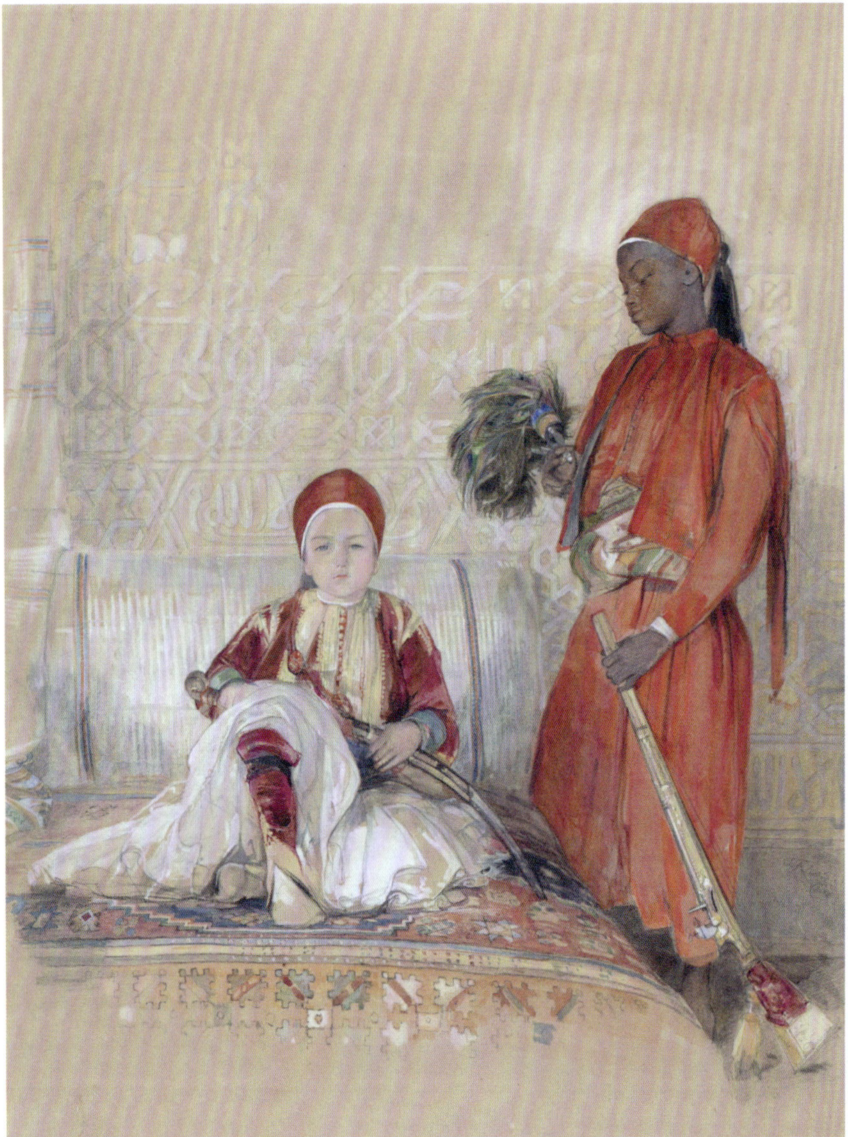

Fig. 132 John Frederick Lewis (1804–1876), *Iskander Bey and his Servant*, c.1848. Watercolour and bodycolour over graphite. Metropolitan Museum of Art, New York, 2019.138.5

However, the most visible colour distinction in the painting is that of skin, a dynamic that was as apparent to audiences in the nineteenth century as it is to those in the present day. The slave markets of Cairo, which were officially outlawed in 1805 but still operated into the middle of the century, were the subject of both deflective outrage and macabre fascination for British travellers. Once again, Lewis is subtle in his image-crafting: there is no overt comment in *The Pipe Bearer* on race in the Ottoman or British worlds. There are no obvious answers as to who these men are and the nature of their relationship. As Briony Llewellyn summarises, 'often with Lewis, we are faced with a contradiction.'[157] The meanings in his paintings are often unresolvable but provoke important questions about the human dimensions so often absent from discussions of Orientalist artwork.

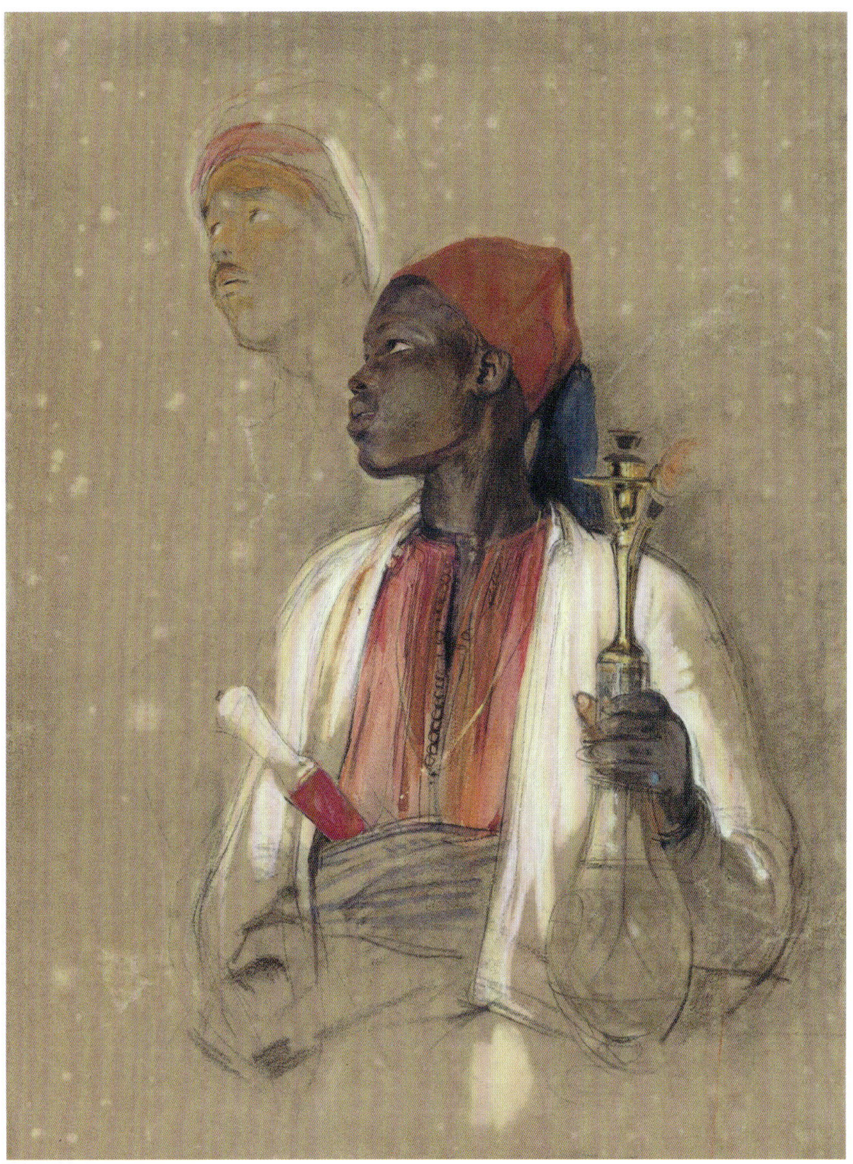

Fig. 133 John Frederick Lewis (1804–1876), Study for *The Pipe Bearer*, 1841–51. Watercolour, gouache and black chalk. Metropolitan Museum of Art, New York, 2014.435.2

Colour was the vehicle used by artists to convey experiences such as sailing down the Nile, watching a desert sunrise and encountering the wealth of colourful Islamic material culture. The pursuit of 'Eastern colour' may have been as much of a construct as the stories in *One Thousand and One Nights*. However, the artist-travellers made it their mission to discover colour in the Middle East.

Object in Focus

Owen Jones, *The History of Joseph and His Brethren* (1865)

In 1865, Owen Jones joined the chromolithography firm Day & Son as a director. Although Day & Son had a strong reputation Jones was, by this time, renowned as a pioneer of colour printing. Decades earlier, in 1836, he had broken his contract with former Day & Son director Louis Haghe to develop his own technique to colour print his first major publication: *Plans, Sections, Elevations and Details of the Alhambra* (1836–45). This new partnership marked the prodigal son's return, but it was also recognition of his superior ability to combine technological advancement with innovative aesthetics.[158]

His first publication in the role was *The History of Joseph and His Brethren* (1865), a lavishly illustrated, gilt-edged gift book. Illustrated gift books were popular amongst middle-class Victorians who displayed the luxurious tomes in their front rooms and parlours.[159] This volume sold for £2.2s, or £175 in today's money. It illustrates, in 52 chromolithographed plates, three chapters from the Book of Genesis that tells the story of Joseph. The volume was bound in a red cloth cover designed by Jones's pupil Arthur Warren and decorated with Egyptian motifs including a winged sun of Thebes and lotus flowers (fig. 134). This colourful volume brought the stories of the Old Testament to Victorian audiences in a way they had never seen them before. Although it is one of Jones's lesser known publications, it is a striking example of the influence of archaeology and Orientalism on Victorian biblical art.

Jones is not typically associated with biblical art. However, in the 1840s, much of his work was concerned with Christian forms of design. During this decade, he published several volumes with Christian and biblical themes: *The Sermon on the Mount* (1844), *The Illuminated Book of Common Prayer* (1845), *The Song of Songs* (1849) and *The Victorian Psalter* (1861). The decoration of these books embraced the Gothic Revival style of A.W.N. Pugin, who exerted a great influence on the young Jones. Pugin believed that true Christian art and architecture should be medieval in style, and had the potential to elevate Christian belief in the modern day.[160] But while Pugin's message had an evangelical tone, Jones instead used Gothic art and architecture as an accessible way to teach Victorians about the universal principles of design.

In contrast to his biblical books of the 1840s, *Joseph and His Brethren* is a singular narrative and, significantly, adopts the Orientalist style that, as we have seen, developed as a result of British artists' engagements with the Middle East. By 1865, Orientalism had made an impact on British visual culture and played a significant role in the Victorian story of colour. In 1832, Jones travelled to Andalucian Spain, where he saw the Alhambra, and then on to Egypt to study traces of pigment on ancient monuments. Many tourists went to Egypt to see the remains of ancient Pharaonic dynasties, and archaeological discovery became a key motivation for travel. At the same time, archaeologists began to uncover evidence of cities mentioned in the Bible such as Sodom, Gommorah and Jericho. Biblical tourism, the opportunity to visit the sites of the Bible, became an equally important reason to visit Egypt and Palestine.[161] This took place during the so-called 'Crisis of Faith' when many Victorian Christians

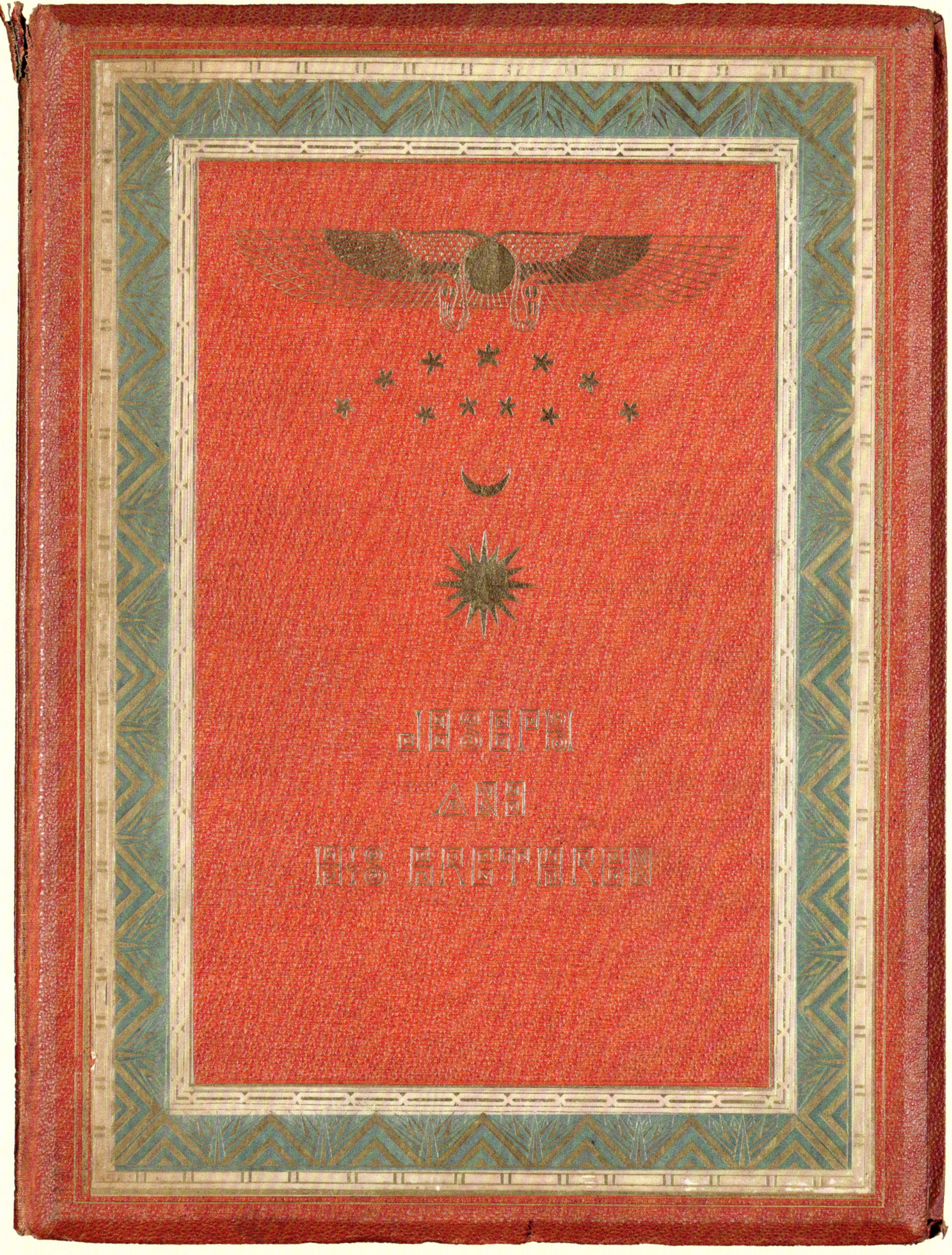

Fig. 134 Cover of *The History of Joseph and his Brethren*, 1865. Bodleian Library, University of Oxford, (OC) 170 n.81

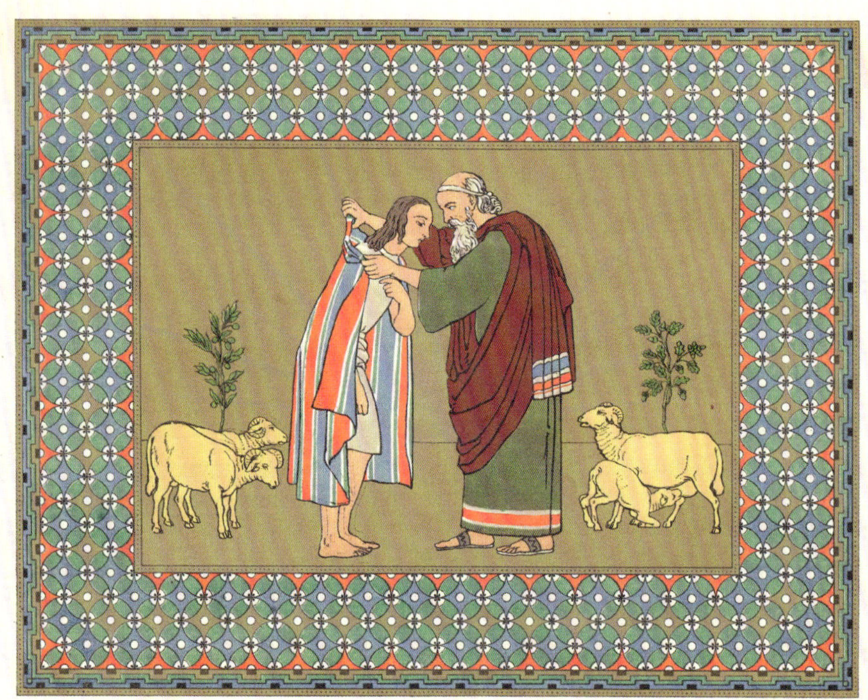

Fig. 135 Plate illustrating Joseph, Israel and the coat of many colours

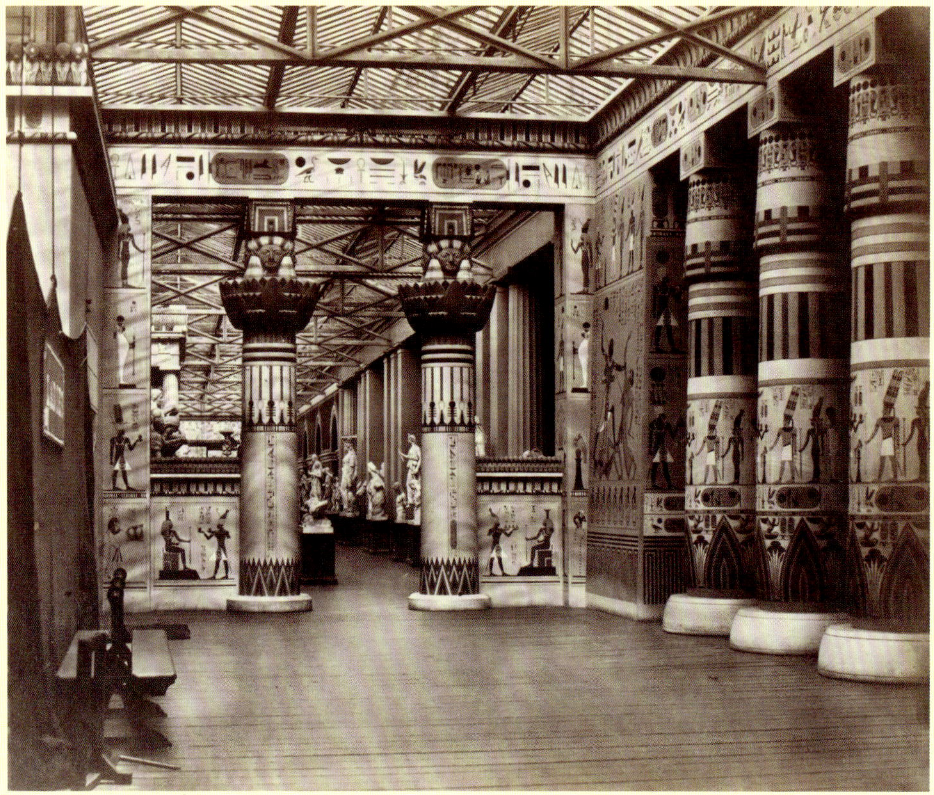

Fig. 136 Phillip Henry Delamotte (1821–1889), The Egyptian Court, Crystal Palace, c.1854. Albumen print. Victoria and Albert Museum, 39305

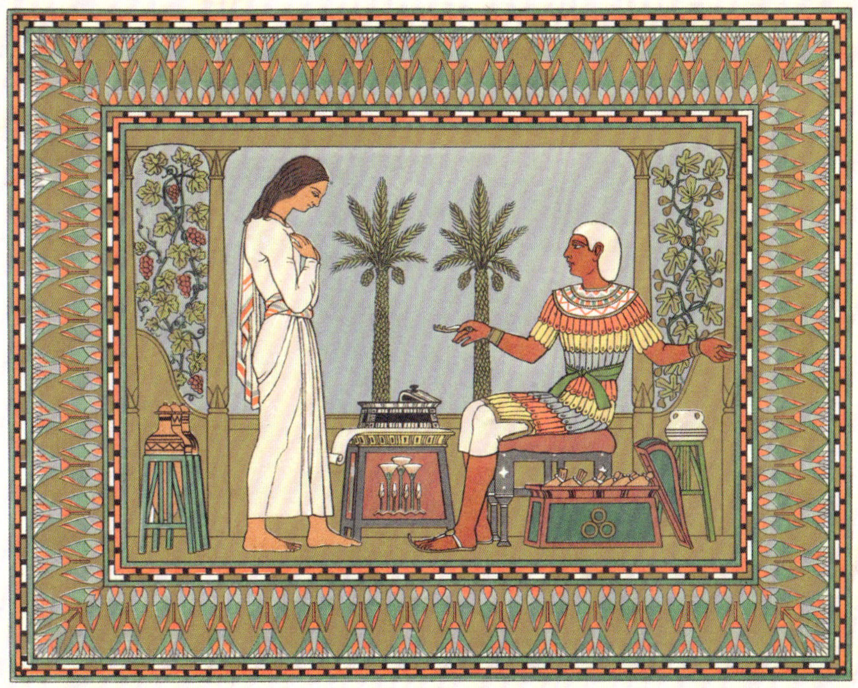

Fig. 137 Plate illustrating 'And Joseph found grace in his sight …'

grappled with revelations such as the theory of evolution and the unearthing of dinosaur remains, and the implication of those discoveries on their beliefs. Biblical tourism was a way for Victorians to use empirical evidence to reinforce their faith and maintain that the stories of the Bible were true. In the same vein, Victorian artists adopted archaeological and Orientalist aesthetics in order to produce religious art that spoke to these modern interpretations of the Bible.

For a man such as Jones who had a reputation as 'the most potent apostle of colour',[162] the story of Joseph seems a natural choice. Joseph's father, Jacob, gives his son 'a coat of many colours'. This gift sends Joseph's brothers into a jealous rage and results in them selling him to slavers (fig. 135). Jones depicts Jacob draping the handmade gift over his son's shoulders. It is a flowing, floor-length coat in red, white, green and blue against a crisp black outline, demonstrating his ability to combine multiple colours in a single image.

After Joseph is sold by his brothers, he is brought to Egypt and eventually becomes a trusted advisor to the Pharaoh. The story's Egyptian setting suited Jones who, following his travels, was a great admirer of ancient Egyptian architecture and design. In 1854, he designed the Egyptian Court at the Crystal Palace in Sydenham along with Egyptologist Joseph Bonomi (fig. 136). They painted the plaster walls of the court in bright primary colours and filled it with replicas of ancient Egyptian architecture and sculpture.

Joseph inhabits a world littered with the material culture of ancient Egypt - similar to the Egyptian Court. In one scene he is shown in the house of the Pharaoh's general, Potiphar. They are surrounded by objects such as vases, stools, tables and chests filled with bottles, which are covered in decoration and colour (fig. 137). Jones used various sources for these objects including collections at the Britsh Museum and books such as Edward William Lane's *Manner and Customs of the Modern Egyptians*.[163] Jones intricately renders an Egyptian interior at the time of Ramses II, when the story of Joseph was believed to have taken place, by piecing together archaeological material

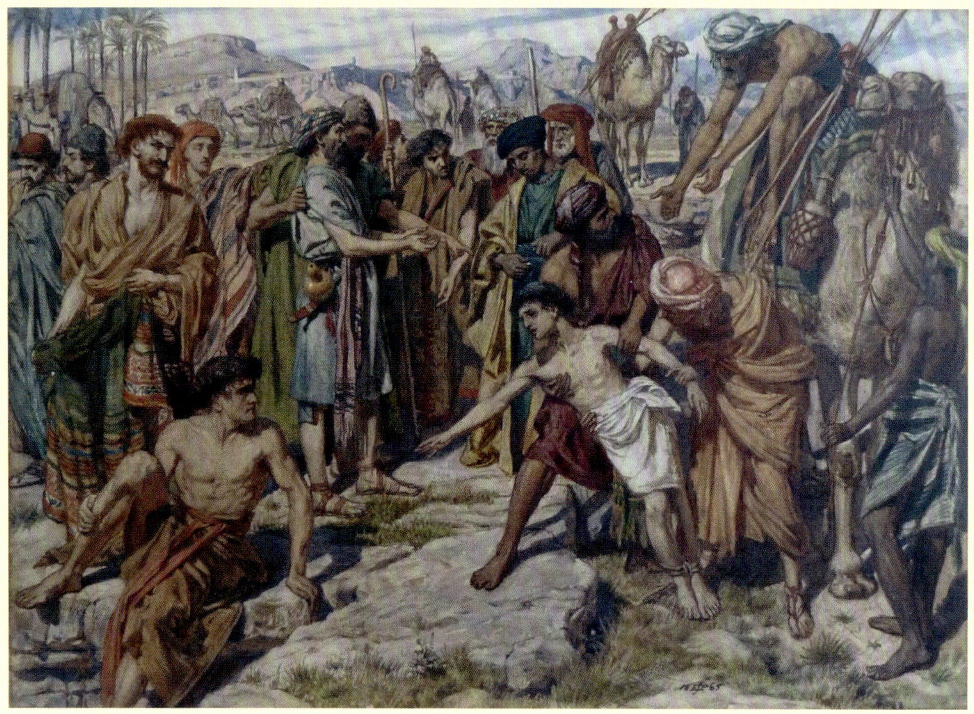

Fig. 138 Edward John Poynter (1836–1919), *Joseph sold by his Brothers to the Ishmaelites*, 1865. Ashmolean Museum, WA1951.134

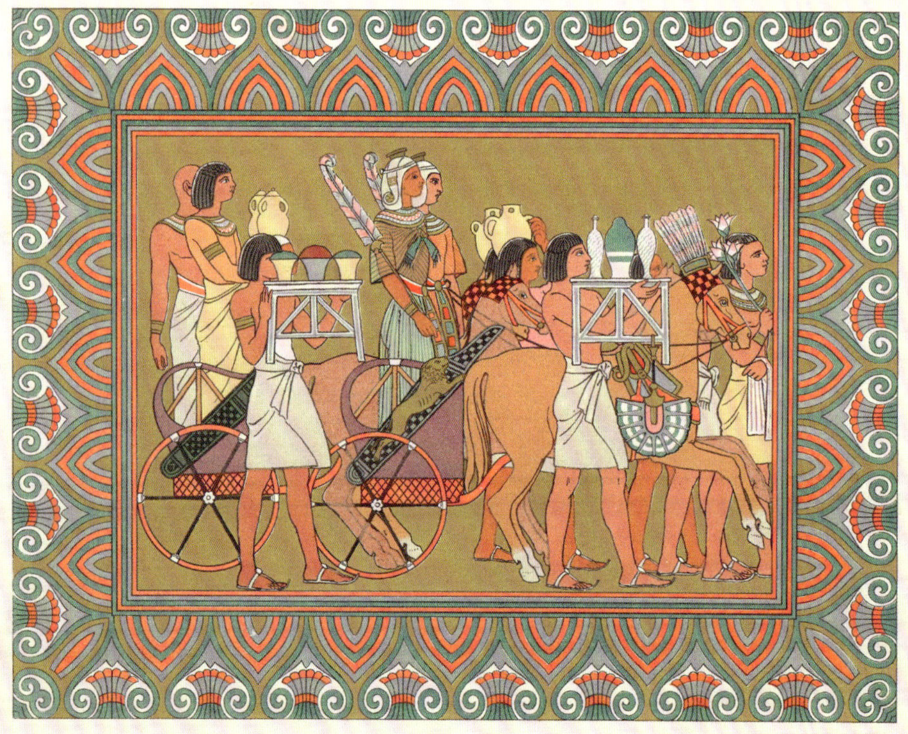

Fig. 139 Each gold page in *Joseph and His Brethren* is bordered by vivid geometric patterns inspired by ancient Egyptian design

and making it appear unified by using a bold colour scheme. These sources were also used by painters such as Edward John Poynter and Lawrence Alma-Tadema, who became known during the 1860s and 1870s for their Egyptian and biblical scenes. Both Poynter and Alma-Tadema also adapted the story of Joseph to create a vision of the biblical past influenced by archaeology (fig. 138).

While the narrative illustration gave Jones an opportunity to explore the impact of archaeology on Victorian visual culture, he did not entirely abandon the design reform principles of his other publications. Each gold page in *Joseph and His Brethren* is bordered by vivid geometric patterns, once again inspired by ancient Egyptian designs (fig. 139). Several of the patterns including the lotus flower designs had already appeared in *The Grammar of Ornament* (1856, fig. 140). The border repeats across two pages, tying the text and illustration together. These borders follow the principles, or 'propositions', of Jones's introduction to *The Grammar of Ornament*. These guiding principles include the dominant yet balanced use of primary colours – outlining gold elements in edging of a darker colour and the appropriate juxtaposition of light and dark tones – all of which can be seen in the border designs.

Joseph and His Brethren appeared at a moment when Victorian artists were rethinking the art of the Bible in light of new discoveries and technologies. Jones created a colourful interpretation of a key narrative from the Old Testament, whose style embraced the overlapping contexts of archaeology, Orientalism and debates about the veracity of the Christian Bible. Like the Ten Commandments, for Jones there were immutable laws that governed the world of design. Chief among them was the role of colour, and he used *Joseph and His Brethren* to highlight its importance in visualising the ancient and biblical worlds.

Madeline Hewitson

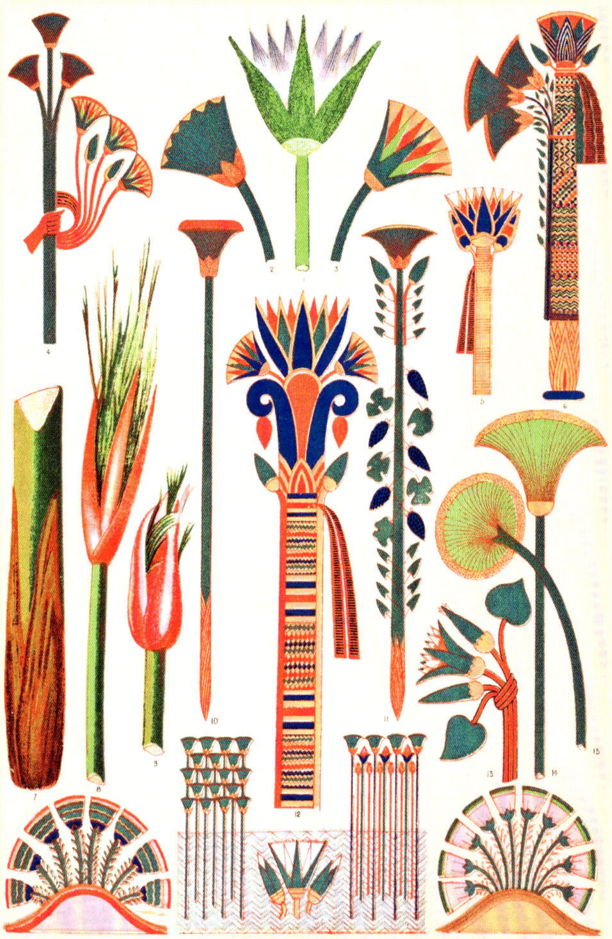

Fig. 140 Owen Jones (1809–1874), 'Egypt No 1' from *The Grammar of Ornament*, 1856

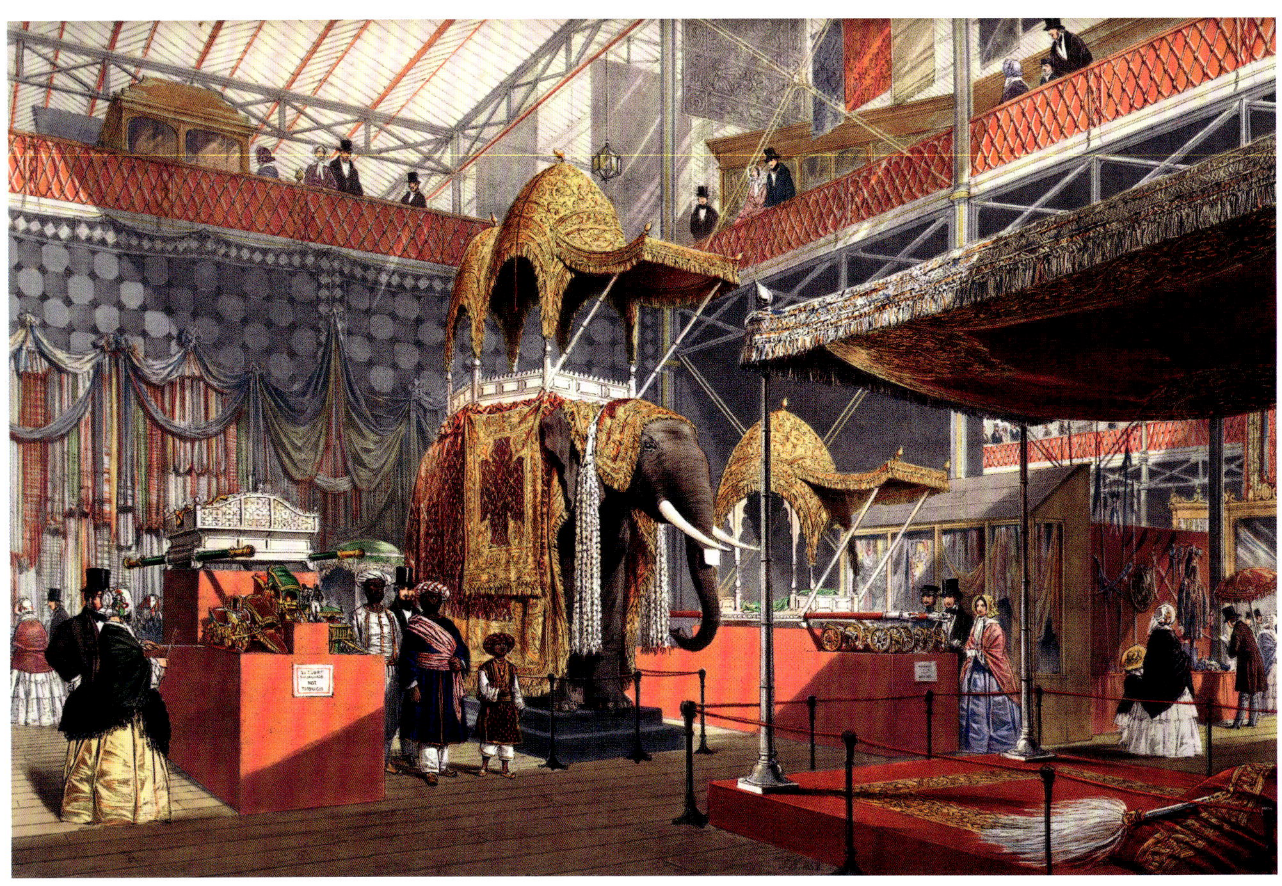

Fig. 141 James Henry Vizetelly (1790–1838), 'India No. 4' from Dickinsons' *Comprehensive Pictures of the Great Exhibition of 1851*, 1854. Hand-coloured chromolithograph. Yale Center for British Art, Paul Mellon Collection

'The gorgeous contributions of India': Sourcing Colour in the British Empire

Matthew Winterbottom and Madeline Hewitson

Since ancient times, the richly coloured textiles of the Indian subcontinent have been highly prized in the West. From the seventeenth century, East India companies imported these and other luxury goods and raw materials, including dyestuffs and pigments, into Europe. The British gained an important foothold in India in 1662 as part of negotiations secured by the marriage of Catherine of Braganza and Charles II. Thereafter the power and influence of the British East India Company steadily grew and expanded until, by the mid-nineteenth century, it controlled large swathes of the subcontinent on behalf of the British government.

The East India Company was a major supporter of the Great Exhibition of 1851, and arranged its magnificent 'Indian Court'. Prominently located around the central chancel of the Crystal Palace, next to Osler & Co.'s famous Crystal Fountain, the Indian Court was one of the largest and most popular in the exhibition. Covering 24,000 square feet, it dwarfed Britain's other colonial courts. The scale and prominence of the displays reflected the importance of India to the British economy.

The colourful displays of Indian works of arts, crafts and manufactured goods at the Great Exhibition amazed and delighted visitors. They brought Indian objects to the attention of the wider public for the first time. The Indian Court was photographed and a series of coloured lithographs allowed those who could not visit the Crystal Palace in Hyde Park to see it in all its richly coloured glory (fig. 141). Dominating the displays and no doubt adding to their popularity was an enormous stuffed elephant wearing a golden howdah and trappings. Also on display was the famous Koh-i-Noor diamond, recently presented to Queen Victoria by deposed Emperor Duleep Singh following Britain's annexation of the Punjab in 1849 – 'the forfeit of Oriental faithlessness, and the prize of Saxon valour', according to one reviewer.[164] Many British artists, designers and manufacturers were inspired by the objects displayed in the Indian Court: for Charles Lockwood Kipling, father of Rudyard, it sparked a lifelong interest in – and promotion of – the arts and crafts of India. Owen Jones described the 1851 displays as the 'gorgeous contributions of India'.[165]

Above all, it was the Indian textiles – with their beautiful combinations of bright colours and stylised patterns – that caught visitors' attention. Textiles and clothing accounted for seven of the 29 classes of materials exhibited. Indian craftsmen, like others across Asia, were considered by many to have an 'innate' sense of colour harmony in art and design. The *Official Catalogue* of the Great Exhibition acknowledged that in 'the management of colours, the skill with which a number of them are employed, and the taste with which they are harmonised ... Europe has nothing to teach, but a great deal to learn.'[166] On seeing the Indian Court, a Russian journalist exclaimed: 'What richness! What perfection of workmanship! What brilliance and harmony of colour!'[167]

In *Gleanings from the Great Exhibition*, Owen Jones compared the 'fruitless struggle to produce in art novelty without beauty – beauty without intelligence; all work without faith' of the British displays to Indian objects that 'were the most perfect in design of any that appeared in the exhibition ... a boon to the whole of Europe.'[168] Jones was a member of the committee that subsequently purchased objects from the Great Exhibition for the School of Design collection that was to become the Victoria and Albert Museum. Nearly a quarter of the committee's £5,000 budget was spent on Indian objects from the Exhibition, with textiles accounting for 65 out of the 139 items purchased.[169] These acquisitions were intended to inspire British designers and manufacturers. They also influenced Jones's work: in his landmark design reform publication *The Grammar of Ornament* (1856) his patterns drew heavily on objects from the Great Exhibition including 'embroidered and woven fabrics'. Perhaps surprisingly, his next major project was to decorate the Crystal Palace when it moved to a permanent home in Sydenham – this included no Indian Court or Indian-influenced designs.

Professor John Forbes Royle, an East India Company employee, was the superintendent of the Indian Court. He was a pioneer in the field of economic botany, which promoted the study of crops that would produce the highest commercial yield. Therefore, his Indian Court included displays of fabrics and dyestuffs such as cotton, indigo and Bengal madder plants, with the aim of enticing manufacturers to purchase the raw materials in bulk. This had the mutually beneficial effect of opening new markets for the East India Company. Beyond the raw products, the displays of finished art manufactures, many of which were made with Indian dyes, were particularly popular with visitors. One critic waxed lyrically about the Court: 'India the glorious glowing land, the gorgeous and the beautiful ... the brightest jewel in Victoria's crown ... We gaze upon the myriad of objects, rare and beautiful, which she contributes, and our thoughts wander back to the day when she was free and powerful.'[170] As Laura Kriegel has observed, the ivory throne at the centre of one display, shown in a coloured lithograph, is empty, inviting visitors to reflect on the subdued 'jewel' in the British Empire's crown.

India was a producer and exporter both of colourful finished textiles – wool, silk and above all cotton – and the raw dyestuffs – mainly vegetable-based, but also animal and mineral in origin – that were used to colour them. Luxurious Kashmir (cashmere) shawls, woven from the finest goat's wool, arrived first in Europe as expensive gifts from Indian rulers. They became sought-after accessories for the European elite in the late eighteenth century and remained highly fashionable until the 1870s. In 1846 the East India Company signed the Treaty of Amritsar with Raja Gulab Singh which established the state of Jammu and Kashmir, a region which produced these shawls. As part of the treaty, Raja Gulab Singh agreed to acknowledge 'the supremacy of the British government' and to present the government annually with 'twelve perfect shawl

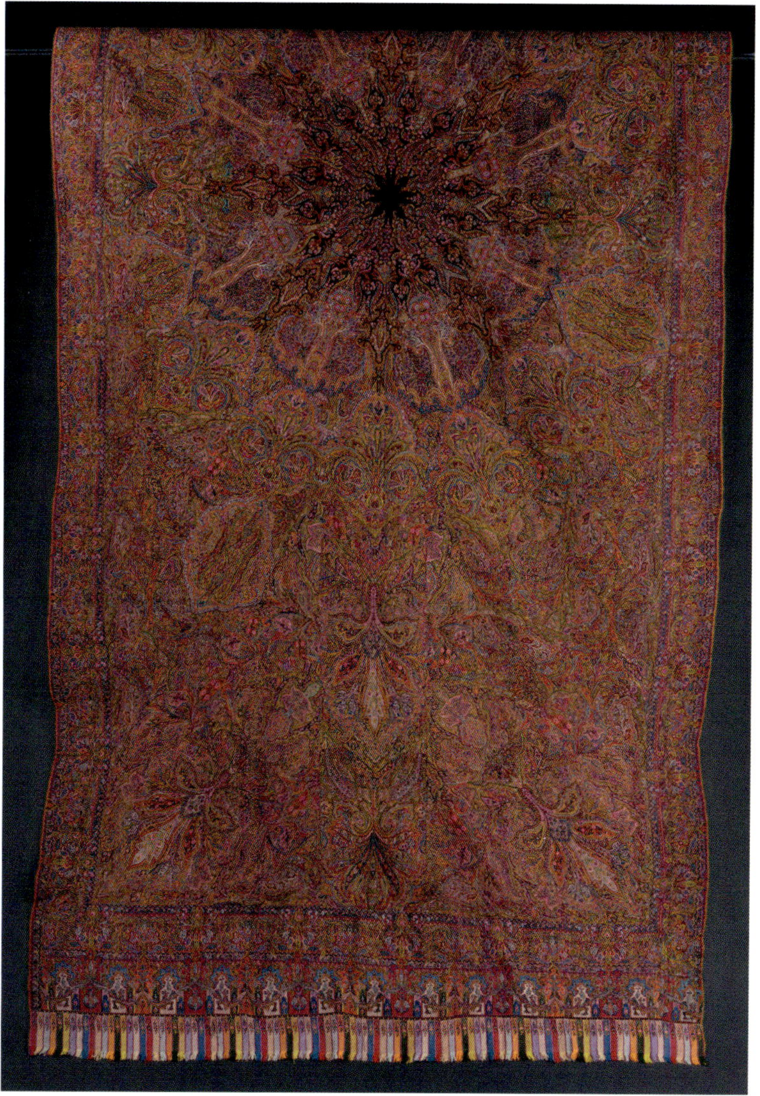

Fig. 142 Kashmir long shawl, 'doruka' type, *c.*1870, woven goat's wool with embroidered accents, vegetable and aniline dyes. One of three pairs of shawls presented annually to the British government by the Maharaja of Jammu and Kashmir and passed on to Queen Victoria. Joan Hart collection

goats of approved breed (six male and six female), and three pairs of Kashmir shawls'. The government passed the shawls on to Queen Victoria. However, as the queen maintained a strict policy of only wearing British-made clothing in public, she seems never to have worn them (fig. 142).

India's traditional dominance in textile production was already under threat by the time of the Great Exhibition. British textile manufacturers were quickly able to copy and mass produce the distinctive colour combinations and stylised patterns of Kashmir shawls. Victorian middle class women were soon able to wear shawls woven in Norwich and Paisley on modern jacquard looms that were a fraction of the price of the original designs from India. Postcolonial theorists such as Homi K. Bhabha later pointed to the complete inversion of the shawl market, from Indian luxury good to British industrial product, in his concept of colonial mimicry.[171] This mimicry was an expression of British desires to imitate Indian colours but also to control the country and ultimately, deplete its resources. In Wilkie Collins's novel *Armadale* (1864–6), the main character Lydia Gwilt is described in several passages wearing a red paisley shawl. The shawl becomes a metaphor for her anxieties, a cheap imitation of the 'real thing' and a haunting reference to the Indian Uprising of 1857 which brought down the East Indian Company and established formal British rule on the subcontinent.[172]

Crippling import duties on Indian textiles coupled with favourable rates for British exports to India deliberately furthered this reversal of textile supremacy. Cheap, mass produced British cloth flooded into Indian markets, devastating many of its established textile centres. The introduction of synthetic aniline dyes in the late 1850s had an equally devastating effect. Dyestuffs such as kermes, madder, fustic, kutch (the traditional source of khaki) and, above all, indigo were highly valuable cash crops. Farmers were forced to grow indigo over necessary foodstuffs for British plantation owners. This led to the Indigo Revolt of 1859, when thousands of Bengali *ryots* (peasant farmers) refused to grow indigo and attacked factories in an attempt to improve contracts and working conditions (fig. 143).[173] However, the twinned factors of technological progress and capitalism hampered their efforts, even if the uprising provided a nominal victory. Synthetic dyes were cheaper and easier to use than traditional vegetable dyes. They were aggressively promoted in India by German dye manufacturers such as AGFA, the predecessor of Bayer. Eventually, the introduction of synthetic indigo in 1897 by the German firm BASF led within a decade to the complete collapse of the local indigo industry in Bengal.

A remarkably colourful Kashmir shawl presented to Queen Victoria in the 1870s uses more than 20 different dyes, including many anilines, and admirably demonstrates how the new synthetic dyes were adopted and used by traditional Indian makers.

The Indian Uprising in 1857 against the oppressive rule of the East India Company deeply shocked British society. In his lecture 'The Deteriorative Powers of Conventional Art over Nations', given at the South Kensington Museum in March 1858, John Ruskin went so far as to link the 'moral baseness' of the recent uprising with the nature of Indian art itself. He began with apparent praise:

> Among the models set before you in this institution, and in the others established throughout the kingdom for the teaching of design, there are, I suppose, none in their kind more admirable than the decorated works of India. They are, indeed, in all materials capable of colour, wool, marble, or metal, almost inimitable in their delicate application of divided hue, and fine arrangement of fantastic line.[174]

However, while Ruskin admitted it was 'quite true' that the art of India was 'delicate and refined', it had 'one curious character distinguishing it from all other art of equal merit in design – it never represents a natural fact ... It either forms its compositions out of meaningless fragments of colour and flowings of line; or if it represents any living creature, it represents that creature under some distorted and monstrous form. To all the facts and forms of nature it wilfully

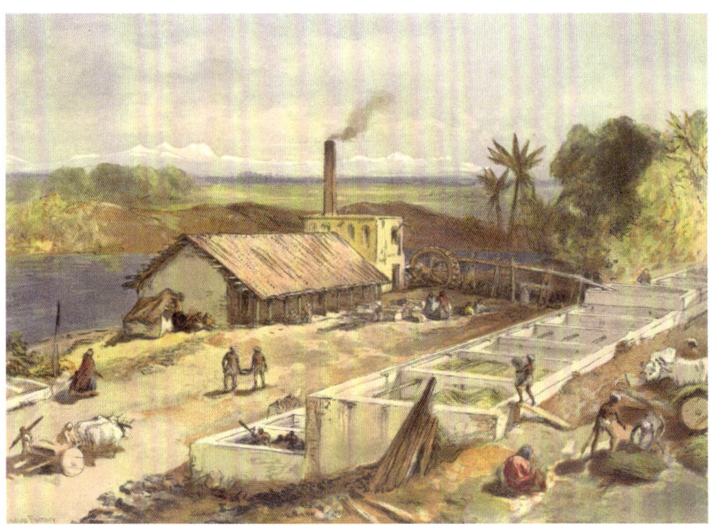

Fig. 143 Watercolour of an indigo factory in Bengal by William Simpson dated 1863

and resolutely opposes itself'.[175] Ruskin's racist conclusion was that this perceived rejection of nature and the use of 'conventional' stylised motifs and patterns, reflected wider moral failings that led to the 'cruelty' and 'barbarism' of the 'Mutiny'.[176]

The legacies of the Uprising were felt long after its events. At the International Exhibition of 1862, the Indian Court was diminished from its position in 1851. Situated in a first floor side gallery and with less than half the display space, it was far less conspicuous. In contrast to the colourful prints made in 1851, no images of the Court were produced for public circulation. It was the aniline coloured textiles of Manchester, Glasgow, Mulhouse and Lyon that captured the public's attention.

India's increasing prominence in imperial rhetoric brought it back into favour in later years. Following the Prince of Wales's tour of India in 1875, the British Court at the International Exhibition of 1876 in Vienna was dubbed the Prince of Wales Pavilion and featured numerous objects he brought back from his trip including a jewelled peacock pen stand and a gold enamelled, diamond and emerald encrusted crown from Lucknow. Themes of Indian craftsmanship and their innate sense of colour was back in circulation amongst European observers.

The Prince of Wales's tour of India had been planned for nearly 20 years. Since 1861, a prophecy had circulated in the Punjab region that 'a king would come from west to east' and 'rule the Country without dipping the end of his little finger in blood'.[177] Proactive advisers who were keen to avoid another Uprising had wanted to send out a member of the British royal family to quell a potential rebellion. However, Indians thought that the prophesised king would be a member of the deposed Sikh dynasty, who had been living in England since 1853. Duleep Singh was one of the most prominent Indian people in Victorian Britain.

Duleep Singh's royal lineage – he was the son of Maharajah Ranjit Singh and his wife Jind Kaur – and the geopolitical machinations that brought him to Britain in 1854 have been explored in several biographical accounts. These attest to the considerable influence Singh retains in Punjabi and Sikh culture. However, his life in Britain was equally storied, partly because of his complicated relationship with Queen Victoria. In her diary, the queen wrote of their first meeting in July 1854:

> we received the young Maharajah Duleep Singh, the son of Rangeit Singh, who was deposed by us, on the annexation of the Punjaub [sic] ... He is 16 & extremely handsome, speaks English perfectly, & has a pretty, graceful & dignified manner. He was beautifully dressed & covered with diamonds ... I always feel so much for these poor deposed Indian Princes.[178]

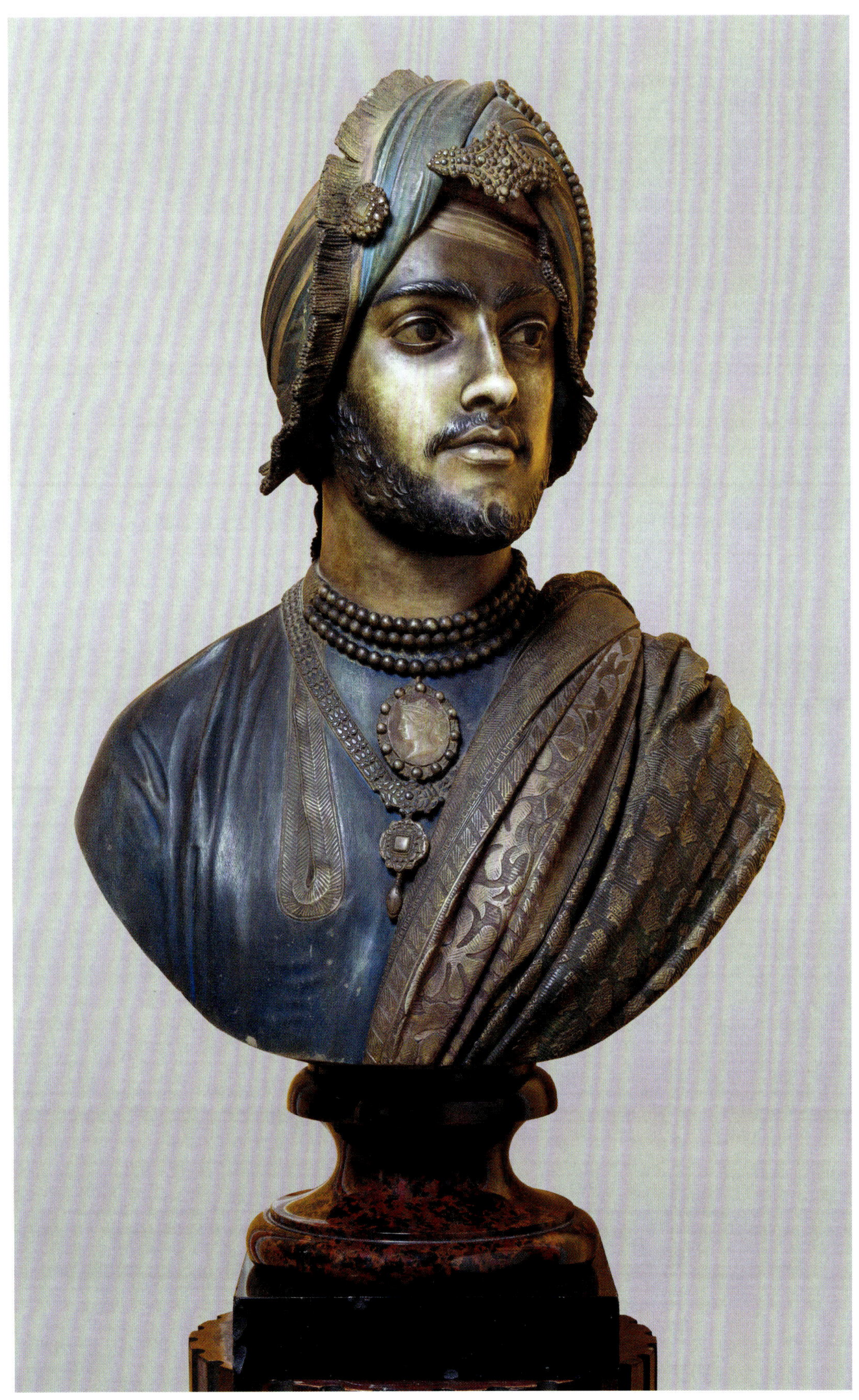

Opposite: Fig. 144 Maharajah Duleep Singh (1838–1893) by Baron Pietro Carlo Giovanni Battista Marochetti (1805–1867). Marble and watercolour. Private Collection. Classé au titre des monuments historiques par arrêté du 24 janvier 2002, N° d'inventaire Palissy : PM78001187

The queen acknowledged Duleep Singh's status as a deposed maharajah, and their equal footing as members of the anointed royal elite. This explains the number of artworks she commissioned from important royal portraitists, as well as the signifiers of his status employed in these works. These signifiers included colourful attire and opulent accessories, which soon became a trope in written and visual descriptions of him.

In 1856, the queen commissioned a bust of Singh for Prince Albert's 37th birthday (fig. 144). A favourite sculptor of the royal family ever since he moved to England from Paris in 1848, Baron Pietro Carlo Giovanni Battista Marochetti used the commission to promote his own views on one of the prevailing artistic debates of the day: the subject of colouring sculpture. As has been seen, the controversial rediscovery of ancient polychromy in the 1850s sparked a number of artistic responses by British sculptors.

Marochetti came down firmly on the side of colouring sculpture and according to diarist Henry Greville was 'full of the subject' as he worked on the commission.[179] Marochetti modelled the bust after several sittings with Singh, and by referring to a portrait by Franz Xaver Winterhalter. William Henry Millais, brother of the Pre-Raphaelite John, was brought in to tint the bust in watercolour – although rumours circulated in the press that Marochetti had used coffee to colour the skin.[180]

Marochetti's polychromatic representation of Singh inevitably clashed with contemporary anthropological concerns about representing racial difference through skin colour. The bust is an orientalising depiction of the maharajah. One critic said that it had the 'sensitive intimacy of a portrait and the disturbing tranquillity of a Ganges' god'.[181] Marochetti's bust is certainly concerned with depicting racial difference and evokes Singh's subjugation, but it is also an image that engages with the possibilities of a colourful expression of royalty and monarchy in Britain, which was a marked contrast to the typically sober dress of Victoria and Albert.

One critic remarked that the bust was 'truthful not only to nature in the flesh tints, but accurate to the tailor's art in the colouring of the robes and the pattern on the turban. Indeed, this last effort of Baron Marochetti's genius is sufficient to charm the heart of a thorough-going mediaevalist and to drive the lovers of the Phidian school to suicidal despair'.[182] Through his colourful sartorial presentation, particularly the emblematic turban, the portrait bust exudes confidence: Singh's strong gaze looks outwards towards the nostalgic, imagined horizon of his birthright. His gaze perhaps also indicates a level of resistance that was concealed in 1856, but which he was later able to express by disavowing his coerced conversion to Christianity and re-embracing Sikhism.

Unfortunately, when Marochetti delivered the polychrome bust to Queen Victoria in August 1856 she remarked that it was 'entirely spoilt by being coloured'. She returned the sculpture and Marochetti duly replaced it with a white marble version.

3

COLOUR FOR COLOUR'S SAKE

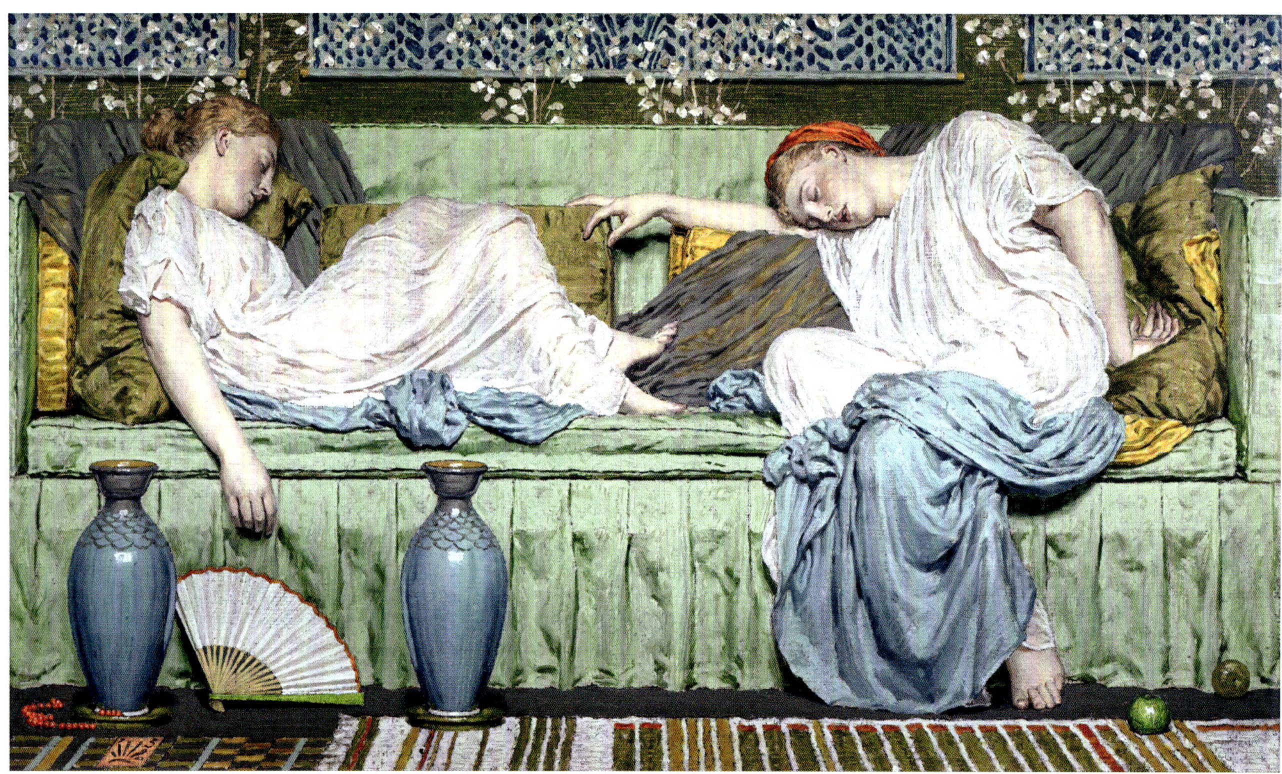

Fig. 145 Albert Moore (1841–1893), *Apples*, 1875. Oil on canvas. Private collection

Colour for Colour's Sake

Stefano Evangelista and Charlotte Ribeyrol

In May 1881, the French art critic and collector Théodore Duret visited an exhibition at the Grosvenor Gallery, a private gallery on New Bond Street founded by Sir Coutts Lindsay and directed by Joseph Comyns Carr. In this new venue of the British avant-garde, Duret particularly admired James McNeill Whistler's *Harmony in Grey and Green, Miss Cicely Alexander* (fig. 160, p. 182) which, he claimed, extolled '*le charme de la couleur en soi*': the charm of colour for colour's sake.[1] And yet this chromophilia, Duret also noted, had been the cause of controversy, forcing the painter to wage 'terrible battles' against his enemies. This was an allusion to the Ruskin-Whistler trial sparked by the gallery's first exhibition in 1877, during which Ruskin accused Whistler, in his painting *Nocturne in Black and Gold, The Falling Rocket* (fig. 146), of 'flinging a pot of paint in the public's face'.[2] For Ruskin, Whistler's materialist handling of colour – made simpler by the recent invention of collapsible metal tubes (fig. 147) – had become a way of deceiving the public by pushing art beyond narrative and representation, aiming instead to capture elusive notions of 'harmonies' and 'atmosphere'. Fearing that Ruskin's comments would damage his reputation, Whistler sued the critic for libel. As Ruskin did not attend the court hearings, the stage was left entirely to Whistler, whose witty defence convinced both audience and jury of the validity of his aesthetics, even if, in the end, he was only awarded a farthing by way of compensation. By spectacularly staging a conflict between aesthetics and morality, the trial revealed the rift between the new avant-gardes and Ruskin's ideal of 'Truth to Nature'. The new generation of painters, writers, musicians and designers no longer adhered to the ethical stance of the ageing critic, which had shaped public discussions of art for almost half a century. Instead, they celebrated 'art for art's sake' – that is to say, in Whistler's words, art 'independent of all clap-trap', appealing 'to the artistic sense of eye or ear' only.[3]

Whistler believed that in the arts the senses should prevail over any 'message' – a stance that was underscored by his decision to call his works 'Nocturnes', 'Arrangements' and 'Harmonies', titles which at the same time gestured towards synaesthesia. Colour, which in itself does not resemble anything, was to play a crucial role in freeing art from both representation and morality. Instead of believing, like Ruskin, that hues were 'sacred' or 'sanctifying', the aesthetes – as the new generation called themselves, in order to emphasise the primacy of perception (*aesthesis* in Greek) in art – selected colours purely for their artistic or sensual effects. As Oscar Wilde put it, the 'recognition of the primary importance of the sensuous element in art, this love of art for art's sake, is the point in which we of the younger school have made a departure

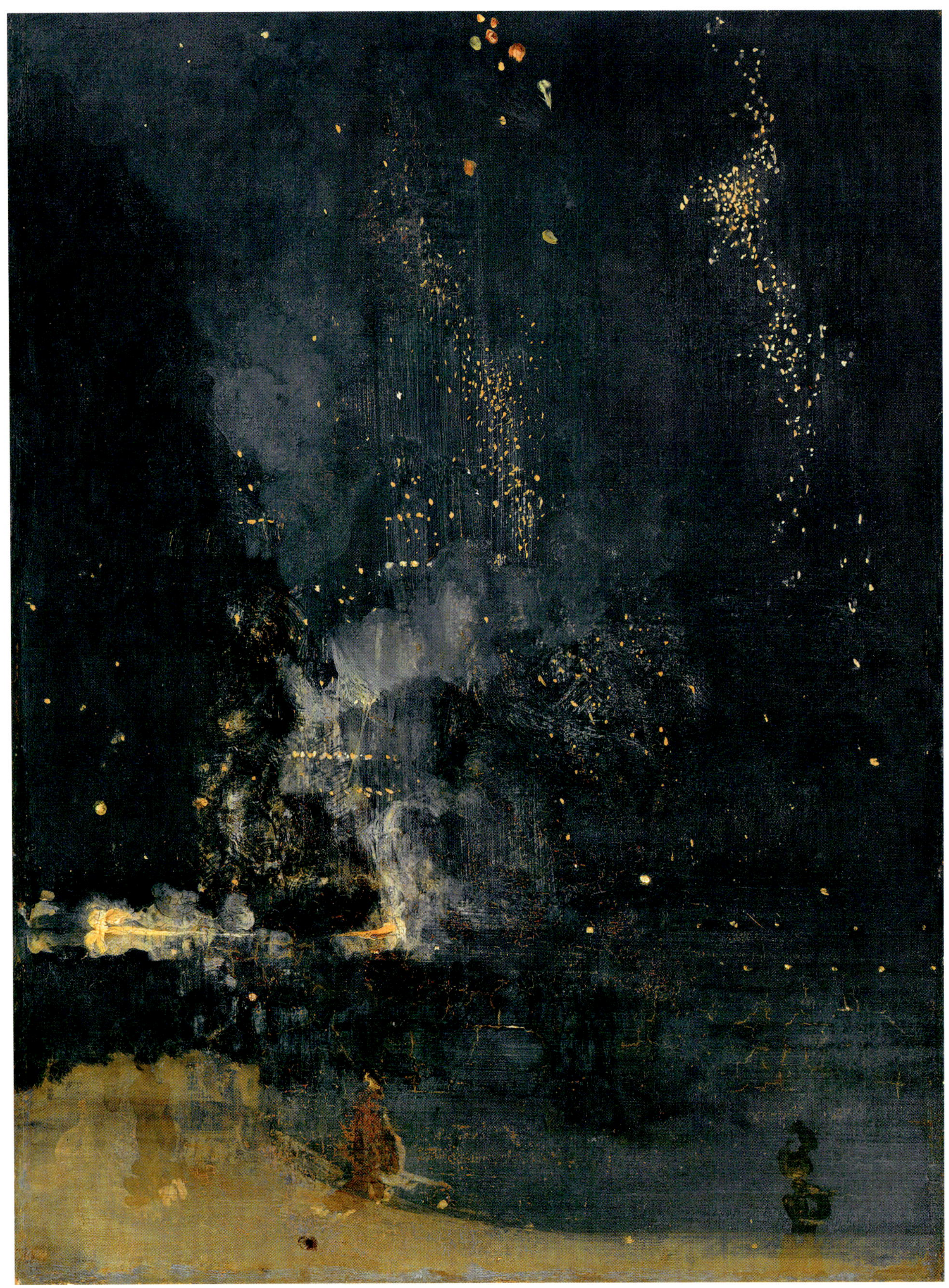

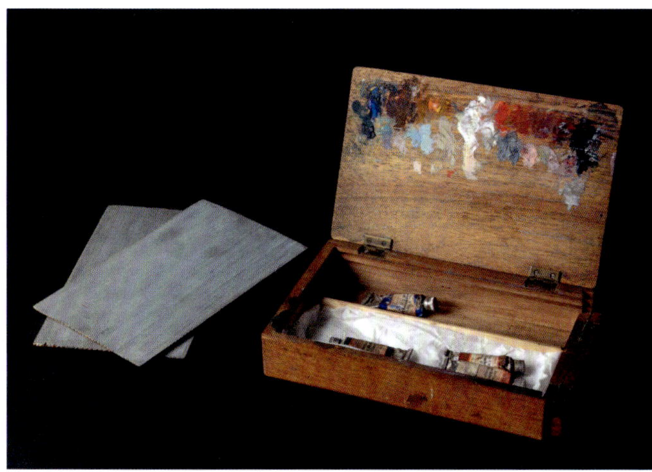

from the teaching of Mr. Ruskin'.[4] The idea of art for art's sake had been imported from France. In particular, the poet and critic Théophile Gautier's celebration of *'l'Art pour l'Art'* – a vision of art divorced from the ugliness of utility – was seized upon in England by the poet A C Swinburne. A close friend of Swinburne, Whistler – who had trained in Paris under the guidance of Gustave Courbet – translated the new ideas into pictorial form.

The emergence of colour for colour's sake was also stimulated by Japanese art, which was first popularised in Europe at the 1862 International Exhibition in London. The exhibition sparked a craze for all things Japanese on both sides of the Channel, which brought an unprecedented number of Japanese objects into Western collections and exercised a major influence on the development of fashion and design. Parisian jeweller Alexis Falize was among the first to integrate vibrant flower and birds motifs inspired by Japanese prints in his precious enamels exhibited in the 1867 Paris Universal Exhibition[5] (fig. 148). In the following years, *japonisme*, as the new taste soon became known, provided artists with ways to challenge Western

Opposite: Fig. 146 James McNeill Whistler (1834–1903), *Nocturne in Black and Gold, The Falling Rocket*, 1872–7. Oil on canvas. Detroit Institute of Art, 46.309

Above: Fig. 147 James McNeill Whistler's paintbox, paint tubes and watercolour palette, The Hunterian, University of Glasgow, GLAHA: 54147, 54156, 54148

Right: Fig. 148 Alexis Falize (1811–1898), Necklace, *c.*1867. Cloisonné enamel and gold. Ashmolean Museum, WA1964.29.1-4

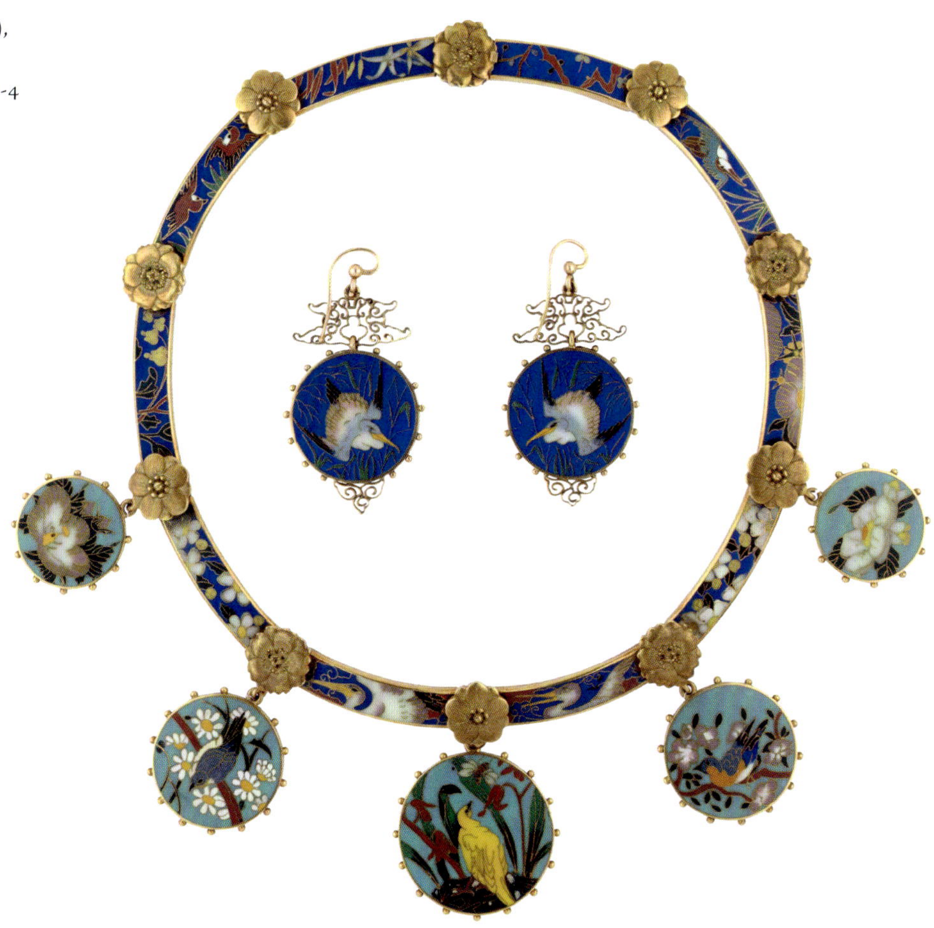

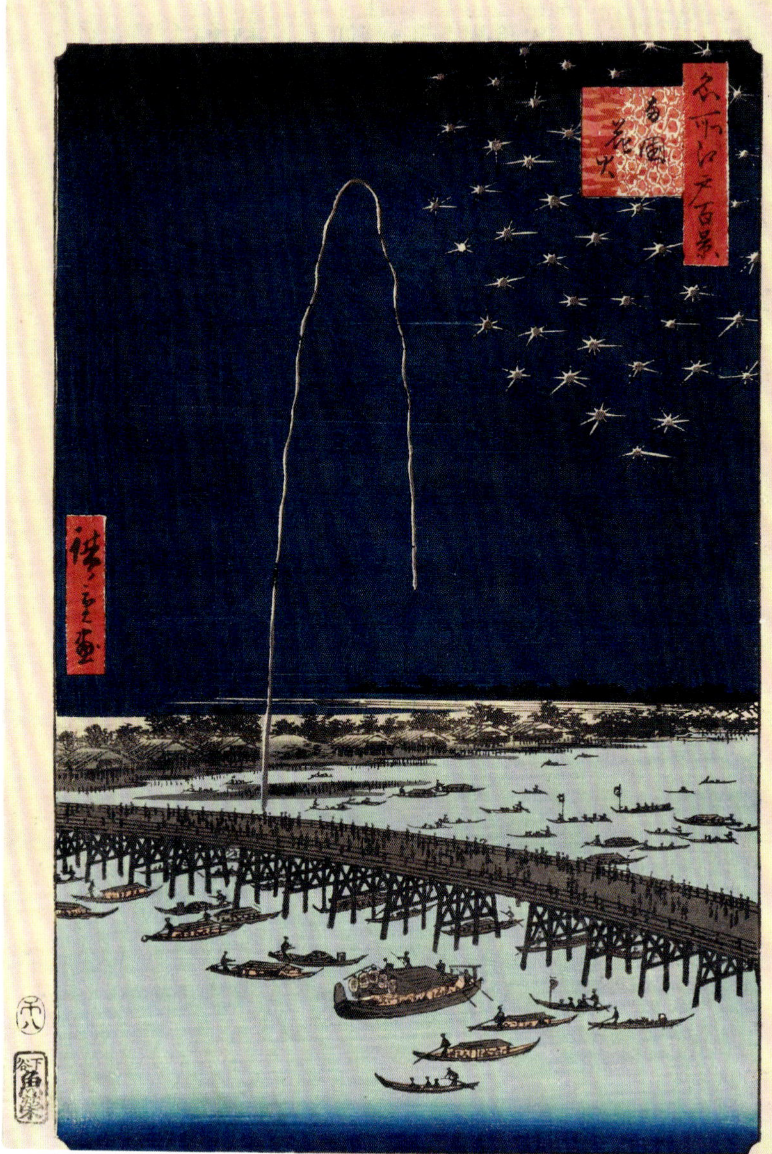

Fig. 149 Utagawa Hiroshige (1797–1858), *Fireworks at Ryōgoku Bridge*, 1858, from *One Hundred Famous Views of Edo.* Colour woodcut. Ashmolean Museum, EAX.4365

rules of representation, as can be seen in works by Whistler and Albert Moore. Whistler, who collected *ukiyo-e* prints (fig. 149), used Japanese art to inspire his innovative rendition of European urban settings. Ruskin failed to appreciate the fashionable aesthetics embodied in the prints of Hiroshige and Hokusai, which, with their flat colours and unusual perspectives, proved difficult to read in terms of traditional Western art history. In this respect Whistler's *japoniste* treatment of Ruskin's beloved Venice in his *Nocturne: Blue and Gold, St Mark's, Venice*, painted after the libel trial, may be seen as provoking the critic further. A fusion of aesthetics of *japonisme* and art for art's sake also pervades Moore's three paintings of 1875: *Apples, Beads* and *A Sofa* (figs 145, 150, 151), which represent the same two sleeping female figures in a frieze-like composition, 'dramatiz[ing] the irrelevance of "subject" in Moore's pursuit of purely aesthetic questions' and 'new chromatic combinations'.[6]

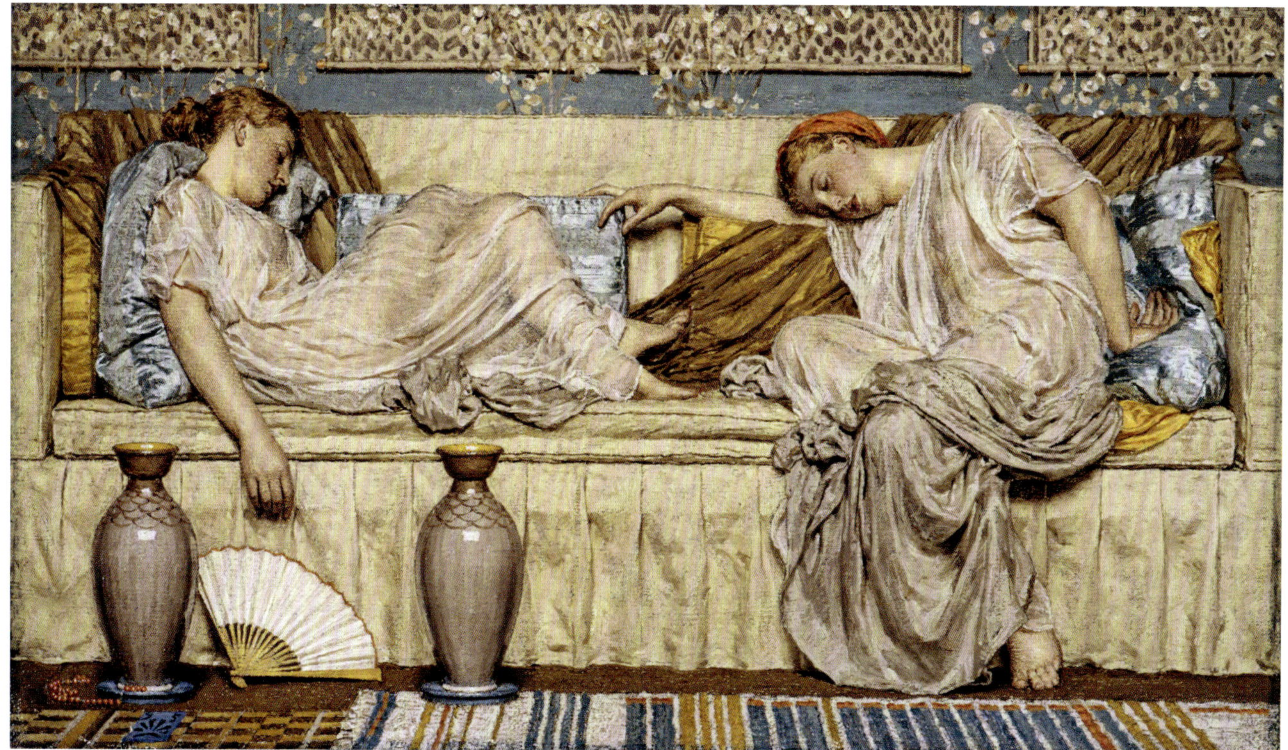

Fig. 150 Albert Moore (1841–1893), *Beads*, 1875. Oil on canvas. National Galleries of Scotland, NG 1019

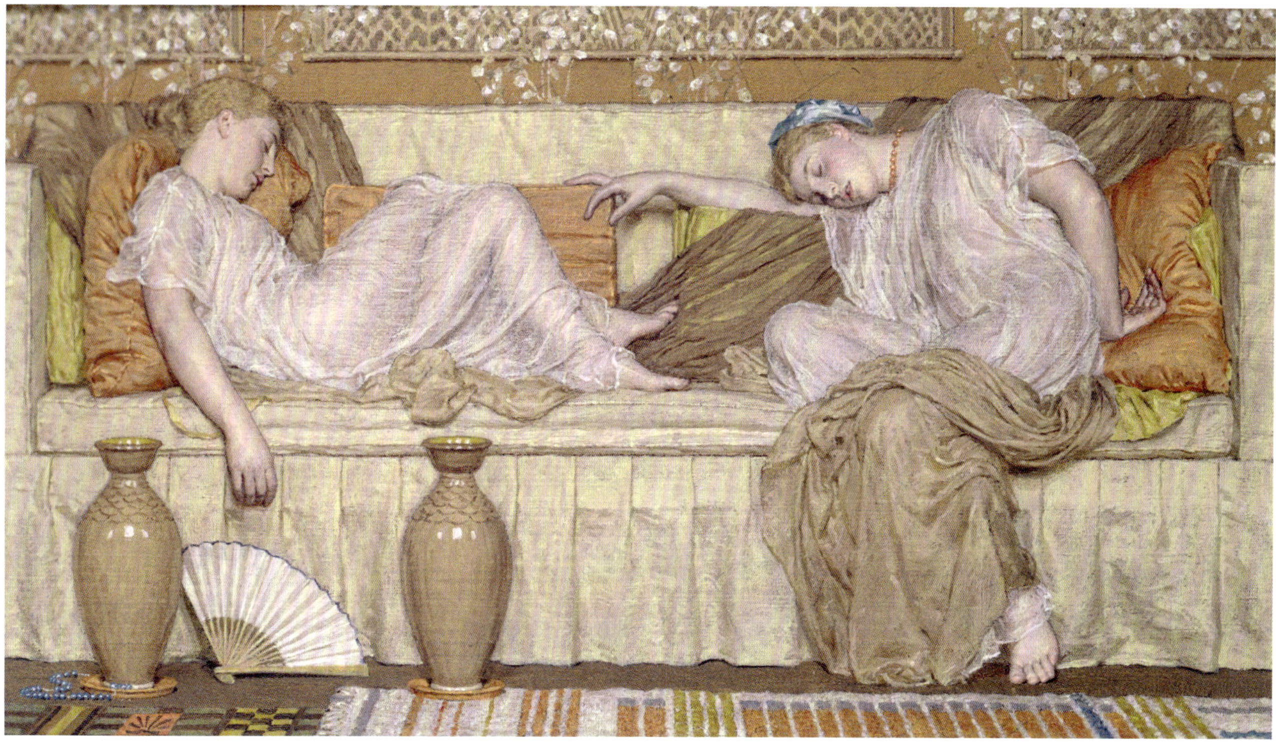

Fig. 151 Albert Moore (1841–1893), *A Sofa*, 1875. Oil on canvas. Private collection

Fascinated by Japan's exotic appeal, aesthetes projected their own artistic creed onto this far-away country, which they idealised as a homeland of the arts that offered a stark, welcome contrast to grim, industrial Britain. In his provocative 'Ten O'Clock' lecture, delivered in London on 20 February 1885, Whistler held up 'the fan of Hokusai' as a symbol of art for art's sake.[7] A few years later, the writer Lafcadio Hearn, who moved to Japan in 1890 and became an influential cultural mediator, described Japan as 'the land of perfect good taste in chromatics'.[8] Like other Western travellers, Hearn was particularly captivated by Japanese blues, not only as used by artists in *ukiyo-e* prints and porcelain, but also in traditional indigo-dyed fabrics visible in Japanese clothes

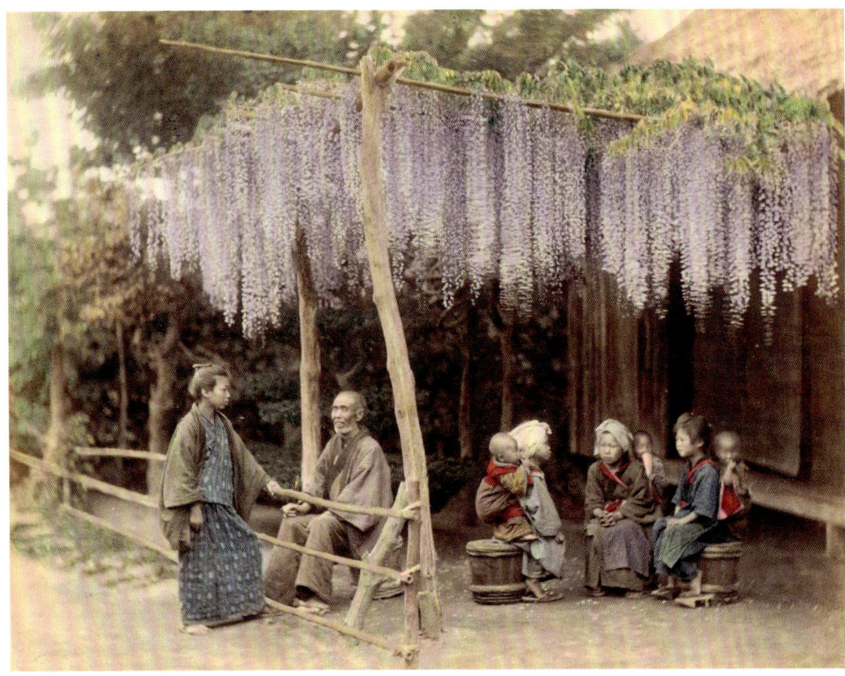

Fig. 152 Raimund von Stillfried-Ratenicz (1839–1911), *Wisteria in Flower*, *c.*1870s. Pitt Rivers Museum, University of Oxford, 1998.99.3

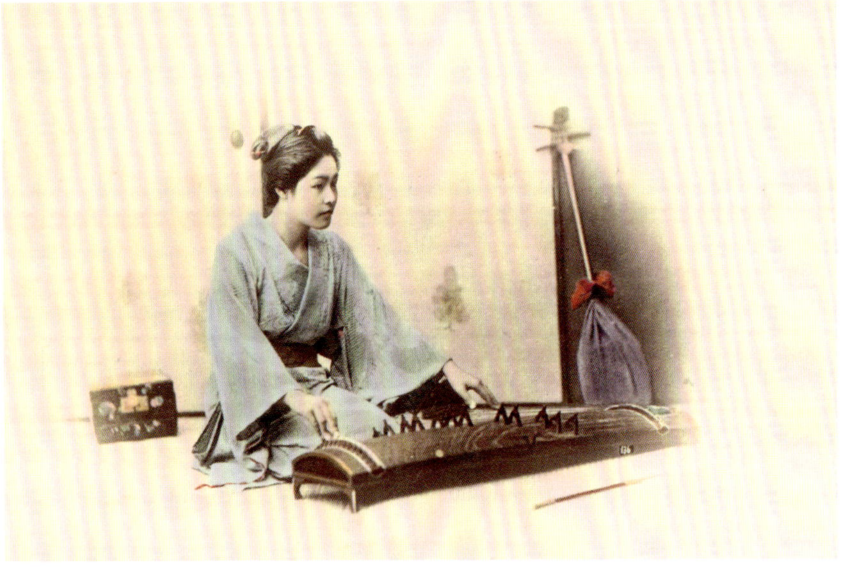

Fig. 153 Raimund von Stillfried-Ratenicz (1839–1911), *Japanese Woman with Koto*, *c.*1870s. Pitt Rivers Museum, University of Oxford, 1998.99.34

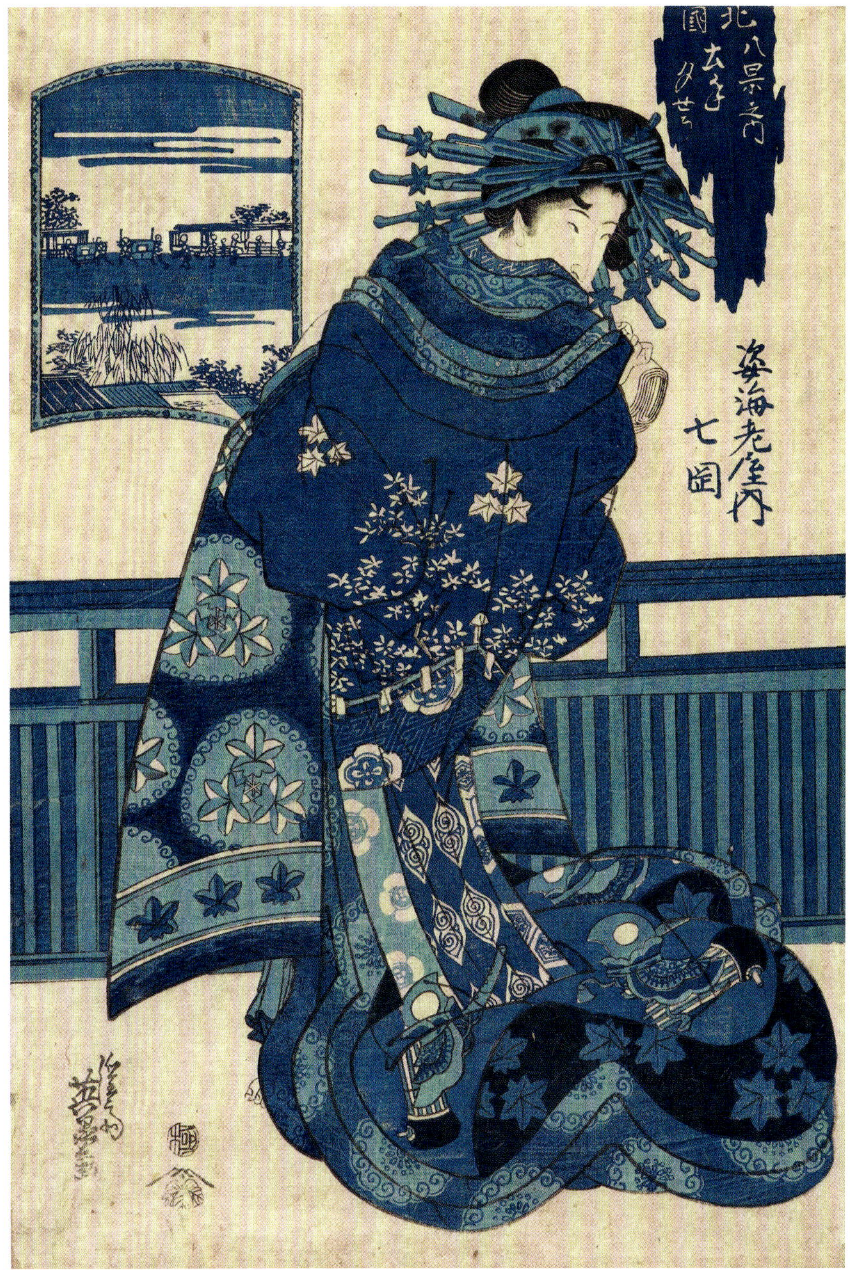

Fig. 154 Keisai Eisen (1790–1848), *The Courtesan Nanaoka of the Sugata Ebi House*, 1810–45. Ashmolean Museum, EA1958.230

and fabric shops (fig. 153). In the literature of *japonisme*, Japan was often envisaged as a blue-tinted fairyland; Hearn described the chromatic tone of a typical Japanese vista as 'given by bluish greys above and dark blues below, sharply relieved by numerous small details of white and cool yellow'.[9] Indeed *aizuri-e*, a technique of Japanese colour printing that became prized in the West, consisted of realising images entirely through different gradations of blue ink, as seen in Keisai Eisen's *The Courtesan Nanaoka of the Sugata Ebi House* (fig. 154). Blue prints were strongly exotic to nineteenth-century Western eyes: they seemed to embody something exquisitely Japanese that had been jealously, almost magically, preserved from the past, free of the contaminating influence

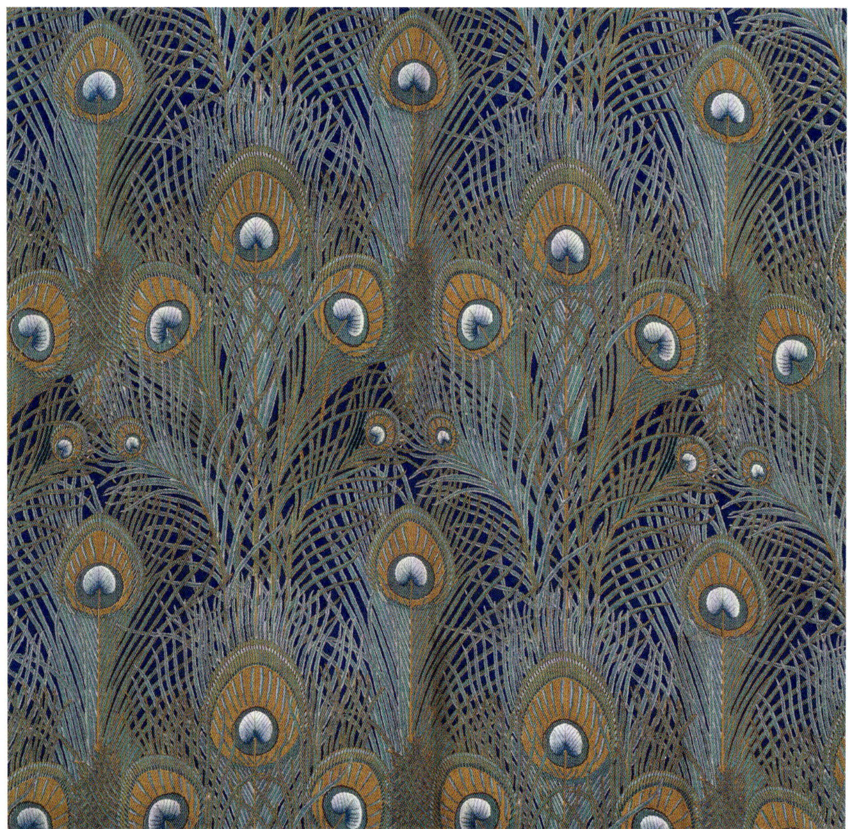

Left: Fig. 155 Hera fabric by Arthur Silver (?) after Christopher Dresser (1834–1904) for Liberty & Co., *c.*1887. Furnishing fabric of roller-printed cotton. Victoria and Albert Museum, London, T.50-1953

Opposite: Fig. 156 James McNeill Whistler (1834–1903), *The Yellow Room*, *c.*1883–4. Watercolour and bodycolour. Lent by the Metropolitan Museum of Art, New York, Marguerite and Frank A. Cosgrove Jr. Fund, 2017, 2017.664

of modern world trade. However, we now know that they were produced using imported Prussian Blue, and were therefore a product of the global movement of pigments. In any case, themes of pleasure and ephemeral beauty favoured by *ukiyo-e* artists chimed powerfully with the British aesthetes' belief that art should first and foremost appeal to the senses.

Originally a mark of the refined tastes of the elite, the blend of aestheticism and *japonisme* found a successful commercial outlet in London department store Liberty & Co., which benefitted from the collaboration of leading designers including Christopher Dresser and E.W. Godwin (fig. 155). Both men were extremely knowledgeable about colour and wrote about its key function in creating aesthetic effects in the interior. In 1877, Godwin was commissioned by Whistler to design his house in Tite Street, Chelsea. Known as the White House, this mansion was meant to embody the ideal of the 'house beautiful', reflecting the refined artistic and cosmopolitan sensibility of its owner. Although the White House was destroyed in the 1960s, a watercolour of its 'Yellow Room' (fig. 156) testifies to its daring chromatic scheme which one sceptical visitor compared to the experience of being 'inside an egg'.[10] In the painting, the purple dress of Maud Franklin, the painter's mistress, stands out against the yellow background, the blue and white china (figs 157, 158) and the Japanese fan decorating the mantlepiece. The White House was the ultimate expression of the fact that, for the aesthetes, the pursuit of beauty did not stop at the fine arts, but constituted a way of life.

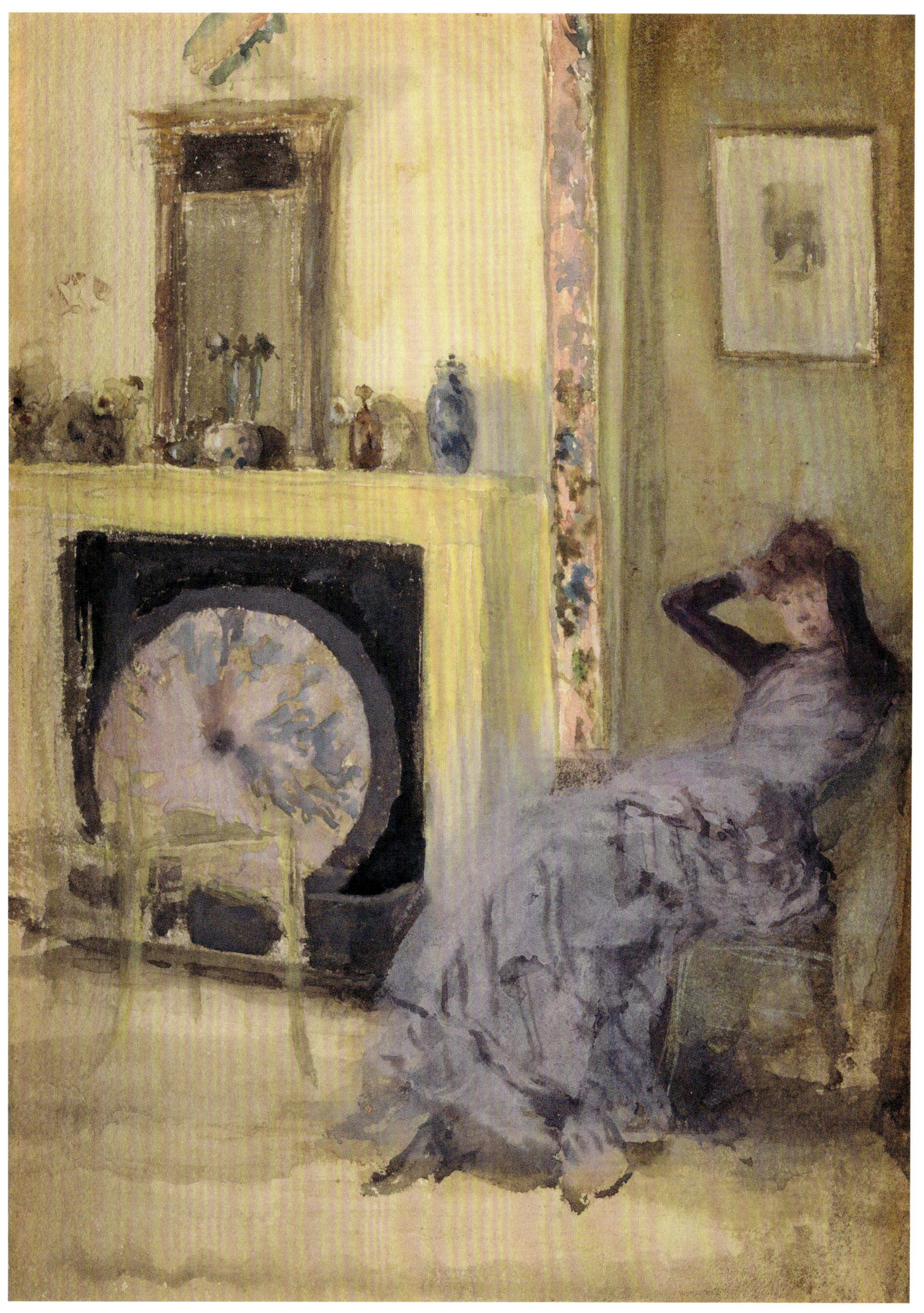

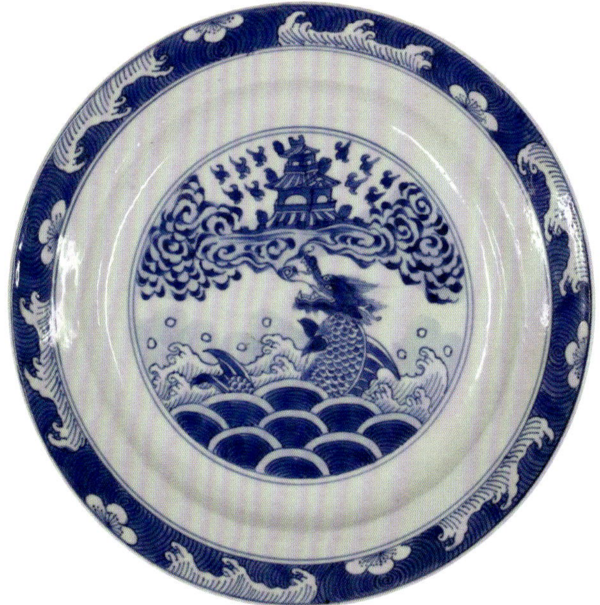

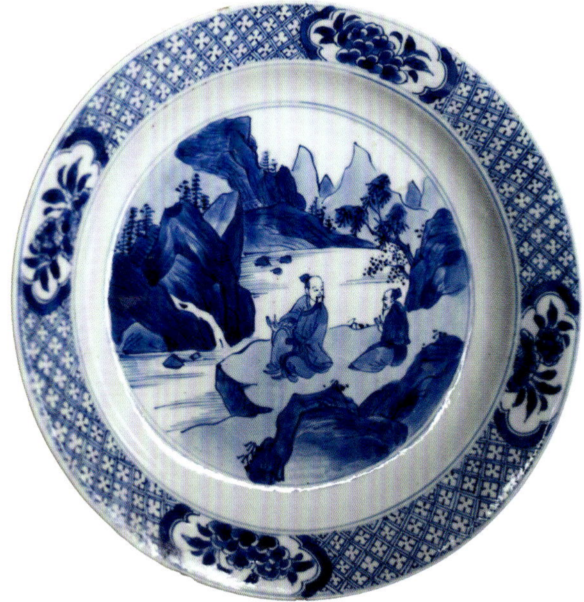

Figs 157, 158 Chinese plates from Whistler's collection, Kangxi period (1662–1722). Porcelain. The Hunterian, University of Glasgow, GLAHA:54006, GLAHA:54531

Unsurprisingly perhaps, the ideal of the aesthetic life soon attracted public mockery, notably in *Punch* (fig. 159). George Du Maurier (who had trained in Paris with Whistler) introduced the characters of the Cimabue Browns, a typically 'aesthetic' family loosely based on the Morrises and the Comyns Carrs. In a cartoon of 1881 he depicted their 'artistic' little girl, who bears the ridiculously pseudo-leonardesque foreign name of Miss Monna Givronda and closely resembles Whistler's Miss Cicely Alexander (fig. 160), explaining to her matter-of-fact grandfather that she prefers the National Gallery to the zoo and German composers to pantomines on Drury Lane. The scene contrasts the down-to-earth outlook of an old generation of empire builders (the grandfather is said to be 'fresh from Ceylon') with the modern cosmopolitan aestheticism embodied by the domestic interior cluttered with sunflowers, De Morgan ceramics (fig. 161), and a Japanese fan and screen.

The same year, Gilbert and Sullivan's *Patience* premiered at the Opera Comique in London. This satirical operetta soon became associated with Wilde, whose North American lecture tour of 1882 was scheduled to coincide with the American tour of *Patience*. Aesthetic hero Reginald Bunthorne was, however, originally based on Swinburne or Whistler, and more generally on Du Maurier's affected aesthetes in *Punch*. Gilbert's libretto singled out for special mockery the new taste for 'greenery-yallery' inspired by the daring chromatic *décor* of the Grosvenor Gallery.[11] Indeed the two colours had become intimately associated with the aesthetic movement and with a related cultural phenomenon that would soon come to dominate discussions of art and literature: *decadence*. In his influential 1868 essay on Charles Baudelaire, Gautier had defined the style of decadence as 'taking colour from every palette' and

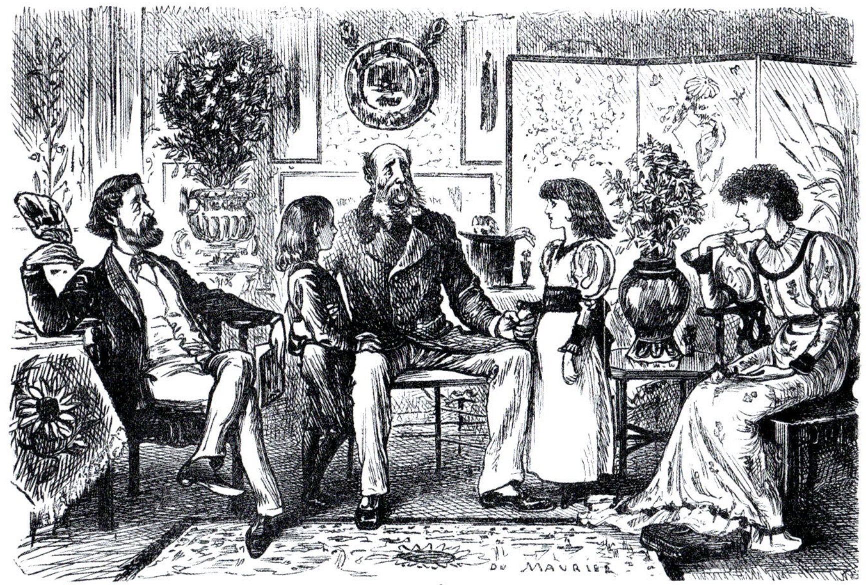

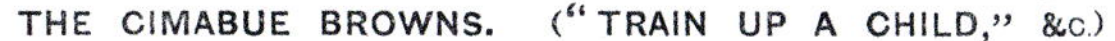

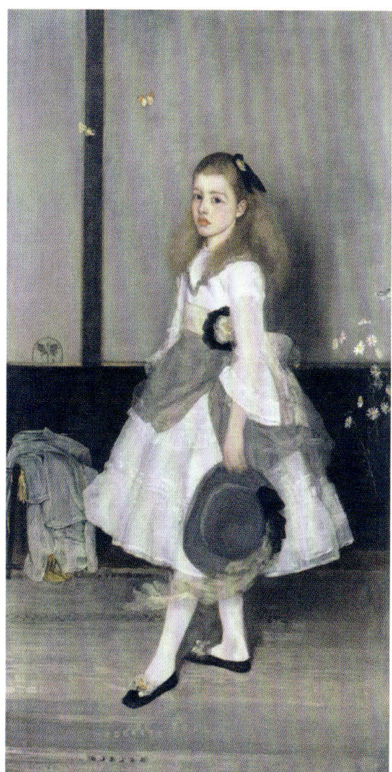

Above left: Fig. 159 George du Maurier (1834–1896), 'The Cimabue Browns. ("Train Up A Child," &c.)', from *Punch*, 22 January 1881

Above right: Fig. 160 James McNeill Whistler (1834–1903), *Harmony in Grey and Green, Miss Cicely Alexander*, 1872–4. Oil on canvas. Tate, N04622

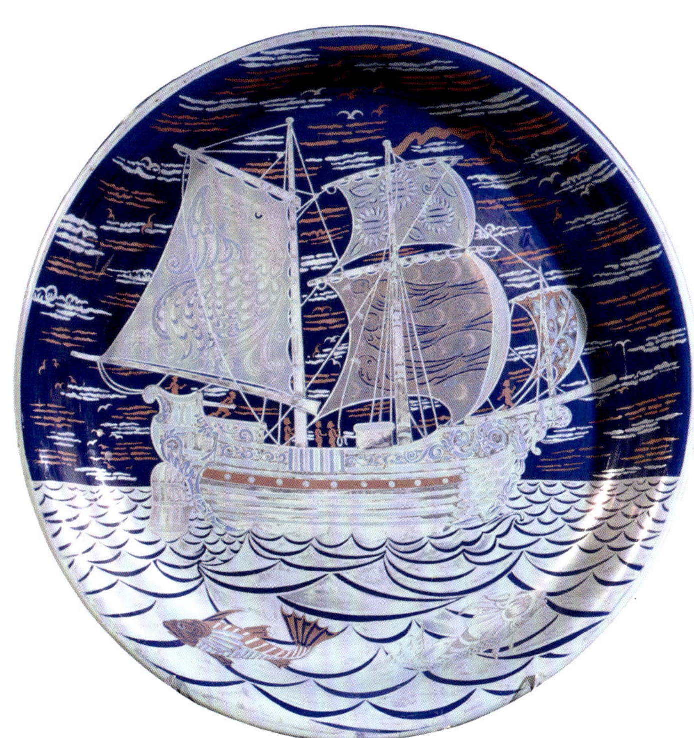

Fig. 161 Moonlight Lustre Galleon Charger by William De Morgan (1839–1917), *c.*1888–1907. Lustre-glazed earthenware. De Morgan Foundation

being reminiscent of 'language already veined with the greenness of decomposition, savouring the Later Roman Empire and the complicated refinements of the Byzantine School, the last form of Greek art fallen into deliquescence'.[12] *Fin-de-siècle* artists seemed to have been particularly drawn to this decadent green, with its complex material history and paradoxical suggestion of both the energy of youth and the discoloration brought about by disease, or the ravaging process of maturation.

Since the Middle Ages green had been regarded as a *couleur maudite*: long shunned by dyers for its chemical instability, it had taken on cultural connotations of subversion and disorder.[13] With the colour revolution and the invention of the first synthetic dyes and pigments, the subversive potential of green was dramatically increased by its potential toxicity. Some of the new vivid greens, like the emerald shade used by the Pre-Raphaelites, had a base of arsenic. The same applied to some fashion items, and particularly to flower wreaths artificially dyed to look greener than nature. In 1861 Matilda Scheurer, a young artificial flower-maker working in London, was reported to have vomited 'green slime' and subsequently died of arsenic poisoning.[14] This event was recorded in the popular press, including in *Punch*, where an 'Arsenic Waltz' cartoon (fig. 162) depicted a *danse macabre* of two skeletons: a man alongside a woman wearing an artificially dyed 'green wreath' on her head. The same arsenic greens were also used in wallpapers which were reported to have caused intoxication in several London homes in the 1860s. These tragedies caused William Morris's own green wallpapers to be viewed with increasing suspicion – his family's fortune had, after all, come from the Devon Great Consols mine, one of the leading producers of copper and arsenic at the time.[15] The scandal took on an international dimension after a report on arsenic poisoning published in the United States in 1874 warned against papered 'walls of death' (fig. 163). Originally indifferent

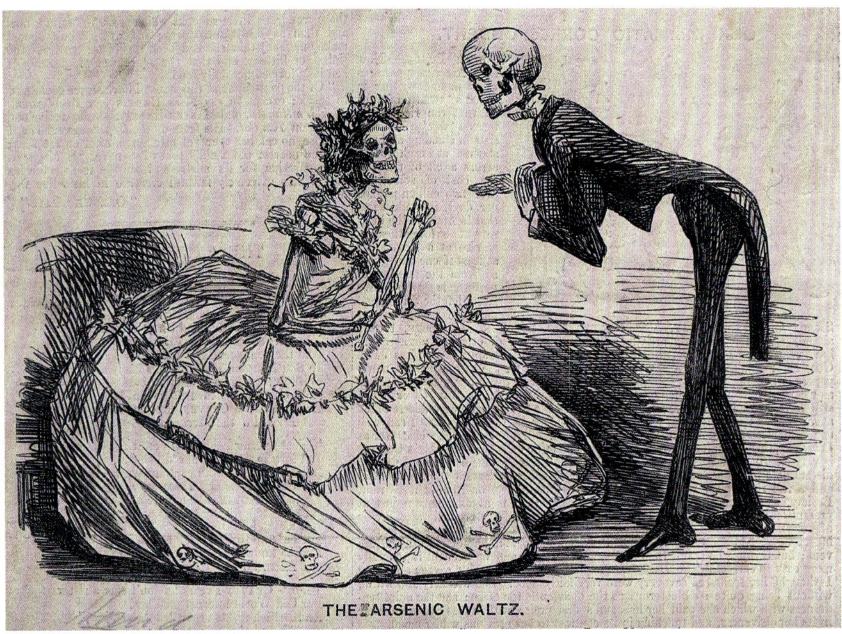

Fig. 162 'The Arsenic Waltz or, The New Dance of Death', from *Punch*, 8 February 1862

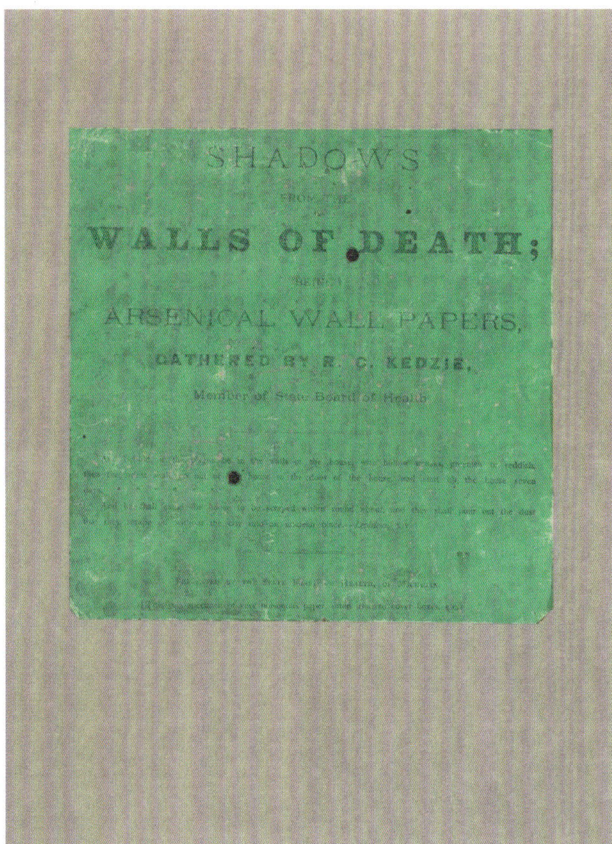

SHADOWS

WALLS OF DEATH;

ARSENICAL WALL PAPERS,

GATHERED BY R. C. KEDZIE,

Member of State Board of Health

Fig. 163 Robert C. Kedzie (1823–1902), *Shadows from the Walls of Death; Facts and Inferences prefacing a Book of Specimens of Arsenical Wall Papers*, 1874, cover and sample page

to the controversy, Morris eventually defended himself by explaining that he only used 'natural and simple' vegetable dyes at his Merton Abbey textile works, in keeping with the precepts advocated by Ruskin and the age-old recipes in Pliny's *Natural History* and Gerard's sixteenth-century *Herball*.[16]

The chromatic scandals of the 1860s and '70s fed into the decadent imagination. Aesthetes turned against nature by repurposing a colour emblematic of life into a decadent symbol of corruption, as exemplified in Joris-Karl Huysmans's *À Rebours* (1884). In this novel, translated into English as either *Against Nature* or *Against the Grain*, the decadent Parisian (anti)hero Des Esseintes experiments with a kaleidoscope of sensual experiences that call into question the relationship between the artistic and the natural. In one of the most memorable episodes, Des Esseintes buys a tortoise in order to set off the colours of one of his Oriental carpets. Disappointed by the result, he covers the animal's carapace with gold and encrusts it with coloured gemstones, effectively turning the creature into a work of art and ultimately causing its death. Des Esseintes's bizarre creation is echoed in some of the experiments undertaken by jewellers during this period, which blurred the line between nature and artifice. The same year *À Rebours* was published, the Portuguese ambassador to London presented Foreign Secretary Lord Granville with a piece of jewellery made up of the bodies of 46 iridescent green South American weevils.[17] Granville only agreed to take the beetles and subsequently commissioned the London

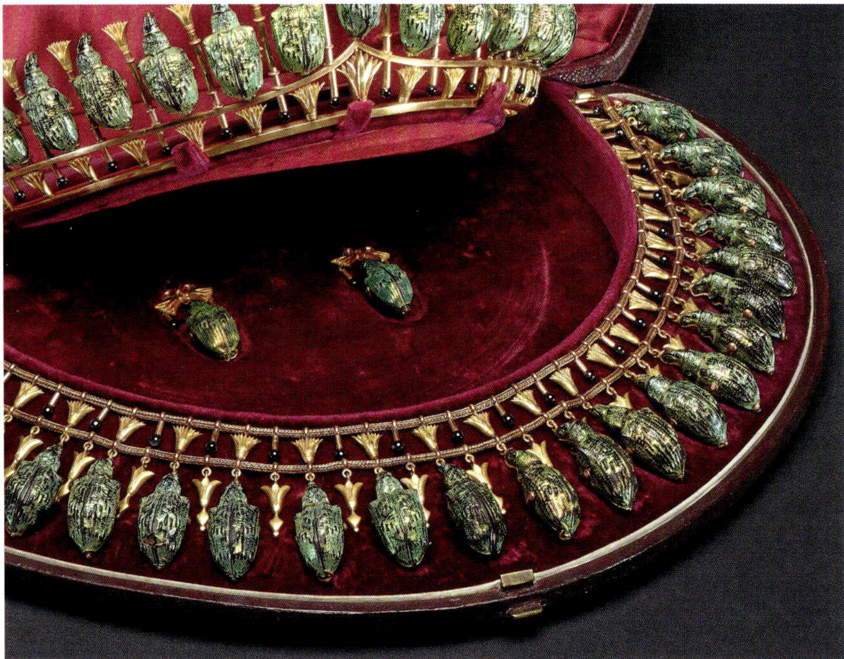

Fig. 164 Detail of Lady Granville's beetle parure by Philipps Brothers & Son, 1884–5. Gold and weevil tissue. British Museum, 2016,8037.1.a-e. Presented by Museum of Applied Arts and Sciences

jewellers Phillips Brothers & Son to mount the insects on a parure inspired by ancient Egyptian artefacts, giving it to his wife, Lady Granville (fig. 164).

The decadent appropriation of the colours of nature is exemplified in another celebrated episode of Huysmans's novel, in which Des Esseintes attempts to cultivate natural flowers that look like artificial ones:

> Not one single specimen seemed real; the cloth, paper, porcelain and metal seemed to have been loaned by man to nature to enable her to create her monstrosities. When unable to imitate man's handiwork, nature had been reduced to copying the inner membranes of animals, to borrowing the vivid tints of their rotting flesh, their magnificent corruptions.[18]

Huysmans's novel caused a stir among the British avant-garde. In *The Picture of Dorian Gray* (1890), Oscar Wilde repurposed *À Rebours* as the strange 'yellow book' that causes Dorian's moral downfall. The much-publicised scandal surrounding the sudden fashion for green carnations (see pp. 197–203) also bears the mark of Des Esseintes's decadent taste for unnatural flowers.

If green carried connotations of physical and moral putrescence, yellow was also associated with organic decay, notably through the natural discoloration of leaves in the autumn. Wilde combined these two most decadent of colours in his poem 'Symphony in Yellow' (1889): inspired by Whistler's studies in colour, Wilde conjured a highly aestheticised image of autumnal London wrapped in yellow fog, in which an omnibus 'Crawls like a yellow butterfly' (perhaps another reference to Whistler, who used the butterfly as his signature). In the last stanza, Wilde revisits the urban river setting used by Whistler in several of his nocturnes:

The yellow leaves begin to fade
  And flutter from the Temple elms,
And at my feet the pale green Thames
  Lies like a rod of rippled jade.[19]

There is a hallucinatory quality in Wilde's vision of insectiform yellow omnibuses and jade-like green river water that brings to mind the colour of absinthe, a highly intoxicating drink that was itself the object of literary and artistic mythologies. The same decadent association of yellow and green suggests mental disorder and social marginality in Eugène Grasset's strikingly modern chromolithograph depicting a young woman injecting herself with morphine (fig. 165).

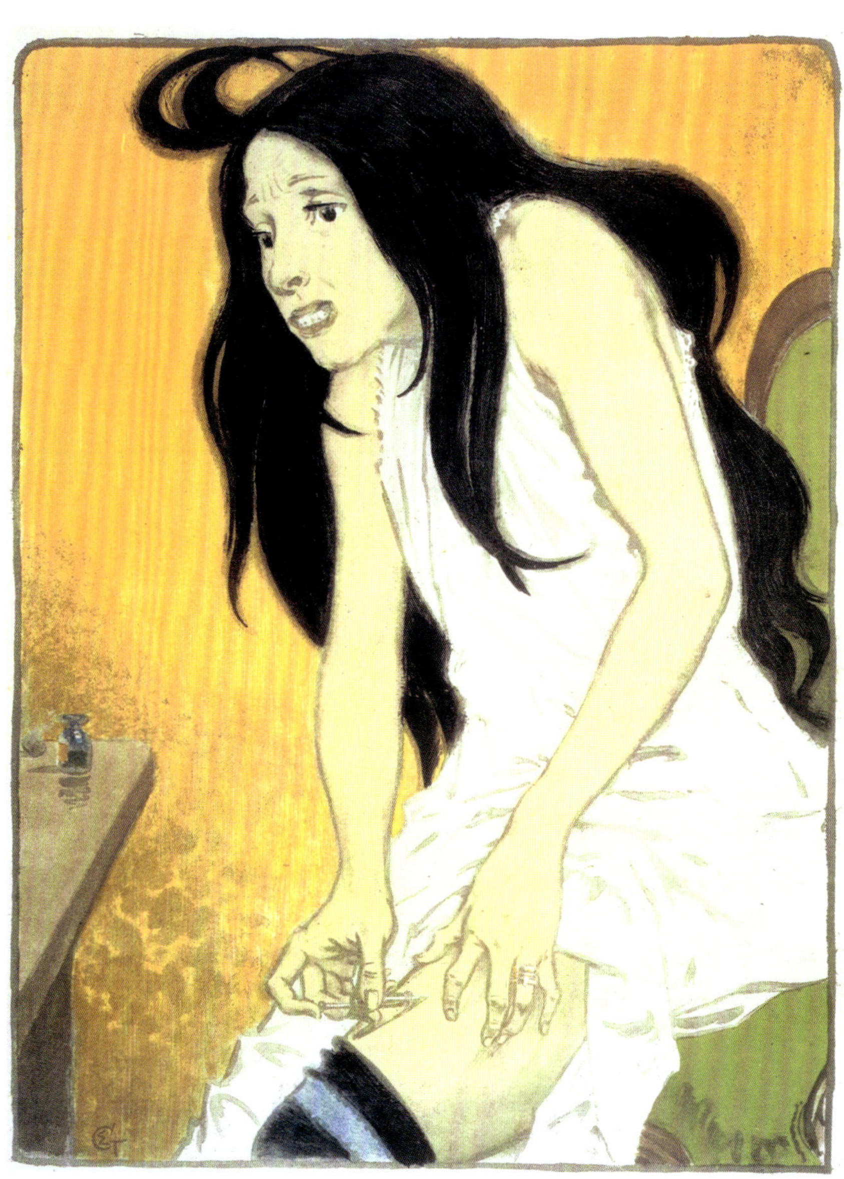

Fig. 165 Eugène Grasset (1845–1917), *La Morphinomane* (The Morphine Addict), 1897. Colour lithograph. Victoria and Albert Museum, E.1094-1963

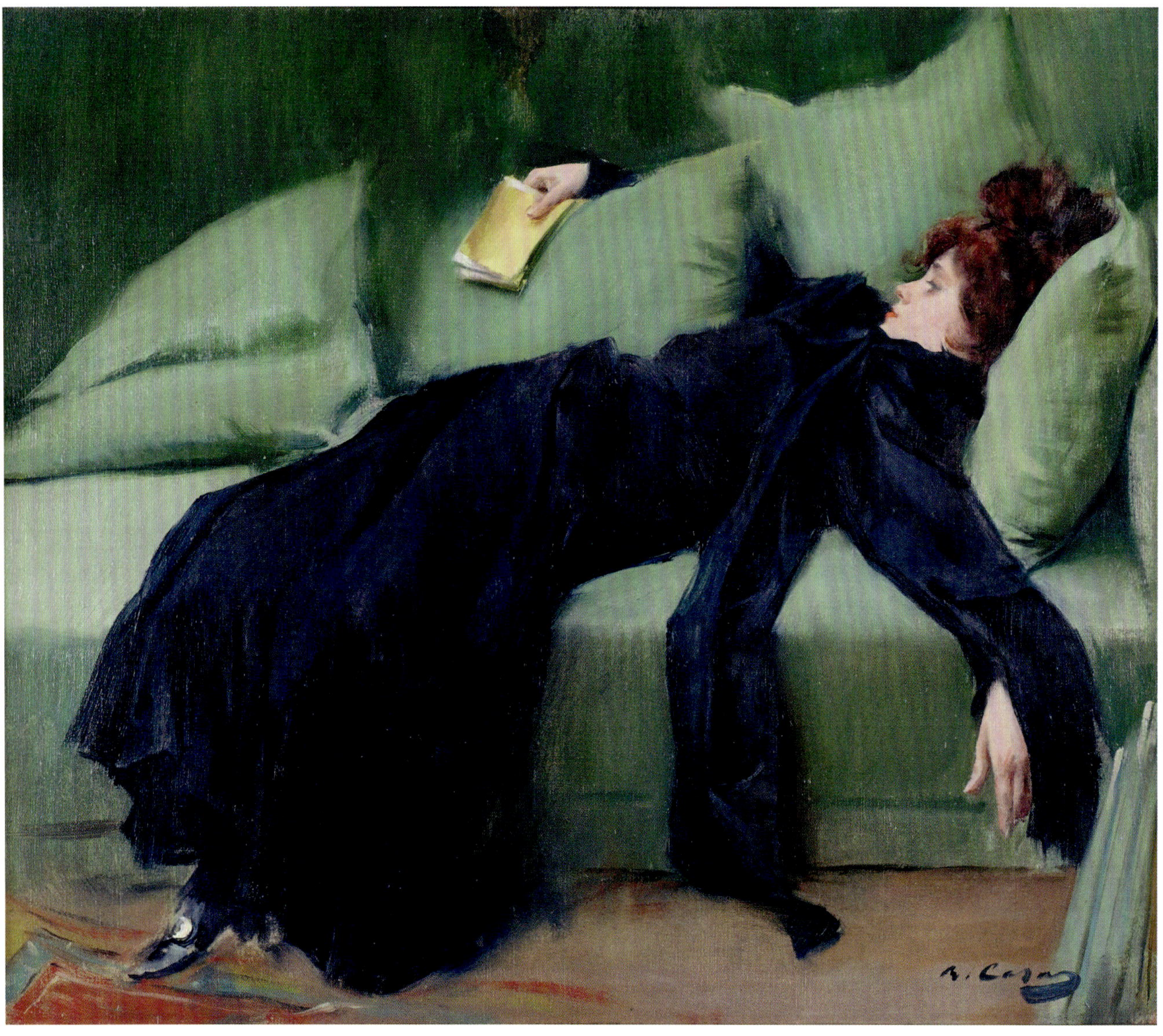

Fig. 166 Ramon Casas (1866–1932), *Decadent Young Woman, After the Dance*, 1899. Oil on canvas. Museu de Montserrat. Donated by Josep Sala Ardiz, 1980, N.R. 200.398

A very different effect is achieved in Ramon Casas's *After the Dance* (fig. 166), which glamorises the decadent colour combination of green and yellow. Casas was a Catalan artist who trained in Paris, where he befriended Henri de Toulouse-Lautrec. The red-haired beauty depicted in this work is Madeleine Boisguillaume, a model of Toulouse-Lautrec, who was particularly drawn to the vivid colours of modern urban life and its more marginal figures, whether waitresses, dancers or prostitutes. But in Casas's painting, the young woman is neither fallen nor virtuous. Her black dress was not designed to be read in moral terms but as a sign of her aesthetic refinement. Within the pictorial composition the dress also serves to heighten the vividness of the green sofa on which she languidly lies following an exhausting night out, a bright yellow book in her right hand. Although the title is not visible, the colour of its cover suggests the wrappings of French novels – maybe, it is implied, one of the racy ones that circulated privately on both sides of the Channel.

Seizing on these cosmopolitan and risqué connotations, the avant-garde periodical *The Yellow Book* first appeared in London on 15 April 1894 (fig. 167). Its deep yellow cover was designed by Aubrey Beardsley, who had already illustrated the first English edition of Wilde's *Salomé* (1894). Uncompromisingly stylish and ready to push cultural boundaries, *The Yellow Book* defined the chromatic identity of this turbulent decade, which came to be known as 'the Yellow Nineties'. In an essay entitled 'Boom in Yellow' (1896), the poet Richard Le Gallienne reflected on the modern triumph of yellow in the public imagination: 'Let us dream of this: a maid with yellow hair, clad in a yellow gown, seated in a yellow room, at the window a yellow sunset, in the grate a yellow fire, at her side a yellow lamplight, on her knee a Yellow Book.'[20] Le Gallienne's snapshot of the Yellow Nineties is marked by an atmosphere of confidence, middle-class prosperity and security. But the publication, two years later, of M P Shiel's *Yellow Danger* – a novel about the perils of reverse colonisation – alerts us to the fact that, in this age of empire, the decadent yellows embraced by the cultural elite could shade into racism and xenophobia.

Le Gallienne's image of a woman reader evokes the fact that Beardsley's covers and advertisements for *The Yellow Book* frequently showed women, which at the time was unusual for a magazine not specifically set up to cater for 'female' interests. The same eye-catching bright yellow was used on posters showcasing new images of femininity: for instance, it featured prominently on Beardsley's advertisement for John Lane's 'Keynote Series' (fig. 168), named after a collection of short stories by George Egerton (pseudonym for Mary

Fig. 167 Copies of *The Yellow Book, An Illustrated Quarterly*, illustrated by Aubrey Beardsley (1872–1898). By Permission of the President and Fellows of Trinity College Oxford

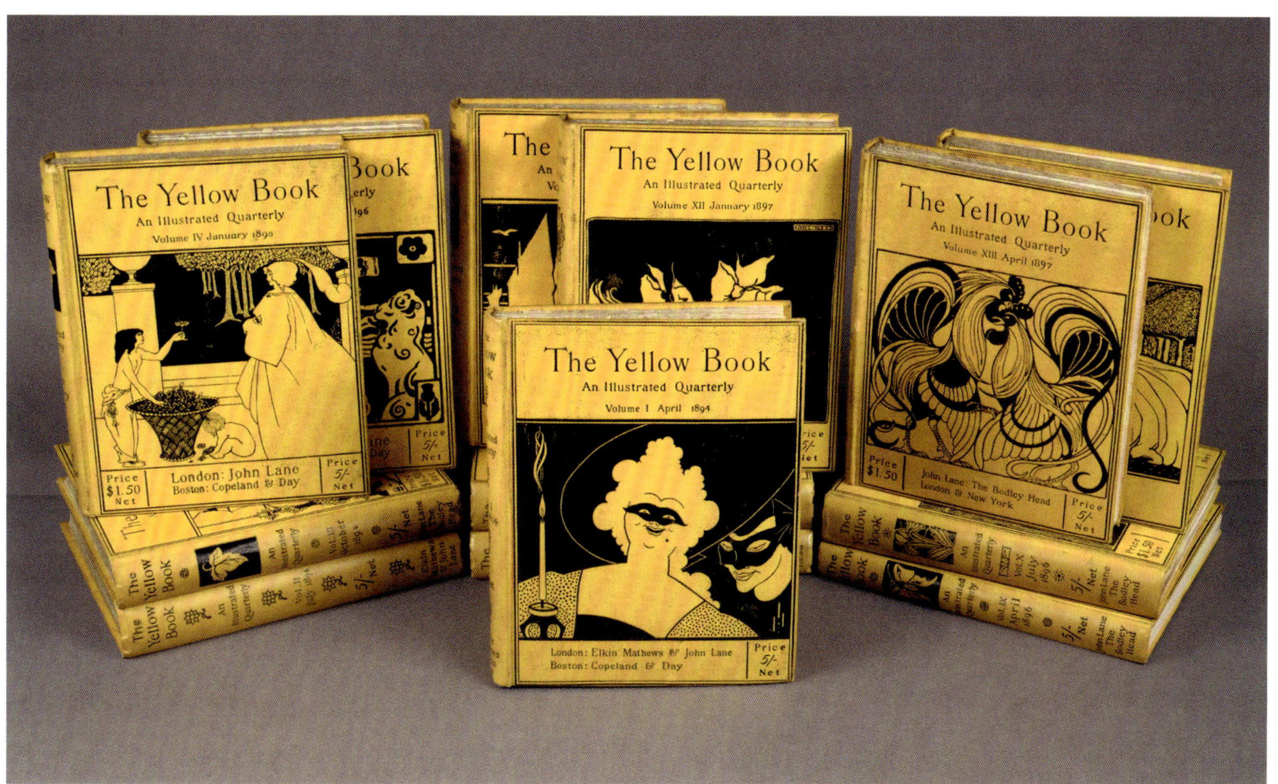

Chavelita Dunne Bright) that focused on sexually and socially emancipated female protagonists. It also carried connotations of freedom in Dudley Hardy's 'Yellow Girl' advertisements for *To-Day* magazine, founded and edited by Jerome K. Jerome (fig. 169).

There was something highly performative about the 'yellow' women of the 1890s. As Du Maurier hinted in his caricatures for *Punch*, performance was key to the aesthetic life from the start, as symbolised by the chromatic exuberance of the peacock – a creature that featured prominently in aesthetic interior decoration in a variety of different guises. The shifting hues of the feathers of the parading bird soon became the symbol of colour for colour's sake – for aesthetes and their detractors alike.

On 2 July 1897 Louise, Duchess of Devonshire, held a Costume Ball at Devonshire House to celebrate Queen Victoria's Diamond Jubilee. For the occasion, she had a gown ornamented with iridescent peacock motifs specially designed by the Paris-based House of Worth, famed for having dressed aesthetic actresses like Sarah Bernhardt and Lillie Langtry. The duchess attended as Zenobia, Queen of Palmyra (3rd century CE), an oriental warrior queen who challenged gender roles by combining both power and beauty

Below left: Fig. 168 Aubrey Beardsley (1872–1898), Keynote Series Poster, 1896. Bodleian Library, University of Oxford, John Johnson Collection, Windows and Bills Advertisement Folder 1 (38)

Below right: Fig. 169 Dudley Hardy (1867–1922), The 'Yellow Girl' poster for *To-Day* magazine, 1893. Chromolithograph. Bodleian Library, University of Oxford, John Johnson Collection

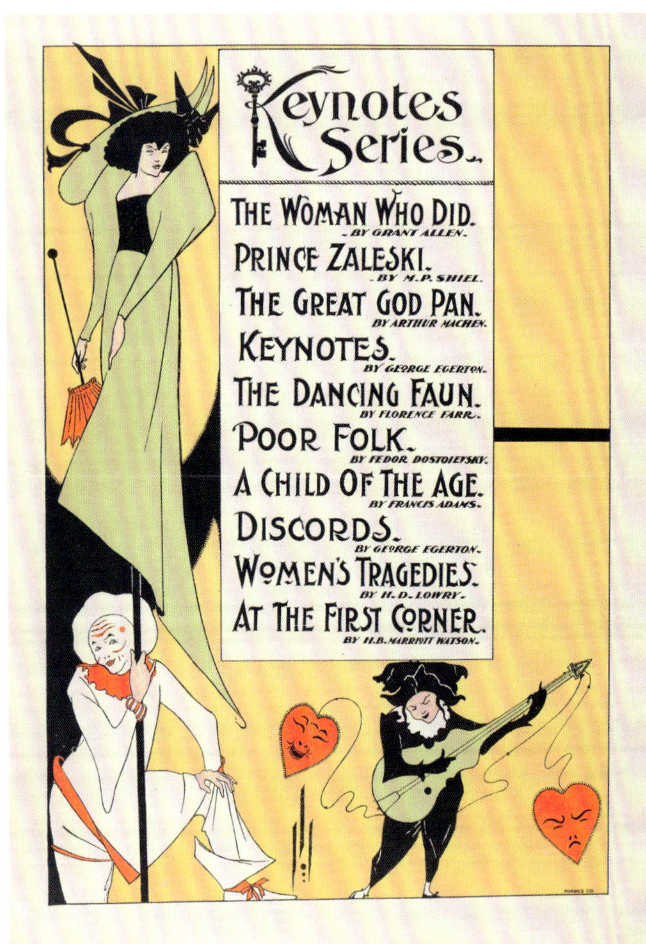

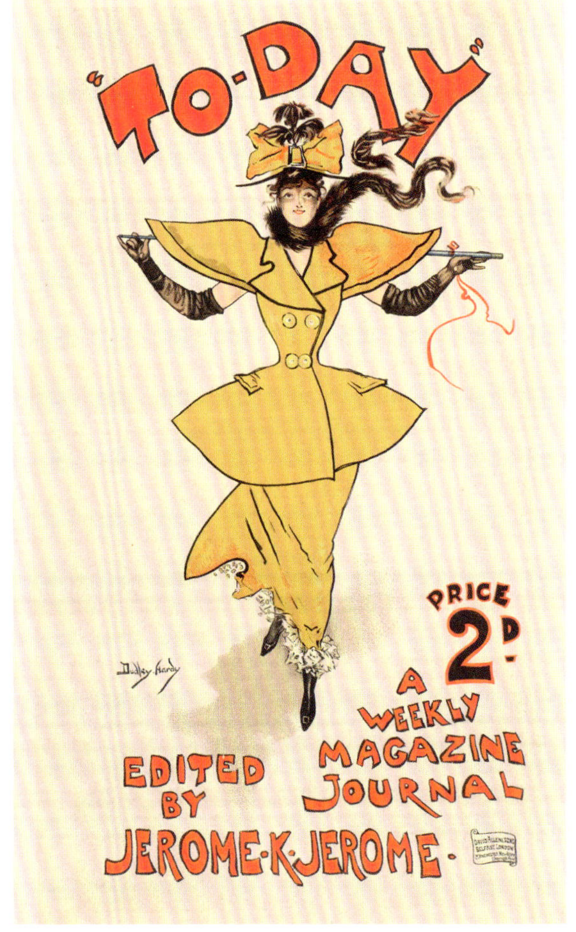

Fig. 170 Henri de Toulouse-Lautrec (1864–1901), 'Troupe de Mlle Églantine', 1896. Colour lithograph. Poster for the troupe when they performed at the Palace Theatre in London in 1896. Victoria and Albert Museum, London, CIRC.554-1962

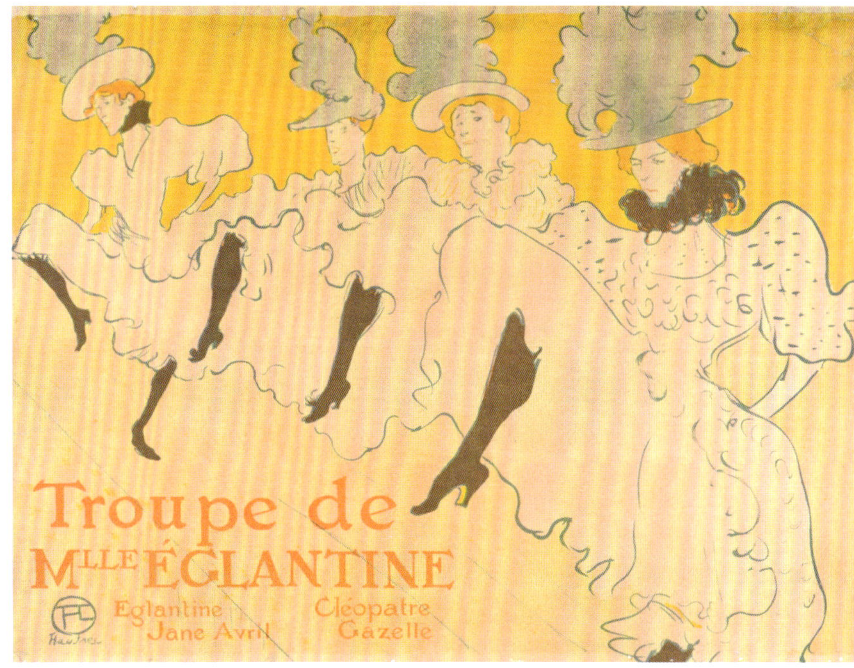

(fig. 8, p. 23). The gown had a bodice of gold cloth and lace, with an over-dress embroidered with stars of emeralds, sapphires, diamonds and other jewels outlined with gold in a design echoing the outspread tail of a peacock. Attached to the shoulders was a train of vivid green velvet lined with turquoise satin and decorated with Egyptian lotus flowers. Although not an aesthetic dress *per se*, this dazzling costume combined exotic references to oriental antiquity with a nod to the 'greenery-yallery' fashion of the 1880s. A far cry from both Ruskin's sacred conception of the hues of nature and the mass-produced anilines, the chromatic eclecticism and opulence of this *fin-de-siècle* peacock dress may be read as a final, decadent flourish at the close of a century which had nevertheless democratised colour for all sections of society.[21]

Object in Focus

James McNeill Whistler, *Nocturne: Blue and Gold, St Mark's Venice* (1880)

In February 1883, a new exhibition, *Arrangement in White and Yellow,* opened at the Fine Art Society on New Bond Street. The title was not simply a reference to the artist's penchant for musically inclined painting titles: the exhibition rooms were themselves chromatically arranged. The walls were covered in white fabric and the floors in yellow matting, with yellow tiles for the mantlepiece, yellow mouldings and borders, yellow furniture, and yellow vases filled with yellow and white roses. The gallery attendants were dressed in yellow and white livery.[22] At the centre of this exhibition full of 'sentient notes of colour' was the infamous James McNeill Whistler, who was exhibiting a series of his Venetian etchings.

The press were quick to tackle Whistler, reserving particular vitriol for the *enfant-terrible* of the Victorian art world. This was a consequence of the scandal his libel case against Ruskin had caused across London society. The art critic had accused Whistler of 'flinging a pot of paint in the public's face' after exhibiting *Nocturne in Black and Gold, The Falling Rocket* (1872–7) at the Grosvenor Gallery.[23] Whistler won, but it was a pyrrhic victory and he was shunned by the cultural elite for airing the grievance in such a public manner. *Punch*'s reaction to *Arrangement in White and Yellow* was to publish a satirical poem entitled 'Whistler in Venice – A Gavotte in Gamboge', which pilloried the artist's work as 'consumedly bilious'.[24] A critic from *Truth* quipped that the exhibition was 'another crop of Mr. Whistler's little jokes'. However, full of characteristic 'American gall'[25], Whistler published his critics' most scathing remarks on the front page of the exhibition catalogue.

In September 1879, in the immediate aftermath of the trial, the Fine Art Society, owned by the publisher William Longman, commissioned Whistler to make a series of 12 etchings in Venice, to help him recover from the bankruptcy caused by the trial and to lay the groundwork for his eventual return to society. Concurrently, perhaps to keep both art-world giants involved with his gallery venture, Longman also set up a subscription fund to help Ruskin recuperate his legal costs.

The etchings and dry points produced after this 14-month exile in Venice have since become crucial in art historical accounts of Whistler's life, and mark a high point in his innovative use of the monochrome medium. However, while Whistler recovered and worked in the Lagoon City, he also produced several oil paintings and returned to the sensorial, subjectless nocturne mode that had originally so offended Ruskin. Whistler embarked on his nocturne series in 1871 with scenes of the Thames at night. The paintings were capable of, as one critic put it, 'moulding our moods and stirring our imaginations, by subtle combinations of colour'.[26]

Six months into his stay he wrote to his friend Matthew Robinson Elden: 'And mind you, all this while, it is not merely the 'Views of Venice' or the 'Streets of Venice', or the 'Canals of Venice' such as you have seen brought back by the foolish sketcher – but great pictures that stare you in the face – complete arrangements and harmonies in color & form that are ready and waiting for the one who can perceive.'[27]

Of the three oil paintings that survive from this period, *Nocturne: Blue and Gold, St Mark's Venice* (fig. 171) reminds viewers of Whistler's enduring

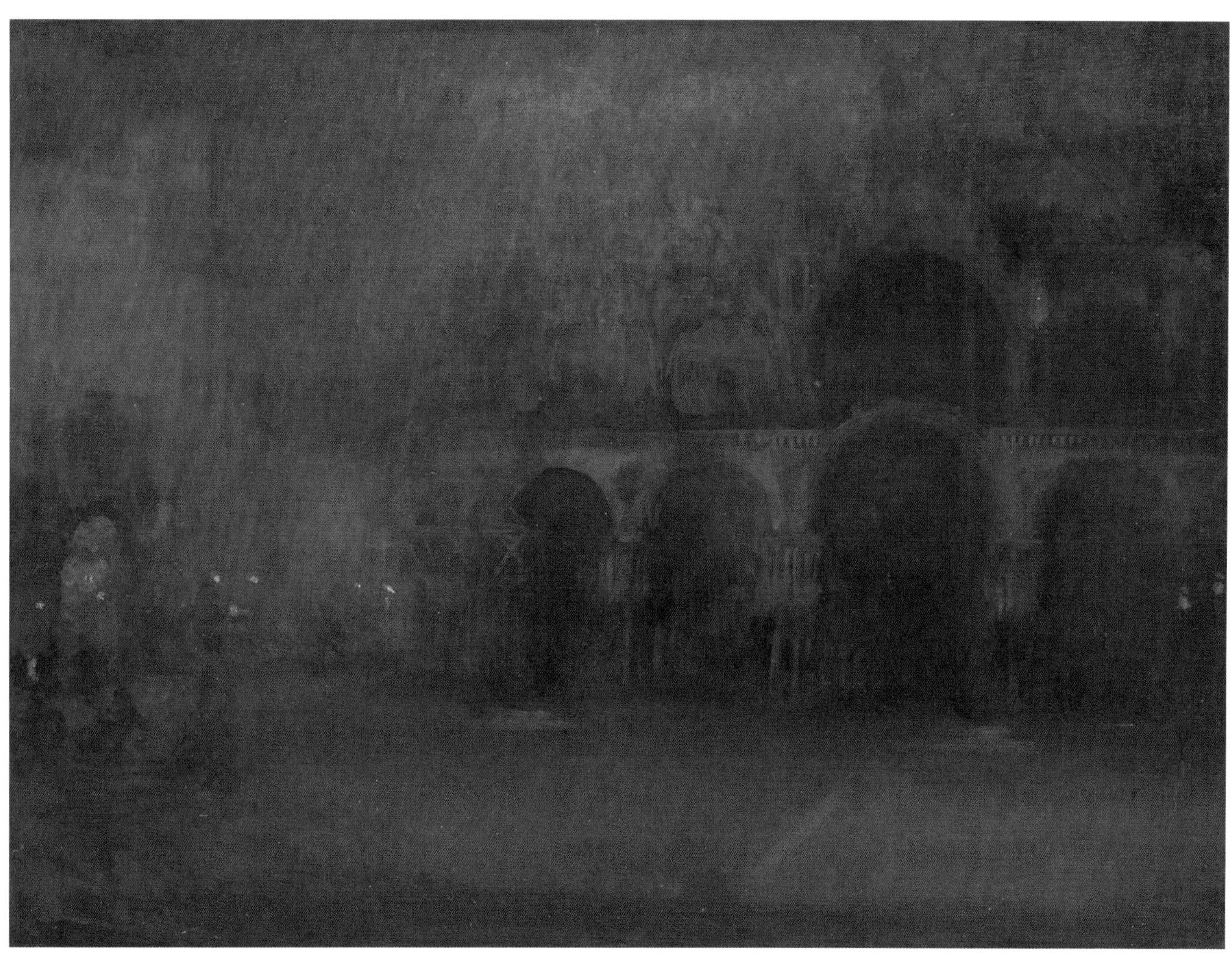

Fig. 171 James McNeill Whistler (1834–1903), *Nocturne: Blue and Gold, St Mark's, Venice*, 1880. Oil on canvas. Amgueddfa Cymru – National Museum Wales. NMW A 210 Bequest: Gwendoline Davies, 1951

interest in colour harmonies. Whistler uses blue and gold to capture an important architectural landmark in the European city synonymous with colour. Although *Nocturne: Blue and Gold* was not initially exhibited at the *Arrangement in White and Yellow* exhibition and – instead debuting at the Society of British Artists' Winter Exhibition in 1886/7 – it forms an important part of Whistler's Venetian oeuvre and should be considered the colourful counterpoint to the better-known black and white etchings. Furthermore, in the story of this exhibition, it shows how far the Victorians' response to Venetian colour had transformed during the generation between Turner and Whistler.

It is unclear why Whistler settled on Venice as his post-trial sanctuary, but it seems a pointed – and psychologically fascinating – choice. Ruskin's fame was inextricably linked to the city because of his landmark publication on Venetian Gothic architecture, *The Stones of Venice* (1851). He was an authority on St Mark's Basilica, calling it a 'gorgeous building' which he approached 'in a kind of awe'.[28] From his first visit as a teenager in 1835 onwards, Ruskin had made detailed architectural drawings of St Mark's, which provided a valuable historic record of the building's decoration. These drawings and later commissioned photographs, which were assembled as part of Ruskin's Oxford teaching collection, revel in the minutiae of architectural detail and demonstrate his keen sense of observation.

Whistler captured his view of St Mark's from the famous Café Florian, in the north-east corner of the piazza. The café was a popular social haunt where he drank with fellow artists and his partner, Maud Franklin. This perspective suggests a more touristic approach to the subject that was markedly different from Ruskin's reverential studies. The viewer sees St. Mark's from a considerable distance – through the unfavourable lighting conditions of the late hour, and also, perhaps, after a few drinks. One critic described it as a 'dissolving view'[29] of St Mark's, while Whistler's friend, the artist Otto Bacher, described its haziness as 'breath on the surface of a pane of glass'.[30] Whistler's approach to St. Mark's – by treating it as a constituent part of an atmospheric urban landscape cloaked in darkness – differed radically from Ruskin's established authority.

In the painting, against the left-hand side of the façade, there are crossed wooden planks which form a scaffolding tower. These were erected as part of major restoration works which commenced in 1877. Ruskin argued bitterly against the renovations, arguing that St Mark's would become 'the ghost – nay, the corpse, of all that I so loved'.[31] He particularly worried about the loss of the coloured marbles from the 'trophy wall' on the western facade. The anti-restoration cause eventually won the day and works were stopped in 1882. However, Whistler seems to have deliberately included a visible symbol of Ruskin's beloved building at its most vulnerable.

Whistler was not a man to forgive and forget. In 1890 he published *The Gentle Art of Making Enemies*: the book included the transcript of the Ruskin libel suit and his account of working for the shipping magnate Frederick Leyland. After the implosion of that relationship over the decoration of Leyland's home, Whistler snuck into the house to paint *Art and Money: or, The Story of the Room* (1877), which zoomorphised the pair as fighting peacocks. Therefore *Nocturne: Blue and Gold* could be viewed as a similar pot-shot in paint. Whistler confidently wrote that he 'learned to know a Venice in Venice that others never seem to have perceived'.[32] At this highly charged moment, the wounded Whistler used *Nocturne: Blue and Gold* to transform the Venice of Ruskin, and by extension Turner, from a space of brightly coloured architectural precision into his own vision of dissolving, atmospheric hues.

Moving beyond Ruskin's Venice, Whistler also uses colour to reference the city's reputation as a cultural meeting point between East and West, and a long-established port city connecting the Far East with western Europe. The artist's choice of dark blue for the starless sky gives the painting the appropriate nocturnal atmosphere, but also recalls the use of indigo and the Japanese *aizuri* technique, examples of which he held in his beloved collection of woodblock prints (fig. 154, p. 179).[33] Records indicate that indigo had been traded from India through Venice for European colour merchants since at least the sixteenth century.[34] While *Nocturne: Blue and Gold* might not initially be considered one of Whistler's *Japonist* paintings, his evocation of Venice as a contact zone for colour exchange suggests hitherto unacknowledged Orientalist connections in this work.

Similarly, Whistler's decision to depict one of the great Italian Byzantine churches points to further Eastern influences. In the nineteenth century, Byzantine art and architecture experienced a significant revivalist movement in Britain, led in no small part by Ruskin's advocacy of St. Mark's.[35] The second hue referenced in the painting's title - gold - is the defining colour of Byzantine architecture and is most evident in the mosaic work in the church interior. Although *Nocturne: Blue and Gold* remains outdoors, other artists such as Frederic Leighton reverently depicted the golden mosaic walls. In Whistler's painting gold is present in a series of small dots, not dissimilar to the falling embers in the painting at the centre of the Ruskin libel case, on either side of the church. These are street lights which project a warm golden glow onto the square. This is an altogether different use of gold, which signals once again a modern and changing Venice. However, the presence of the Byzantine age is still felt in the richness of colours in the painting. The receding blackness of the rounded doorways is also, perhaps, an enticing invitation to explore its golden interiors. *Nocturne: Blue and Gold* suffuses two Eastern aesthetics - blue tinted Japanese woodblocks and the echoes of Byzantine gold - to offer a new way to consider Venice as a crucible for global colour cultures.

Taking on one of Venice's best-known subjects during a moment of professional reinvention, Whistler reasserted his *nocturnes* as a forward-looking, modern vehicle for colour. Venice, as the city of colour, was the bold choice for taking this stance. In the face of censure by Ruskin and other critics, *Nocturne: Blue and Gold* remains testament to a transformation in painting during the Victorian era.

Madeline Hewitson

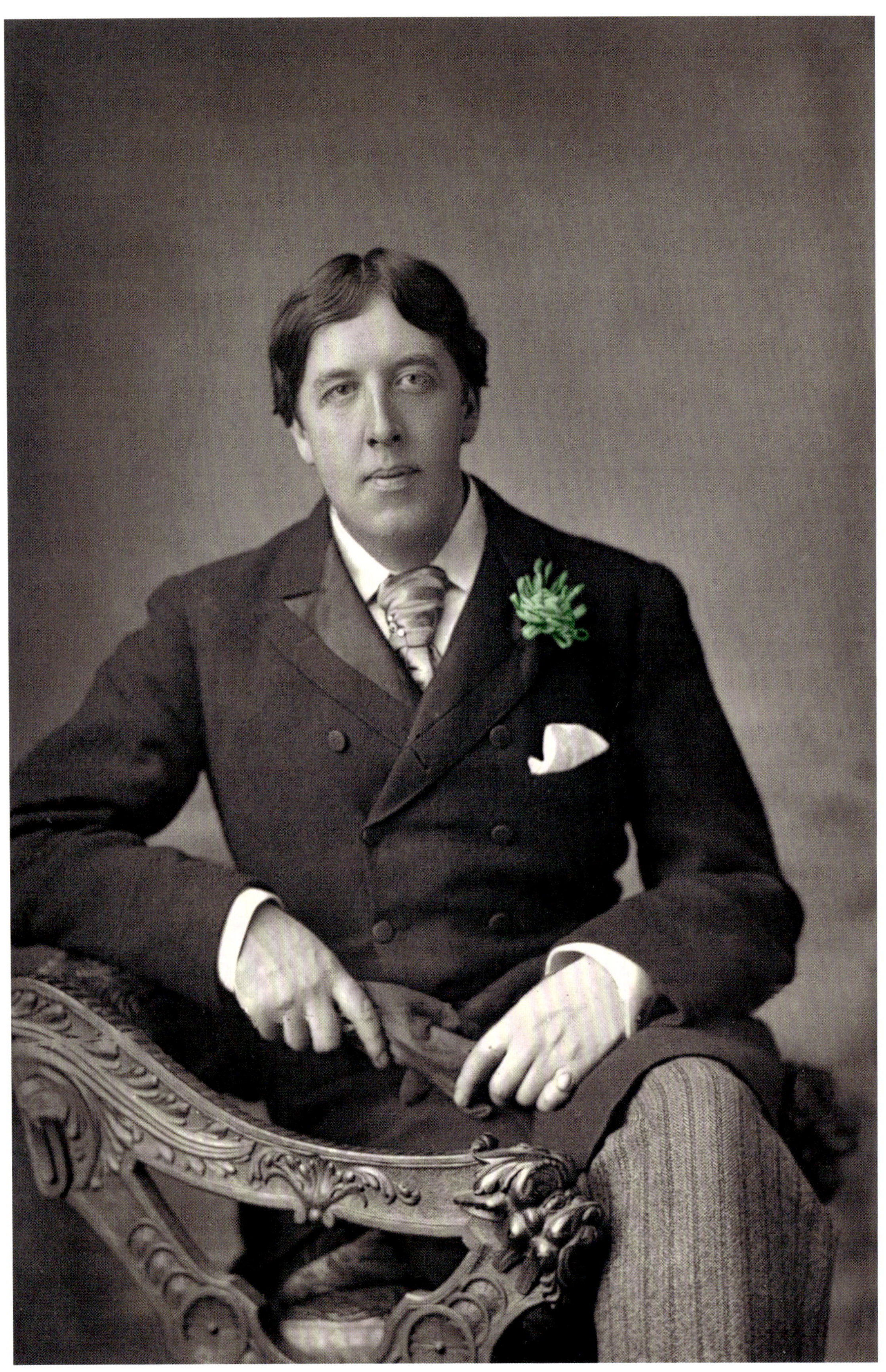

Queer Colours

Stefano Evangelista

The closing decades of the nineteenth century saw profound changes in the way that homosexuality was viewed in society and in the arts. The very word homosexual was a modern coinage, invented to describe what was increasingly regarded as a phenomenon that ought to be studied and understood with the new tools of modern medicine and psychology, rather than simply condemned. Spearheaded by the emerging discipline of sexology, this scientific interest in homosexuality overlapped with scholars' attempts to research how love between people of the same sex manifested itself in different times and places – in Sappho's Greece, for instance, in the Italian and English Renaissance, or in the countries of Asia and the Middle East that imperial expansion had brought closer to home. At the same time, modern artists and writers also looked for ways to represent queer identities in a positive light, sidestepping or indeed overturning prejudice and censure.

In this large effort to bring homosexuality to unprecedented visibility, changing understandings of colour also played an important role. As early as 1871, Charles Darwin had already established a link between colour and sexual selection: in the *Descent of Man*, he noted that certain male animals use the colour of their fur or plumage to make themselves attractive to potential sexual partners. It seemed logical, therefore, that later in the century sexologists should have wondered whether, in humans too, colour was attached to sexual behaviour. In his pioneering study *Sexual Inversion*, compiled and revised from the 1890s to 1915, the English sexologist Havelock Ellis made a point of recording the favourite colour of many of the homosexual men and women that he interviewed for his case studies. For instance, of case XII, a 24-year-old man who said that he became aware of the prevalence of homosexuality in England thanks to publicity surrounding the Oscar Wilde case, Ellis noted:

> He has a special predilection for green; it is the predominant colour in the decoration of his room, and everything green appeals to him. He finds that the love of green (and also of violet and purple) is very widespread among his inverted friends.[36]

Was green a particularly queer colour? Unsurprisingly, the evidence gathered in *Sexual Inversion* was contradictory to say the least, pointing to a whole range of colour preferences among interviewees. Ellis nonetheless reported the opinion of one of his colleagues, that 'inverts [the common way of referring to homosexuals before this word became widespread in English] exhibit a preference for green garments'.[37] He elaborated:

Fig. 172 Oscar Wilde (1854–1900), Irish poet and playwright. Photograph by Downey

> This decided preference for green is well marked in several of my cases of both sexes, and in some at least the preference certainly arose spontaneously. Green ... is very rarely the favourite colour of adults of the Anglo-Saxon race, though some inquirers have found it to be more commonly a preferred colour among children, especially girls, and it is more often preferred by women than by men.[38]

Case XII's queer taste for green confirmed the basic premise of Ellis's theory of inversion: that homosexual men are individuals in whom female psyches are trapped inside male bodies (and the other way round for homosexual women). Here, the adult male 'invert' displays an anomalous colour taste that is otherwise normally associated with women and little girls. By the same token, Ellis noted that 'of recent years there has been a fashion for a red tie to be adopted by inverts as their badge' – red being, according to his findings, more common as a favourite colour among 'normal women' than among men.[39] He quoted a report that the male street-walkers of Philadelphia and New York wore red neckties in order to make themselves immediately recognisable to potential clients. Indeed, this use of red ties had become so well known among the general public in the United States that it attracted mockery in student circles and lewd comments in the streets.

Such observations about the connections between colour and sexual identity are more interesting for their anecdotal than their scientific content. Ellis's sexological reading of the meaning of green appears to be largely determined by cultural factors: old connotations of green as a colour of danger and unreliability can be traced back at least to the Old Masters. In *Sexual Inversion*, these links are repurposed to signify the double life of nineteenth-century queer men and women, who were forced to keep their inner feelings hidden from society. Oscar Wilde had played on the same associations when he subtitled his story *Pen, Pencil and Poison* (1889), an essay about the English artist, critic and murderer Thomas Wainewright, 'A Study in Green'. More revealing are Ellis's observations of how certain homosexual individuals might have used colour codes, through the medium of fashion accessories, to constitute communities and form a shared identity in an extremely hostile environment. His scientific enquiries also give us a glimpse into the cultural construction of the turn-of-the-century homosexual as a chromophile – an individual marked by a heightened sensitivity to colour.

However clumsy Ellis's theories of sex might appear from a twenty-first-century perspective, his views were decidedly progressive for the time. His aim was to show that homosexuality was a congenital condition, and not a moral perversion or disease. In *Sexual Inversion* he endorsed his collaborator John Addington Symonds's idea that homosexuality could be compared to colour-blindness: both were, quite simply, naturally occurring deviations from the norm. Confusingly, perhaps, he also compared homosexuality to synaesthesia: 'Just as the colour-hearer instinctively associates colours with sounds, like the young Japanese lady who remarked when listening to singing, "That boy's voice is red!" so the invert has his sexual sensations brought into relationship

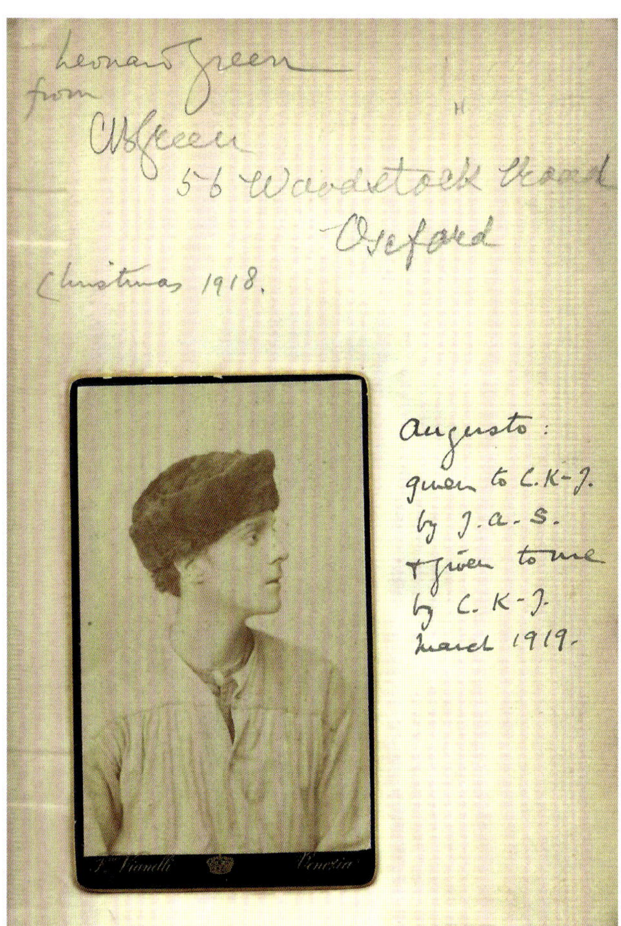

Fig. 173 Photograph of Augusto Zanon pasted into a copy of *In the Key of Blue* (1893) by John Addington Symonds. Collection Raimondo Biffi

with objects that are normally without sexual appeal.'[40] The point of these comparisons was to stress that homosexual individuals were not to blame for their tastes and behaviours.

By the time that *Sexual Inversion* finally went to press, after many delays, Symonds had already been dead for over three years. Nonetheless, he was a prominent presence in the book. He was, in fact, listed as co-author in the first English edition of 1897, which also contained his anonymised sexual autobiography and his pamphlets campaigning for social tolerance and legal reform. Symonds, who embraced his homosexual identity late in life, when he was already a married man with four daughters, was fascinated by his own sexual psychology and repeatedly wrote about the lives and works of famous gay men from the past. As a historian of art and an aesthete, Symonds was also interested in colour. His remarkable work *In the Key of Blue* (1893), composed during the most intense phase of his collaboration with Ellis, was his way of bringing together these long-standing interests.

In the Key of Blue starts as an essay on the nomenclature of colour in literature, but it soon shades into a series of impressionistic prose sketches which have as their object a young Venetian porter named Augusto Zanon (fig. 173). Like other wealthy homosexual men from northern Europe, Symonds regularly travelled to Italy, partly for the arts, partly to look for sexual partners among the country's poorer social milieus. He befriended Zanon on one of these trips. In this highly experimental work Symonds behaved like a painter, using Zanon as his model: he staged the young man, dressed in the blue costume that was then characteristic of Venetian workers, against various backgrounds in the city and its surrounding countryside, translating into words the alluring effects produced by pairing Zanon's blues with other colours and observing them in different lights. The first of a number of inset poems addresses the vision of Zanon in the alluring intimacy of the Venetian night:

> A symphony of black and blue –
> Venice asleep, vast night, and you.
> [...]
> Pitch-dark! You were the one thing blue;
> Four tints of pure celestial hue:
> The larkspur blouse by tones degraded
> Through silken sash of sapphire faded,
> The faintly floating violet tie,
> The hose of lapis-lazuli.[41]

Catherine Maxwell has rightly described *In the Key of Blue* as 'an open love letter.'[42] Indeed Symonds celebrates the beauty of Zanon's male body and his own desire for it, simultaneously inviting readers to partake of his longing. Symonds places a strong emphasis on the materiality of colour, in particular on the degradation and fading effects produced by the wear of the blue fabric through use and gesture, in order to show that the active body of the worker participates in the very creation of colour and what makes it attractive to his eyes. The extreme artfulness of the literary composition serves to deflect the overload of homoeroticism by aestheticising and abstracting what are in fact very visceral emotions. Colour is therefore crucial to the way that Symonds manages the very delicate task of bypassing Victorian moral censorship. Eschewing realistic representation, his impressionistic handling of colour gestures towards a different way of imagining masculinity and social relations. This is how, seen through Symonds's eyes, the blues of the hard-wearing clothes of Venetian working men become distinctly queer colours, associated with an attraction for working-class masculinity – bodies, like clothes, that are erotically marked by the 'stains of labour', as he writes in the essay.[43] Blue thus manifests a utopianism that Symonds shared with other homosexual activists of the time such as Edward Carpenter. He believed that the emancipation of homosexuality would stimulate cross-class partnerships, as opposed to the socially homogenous unions of heterosexual marriage. As Symonds wrote to the poet Richard Le Gallienne, who published a review of *In the Key of Blue*: 'Augusto, for me, is a good deal more than a lay figure. He is a downright good fellow and good friend.'[44]

Merging acoustic and visual sensations, Symonds's title, *In the Key of Blue*, plays with the synaesthetic imagination beloved by writers associated with the aesthetic and decadent movements. Colour is shorthand for a literature that aspires to the condition of music – to paraphrase a famous aphorism that Symonds's contemporary Walter Pater coined in relation to Giorgione (significantly, a Venetian painter) – that is, for a style that moves beyond descriptive realism, aiming instead primarily to convey the qualities of atmosphere, mood or sensation.[45] By speaking of 'symphonies and harmonies of blue', Symonds openly alludes to James McNeill Whistler and, through Whistler, to Théophile Gautier's classic colour poem 'Symphonie en blanc majeur' (1852), which Symonds transposes in a queer key.[46] The allusion to Whistler is also very strong on the book's strikingly aesthetic cover, designed by the English artist Charles Ricketts. This features an elegant gilt floral motif consisting of laurel and hyacinths, symbolising Symonds's blending of poetic and chromatic sensibility (the colbalt blue of certain hyacinths recalls the hue of the Venetian fabrics described by Symonds) (fig. 174). The first edition included a number of copies bound in blue cloth, now extremely rare, which echo one of Whistler's most characteristic colour schemes. Notably, Whistler used this combination in *Nocturne in Blue and Gold: St Mark's, Venice* (1880), where he attempted to capture the atmosphere of Venice at night through the modern cosmopolitan influences of Impressionism and *japonisme* (fig. 171). The same combination dominates his celebrated 'Peacock Room', also known as the 'Harmony in Blue

Fig. 174 John Addington Symonds (1840–1893), *In the Key of Blue*, 1893. From the collection of Prof. Shane Butler

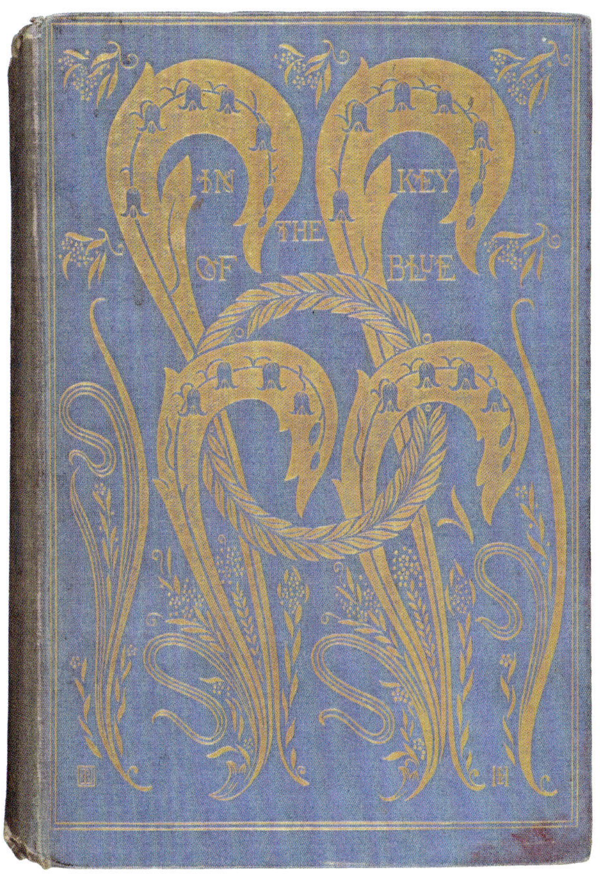

and Gold', which he executed in 1876–7 for the British shipping magnate and arts patron Frederick Richards Leyland. Like the 'Peacock Room', *In the Key of Blue* is also a 'total' work of art of sorts: its physical form and literary content partake of the same aesthetic values.

In the Key of Blue should be viewed as a collaboration between two queer artists. Ricketts, who also illustrated Wilde's *A House of Pomegranates* (1891) and *The Sphinx* (1894), was the life-long partner of artist Charles Shannon. The two men were a firm point of reference in London's queer artistic circles. They were particularly close to the lesbian poetic partnership of Katharine Bradley and Edith Cooper, who operated under the pseudonym of Michael Field. Michael Field's works also strove to integrate visual and poetic idioms in interesting ways, including by experimenting with coloured type in their collection of Sapphic lyrics *Long Ago* (1889). Ironically, however, in the case of *In the Key of Blue*, writer and illustrator(s) disagreed about the blue cover. Symonds was very pleased with it, preferring it to the cream version in which the majority of the copies were bound. While Ricketts, so the story goes, objected to it, fearing that it could give rise to an unfortunate pun:[47] 'Reckitt's Blue' was the name of a popular commercial brand of laundry powder produced by the English firm Reckitt & Sons, which was used to improve old or yellowing white fabrics by adding a trace of blue produced with synthetic ultramarine (in a process similar to the blue rinse used to colour white hair). The easy slip between Ricketts' blue and Reckitt's Blue would risk puncturing the exquisiteness of the book project.

There is something amusing in Ricketts's fear of being derided by colour association. But in a period when homosexuality attracted social stigma and could be criminally punished, homosexual individuals had good reason to be anxious about their public reputations. Playing with colour was a way of both revealing and concealing. Despite Havelock Ellis's tales of students attracting homophobic slurs for wearing red neckties, the most talked-about coloured symbol of homosexuality was the green carnation – an innocent chromatic *divertissement* that became an icon of the 1890s craze to perform and transgress. It was Oscar Wilde who brought the artificially dyed flower to prominence when, at the premiere of his comedy *Lady Windermere's Fan* in February 1892, he appeared in the St James's Theatre wearing a green carnation in his lapel. The provocative fashion soon spread among aesthetes belonging to Wilde's circle and was duly noted by the press, which speculated about its meaning.

While it remains open to debate whether the green carnation was ever used as a badge of homosexuality, its green is decidedly also a queer colour inasmuch as it cannot easily be pinned down to a fixed meaning. It is a social provocation; it expresses a wish to subvert normative behaviours. And, of course, it flaunts a taste for the unnatural that could all too easily be associated with the allegedly abnormal passions of the 'invert', but that was also many other things besides. The green carnation also embodies the decadent paradox that nature imitates art, on which Wilde expounded in his critical writings.

Only a few days after the much talked-about premiere of *Lady Windermere's Fan*, Wilde's friend, the writer Violet Hunt, had already seized on the growing furore in a brief sketch entitled 'Green Carnation' (1892), which featured an erotic triangle involving a woman and two men who exchange a green carnation as a token of their love for one another. And in 1894, Robert Hichens's novel *The Green Carnation* contained thinly veiled caricatures of Wilde and his lover Alfred Douglas. The novel opens with Reggie Turner – a Douglas epigone – sporting the flower in his buttonhole and admiring his reflection in the mirror. In the second chapter Lady Locke asks her cousin Lady Windsor if such carnations bloom on cottage walls: 'My dear Emily, green carnations never bloom on walls at all. Of course they are dyed. That is why they are original. Mr Amarinth says Nature will soon begin to imitate them, as she always imitates everything, being naturally uninventive.'[48] And when asked who started the fashion of the green carnation, Lady Windsor makes the following reply: 'That was Mr. Amarinth's idea. He calls it the arsenic flower of an exquisite life. He wore it, in the first instance, because it blended so well with the colour of absinthe. Lord Reggie and he are great friends. They are quite inseparable.'[49] Green carnations were not arsenic-based: they were dyed by immersing their stems in a harmless aniline malachite green.[50] But in their *fin-de-siècle* mythology they often acquired poisonous connotations that echoed the much-publicised mid-century anxieties about toxic greens, while at the same time channelling homophobic feelings.[51]

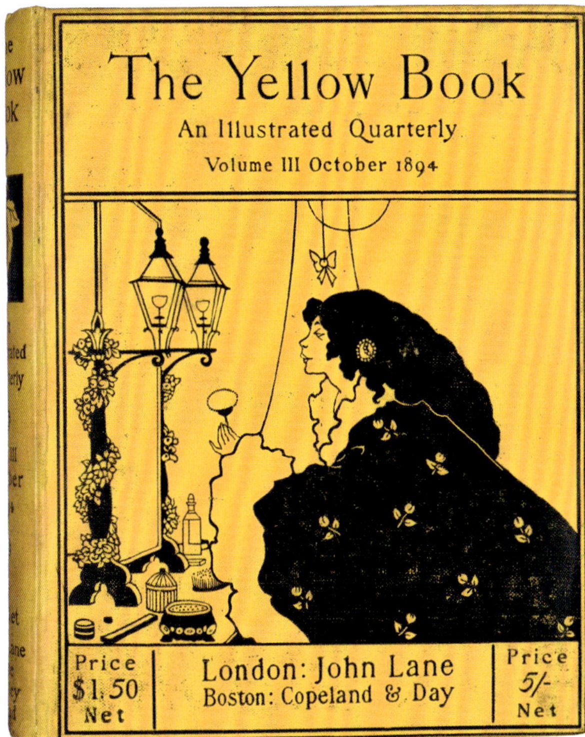

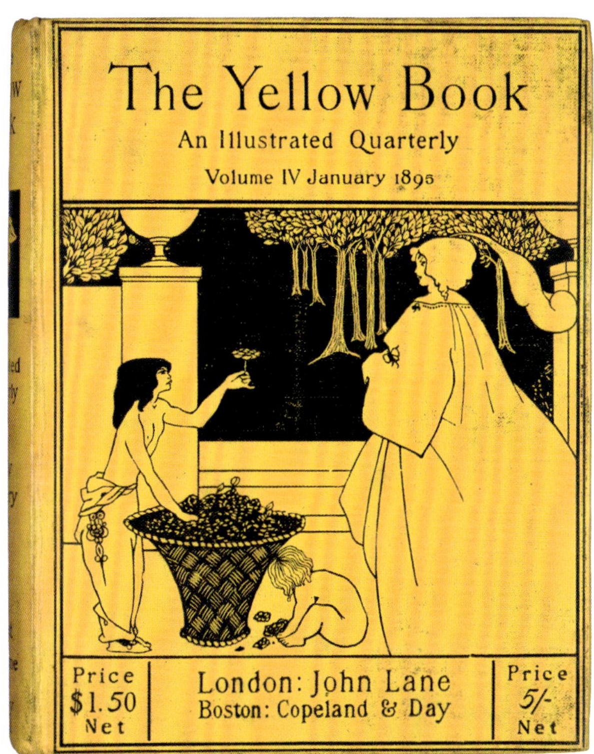

Fig. 175 *The Yellow Book*, By Permission of the President and Fellows of Trinity College Oxford

This was the danger of flirting with visibility. Oscar Wilde became the public face of the queer culture of the *fin de siècle* following his conviction for 'gross indecency' in May 1895. When he was first arrested he was seen holding a book with a yellow cover – a detail emphasised in several press reports. Yellow was the traditional colour of the wrappings of French novels, connoting lasciviousness in the Victorian public imagination. It was also the signature colour of England's most famous decadent magazine, *The Yellow Book*, which had been launched the previous year. Looking back on its power to symbolise the *zeitgeist* of the 1890s, the writer and bibliophile Holbrook Jackson remarked that yellow 'was associated with all that was *bizarre* and queer in art and life, with all that was outrageously modern.'[52] This use of the adjective 'queer' in 1913, in close association with the idea of modernity, is deeply suggestive. The covers of *The Yellow Book*, designed by Aubrey Beardsley, often sported androgynous figures and emancipated women displaying a progressive gender-bending ethos (Beardsley, who had illustrated Wilde's *Salomé*, was also notorious for his penchant for obscenities) (fig. 175). No matter that Wilde had never published in *The Yellow Book* and that the volume he was carrying on that fateful day was something altogether quite different: once rumours got out that Wilde had been caught with a copy of *The Yellow Book*, the editors started to panic that its colour symbolism had become unsustainably toxic and risky. They even sacked Beardsley in an attempt to clean up their reputation. But by then it was already too late. *The Yellow Book* ceased publication before the end of the decade, officially bringing the 'yellow nineties' to a close.

Object in Focus

Fin-de-siècle Tanagras

In his 1892 essay 'Degeneration', the social critic Max Nordau lamented that *fin-de-siècle* interiors were increasingly 'covered with Morris draperies, on which strange birds flit amongst crazily ramping branches', as well as being cluttered with all sorts of *bibelots*.[53] In the drawing rooms of such decadent dwellings could be found:

> a display of antiquities or articles of vertù, big or small, and for the most part warranted not genuine; a figure of Tanagra near a broken jade snuff-box, a Limoges plate beside a long-necked Persian waterpot of brass, a bonbonnière between a breviary bound in carved ivory, and snuffers of chiselled copper.[54]

A 'figure of Tanagra' is here given pride of place among an eclectic and foreign array of artworks. Often representing draped women standing, sitting or dancing, these polychrome terracotta statuettes dating from the fourth century BCE were then referred to as 'Tanagras' because the vast majority of the figurines came from tombs excavated in the 1870s on the site of Tanagra in Boeotia, Greece.

Although similar figurines from Athens, Alexandria or Corinth already featured in private and public collections – the celebrated *Danseuse Titeux* now in the Louvre was found on the Acropolis as early as 1846 – the excavations in Boeotia and the display of numerous Tanagras at the Paris Universal Exhibition of 1878 sparked new interest in the statuettes, from artists and amateurs alike. In 1874 antiquities collector and dealer Charles Merlin had supplied the British Museum with several of these Tanagras, including a figurine of a standing woman draped in a blue chiton and pink himation, holding a fan in her left hand (fig. 176). By the 1890s their popularity had grown so much that numerous fakes were produced to satisfy demand for these domestic and decorative antiquities – hence Nordau's suspicion that such figurines found in decadent interiors were probably 'not genuine'.

Whether authentic or not, the British Museum statuettes were widely praised for their dainty elegance. The world of Tanagra was not the mythological realm of martial gods and heroes, but rather the more feminine sphere of the fashionable 'Parisiennes' of the Hellenic past.[55] Mainly produced at the time of Alexander the Great, the figurines contrasted with the 'heroic marble idealisations of that gigantic age', challenging traditional conceptions of Greek heritage.[56] Classical scholarship was at the time very much the domain of men, and yet the discovery of 'the dainty little ladies from Tanagra', which most male academics did not take very seriously, opened up the field to women like Caroline Hutton, one of the first females to study classics at Girton College, Cambridge.[57] Hutton chose a statuette from Corinth (fig. 177) acquired by the British Museum in 1895 as the tinted frontispiece to her book *Greek Terracotta Statuettes* (1899), which she strategically aimed not just at academics but at 'that wider public … mostly attracted by their aesthetic charm'.[58] In her text, Hutton pointed to the statuettes' ability to give a broader account of the lives of the ladies of Ancient Greece than previous scholars had ever allowed:

> we see the Greek woman of the upper classes, we learn how she dressed, the shape, colour and fashion of her different garments, and how coquettishly and with what infinite variety she arranged a costume which, in itself, is extremely

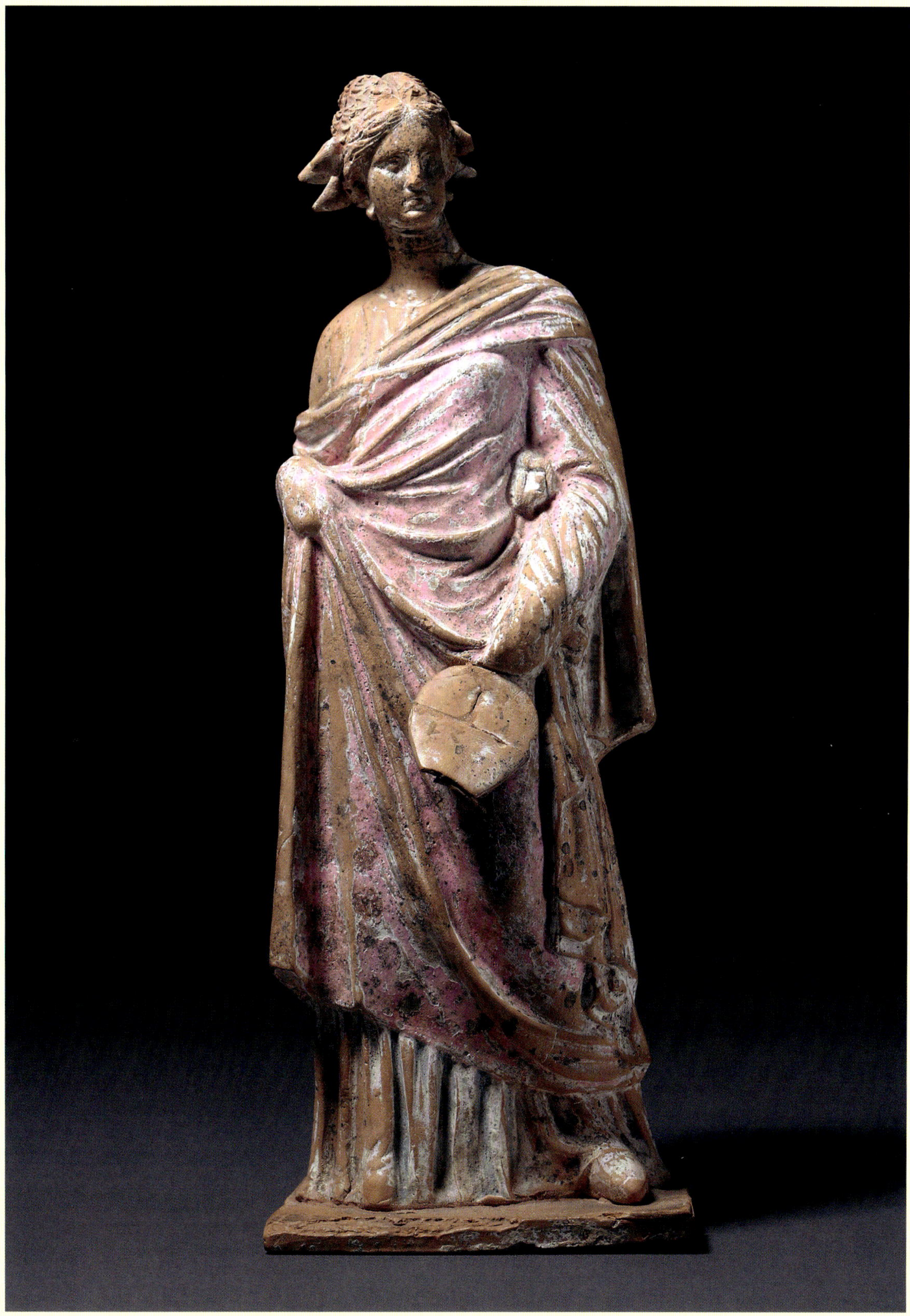

Fig. 176 Figure of standing woman, Boeotia, 300–250 BCE. Terracotta. British Museum, 1874,0305.65. Purchased from Charles Merlin

> simple, and whose elements never varied; and we also learn how she amused herself. Such details are all the more interesting because classical authors tell us so little about her daily life, and the general impression is that we know nothing of it … But why do more than half the Tanagra ladies wear hat and shawl if 'they were not allowed to breathe the outer air, and brooding on their own dull thoughts, must stay within'?[59]

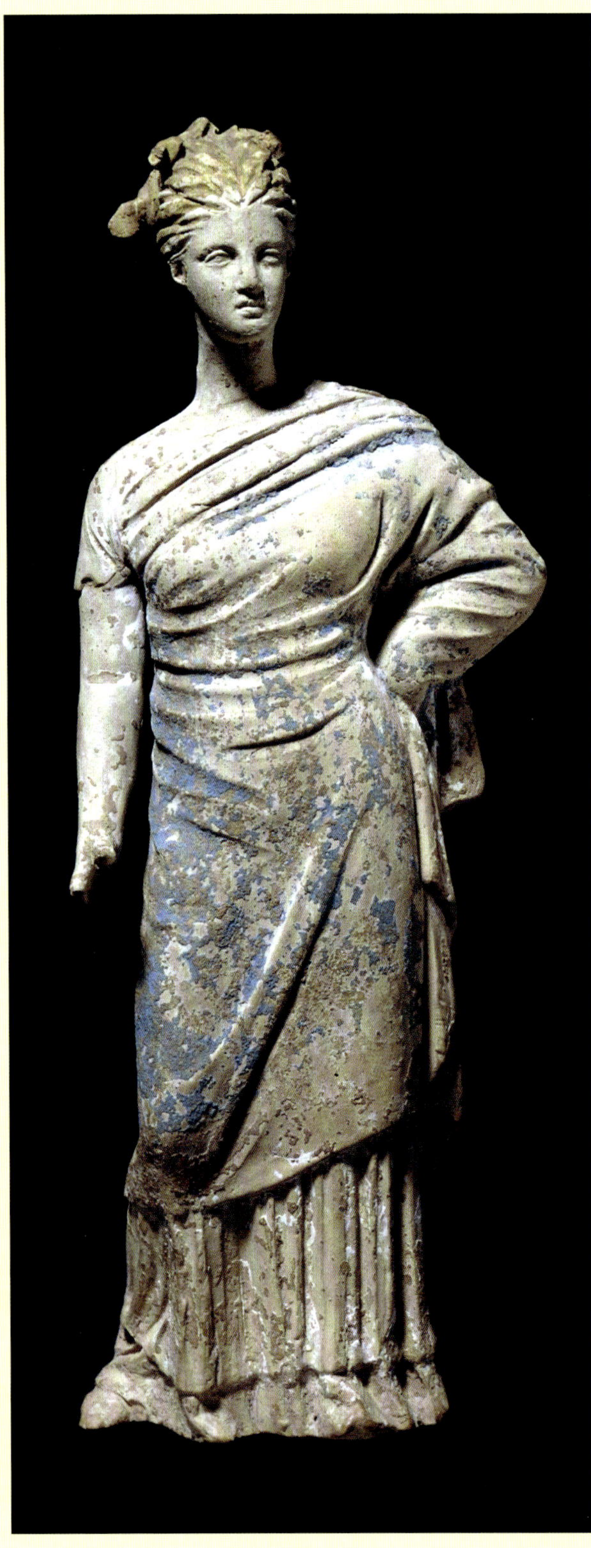

Fig. 177 Figure of standing woman, Corinth, 300–250 BCE. Terracotta. British Museum, 1895,1029.7. Purchased from Jean P. Lambros

The subtle polychromy of the terracotta statuettes – often combining touches of Egyptian blue, ochres, rose madder or cinnabar – also jarred with the supposedly pristine whiteness of the more monumental and masculine sculptures of the fifth century BCE, the glorious Age of Phidias and Pericles.[60] These colours, generally well preserved because most of these figurines had been found in sealed tombs, proved as inspiring to artists and writers as were the elegant folds of their draperies. In France, the historical genre painter and sculptor Jean-Léon Gérôme became so obsessed with the statuettes that he copied them in both paint and marble, even creating his own Tanagra type, 'the Hoop Dancer'. His 1893 painting *Sculpturae vitam insufflat pictura* (fig. 178) depicts a female *coroplast* (the Greek name for a modeller of terracottas) at work on a range of brightly coloured 'hoop dancers' in a shop visited by three female customers who are themselves based on original Tanagras. Lawrence Alma-Tadema, who admired Gérôme's work and paid tribute to his 'Hoop Dancer' in *The Golden Hour* (1908), drew inspiration from several of these figurines to recreate the domestic life of the ancient Hellenes.

Although Oscar Wilde had claimed the 'sombre colouring' of Alma-Tadema's *Phidias Showing the Parthenon Frieze to his Friends* was 'un-Greek', he too embraced the Tanagra type, singling out their faded colours as a potential link between past and present in his essay 'The Critic as Artist' (1891):[61]

> In those days the artist was free. From the river valley he took the fine clay in his fingers, and with a little tool of wood or bone, fashioned it

into forms so exquisite that the people gave them to the dead as their playthings, and we find them still in the dusty tombs on the yellow hillside by Tanagra, with the faint gold and the fading crimson still lingering about hair and lips and raiment … Through form and colour he re-created a world.[62]

Wilde probably started collecting Tanagras in the late 1870s while still an undergraduate at Oxford, following a trip to Greece with John P. Mahaffy. According to his biographer Richard Ellmann, his college rooms were 'filled with exquisite objects, not only blue china but Tanagra statuettes brought back from Greece, Greek rugs bought with the help of William Ward, photographs of his favourite paintings, and his famous easel sporting its unfinished painting'. The scene anticipates Nordau's depiction of the eclectic decadent interior.[63]

In *The Picture of Dorian Gray* (1890), Wilde also compares Sybil, Dorian's beloved actress, to a Tanagra figure in Basil Hallward's studio.[64] Like the fictional painter, many *fin-de-siècle* artists collected and copied the Greek statuettes: James McNeill Whistler and Albert Moore were amongst the earliest enthusiasts in Britain. The two men met around 1864. In 1865, at the Royal Academy Exhibition, Moore presented his first major 'classical' work *The Marble Seat*, a painting inspired by the east pediment frieze of the Parthenon.[65] Emulating Moore's model, Whistler then began to depict draped women in subdued chromatic harmonies. Their common passion for

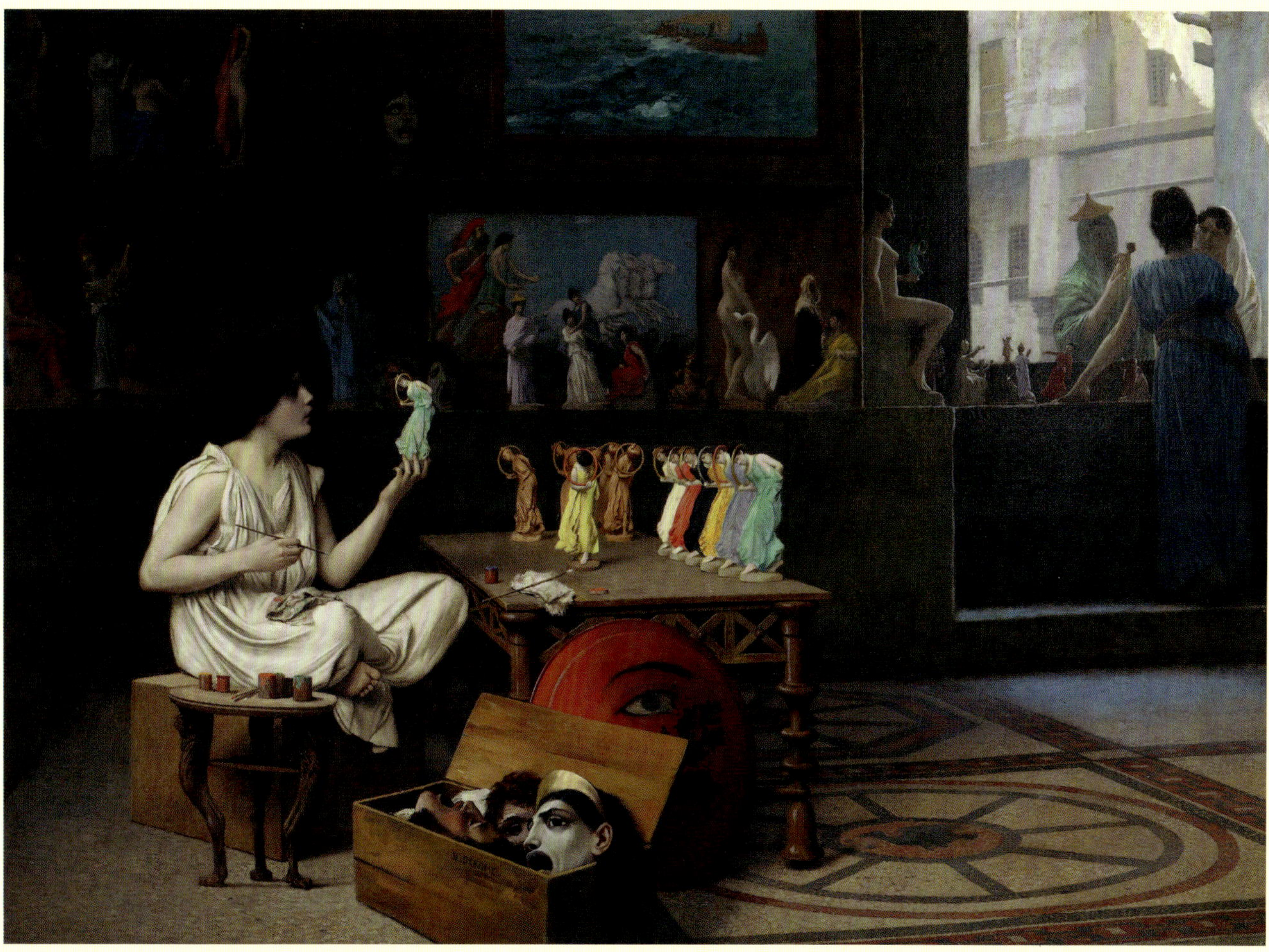

Fig. 178 Jean-Léon Gérôme (1824–1904), *Sculpturae vitam insufflat pictura*, 1893. Oil on canvas. The Art Gallery of Ontario, Toronto , inv. 69/31

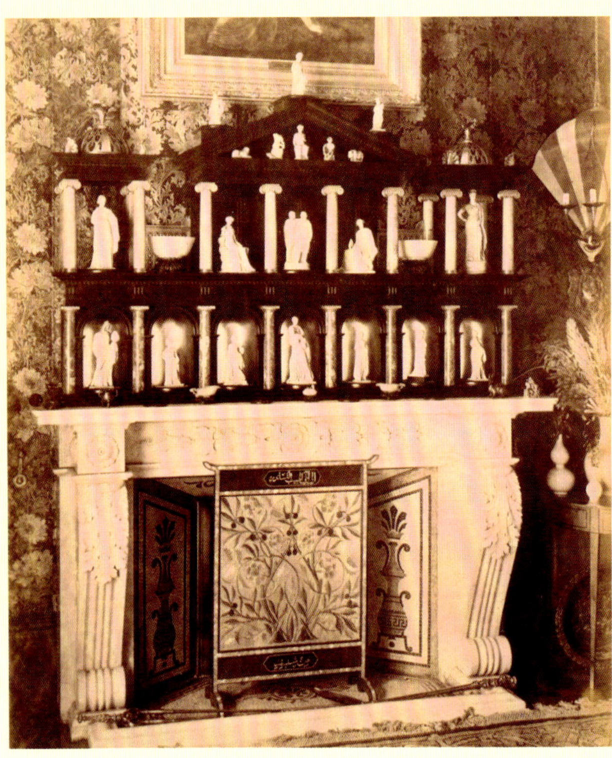

Fig. 179 Bedford Lemere & Co., Interior of 1 Holland Park, Fireplace with Tanagra Figures, *c.*1898. Private Collection / The Stapleton Collection

Fig. 180 Albert Moore (1841–1893), *Pomegranates*, 1866. Oil on canvas. Guildhall Art Gallery, City of London Corporation, 1512

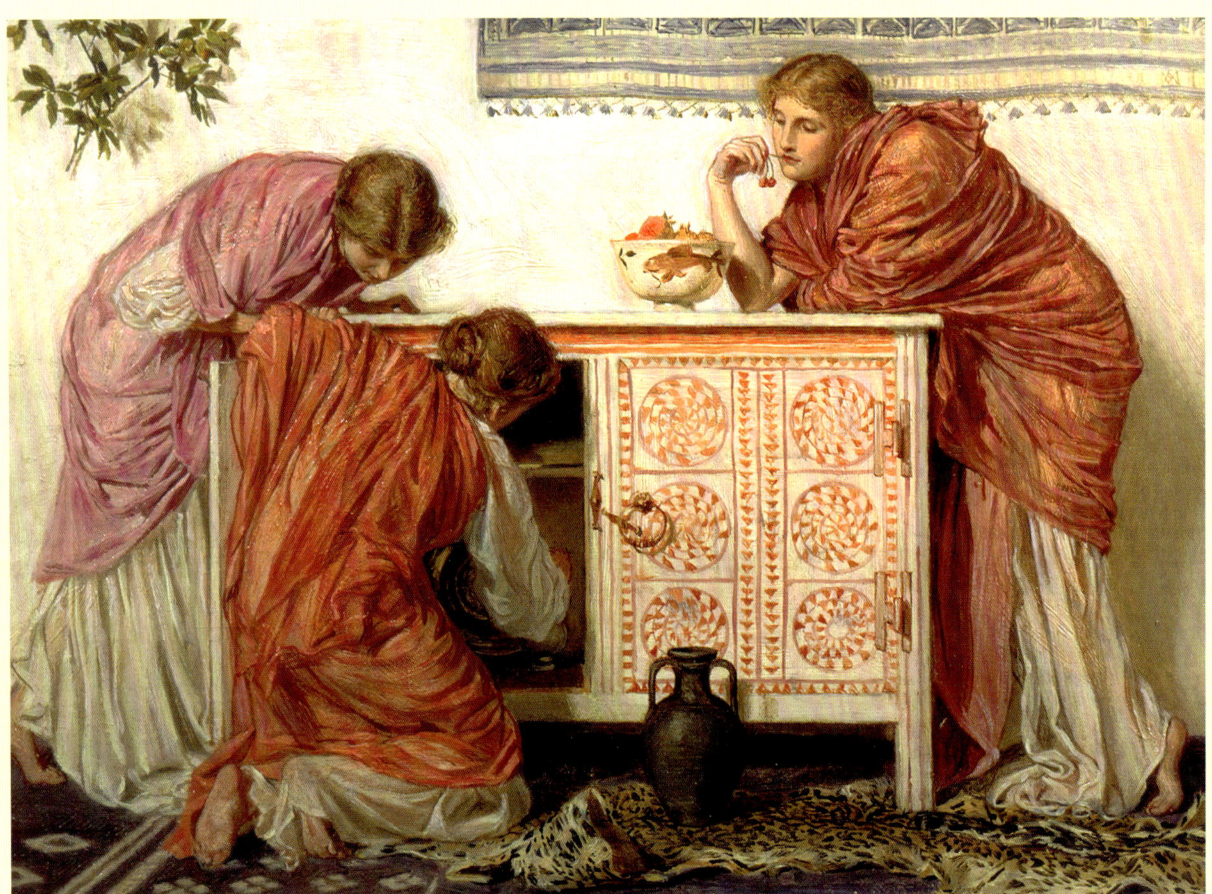

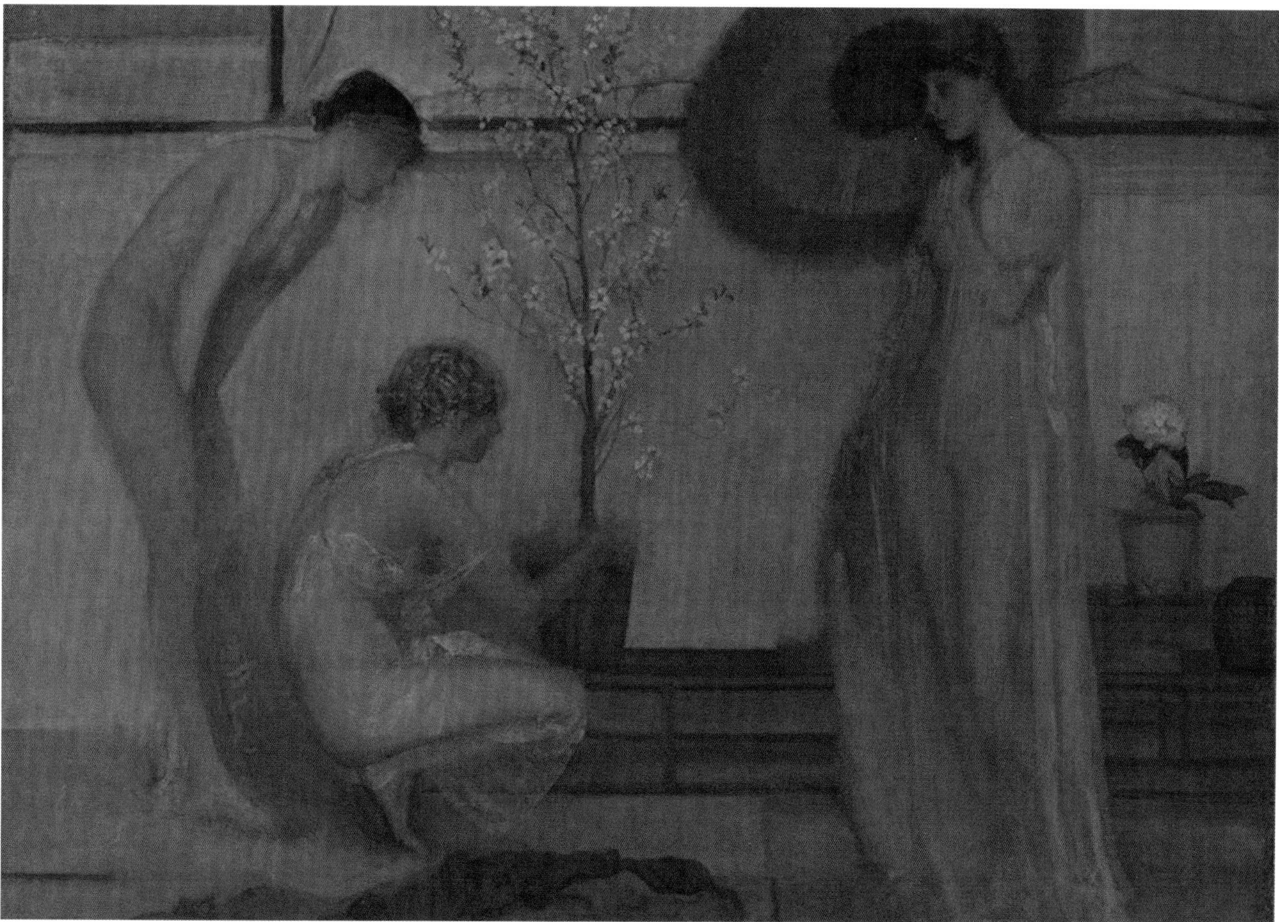

Fig. 181 James McNeill Whistler (1834–1903), *Three Figures: Pink and Grey,* 1868–8. Oil on canvas. Tate, N05971

Tanagras was fostered by the wealthy Ionides family, patrons of Greek ancestry with privileged access to the antiquities being excavated in the country. Whistler even owned a photograph album of Alexandre Constantine Ionides's collection of terracotta figures displayed in the 'antiquities' rooms of his Aesthetic house in Holland Park (fig. 179). There the statuettes were placed on a black marble overmantel designed by artist Walter Crane to resemble a Greco-Roman temple, in compartments formed by classical columns of red and yellow Sienna marble.[66]

Whistler and Moore's shared fascination with the flowing draperies and pastel hues of Tanagras reached its peak in the 1870s. At the time, Whistler occupied a studio on Great Russell Street, opposite the British Museum, which gave him easy access to several of these figurines. The frieze-like arrangement of Moore's *Pomegranates* (fig. 180), which shows three women dressed in himation draperies ranging from pink to red – and looking into a chest of similar hue – is strikingly close in both composition and tone to Whistler's *Three Figures: Pink and Grey* (fig. 181), in which the subtle harmony of pinks and greys is only relieved by the bright red of the flower pot and one of the women's headscarves. This oil on canvas was based on one of six oil sketches known as the 'Six Projects', which were produced by Whistler in 1868 as part of a plan for a frieze commissioned by businessman F.R. Leyland. That same year, the poet A.C. Swinburne praised the non-narrative 'melody of ineffable colour' displayed in both Whistler and Moore's classical paintings of floral

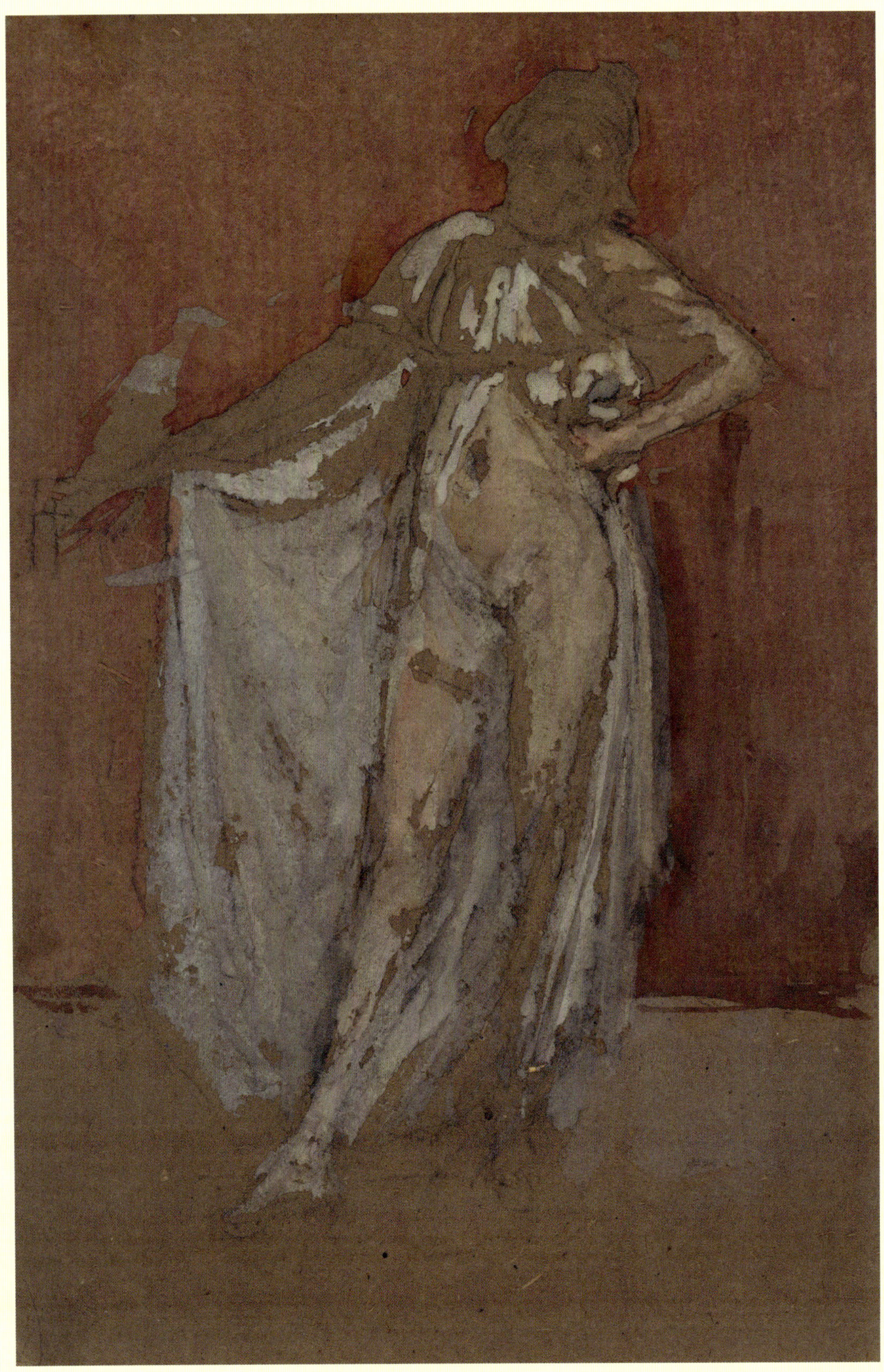

Fig. 182 James McNeill Whistler (1834–1903), *A Dancing Woman in a Pink Robe*, 1888–95. Watercolour and bodycolour. The Hunterian, University of Glasgow GLAHA:46134

women: 'In all of these the main strings touched are certain varying chords of blue and white, not without interludes of the bright and tender tones of floral purple or red.'[67]

Both paintings bear the influence of two-dimensional Japanese prints, which Moore and Whistler often freely fused with Hellenic motifs. The suspended foliage in the left-hand corner, the carp bowl and the circular motifs decorating the cabinet in *Pomegranates* are all strongly evocative of Japanese art and, in particular, of *ukiyo-e* prints.[68] The parasol and cherry blossom in Whistler's *Three Figures* are equally *japonistes*. The mirrors and fans ornamenting many Tanagras encouraged such parallels between Ancient Greece and Japan, which lay at the core of Whistler's eclectic conception of beauty expounded in his 1885 'Ten O'Clock Lecture': 'The story of the beautiful is already complete - Hewn in the marbles of the Parthenon - And broidered, with the birds, upon the fan of Hokusai.'[69]

Although their styles eventually diverged from the 1880s, Whistler and Moore's friendship never faltered, the American painter even asking Moore to testify in his favour at the libel trial against John Ruskin in 1878. Whistler's fascination with Tanagras also remained undimmed, as shown by some of his later pastels and watercolours, including *Dancing Woman in a Pink Robe* (fig. 182). The figure is in the same delicate shade of pink (emphasised by the porphyry-red background) as some of his earlier work, but it no longer displays the sculptural quality favoured by Moore. Whistler's *Dancing Woman* explores the possibility of movement, probably as a response to the colourful performances of Loïe Fuller, whom the painter had seen in 1892 and whom the sculptor Auguste Rodin compared to a 'Tanagra in action'.[70] Fuller soon became so famous across Europe that her dancing body was commodified into an *objet d'art* in the style of a modern *Danseuse Titeux*. Echoing Wilde's comment in 'The Critic as Artist', all artists who were inspired by the flowing figures from Tanagra 're-created a world' - an antique past no longer white and distant, but alive with colour.

Charlotte Ribeyrol

Object in Focus

Japanese Board Game

Snakes and ladders-type board games, known as *sugoroku* ('double sixes'), had been popular in Japan since the thirteenth century, when they were used as Buddhist teaching tools. From the eighteenth century, developments in woodblock printing technology enabled the mass production of cheap and colourfully illustrated *sugoroku* on a whole range of topics including kabuki theatre, flower arranging and classical literature. Their affordability and accessibility made these games not only a best-selling form of entertainment, but also a highly effective tool for informal education and propaganda.

This 'Board Game of Japanese Reforms' (fig. 183) illustrates a range of sophisticated activities players could aspire to take part in as model citizens in the rapidly modernising Japan of the late nineteenth century. In the 1850s, Japan was forced to open up trade with foreign powers after more than two centuries of limited contact with the outside world. Determined not to become a victim of the expansionist policies of the United States and the European nations, the Japanese government embarked on a programme of modernisation and Westernisation that was intended to transform Japan from a pre-industrial, feudal country into a powerful, modern nation state. This modernisation process was known as 'civilization and enlightenment' (*bunmei kaika*), and almost every element of Japanese society was affected: there was a new constitution, new laws, new schools, new clothes and new customs. Japanese delegations were sent abroad to devour the latest information about Western technology and systems, while foreign technical experts were invited to Japan to share their knowledge. Steam ships, railways, gas lights, brick buildings, Western classical music and dance parties became symbols of modern Japan and its strengthening position in the world.

From the 1860s to the 1890s woodblock prints depicting new machines and buildings, fashions and customs – often shown in an idealised version – played an important role in communicating the modernisation process to Japanese citizens who were attempting to adjust to the rapid changes in their society. Inexpensive and fun, with their colourful, easily understood visuals, these 'civilization and enlightenment pictures' (*bunmei kaika-e*) were an easy way to instruct the population in proper 'enlightened' behaviour. The authorities encouraged their publication, and educational *sugoroku* like this one were typically distributed free or at minimal cost in magazines and newspapers, especially at New Year. The games were folded up and placed inside illustrated sleeves printed with a title and sometimes the name of the artist. Although *sugoroku* were issued in substantial numbers, the fact that they were designed to be used means that very few survive today. Indeed, the substantial wear and tear visible in this example suggests that this 'board' was actually used.

The 'Board Game of Japanese Reforms' demonstrated 15 modern pastimes that exemplified ideal behaviour for 'good subjects', according to the government's edict, and was clearly aimed at women and children. Players started at the lower central square, where a group of women dressed in the latest Western fashions and hairstyles are organising a charity event. Coloured cartouches in each of the game squares contain instructions for players to move on to other squares, depending on the throw of the dice.

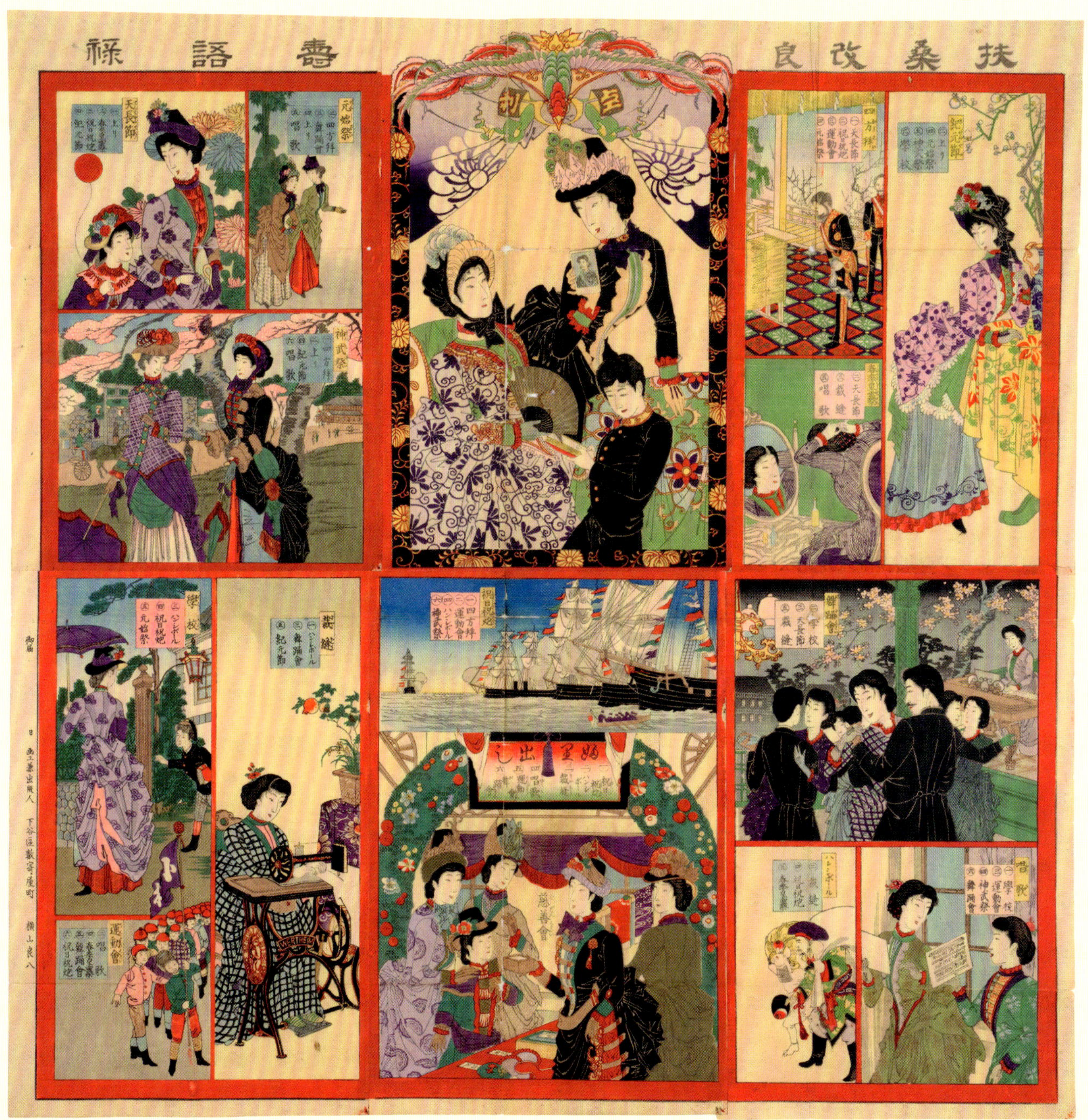

Fig. 183 Yōshū Chikanobu (1838–1912), 'Board Game of Japanese Reforms' (*Fusō kairyō sugoroku*), 1887. Colour woodblock print published by Yokoyama Ryōhachi

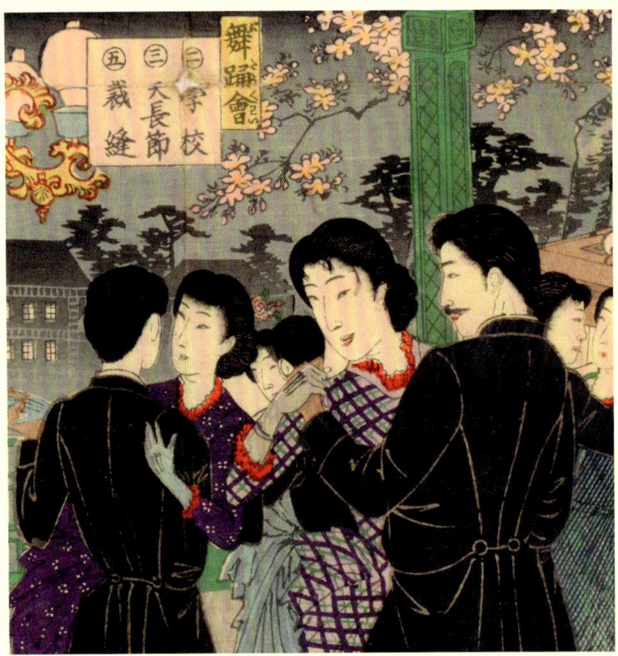

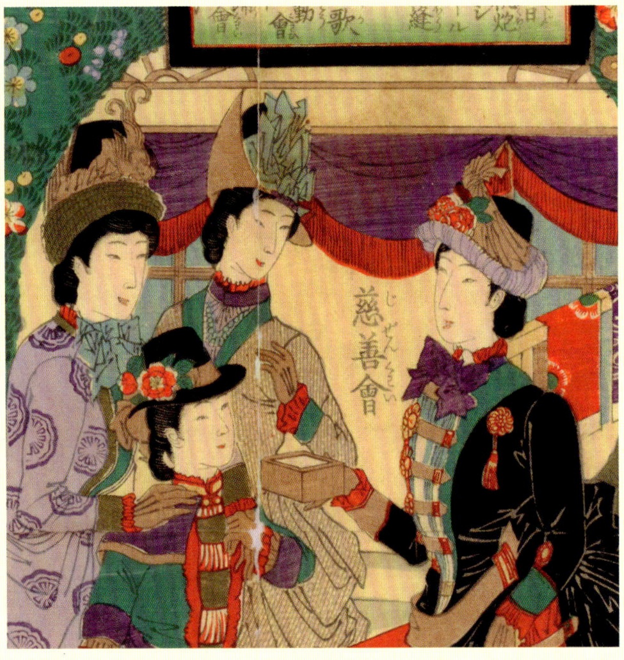

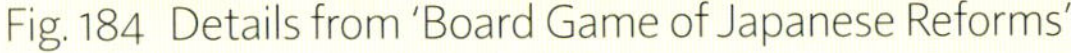
Fig. 184 Details from 'Board Game of Japanese Reforms'

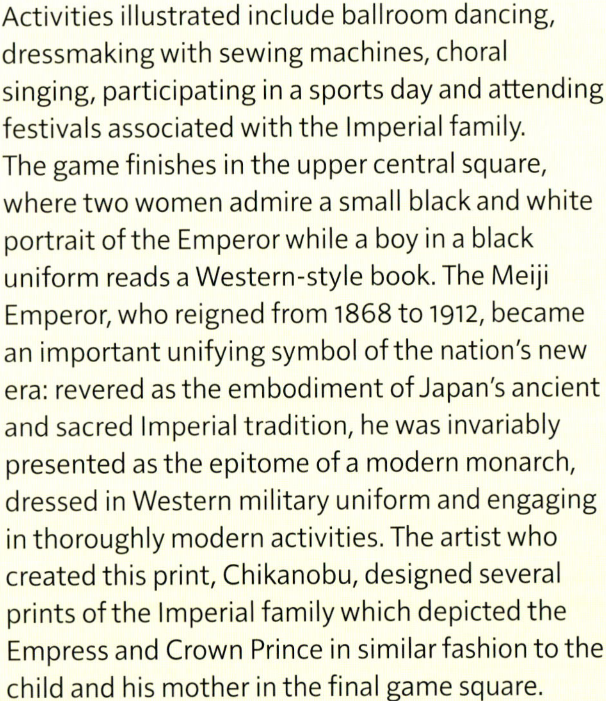
Activities illustrated include ballroom dancing, dressmaking with sewing machines, choral singing, participating in a sports day and attending festivals associated with the Imperial family. The game finishes in the upper central square, where two women admire a small black and white portrait of the Emperor while a boy in a black uniform reads a Western-style book. The Meiji Emperor, who reigned from 1868 to 1912, became an important unifying symbol of the nation's new era: revered as the embodiment of Japan's ancient and sacred Imperial tradition, he was invariably presented as the epitome of a modern monarch, dressed in Western military uniform and engaging in thoroughly modern activities. The artist who created this print, Chikanobu, designed several prints of the Imperial family which depicted the Empress and Crown Prince in similar fashion to the child and his mother in the final game square.

It was appropriate that a board game about modernising reforms should use a vivid new palette of colours quite different from the range of tones typical of traditional woodblock prints. Players would have noticed the startling red borders of the game squares, and the rich yellows, purples, pinks and greens within, even before making out the details of the various pastimes depicted. To this original audience in 1887 these brilliant colours – typical of 'civilization and enlightenment pictures' – were as contemporary as their content, and reflected the dramatic progress of Japanese society. From the birth of Japanese colour printing in the eighteenth century, woodblock printmaking had depended on natural dyes, mostly derived from flowers, plants and minerals. By the late eighteenth century, printmakers were using these to achieve a highly sophisticated range of colour effects. However, many traditional pigments were unstable, with vegetable dyes often highly fugitive and mineral-based pigments quick to deteriorate.

Since the 1820s the early synthetic dye Prussian Blue, imported from Germany, had transformed Japanese printmaking. Cheap, stable and easy to use, it gave artists unprecedented freedom in their depiction of seas, rivers and skies, ushering in a 'Blue Revolution' and contributing to the emergence of the landscape print genre.[71] So popular was the new pigment that many publishers produced works printed predominantly, or even entirely, in shades of blue. The celebrated print designer Katsushika Hokusai was one of the first Japanese artists to embrace the novel colour: his 'Great Wave off Kanagawa' of 1831 is one of many Hokusai designs to make dramatic use of Prussian Blue.

From the late 1860s, however, another colour revolution unfolded.[72] Although traditional pigments were widely used well into the Meiji era, the opening of Japan to international trade released a flood of imported aniline and other synthetically manufactured pigments. As with Prussian Blue, these new colourants spread rapidly in Japan because they were bright and easy to use. Smaller quantities of dye were now needed to achieve the desired colours, and so printing also became less labour intensive and consequently more affordable.

The first chemical pigment to enter Japan through the hands of merchants in Yokohama in 1864 was magenta (also known as fuchsine or rosaniline). Red had traditionally been made with a natural dye derived from safflower, but after 1869 this was almost completely replaced by magenta, and also by carmine, an organic colorant derived from cochineal beetles. Carmine cochineal remained the primary red in Japanese prints for the next two decades. Very quickly, red became the predominant colour in woodblock prints, often used over large areas: as solid red backgrounds or in wide bands of red gradation, down from the upper edge of a print, or up from the horizon. 1875 saw the arrival of a new synthetic dye called methyl violet. This 'true' violet created a rich purple without any need for mixing. This was particularly useful since purple was the colour of the Imperial household, and the colour became wildly popular. Two years later, in 1877, the synthetic pigment eosine was introduced - used by itself to give a bright pink, but also with cochineal carmine to give a deep, bluish red. From 1889 a succession of red synthetic naphthol dyes appeared - these produced an even more assertive, albeit rather unstable, red.

The new reds were accompanied by equally brilliant - although not aniline - yellows and greens. These colours had long been made in Japan from the mineral orpiment (arsenic sulphide), and orpiment mixed with Prussian Blue. From the mid-nineteenth century, however, it became possible to obtain arsenic sulphide pigments through a synthetic industrial process, which made them cheaper to use. While Prussian Blue continued to be an important element of printmaking it was no longer a novelty, and the colour blue was rarely a predominant feature of late nineteenth-century prints.

The effect of Meiji-period dyes can be startling, and they have often been criticised as 'garish' and 'strident'. Yet they can also be seen as lively examples of the Japanese quest to express enlightenment and sophistication in the final decades of the century. The colour choices made by print designers and publishers can be seen as part of a wider negotiation of modern national identity, as Japan emerged onto the world stage. Just as the Prussian-blue skies and oceans of the early nineteenth century have been linked to Japan's growing awareness of the world beyond its borders, so the brilliant synthetic colours of late-nineteenth century prints can be seen to express the rapid progress of a nation galloping its way into modernity.

Publishers' rapid adoption of new pigments chimes with the country's technological innovation, foreign trade, and its entrance into the international arena as a leading modern power. Yet these state-of-the-art colours were also linked to Japanese history and to Japan's sense of national identity. In particular, the reds and purples that dominated 'civilisation and enlightenment pictures' also symbolised Japan's ancient traditions: red being the colour of festivity, healing, the sun and Japan itself - land of the sun goddess; purple being the colour of the Emperor and the Imperial family. It is interesting to note that, by the turn of the century, synthetic pigments began to be used in a more subtle, naturalistic way, and 'enlightenment' subjects largely disappeared: as Japan's national confidence grew, there was no longer any need to trumpet its advances in woodblock prints.

Clare Pollard

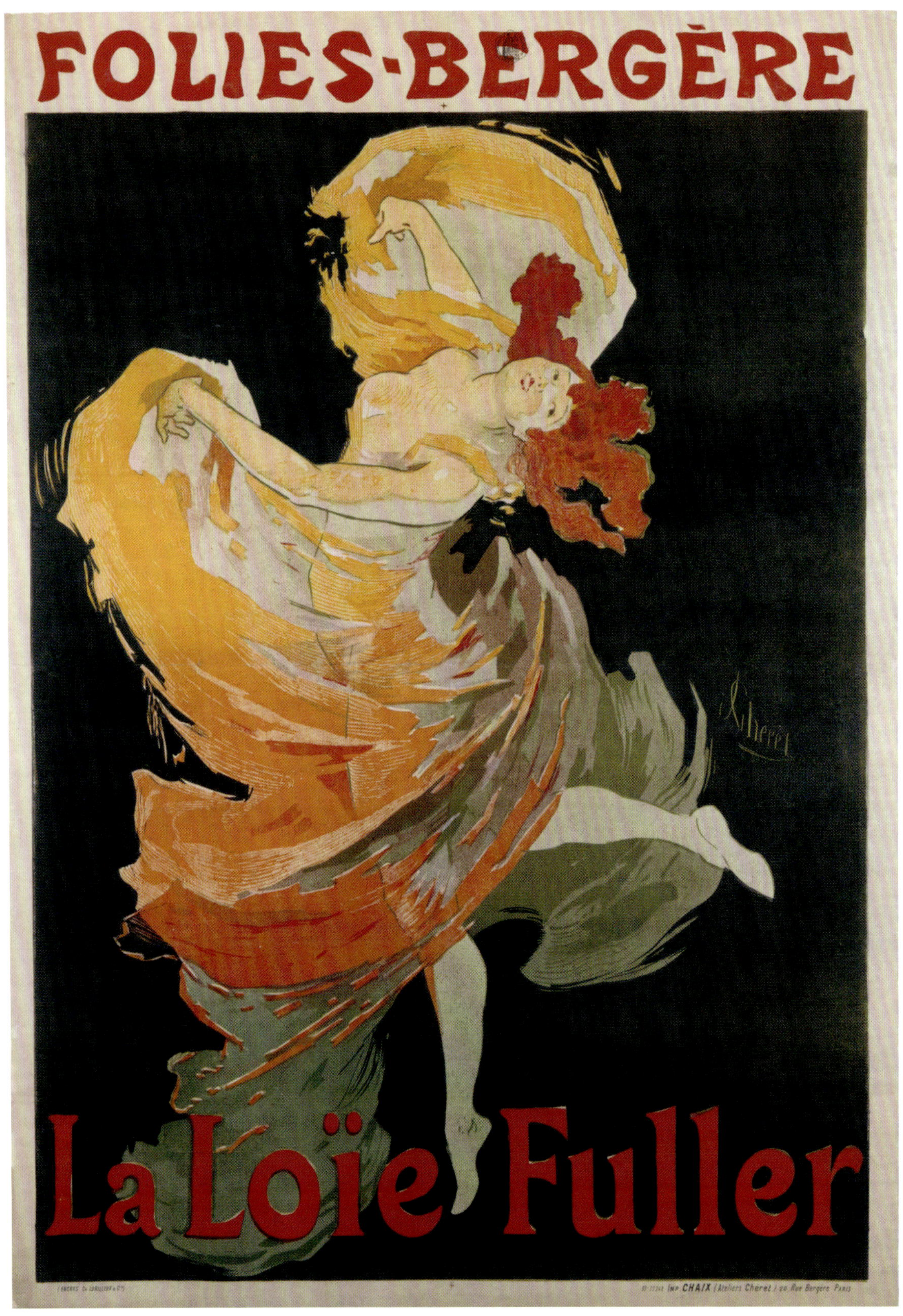

Fig. 185 *La Loïe Fuller*. Poster advertising Loïe Fuller at the Folies Bergères, designed by Jules Chéret (1836–1932), printed by Imprimerie Chaix, Paris, 1893. Colour lithograph. Victoria and Albert Museum, E.113-1921

The Electric Fairy: Loïe Fuller (1862–1928)

Matthew Winterbottom

On 5 November 1892, Marie Louise Fuller, a stout, unknown vaudeville performer from Illinois, premiered her 'Serpentine Dance' at the famous Folies Bergère cabaret music hall in Paris (fig. 185). The audience was captivated, and Fuller became an overnight sensation. The poet Stéphane Mallarmé described how Fuller had 'transformed the Folies Bergère', creating a 'success without precedence in this theatre.'[73] 'La Loïe' became the darling of Paris, playing for an unprecedented 300 consecutive performances. Mallarmé wrote: 'Every night, the regular boulevard public is submerged in a crowd of scholars, painters, sculptors, writers, ambassadors ... All these people, forgetting their social rank and dignity, climb on tabletops like a group of kids.'[74] A reviewer described changes in the clientele of the Folies Bergère: 'One now sees black dress coats ... carriages decorated with coats of arms; the aristocracy is lining up to applaud Loïe Fuller.'[75]

Her success also brought fame beyond Paris: Fuller was the most famous American in Europe during the 1890s and 1900s. Loved by both the working classes and the aristocracy, Fuller's performances transcended high and low culture. Among her friends were famous artists, actors, writers and royals. Seen as the living embodiment of 'La Art Nouveau' and a symbol of Modernism, she was the inspiration for countless artworks, poems and even early films (figs 186,

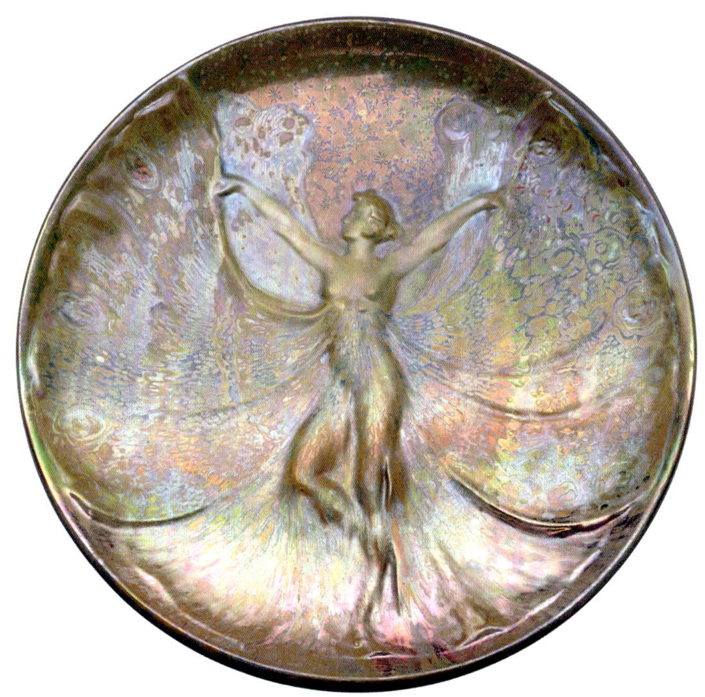

Fig. 186 Charger, designed by Lucien Lévy-Dhurmer (1865–1953), 1901. Earthenware. Indianapolis Museum of Art at Newfields, USA

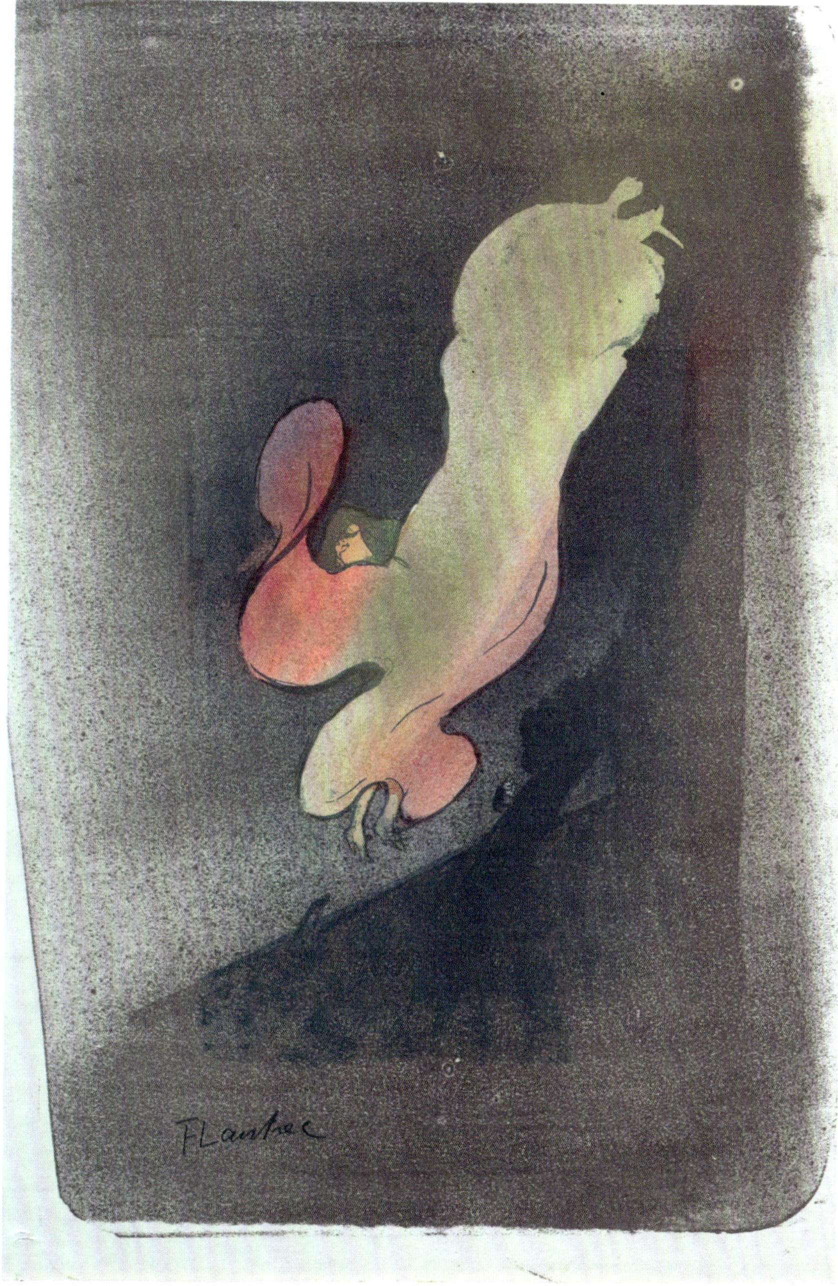

Fig. 187 Henri de Toulouse-Lautrec (1864–1901), *Miss Loïe Fuller*, 1893. Colour lithograph. The Cleveland Museum of Art, Gift of Ralph King 1925.1202

187). A journalist for *The Architectural Record* wrote: 'Miss Fuller's impression upon the world will not have been a transient one. She has contributed towards the creation of a new style; she has come upon the scene at the right moment.'[76]

Loïe Fuller was the only woman to have her own pavilion at the celebrated 1900 Paris Exposition, an event that attracted more than 50 million visitors. Jean Cocteau recalled seeing her there 'atop a pedestal manoeuvring great waves of supple silk … creating innumerable orchids of light and fabric unfurling, rising, disappearing, turning, floating … Let us all hail this dancer who … created the phantom of an era'.[77]

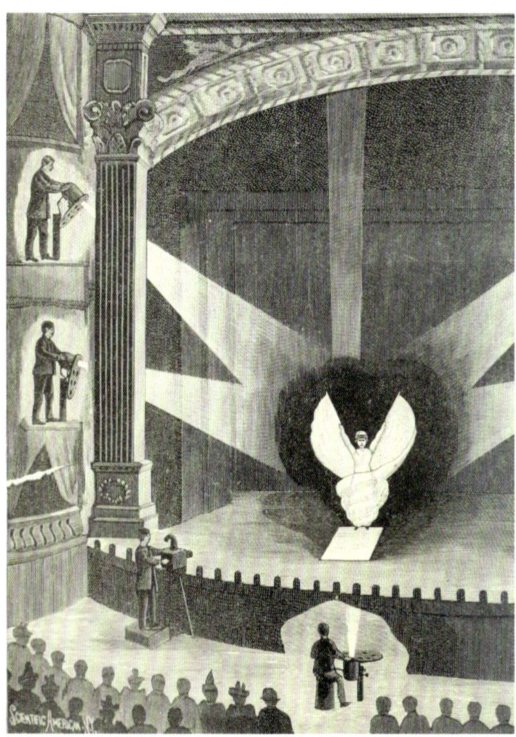

Fig. 188 Frontispiece to Albert A. Hopkins and Henry Ridgely Evans, *Magic: Stage Illusions and Scientific Diversions, Including Trick Photography*, 1897

Fuller created 128 different dances over her 40-year career. She wrote that it was 'generally agreed that I have created something new, something composed of light, colour, music, and the dance, more especially of light and the dance'.[78] Through her choreographic and technical inventiveness and brilliance, Fuller is now recognised as a pioneer of modern dance and theatrical lighting techniques and stagecraft. Many of her innovations and techniques are still in use today.

Colour was central to the success of Fuller's performances. Her voluminous costumes were made using dozens of metres of diaphanous white silk, with concealed cane rods to extend the sleeves. Using strength and skill, Fuller moved her body to create shifting sculptural forms, the billowing silk swirling around her in shapes that recalled butterflies, flowers, waves, clouds and flames. Enhancing this spectacle were the jewel-like colours of the lights – constantly changing and merging – that lit the swirling silk on an otherwise darkened stage. The effect was ethereally beautiful and extraordinarily effective. The names of many of her dances – Serpentine, Violet and Butterfly, Opal, Lily and Fire – reflected the changing forms and colours she created for the audience.

In addition to devising the choreography, Fuller also invented and patented complex electrical lighting systems using rotating disks to project coloured lights onto the stage from many angles (figs 188, 189). Glass panels fitted directly into the stage floor provided dramatic up-lighting effects. Fuller corresponded with Thomas Edison about lighting techniques; her early and innovative use of electricity gave her the moniker '*La fée élétricité*', or the Electric Fairy.[79]

Fuller also patented the chemical gel filters that coloured the spotlights, and even the phosphorescent salts that made her silk costumes glow on stage. She wrote: 'I am astounded when I see the relations that form and colour assume.

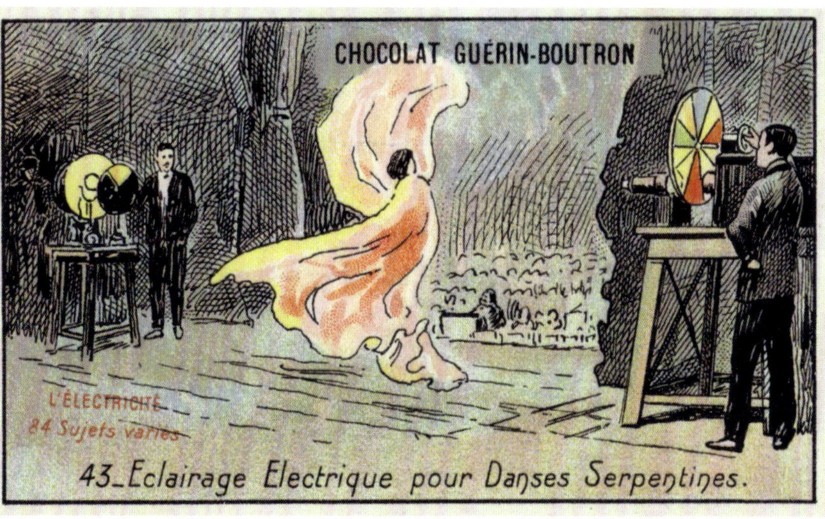

Fig. 189 *Electric lighting for the serpentine dance*, *c.*1900. Colour lithograph

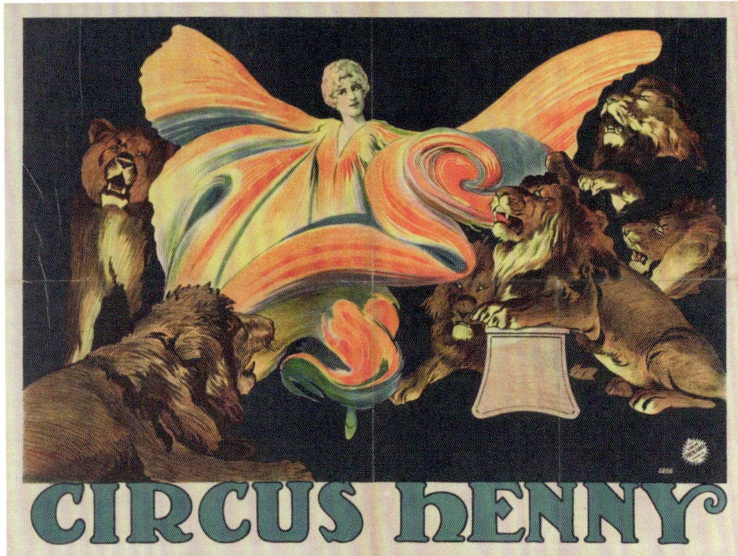

Fig. 190 Serpentine Dance with Lions at the Circus Henny, coloured lithograph, Friedländer, Hamburg, 1919. 96 x 71 cm

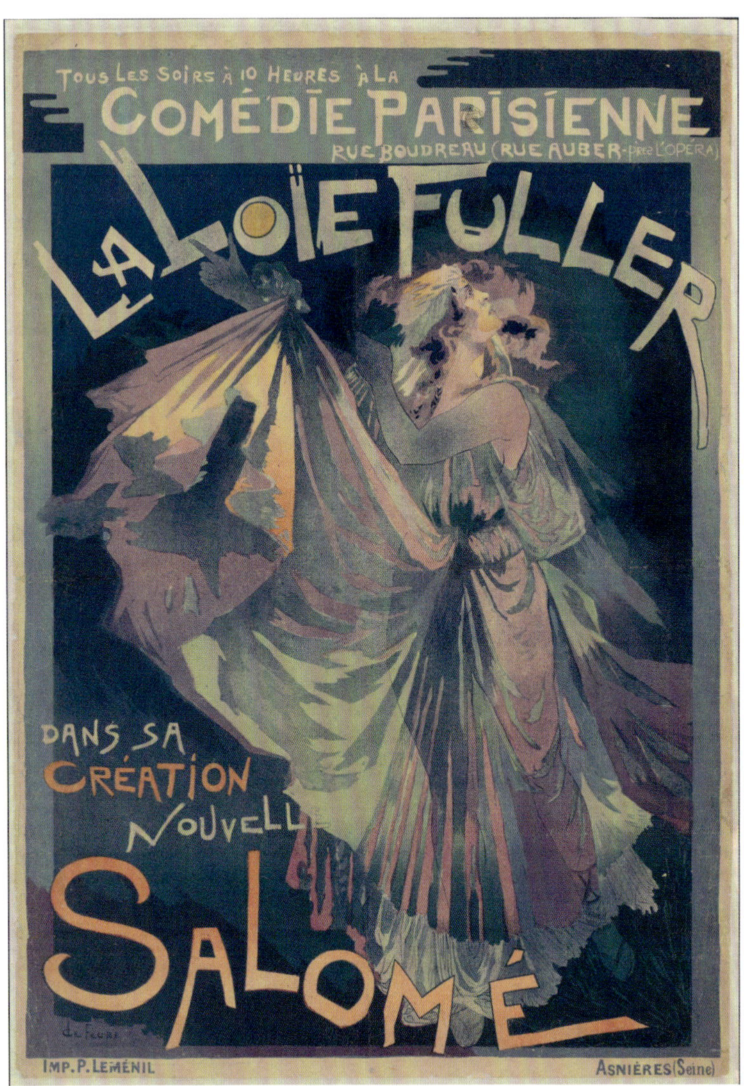

Fig. 191 Georges de Feure (1868–1943) *La Loïe Fuller dans sa Création Nouvelle Salomé*, 1900. Colour lithograph poster advertising the dancer Loïe Fuller performing at 10pm every night at the Comédie Parisienne. Victoria and Albert Museum, London, E.161-1921

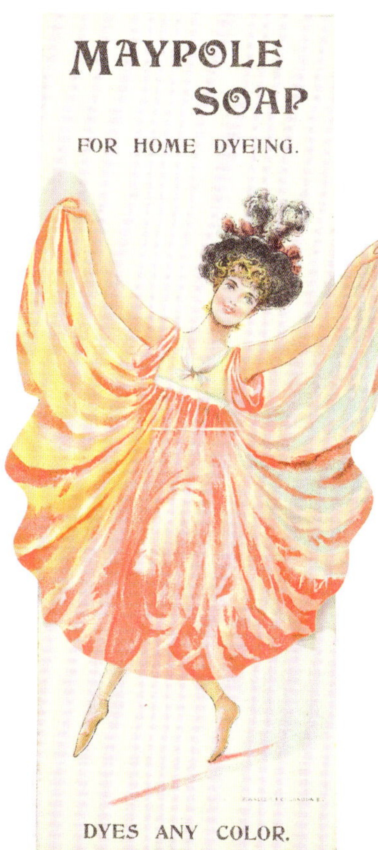

Fig. 192 'Maypole Soap for Home Dyeing' advertisement card, *c.*1899. Colour lithograph. Bodleian Library, University of Oxford, John Johnson Collection, Soap 1 (74)

The scientific admixture of chemically composed colours, heretofore unknown, fills me with admiration, and I stand before them like a miner who has discovered a vein of gold, and who completely forgets himself as he contemplates the wealth of the world before him.'[80]

Fuller's dances inspired hundreds of similar acts in theatres and music halls across Europe and America. Audiences could see novelty performances of dancing dogs dressed like Fuller, and even young women performing their versions of her Serpentine Dance in cages with lions and tigers (fig. 190).[81]

Fuller's name and image were recognisable far beyond *fin-de-siècle* Paris: stores sold flowing silk 'Loïe' shirts, blouses and even men's ties, and colourful cocktails were named after her. Fuller's image was used to advertise all manner of household products, from perfume to home dyes (fig. 192). Although most consumers would never have seen her perform in person, they might have seen a low-budget version at their local music hall, or a film featuring her (or one of her imitators) in the cinema. These early black and white films were often tinted using aniline dyes, but they could not convey the ethereal beauty and subtle colour effects of the original live performances.

In 1900, the critic Arsène Alexandre wrote: 'Loïe Fuller has triumphed first of all because she is an inventor: she created a new form of art. Was it dance? Dancers would have told you no … Was it colour? Painters would have told you with a bit of envy – but loyal and admiring envy – that it was something more that they could neither analyze nor pin down.'[82]

Object List

All measurements in millimetres, height × width × depth

1
Queen Victoria's Mourning Dress and Widow's Cap, c.1898
Mourning outfit: silk, cotton, chiffon; bodice = bust 1150 dia., waist 1170 dia., back 360 width; jacket = bust 1320 dia. , waist 1420 dia. , back 410 width; skirt = waist 1150 dia. Widow's cap: silk net, 230 × 160
Historic Royal Palaces

2
John Everett Millais (1829–1896)
Portrait of John Ruskin, 1853–4
Oil on canvas, 713 × 608
Ashmolean Museum. Accepted by HM Government in lieu of Inheritance Tax and allocated to the Ashmolean Museum, 2013.

3
Joseph Mallord William Turner (1775–1851)
Venice, from the Porch of Madonna della Salute, c.1835
Oil on canvas, 914 × 1222
Lent by The Metropolitan Museum of Art, Bequest of Cornelius Vanderbilt, 1899 (99.31)

4
Joseph Mallord William Turner's watercolour palette case, c.1800–51
Wood, paint, glass metal, 53 × 355 × 292
Ashmolean Museum. Presented by John Ruskin, 1861.

5
George Field (1777–1854)
Chromotography; Or, A Treatise on Colours and Pigments, and of Their Powers in Painting, 1835
Printed book
Bodleian Libraries, University of Oxford, 2 DELTA 195

6
Joseph Mallord William Turner (1775–1851)
Venice: the Grand Canal, 1840
Watercolour over graphite with bodycolour and pen and red ink, 460 × 604
Ashmolean Museum. Presented by John Ruskin, 1861

7
John Ruskin (1819–1900)
Study of the Marble Inlaying on the Front of the Casa Loredan, Venice, 1845
Watercolour on paper, 342 × 297
Ashmolean Museum. Presented by John Ruskin to the Ruskin Drawing School (University of Oxford), 1875

8
John Brett (1831–1902)
Gentian, 1862
Watercolour on paper, 107 × 146
Birkenhead, Williamson Art Gallery and Museum

9
John Ruskin (1819–1900)
Study of Dawn: Purple Clouds, 1868
Watercolour on paper, 153 × 223
Ashmolean Museum

10
John Ruskin (1819–1900)
Study of a Kingfisher, with dominant reference to colour, 1871
Watercolour on paper , 604 × 450
Ashmolean Museum. Presented by John Ruskin to the Ruskin Drawing School (University of Oxford), 1875

11
John Everett Millais (1829–1896)
The Woodsman's Daughter, 1851
Oil on canvas, 1050 × 793 × 77
Guildhall Art Gallery, London

12
Dante Gabriel Rossetti (1828–1882)
Beatrice at a Marriage Feast Denying her Salutation to Dante, 1855
Watercolour and pen on paper, 550 × 725
Ashmolean Museum

13
John Everett Millais (1829–1896)
Mariana, 1851
Oil on mahogany, 597 × 762
Tate: Accepted by HM Government in lieu of tax and allocated to the Tate Gallery 1999

14
Edward Burne-Jones (1833–1898) for Morris & Co.
Angel with Lute (panel from St. James's Church, Marylebone), 1873–5
Glass, lead, wood, 2793 × 738 × 43
The Whitworth, The University of Manchester

15
John Hardman Powell (1827–1895) for Hardman & Co.
Flagon, 1858–9
Ruby glass mounted in silver-gilt, embellished with cabochons and enamels, 325 × 150 × 130
Victoria and Albert Museum. Formerly in the collection of Charles and Lavinia Handley-Read

16
Augustus Welby Northmore Pugin (1812–1852) for John Hardman & Co.
Headband, 1848
Enamelled gold set with a ruby, diamonds, turquoises and pearls , 31 × 155 × 5
Victoria and Albert Museum

17
Augustus Welby Northmore Pugin (1812–1852)
Gothic Brooch, c. 1848
Gold and enamel, 70 × 120 × 80
Ashmolean Museum. Purchased, with funds given by Barrie and Deedee Wigmore, 2023

18
Paste-set silver brooch in the shape of a heart given to Jane Morris by Dante Gabriel Rossetti, c. 1840–65
Silver set with glass, 34 × 29 × 6
Victoria and Albert Museum. Bequeathed by May Morris

19
Augustus Welby Northmore Pugin (1812–1852)
Design for Wallpaper for Palace of Westminster, 1851
Pencil with blue, red, brown, yellow, green and pink washes on paper
Victoria and Albert Museum

20
Augustus Welby Northmore Pugin (1812–1852) for Minton & Co.
Tiles from the Stove in the Medieval Court, 1851
Earthenware with majolica glaze, 290 × 290
Ashmolean Museum. Bequeathed by Peter Rose and Albert Gallichan, 2021

21
Frederick Sandys (1829–1904)
Scene from the Oeuvres of Christine de Pisan, 1850–60
Watercolour on paper, 88 × 89
Lent by Birmingham Museums Trust on behalf of Birmingham City Council

22
Christine de Pisan (b. 1364)
Lovers in Conversation (Cent ballades d'amant et de dame), c.1410–14
Illuminated manuscript, 230 × 570 × 400
The British Library

23
Jean Froissard (1337–1405)
Chroniques, vol. IV, part 2 (Dance of the Wodewoses), c.1470–2
Illuminated manuscript, 290 × 660 × 460
The British Library

24
Elizabeth Eleanor (Lizzie) Siddal (1829–1862)
Madonna and Child
Watercolour on paper, 604 × 450
Ashmolean Museum. Bequeathed by John N. Bryson, 1977

25
Jane Morris (1839–1914)
Daisy Wall Hanging, 1862
Embroidered wool, 1670 × 2960
Society of Antiquaries (Kelmscott Manor)

26
Dante Gabriel Rossetti (1828–1882) and Eleanor Elizabeth (Lizzie) Siddal (1829–1862)
Medieval-style jewel casket belonging to Jane Morris, c.1859
Painted cedar wood bound with studded iron bands, 177 × 292 × 177
Society of Antiquaries (Kelmscott Manor)

27
Phoebe Anna Traquair (1852–1936)
Two Pages, Illuminated, 'Sonnets from the Portugese' by Elizabeth Barrett Browning, 1894–6
Pen and ink and bodycolour over pencil on vellum, 188 × 155 and 188 × 157
National Galleries of Scotland. Phoebe Anna Traquair Bequest, 1936

28
Alfred William Hunt (1830–1896)
A November Rainbow, Dolwyddelan Valley, November 11, 1866, 1 p.m., 1866
Watercolour on paper, 503 × 755
Ashmolean Museum. Purchased with the assistance of the Art Fund, 1922

29
Utagawa Hiroshige (1797–1858)
A Fine Evening on the Coast in Tsushima Province, 1856
Nishiki-e (full colour) woodblock print, with *bokashi* (tonal gradation), 353 × 244
Ashmolean Museum. Presented by Mrs E.M. Allan and Mr and Mrs H.N. Spalding from the Herbert H. Jennings Collection, 1952

30
Christopher Dresser (1834–1904) for Minton & Co.
Vase with beetle on the side, 1872
Porcelain, 245 × 120 × 120
Ashmolean Museum. Bequeathed by Peter Rose and Albert Gallichan, 2021

31
Kate Greenaway (1846–1901)
Two dodecagonal ornamental designs with pencil drawings of flowers and leaves, 1864
Watercolour and pencil, 323 × 475
Victoria and Albert Museum

32
Humming bird fan and case
M. & E. Natté, Rio de Janeiro, 1880s
Feathers, ivory, card, Fan: 340 × 430 × 40; case 350 × 470 × 25.
Manchester Art Gallery

33
Harry Emanuel (1831–1898)
Humming bird necklace and case, 1865
Gold, feathers, leather, silk, 32 × 233
British Museum, 1993,0205.1. Purchased from Roger Garlick

34
Henry Stacy Marks (1829–1898)
Studies of a white-crested laughing thrush, a cock of the rock and a yellow macaw, 1877
Watercolour over graphite on wove paper, 604 × 450
Ashmolean Museum. Presumably presented by John Ruskin to the Ruskin Drawing School (University of Oxford), where it was first recorded in 1906

35
Frederick Sandys (1829–1904)
Vivien, 1863
Oil on canvas, 640 × 525
Manchester Art Gallery

36
John Gould (1804–1881)
A monograph of the Trochilidæ, or family of humming-birds, 1861
Printed book with coloured lithographs, 250 × 760 × 567
Bodleian Libraries, University of Oxford, CR.D.14/4. vol. 4

37
Anna Atkins (1799–1871)
Cyanotype Herbarium, the First Fascicule of 'Photographs of British Algae', 1843
Cyanotypes on paper, 260 × 207 × 20
The Provost and Fellows of Oriel College

38
Patrick Syme (1774–1845) and Abraham Gottlob Werner (1749–1817)
Werner's Nomenclature of Colours, with Additions by P. Syme, 1814
90 × 230 × 205
Bodleian Libraries, University of Oxford, Rigaud e.402

39
Sarah Angelina Acland (1849–1930)
A Study of a Fish, 1877
Watercolour on paper, 138 × 177
Ashmolean Museum. Presumably presented by John Ruskin to the Ruskin Drawing School (University of Oxford), where it was first recorded in 1906

40
Arthur Hughes (1832–1915)
April Love, 1855–6
Oil on canvas, 889 × 495
Tate: Purchased 1909

41
Simpson, Maule & Nicholson
Coal Tar Dyes, c.1895
Paper and dyes, 350 × 270
Bodleian Libraries, University of Oxford, John Johnson Collection, Soap 1 (41) subsect. Dye

42
Berline Aniline Company
2 Folders of Dyed Samples, c.1899
Woven wool and silk on printed paper, 1330 × 185 × 3; 1570 × 240 × 3
Museum of the History of Science, Oxford

43
Portrait of a Man in Studio Setting, c.1850–9
Painted ambrotype in a leather case, 94 × 172
Private collection

44
Studio of Beard Patentee
Portrait Bust of a Man, c.1845
Ninth-plate daguerreotype with applied colour in vertical leather case, 152 × 62
Private collection

45
Ambrotype Photograph, 1860–5
Glass, gilt, velvet, wood, 90 × 80
Manchester Art Gallery

46
Aniline fringed chromolithographed greeting cards, c.1880–9
Card and silk; card 1, 160 × 110; card 2, 100 × 80; card 3, 125 × 70; card 4, 90 × 65; card 5, 150 × 115; card 6, 125 × 105; card 7, 140 × 105; card 8, 170 × 120
Private Collection

47
Women's purple velvet bonnet, 1862
Velvet, net, cotton, velvet, artificial flowers, cotton, glass beads, feathers, 280 × 170 × 100
Manchester Art Gallery

48
Lilac boots, 1864
Silk, 245 × 155 × 70
Fashion Museum Bath

49
Maxen Gantiez
Shoes worn by Mary Chamberlain, c.1890–9
Silk, 235 × 115 × 65
Fashion Museum Bath

50
Crinoline, 1865–7
Wool, cotton, steel, tape, 800 × 720 × 650
Manchester Art Gallery

51
Flack & Smith
Boots, c.1890–9
Silk, 265 × 240 × 80
Fashion Museum Bath

52
Corset, 1888–9
Cotton satin, 350 × 200 × 350
Manchester Art Gallery

53
Slippers, c.1860–9
Wool, 160 × 40 × 55
Fashion Museum Bath

54
Raspberry pink stockings, c.1880–9
Silk, 675 × 200
Fashion Museum Bath

55
Blue stockings, c.1880–9
Silk, 765 × 180
Fashion Museum Bath

56
Purple stockings, c.1880–9
Wool, 680 × 240
Fashion Museum Bath

57
Pink stockings, c.1880–9
Silk, 730 × 195
Fashion Museum Bath

58
Women's boots, c.1870–9
Bold blue satin over linen, leather, 240 × 220 × 125
Manchester Art Gallery

59
Men's Berlin work slippers, 1863–4
Wool, canvas, leather, 280 × 180
Manchester Art Gallery

60
Magenta and black stockings, 1862
Wool, 540 × 205
Manchester Art Gallery

61
Pink black and gold striped stockings, 1862
Wool, 315 × 155
Manchester Art Gallery

62
Dress, 1865–70
Silk, cotton, muslin, glass beads, 1450 × 1750 × 4830
Manchester Art Gallery

63
Silk parasol, c.1870
Silk, metal, ivory, bamboo, cotton, 8 diameter
Manchester Art Gallery

64
Edward Burne-Jones (1833–1898)
Head of a Woman, c.1890
Gold paint on purple prepared ground, 604 × 450
Ashmolean Museum. Presented by Mrs Helen Mary Gaskell, CBE, 1939

65
Purple and gold Psalter, Rheims area, c.9th century
Parchment manuscript
120 × 300 × 198
Bodleian Libraries, University of Oxford, MS. Douce 59

66
Henry Wyndham Phillips (1820–1868)
Portrait of Owen Jones, 1856
Oil on canvas, 1360 × 950
RIBA Collections

67
William Burges (1827–1881)
The Great Bookcase, 1859–62
Painted wood and pietra dura, 3175 × 1739 × 495
Ashmolean Museum

68
Minton & Co.
Fountain, c.1862
Earthenware with majolica glazes, 1400 × 1070
Victoria and Albert Museum. Bequeathed by Mrs Annemarie Aschenagi

69
George Frederic Watts (1817–1904)
The Wife of Pygmalion, c.1868
Oil on canvas, 649 × 520
The Faringdon Collection Trust, Buscot Park

70
The Oxford Bust, 50–200 CE (head); 1500–1640 (bust)
Marble, 660 × 295 × 550
Ashmolean Museum. Presented by the Dowager Countess of Pomfret in 1755

71
John Gibson (1790–1866)
Tinted Venus, 1851–6
Polychrome marble with wax coating and marble base, 1760 × 650 × 440 × 450
National Museums Liverpool, Walker Art Gallery

72
Lawrence Alma-Tadema (1836–1912)
Pheidias and the Frieze of the Parthenon, 1868–9
Oil on canvas, 1118 × 1487
Lent by Birmingham Museums Trust on behalf of Birmingham City Council

73
John Bell (1811–1895)
A Daughter of Eve: A Scene on the Shore of the Atlantic (The American Slave), 1862
Bronze or bronze-patinated electrotype, silver and gold plate, 1525 × 400 × 360
National Trust, Cragside, NT 1228372

74
Owen Jones (1809–1874)
The History of Joseph and His Brethren, 1865
Printed book with chromolithographs
40 × 300 × 440
Bodleian Libraries, University of Oxford, (OC) 170 n.81

75
Edward John Poynter (1836–1919)
Israel in Egypt, 1867
Oil on canvas, 1759 × 3552 × 88
Guildhall Art Gallery, London

76
Minton & Co.
Majolica peacock, 1873
Ceramic, 1485 × 665 × 610
National Museums Liverpool, Walker Art Gallery

77
C.F. Hancock
The Devonshire Parure, 1856
Enamelled gold and gems
Necklace: 125 × 260, Stomacher: 295 × 185 × 12, Hair comb: 180 × 165 × 50, Bandeau: 350 × 41 × 4, Bracelet: 75 × 65 × 33, Diadem: 170 × 70, Coronet: 185 × 205 × 86
The Devonshire Collections, Chatsworth

78
Two-handled vase painted with scenes from the Portland vase, Staffordshire, *c*.1845–60
Bone china, 400
British Museum, 2019,8011.1. Presented by Richard Dennis

79
Hill Pottery
Vase cast in the form of the Portland vase, *c*.1860–70
Bone china, 245
British Museum, 2021,8005.1. Given in memory of Ian Jenkins OBE (1953–2020), British Museum curator, by his colleagues: Andrew Burnett, Frances Carey, Jill Cook, Lesley Fitton, Antony Griffiths, Judy Rudoe and Kim Sloan

80
William Holman Hunt (1827–1910)
The Afterglow in Egypt
Oil on canvas, 820 × 370
Ashmolean Museum. Bequeathed by Mrs Thomas Combe, 1893

81
John Frederick Lewis (1804–1876)
The Pipe Bearer, 1856
Oil on panel, 670 × 545
Lent by Birmingham Museums Trust on behalf of Birmingham City Council

82
Frederic Leighton (1830–1896)
Interior of a Mosque or the Mimbar of the Great Mosque at Damascus, 1873
Oil on canvas, 310 × 245
Government Art Collection

83
Edward Lear (1812–1888)
Baalbek from Lebanon, 1858
Watercolour and pen and black ink with graphite indications, 193 × 524
Ashmolean Museum. Presented by Craddock and Barnard, 1936

84
Shawl Presented to Queen Victoria, *c*.1875
Wool and silk, 3670 × 1490
Joan Hart Collection

85
Man's Smoking Jacket and Hat, *c*.1890
Wool, silk, velvet, 925 × 1180 × 1740
Joan Hart Collection

86
Challis dressing gown, *c*.1870–9
Wool, cotton, linen, 1340 × 730 × 257
Joan Hart Collection

87
Baron Carlo Marochetti (1805–1867)
Maharajah Duleep Singh, 1856
Marble, wax, 806 × 470 × 285
Private Collection. Classé au titre des monuments historiques par arrêté du 24 janvier 2002, N° d'inventaire Palissy: PM78001187

88
Sophie Anderson (1823–1903)
Scheherazade, date unknown
Oil on canvas, 500 × 410
The New Art Gallery Walsall

89
Albert Moore (1841–1893)
Beads, 1875
Oil on canvas, 298 × 516
National Galleries of Scotland. Purchased 1910

90
Albert Moore (1841–1893)
Apples, 1875
Oil on canvas, 290 × 510
Private collection

91
Albert Moore (1841–1893)
A Sofa, 1875
Oil on canvas, 292 × 508
Private collection

92
House of Worth Dress, 1897
Under-robe of cloth of silver, wrought all over with silver thread and brilliants; over-dress of green and gold shot-silk gauze, embroidered to the waist with green and gold metalwork, decorated with jewels;

train of green velvet, embroidered in gold thread; bodice of gold cloth and lace over a whalebone corset. Bust 890, waist 670, hip 1040 with padding, dress shoulder to floor 1470
The Devonshire Collections, Chatsworth

93
Elkin Matthews and John Lane (illustrated by Aubrey Beardsley)
The Yellow Book, 13 vols., 1894–7
Printed books, 208 × 75 × 25
By Permission of the President and Fellows of Trinity College Oxford

94
Marguerite de Lubert (1702–1785)
Histoire Secrète du Prince Croqu'étron, 1873
Printed book, 142 × 89 × 5
By Permission of the President and Fellows of Trinity College Oxford

95
J.P.R. Cuisin (1777–1845)
Les amours secrètes d'une comtesse de l'Empire, *c.*1850
Printed book with coloured lithographs, 141 × 96 × 22
By Permission of the President and Fellows of Trinity College Oxford

96
Aubrey Beardsley (1872–1898)
Keynote Series Poster, 1896
Printed poster, 620 × 475
Bodleian Libraries, University of Oxford, John Johnson Collection, Windows and Bills Advertisement Folder 1 (38)

97
Henri de Toulouse-Lautrec (1864–1901)
Poster for 'Troupe de Mlle Églantine' when they performed at the Palace Theatre in London in 1896, 1896
Colour lithograph, 618 × 810
Victoria and Albert Museum. Given anonymously

98
James McNeill Whistler (1834–1903)
The Yellow Room, 1883–4
Watercolour and gouache on paperboard, 248 × 178
Lent by The Metropolitan Museum of Art, Marguerite and Frank A. Cosgrove Jr. Fund, 2017. (2017.664) (Frame) Lent by The Metropolitan Museum of Art, Gift of Tracy Gill and Simeon Lagodich, 2018 (2018.653)

99
Eugene Grasset (1845–1917)
La Morphinomane (The Morphine Addict), 1897
Colour lithograph, 576 × 425
Victoria and Albert Museum

100
Phillips Brothers, London
Lady Granville's beetle parure and case, 1884–5
Gold, weevils, silk, leather, wood die-stamped, 210 × 295
British Museum, 2016,8037.1.a-e. Presented by Museum of Applied Arts and Sciences.

101
Ramon Casas (1866–1932)
Jove decadent. Després del ball, 1899
Oil on canvas, 585 × 674 × 43
Museu de Monstserrat. Donated by Josep Sala Ardiz, 1980

102
Yellow moire and chiffon cape with yellow satin lining, *c.*1898
Silk, 760 × 450 × 850
Fashion Museum Bath

103
Dudley Hardy (1867–1922)
The Yellow Girl poster for To-Day Magazine, 1893
400 × 300
Bodleian Libraries, University of Oxford, John Johnson Collection, Window and Bills Advertisement Folder 1 (3)

104
Japanese Boardgame, 1887
Colour woodblock print, 737 × 731
Ashmolean Museum. Presented by Ellis Tinios, 2020

105
Baron Raimund von Stillfried-Ratenicz (1839–1911)
Wisteria in Flower / Japanese Woman with Koto, *c.*1870–9
Hand tinted photograph, 720 × 2295 × 150
Pitt Rivers Museum

106
Japanese Textile Sample Book, *c.*1870–1900
Paper and textile, 330 × 210 × 20
Ashmolean Museum. Presented by Miss I. B. Keith, 1957

107
Alexis Falize (1811–1898)
Necklace, *c.*1867
Gold and enamel, 35 × 400
Ashmolean Museum. Presented by Misses M.D. and B.P. Legge, in accordance of the wishes of their sister, Miss C.M. Legge, 1964

108
Alexis Falize (1811–1898)
Earrings, *c.*1867
Gold and enamel, 45 × 29
Ashmolean Museum. Presented by Misses M.D. and B.P. Legge, in accordance of the wishes of their sister, Miss C.M. Legge, 1964

109
Alexis Falize (1811–1898)
Bracelet, *c.*1867
Gold and enamel, 30 × 29
Ashmolean Museum. Presented by Misses M.D. and B.P. Legge, in accordance of the wishes of their sister, Miss C.M. Legge, 1964

110
Hunt & Roskill
Bracelet, *c.*1867
Gold and enamel, 22 × 182
Ashmolean Museum. Presented by Misses M.D. and B.P. Legge, in accordance of the wishes of their sister, Miss C.M. Legge, 1964

111
Keisai Eisen (1790–1848)
High ranking courtesan from Sheibi House, 1810–45
Aizuri-e woodblock print on paper, 555 × 404
Ashmolean Museum. Bequeathed by Oswald J. Couldrey, 1958

112
Toyohara Kunichika (1835–1900)
The Gang of Five Returning in the Morning Like Wild Geese, 1863
Nishiki-e woodblock print with ink and colour on paper, 554 × 402
Ashmolean Museum. Presented by Christ Church College, University of Oxford, 1983

113
Utagawa Hiroshige (1797–1858)
Fireworks at Ryōgoku Bridge, Edo, 1858
Nishiki-e (full colour) woodblock print, with *bokashi* (tonal gradation), 357 × 237
Ashmolean Museum. Presented by Mrs E. M. Allan and Mr and Mrs H. N. Spalding from the Herbert H. Jennings Collection, 1952

114
William De Morgan (1839–1917)
Moonlight Lustre Galleon Charger, 1888–1907
Earthenware, 466 × 60
Trustees of the De Morgan Foundation

115
John Addington Symonds (1840–1893) (cover design by Charles Ricketts)
In the Key of Blue, 1893
Printed book, 43 × 143 × 198
From the collection of Professor Shane Butler

116
James McNeill Whistler (1834–1903)
Nocturne: Blue and Gold, St Mark's, Venice, 1880
Oil on canvas, 754 × 905
Lent by Amgueddfa Cymru – Museum Wales. NMW A 210 Bequest: Gwendoline Davies, 1951

117
James McNeill Whistler's Paintbox, 1800–1900
Wood, 50 × 190 × 150
The Hunterian, University of Glasgow

118
Winsor & Newton
James McNeill Whistler's paint tubes, n.d.
Metal, paper label, oil paint, Dimensions
The Hunterian, University of Glasgow

119
James McNeill Whistler's watercolour palette, 1800–1900
Metal, 9 × 205 × 225
The Hunterian, University of Glasgow

120
Tanagra Figure, 300–250 BCE
Terracotta with pigments, 26 × 120 × 80
British Museum, 1895,1029.7. Purchased from Jean P. Lambros

121
Tanagra Figure, 300–250 BCE
Brown terracotta with pigments, 240 × 90 × 70
British Museum, 1874,0305.65. Purchased from Charles Merlin

122
James McNeill Whistler (1834–1903)
A Dancing Woman in a Pink Robe, 1888–95
Chalk and watercolour on brown paper laid down on card, 275 × 183
The Hunterian, University of Glasgow

123
James McNeill Whistler (1834–1903)
Three Figures: Pink and Grey, 1868–78
Oil on canvas, 1391 × 1854
Tate: Purchased with the aid of contributions from the International Society of Sculptors, Painters and Gravers as a Memorial to Whistler, and from Francis Howard 1950

124
Albert Moore (1841–1893)
Pomegranates, 1866
Oil on canvas, 468 × 572 × 51
Guildhall Art Gallery, London

125
Jody Sperling
'Night Winds' from *Roman Sketches* performed by Jody Sperling
Recorded 11 May 2007 by Penny Ward
Video

Notes

1. GLOWING COLOUR

1 Blaszczyk (2012).
2 Dickens (1854), p. 169.
3 Ruskin (1903–12), v, pp. 321–2.
4 Ruskin (1903–12), XXXIV, p. 32–3.
5 Quoted in Mosley (2001), p. 72.
6 'The Great Exhibition: About Dyes and Beauty and Coal-Tar Mauve and Magenta How Made Extraordinary Specimen of Aniline Art and the New Colors', *New York Times*, 28 July 1862, p. 2.
7 Fuchsine (soon known as Magenta) was used to colour wine in particular.
8 Henry T. Finck (1880) quoted in Gaskill (2018), p. 13.
9 Harvey (1995).
10 For an account of early experimentations with colour photography, see Boulouch (2011).
11 The expression 'colour sense' was coined by none other than the four-time Prime Minister W.E. Gladstone.
12 On the cinematic effect of Loïe Fuller's performances, see Ronetti (2021/3).
13 'Now, if any woman rather shrewder than her fellows, [should] ask me, 'How shall I know which combination best suits my especial needs' I answer, 'Try it in a bonnet. No colours suit a room that are not pleasing in dress.' Haweis (1881), p. 366.
14 See Roque (2009) and Kalba (2017).
15 Merrifield (1851) and Loske (2016).
16 Batchelor (2000), pp. 22–3.
17 Goethe (2006), p. 30.
18 'A man of no talent, a bad colourist, would be ready to give you mathematical reasons for every colour he put on the canvas.' Ruskin (1903–12), XII, p. 500.
19 Townsend (2004), p. 188, also quoted in Dootson (2018), p. 1.
20 Townsend (2004) and Prettejohn (2000), pp. 148–52.
21 Wilde (2005), p. 255.
22 Matthews (1999), p. 180.
23 Schaffer (2000), p. 104.
24 Davis (2014).
25 Dootson (2018), p. 99.
26 Quoted in Dootson (2018), p. 99.
27 Most recently Levi and Tucker (2020) and Hughes (2021).
28 Ruskin (1903–12), VII, p. 414 n. 3.
29 Ibid., XV, p. xxii.
30 Ibid., p. 83, quoted in Hughes (2021), p. 184.
31 Ibid., p. 133.
32 Ibid., pp. 157–8, quoted in Hughes (2021), pp. 187–8.
33 Haslam (2000).
34 Hewison (1984) quoting from Ruskin (1903–12) XXI, p. xxvii.
35 Ruskin (1903–12), XX and XXII.
36 Ibid., XV, p. 415.
37 Ibid., pp. 11–12.
38 Ibid., XXII, pp. 55–6.
39 Ibid., XVI, p. 371, quoted in Wildman (2021), p. 138.
40 Ibid., XXI, p. 106, quoted in Wildman (2021), p. 138.
41 Goncourt (1989), III, p. 617, quoted in part and differently translated in Gage (1987), pp. 192–3; see also Warrell (2003), p. 254.
42 'cette pauvre petite priere a notre Dieu Turner', repr. Warrell (2003), p. 255.
43 Gowing (1966), p. 5.
44 Ibid., pp. 15, 19
45 Quoted in Warrell (2003), p. 14.
46 Quoted in Gage (1987), p. 193 from Ruskin (1903–12), XXXV, p. 295.
47 Warrell (2003), pp. 49–51.
48 Gowing (1966), p. 19.
49 Wilton (1979), nos 1162, 1190.
50 Butlin and Joll (1984), no. 349.
51 Ibid., no. 365.
52 Ibid., nos 383 (Tate) and 384 (V&A).
53 Smiles (2020), p. 64.
54 Butlin and Joll (1984), no. 402 (Tate); see also Smiles (2020), pp. 173–4.
55 Quoted in Brown (2014), p. 116.
56 Butlin and Joll (1984), no. 368 (Huntington Library, San Marino).
57 Ruskin (1903–12), I, p. 447, quoted in Hewison (2000), p. 67.
58 Quoted in Warrell (2003), p. 251.
59 Ibid.
60 Burne-Jones (1904), vol. 1, p. 97.
61 Ibid.
62 Ibid.
63 Morris (1988), II, p. 228.
64 Ruskin (1903–12), v, pp. 321–2.
65 Ibid., XX, p. 140.
66 Ibid., VIII, pp. 176–7.
67 Ibid., XXXIII, p. 165.
68 Spielmann, quoted in Millais (1899), p. 106.
69 Ruskin (1903–12), XII, p. 320.
70 Patmore (1857), p. 584.
71 Ibid., pp. 583–4. On the reception of these murals and more generally of Pre-Raphaelite medievalism, see Cruise (2010), pp. 121–40.
72 Ruskin (1903–12), XII, p. 500.
73 Patmore (1857), p. 583.
74 Ruskin (1903–12), IX, p. 285.
75 Faxon (1992), pp. 99–100.
76 Marsh (2019), p. 115.
77 Humphreys (1849), p. 176.
78 Ruskin quoted in Allitt (1997), p. 46.
79 Anon. (1846), p. 215.
80 Anon. (1845), pp. 200–1.
81 On the historical jewellery presented at the 1862 International Exhibition, see Gere and Rudoe (2014), pp. 83–105.
82 Burges (1862), p. 10.
83 Kirkup quoted in Holbrook (1911), p. 98.
84 Morris quoted in Peterson (1982), p. 8.
85 Ruskin (1903–12), VIII, p. 81.
86 Marshall (2021), p. 3.
87 Garcia (2019).
88 Tupper (1856), p. 43.
89 'Banquet at the Royal Academy', *The Times*, 1 May 1871, p. 6.
90 Keats (1820), p. 41.
91 Haydon (1929), p. 231.
92 Darwin (1849), p. 20.
93 Syme (1814), p. 11.
94 Darwin (1879), p. CDIII.
95 Ibid.
96 Letter to Asa Gray, 3 April 1860.
97 *Punch*, 23 April 1870.
98 Dorment (1977), p. 5.
99 Tennyson (1859), p. 101.
100 Ibid., p. 107.
101 Ibid., p. 89.
102 Holmes (2020), p. 3.
103 Ruskin (1903–12), XXV, p. 263.
104 Smith (2006), p. 3.
105 Ruskin (1903–12), XV, p. 156.
106 Jacklin (2017), p. 101.
107 Great Britain Department of Science and Art (1854), p. 23.
108 Dresser (1862), p. 189.
109 Braga (2021), n.p.
110 Wakefield (1811), p. 209.
111 Atkins (1843), 'Introduction'
112 Schaaf (1979), pp. 209–24.
113 Sanger Shepherd and Company Limited was a photography and electrical goods company active from 1900 until 1927.
114 Museum of the History of Science, Oxford,

Collections Online, *Colour Photograph (Sanger Shepherd Lantern Slide) of a Peacock Feather, by E. Sanger Shepherd & Co., London, 1899*. https://www.hsm.ox.ac.uk/collections-online#/item/hsm-catalogue-8596 (last accessed 17 March 2022)

115 Flints (2015), p. 179.

116 Original material about Acland can be found in the Bodleian's special collections, such as the Acland family papers and the Henry Minn collection. The collection of the Museum of the History of Science, Oxford includes colour lantern slides and the colour processes Sanger Shepherd and Autochrome, amongst others, demonstrating Acland's experimentation with different colour formats. Her diaries and notebooks are part of the Robert T. Gunther Collection.

117 Schaaf (2018). Other recent publications include Garascia (2021). Atkins's central role for the early development of the photographic medium was also celebrated in the exhibition *Blue Prints: The Pioneering Work of Anna Atkins*, 19 October 2018–17 February 2019 at the New York Public Library. The Photo Oxford Festival *Women & Photography. Ways of Seeing and Being Seen* featured her work in 2020.

118 Hudson (2012b). The book reproduces and examines more than 220 examples of Acland's work from the collections of the Bodleian Library and Museum of the History of Science, Oxford. Also see Hudson (2012a).

119 Recent research on early women photographers was presented in the *Colour Fever* online symposium, 25 October–5 November 2021 at the V&A Research Institute and the online conference *Let Us Now Praise Famous Women: Discovering the Work of Female Photographers*, 24 October 2020 at the Bodleian Library, Oxford; see also texts in Bender and Simonsen (2021).

120 'Revolting Cruelty to Seals', *The Animal World*, April 1875, p. 52

121 Tree (1991), p. 175.

122 Ibid.

123 Gould (1861), p. 25.

124 Queen Victoria (1851), XXXI, p. 288.

125 Poliquin (2012), p. 43.

126 British Museum (1884), p. 20.

127 Rudoe and Gere (2010), p. 227.

128 Wallace (1877), p. 784.

129 Bullock, (1800), p. 30.

130 Tolini (2002).

131 Nietzsche (1872).

132 Cowie (2022), p. 17 .

133 Boase (2021), p. 3.

134 Atkinson (1896), p. 4.

2. COLOUR FOR ALL

1 Salter (1871) pp. 162–3, quoted in Ribeyrol (2020).

2 Travis (2014), p. 38.

3 See Garfield (2000).

4 Ibid., p. 61.

5 Dickens (1859), pp. 168–71, quoted in Garfield (2000), pp. 65–6.

6 Ibid.

7 'The Mauve Measles', *Punch*, 20 Aug. 1859, p. 81, quoted in Garfield (2000).

8 Mason (1916).

9 Garfield (2000), p. 76.

10 'The Triumph of Colour', *Trewman's Exeter Flying Post*, 26 June 1861, p. 3.

11 Timbs (1863), p. 71.

12 Hofmann (1863), p. 120.

13 Turnbull (1951), p. 267.

14 Ibid., p. 46.

15 Garfield (2000), p. 90.

16 See 'Indigo in Bihar', *Nature*, 101 (1918) pp. 388–9.

17 Cesaratto, et al. (2018).

18 Ruskin (1903–12), XIX, pp. 379–80, quoted in Ribeyrol (2016), p. 9.

19 Taine (1957), pp. 9–20.

20 'The Triumph of Colour', *Trewman's Exeter Flying Post*, 26 June 1861, p. 3.

21 'The Fashions-Stockings', *The Lady's Newspaper & Pictorial Times*, 26 January 1861, p. 51.

22 'Mythology and Socks', *Punch*, 7 October 1868, p. 160.

23 William Crooke, 'Poisonous Dyes', *Huddersfield Chronicle*, 17 October 1868, p. 8.

24 Quoted in Vettese Forster and Christie (2013), p. 10.

25 Ibid.

26 Haweis (1879), pp. 108–9.

27 Quoted in Cobbold (2020), pp. 30–55.

28 Lanman (2000).

29 Lecture given 29 October 1889 at a meeting sponsored by the Applied Art Section of the National Association for the Advancement of Art at the Museum of Science and Art, Edinburgh; published in *The Decorator and Furnisher*, vol. 19, no. 6 (March 1892).

30 Ibid.

31 Holman Hunt (1880).

32 Letter dated 11 June 1891, Glasgow University Library (MS Whistler W584, 06591).

33 'Beautiful Tar', *Punch*, 15 September 1888, p. 123.

34 Quoted in Dishon (2014), p. 39.

35 Bryant (2014), p. 63.

36 Quoted in ibid., p. 40.

37 Crace (1862), p. 342.

38 Ibid.

39 Dishon (2014), p. 32.

40 Ibid.

41 *The Athenæum*, 3 February, 1866, p. 172.

42 Browning (1897), II, p. 155.

43 Ibid., p. 148.

44 Matthews and Gibson (1911), p. 182.

45 Hatt (2014), p. 189.

46 Ibid.

47 *Cornhill Magazine*, VI (July–September 1862), p. 279.

48 See Nichols (2015).

49 Droth, Edwards and Hatt (2014), pp. 200–1.

50 'The International Exhibition', *The Illustrated London News*, 5 July 1862, pp. 17–18.

51 Atterbury and Batkin (1989), p. 151.

52 George Wallis, 'The Art Manufactures of Birmingham and the Midland Counties', *Midland Counties Herald*, June 1862, quoted in *Catalogue of Some of the Principal Pieces Exhibited by Elkington and Co.: Manufacturers of Artistic Works in Silver, Bronze, and other Metals: London International Exhibition, Class 33* (Birmingham, 1862), p. 11.

53 Wallis, op. cit., pp. 11–12.

54 Droth (2014), pp. 251–4.

55 Harvey (2019), p. 79.

56 Atterbury and Batkin (1989), p. 112.

57 Waring and Thompson (1863), pl. 203.

58 Droth (2014), pp. 212–18.

59 'Woven, Spun, Felted, and Laid Fabrics, when Shown as Specimens of Printing or Dyeing', *The International Exhibition of 1862: The Illustrated Catalogue of the Industrial Department* (London, 1862), p. 22.

60 *The Ladies Treasury*, 1 November 1862, p. 342.

61 'Mineralogy and Chemistry, and Their Applications, in the International Exhibition', *The Illustrated London News*, 12 July 1862, p. 50.

62 Dickens (1862), pp. 560–61.

63 *Examiner*, 9 August 1862.

64 Dickens (1862), pp. 560–61.

65 *Examiner*, 9 August 1862.

66 Dickens (1862), p. 563.

67 *The Illustrated Exhibitor, a Tribute to the World's Industrial Jubilee; Comprising Sketches, by Pen and Pencil, of the Principal Objects in the Great Exhibition of the Industry of All Nations*, 1–30 (June–December 1851) p. 91.

68 Ibid.

69 Donnelly (2014), p. 108.
70 Quoted in ibid.
71 See Winterbottom (2017), pp. 14–25. Also Ribeyrol (2023), p. 27.
72 Ribeyrol (2023), p. 12.
73 William Burges, 'The International Exhibition', *The Gentleman's Magazine and Historical Review*, 213 (July 1862) p. 10.
74 William Burges, 'The Japanese Court in the International Exhibition', *The Gentleman's Magazine and Historical Review*, 213 (Sep 1862) p. 254.
75 Winterbottom (2017); Ribeyrol (2023).
76 FitzHugh (1997), pp. 23–45.
77 Pliny, *Natural History*, 34.54.
78 Gettens and Stout (1966); Carlyle (2001); Townsend (2002).
79 Colourmen were the salespeople who bridged the gap between industry and artists.
80 Field (1835), p. 179.
81 See 'More brilliant tints than fancy could conceive' – Exhibiting Colour: The 1862 International Exhibition by M. Winterbottom, in this volume.
82 Eastlake (1847); Merrifield (1849).
83 Ribeyrol (2023), Introduction.
84 Carlyle (1993); Townsend et al. (1995).
85 Carlyle (2001); Townsend (1995); Townsend (1993); Katz (1995); Jacobi (2007).
86 Townsend, Ridge and Hackney (2004), pp. 51–75.
87 Winterbottom (2017).
88 Ball (2001).
89 Townsend et al. (1995).
90 Ruskin (1903–12), v, p. 321.
91 See 'More brilliant tints than fancy could conceive' – Exhibiting Colour: The 1862 International Exhibition by M. Winterbottom, in this volume.
92 Bastide (1967), p. 312.
93 Scharf (1854), p. 43.
94 Prettejohn and Trippi (2016).
95 Spies (2016), p. 97.
96 Greville (1897), p. 78.
97 Martin, (2016), n.p.
98 Lafont (2017), pp. 89–113.
99 The exhibition 'The Colour of Anxiety: Race, Sexuality and Disorder in Victorian Sculpture' (Henry Moore Institute, 25 November 2022 – 26 February 2023) explores these themes in greater depth.
100 Beach (2022), pp. 77–112.
101 For a complete exhibition history of this sculpture, see Warren (2022), n.p.
102 Droth and Hatt, (2016).
103 Elyse and Walters (2022).
104 Hatt (2016), n.p.
105 See Loske (2016), pp. 1–16.
106 'The International Exhibition', *The Critic*, 12 April 1862, pp. 96–7.
107 Quoted in Moser (2012), p. 163.
108 Moser (2012), p. 163.
109 Wallace (1997), p. 6.
110 Lewes in Jones (1854), pp. 31–2.
111 Winckelmann (2006), p. 195.
112 Winckelmann quoted in Smith (2021), p. 14.
113 Jockey (2013), p. 172.
114 Eastlake (1870), p. 210.
115 Westmacott, (1859) p. 231.
116 Hatt (2014), p. 186.
117 *The Art Journal*, July 1862 quoted in Smith (1996), p. 121.
118 Gibson quoted in Eastlake (1870), pp. 211–12.
119 'Gibson as Pygmalion' in Eastlake (1870), p. 211.
120 Gibson quoted in ibid., p. 213.
121 Ibid., p. 128.
122 Watts's admiration for Phidias was such that Charles Couzens painted his portrait in front of a portion of the Parthenon's East Frieze. See Jenkins (2016), p. 50.
123 Prettejohn (2004), p. 56.
124 Jenkins (1984), p. 181.
125 Watts quoted in Prettejohn (2012), p. 68.
126 Swinburne (1875), pp. 359–60.
127 Prettejohn (2009), p. 107.
128 Dowling (1989), pp. 1–8 and Ribeyrol (2013).
129 For a detailed analysis of *Israel in Egypt*, see Moser (2020), pp. 154–64.
130 Prettejohn (2022), p. 68.
131 'Exhibition of the Royal Academy', *The Illustrated London News* 50/426 (11 May 1867) p. 478.
132 Prettejohn (2022), p. 74.
133 Cook (1869), p. 156.
134 Riggs (1869), n.p.
135 Russell (1869), p. 65.
136 Blunt (1879), pp. 155–6.
137 Burton (1856), p. 217.
138 Thackeray (1888), p. 178.
139 Landow (1982), p. 646.
140 Dadd (1843).
141 See Said (2003) and Nochlin (1989), pp. 33–59.
142 Pratt (1991), p. 33.
143 Eaton (2013), p. 5.
144 Wright (1896), p. 184.
145 'Memoirs and Letters of the Late Thomas Seddon, Artist', *The Leader* 437 (7 August 1858).
146 Wilcox (2001), p. 13.
147 Boden (2020), pp. 120–23.
148 Barrington (1906), p. 134.
149 Barringer (1999), p. 120.
150 'Egyptian Cotton; Its Modern Origin and the Importance of Supply', *New York Times* (26 June 1864), p. 5.
151 Balfour-Paul (1997), p.xiii.
152 Thackeray, (1888), p. 438.
153 Sattin (2010), p. 182.
154 Llewellyn (2019), p. 29.
155 Roget (1891), p. 144.
156 Mann (2011), pp. 93–6.
157 Llewellyn (2019), p. 34.
158 Ferry, (2003), pp. 175–88.
159 See Beckwith (1987).
160 See Pugin (1853).
161 Gange and Ledger-Lomas (2013), p. 3.
162 'The Late Mr. Owen Jones' *The Illustrated London News* 64 (9 May 1874), pp. 445–6.
163 See Moser (2020).
164 'Major Mackeson Brings Koh-i-noor, the Famous Diamond, to England', *Times*, 1 July 1850, p. 4.
165 Dentith (2000).
166 Swift (2012), p. 11.
167 Ibid, p. 5.
168 Driver and Ashmore (2010).
169 Ibid, p. 357.
170 'India and Indian Contributions to the Industrial Bazaar' *The Illustrated Exhibitor : A Tribute to the World's Industrial Jubilee / Comprising Sketches, by Pen and Pencil, of the Principal Objects in the Great Exhibition of the Industry of All Nations*, 18 (4 October 1851), p. 1. Web.
171 Bhaba (1984), p. 125.
172 Choudhury (2016), p. 817.
173 Eaton (2013), p. 15.
174 John Ruskin, 'The Two Paths: Being Lectures on Art, and Its Application to Decoration and Manufacture', delivered in 1858–9 and published by Smith, Elder & Co. in 1859.
175 Ibid, p. 4.
176 Crinson (1996), p. 23–6.
177 Taylor (2018), p. 138.
178 http://www.queenvictoriasjournals.org/search/displayItem. do?Format Type= fulltextimgsrc&QueryType =articles&ResultsID= 3361070850657&filterSequence= 0&PageNumber=1&ItemNumber =2&ItemID=qvj07854&volume Type=PSBEA
179 Barrington (1904), vol. 1.
180 *The Illustrated London News* (10 May 1856), p. 509.
181 *Gazette des Beaux-Arts* (July 1862), p. 376.
182 *The Homeward Mail*, 3 September 1858, p. 952.

3. COLOUR FOR COLOUR'S SAKE

1 Duret (1881), p. 554.
2 Ruskin quoted in Whistler (1967), p. 1.
3 Whistler (1967), pp. 127–28.
4 Wilde (1906), p. 5.
5 Phillips (2011), pp. 210–11.
6 Asleson (2000), pp. 130–1.
7 Whistler (1967), p. 159.
8 Hearn (1905), p. 230.
9 Ibid.
10 Quoted in Gere and Hoskins (2000), p. 72.
11 Gilbert (1881), p. 38.
12 Gautier translated in Potolsky (2013), p. 51 (translation modified).
13 Pastoureau (2013), p. 97.
14 David (2015), p. 70.
15 Hawksley (2016).
16 Morris quoted in Lazarus (1886), p. 397.
17 Rudoe (2017), pp. 50–1.
18 Huysmans (1922), pp. 142–3.
19 Wilde (1913), p. 168.
20 Le Gallienne (1896), p. 87.
21 Schaffer (2000), p. 104.
22 Singletary (2017), p. 25.
23 Ruskin (1877), pp. 181–213.
24 'Whistler in Venice – A Gavotte in Gamboge', *Punch* (3 March 1883), p. 107.
25 Ibid.
26 'Banquet at the Royal Academy', *The Times* (1871), p. 6.
27 Whistler (1880), MS Whistler E61.
28 Ruskin (1903–12), X, pp. 83–4.
29 'Society of British Artists', *The Era* (11 December 1886), p. 13.
30 Bacher (1909), p. 31.
31 Ruskin (1903–12), XXIV, pp. 406–9.
32 Whistler (1880), MS Whistler LB 3/8.
33 Evangelista (2016), p. 89.
34 Nadri (2016), p. 91.
35 See Bullen (2003).
36 Ellis (1915), p. 120.
37 Ibid., p. 299.
38 Ibid.
39 Ibid.
40 Ibid., pp. 317–18.
41 Symonds (1893), p. 7.
42 Maxwell (2010), p. 238.
43 Symonds (1893), p. 4.
44 Symonds (1967–69), 3:827.
45 Pater (1980), p. 106.
46 Symonds (1893), p. 4.
47 Babington (1925), p. 83.
48 Hichens (1894), pp. 22–23.
49 Ibid., p. 21.
50 The chemical process is described in *The Artist* (1892), pp. 114–15. The author thanks Catherine Maxwell for this reference.
51 Beckson (2000); Matthews David (2022).
52 Jackson (1922), p. 46.
53 Nordau (1895), p. 10.
54 Ibid. For a further discussion of the Tanagra craze of the late 19th century see also Anderson (2020) and Jeammet (2003).
55 Reinach (1889), p. 54.
56 Huish (1898), p. 103.
57 Hutton (1899), p. 44.
58 Ibid., p. 1.
59 Ibid., p. 45.
60 On the polychromy of Tanagra figures, see Bourgeois and Jeammet (2020) pp. 3–28.
61 Quoted in Ross (2013), p. 106.
62 Wilde (2007), p. 132.
63 Ellmann (1988), p. 84.
64 Wilde (2005), p. 233.
65 Asleson (2000), p. 77.
66 Anderson (2020), p. 13.
67 Swinburne (1875), pp. 372–3. See also p. 360.
68 Asleson (2000), p. 85.
69 Whistler (1967), p. 159.
70 Garnier (2008), p. 79.
71 See Smith (2005).
72 See Yan-Bing Luo et al. (2018).
73 Quoted in Garelick (2009), p. 3.
74 Ibid.
75 Unsigned review, *L'Écho de Paris* (26 November 1892), quoted in Garelick (2009).
76 Anet (1903), p. 278.
77 Quoted in Garelick (2009), p. 14.
78 Fuller (1913), p. 62.
79 Garelick (2009), p. 6.
80 Fuller (1913), p. 37.
81 Hindson (2008), pp. 50–1.
82 Quoted in Andrew (2020).

Bibliography

Allitt, Patrick, *Catholic Converts: British and American Intellectuals Turn to Rome* (Ithaca, 1997)

Anderson, Anne, 'Tanagra Mania: Collecting, Displaying and Emulating Greek Tanagra Figures in the *Fin de Siècle*', in eds. Diana Davis et al., *Ceramics as Sculpture, The French Porcelain Society Journal* 8 (2020), pp. 1–30

Andrew, Nell, 'The Idea in Motion: Loïe Fuller at the Banquet', Moving Modernism: The Urge to Abstraction in Painting, Dance, Cinema, Oxford Studies in Dance Theory (New York, 2020; online edn, Oxford Academic, 23 Apr. 2020), https://doi.org/10.1093/oso/9780190057275.003.0002, accessed 5 April 2023

Anet, Claude, 'Loie Fuller in French Sculptre', *The Architectural Record* (March 1903)

Anon., 'On Decorative Colour', *The Ecclesiologist* 4 (1845), pp. 199–203

Anon., 'On Flowers as Employed in the Adornment of Churches', *The Ecclesiologist* 6 (1846), pp. 215–17

Anon., 'Memoirs and Letters of the Late Thomas Seddon, Artist', *The Leader* 437 (7 August 1858)

Anon., 'The International Exhibition', *The Critic*, 12 April 1862, pp. 96–7

Anon. 'The Great Exhibition: About Dyes and Beauty and Coal-Tar Mauve and Magenta How Made Extraordinary Specimen of Aniline Art and the New Colors', *New York Times*, 28 July 1862, p. 2

Anon., 'Egyptian Cotton; Its Modern Origin and the Importance of Supply', *New York Times*, 26 June 1864, p. 5

Anon., 'The Society of Painters in Water Colours', *Art Journal* 28 (1866), p. 174

Anon., 'Exhibition of the Royal Academy', *Illustrated London News* 50/426 (11 May 1867), p. 478

Anon., 'Banquet at the Royal Academy', *The Times* (1871), p. 6

Anon., 'Variations in Violet and Green' (14 November 1871)

Anon., 'The Late Mr. Owen Jones' *The Illustrated London News* 64 (9 May 1874), pp. 445–6

Anon., 'Revolting Cruelty to Seals', *The Animal World* (April 1875), p. 52

Anon., 'Whistler in Venice – A Gavotte in Gamboge', *Punch* (3 March 1883)

Anon., 'Society of British Artists', *The Era* (11 December 1886)

Anon., 'From Month to Month. A Summary', *The Artist and Journal of Home Culture* (1 April 1892), pp. 113–15

Asleson, Robyn, *Albert Moore* (London, 2000)

Atkins, Anna, *Photographs of British Algae: Cyanotype Impressions*, 1843, n.p.

Atkinson, Blanche, *A Woman's Question* (London, 1896)

Atterbury, Paul, and Maureen Batkin, *The Parian Phenomenon: A Survey of Victorian Parian Porcelain Statuary & Busts* (Shepton Beauchamp, 1989)

Axel, Brian Keith, *The Nation's Tortured Body: Violence, Representation and the Formation of a Sikh 'diaspora'* (Durham and London, 2001)

Babington, Percy L., *Bibliography of the Writings of John Addington Symonds* (London, 1925)

Bacher, Otto, *With Whistler in Venice* (New York, 1909)

Balfour-Paul, Jenny, *Indigo in the Arab World* (London and New York, 1997)

Ball, Philip, *Bright Earth: The Invention of Colour* (London, 2001)

Barringer, Tim, *Reading the Pre-Raphaelites* (New Haven and London, 1999)

Barrington, Emilie, *The Life, Letters and Works of Frederic Leighton*, 2 vols (London, 1906)

Bastide, Roger, *Colour, Racism and Christianity* (Paris, 1967)

Batchelor, David, *Chromophobia* (London, 2000)

Beach, Caitlin Meyhee, *Sculpture at the Ends of Slavery* (Oakland, 2022)

Beckson, Carl, 'Oscar Wilde and the Green Carnation', *English Literature in Transition, 1880–1920* 43/4 (2000), pp. 387–97

Beckwith, Alice H.R.H., *Victorian Bibliomania: the illuminated book in nineteenth-century Britain* (Providence, 1987)

Bender, Geoff and Rasmus R. Simonsen, eds., *Photography's Materialities: Transatlantic Photographic Practices over the Long Nineteenth Century* (Leuven, 2021)

Blaszczyk, Regina, *The Color Revolution* (Cambridge, MA, 2012)

Blunt, Anne, *A Pilgrimage to Nejd, the Cradle of the Arab Race. A Visit to the Court of the Emir and 'Our Persian Campaign'* (London, 1879)

Boase, Tessa, *Etta Lemon: The Woman Who Saved Birds* (Essex, 2021)

Boden, Madeline Stacey, 'A Relief from Classicism: Frederic Leighton in the Near East, 1857–1895' (unpublished PhD Thesis, University of York, 2020)

Boulouch, Nathalie, *Le ciel est bleu: une histoire de la photographie couleur* (Paris, 2011)

Bourgeois, Brigitte, and Violaine Jeammet, 'La polychromie des terres cuites grecques: approche matérielle d'une culture picturale', *Revue archéologique* 69/1 (2020), pp. 3–28

Braga, Ariane Varela, 'Microorganisms, Microscopes, and Victorian Design Theories', *British Art Studies* 21 (2021), https://doi.org/10.17658/issn.2058-5462/issue-21/avbraga/001 (accessed 1 March 2023)

British Museum, *A Guide to the Gould Collection of Humming-birds* (London, 1884)

Brown, David Blayney, et al., *Late Turner – Painting Set Free*, exh. cat., Tate (London, 2014)

Browning, Elizabeth Barrett, *The Letters of Elizabeth Barrett Browning*, (London, 1897)

Bryant, Julius, '"The Progress and Present Condition of Modern Art": Fine Art at the 1862 Exhibition', *The Journal of the Decorative Arts Society 1850 – the Present* 38 (2014)

Bullen, J.B, *Byzantium Rediscovered* (London, 2003)

Bullock, William, *A Companion to the Liverpool Museum* (Liverpool, 1800)

Burges, William, 'The International Exhibition', *Gentleman's Magazine* 213 (September 1862), pp. 3–12

Burne-Jones, Georgina, *Memorials of Edward Burne-Jones*, 2 vols (London, 1904)

Burton, Richard, *Personal Narrative of a Pilgrimage to El-Medinah and Meccah*, 3 vols (London, 1856)

Butlin, Martin and Evelyn Joll, *The Paintings of J.M.W. Turner*, 2 vols (London and New Haven, 1984)

Carlyle, Leslie, 'Authenticity and Adulteration: What Materials Were 19th Century Artists Really Using?' *The Conservator* 17/1 (1993), pp. 56–60

Carlyle, Leslie, *The Artist's Assistant: Oil Painting Instruction Manuals and Handbooks in Britain, 1800–1900, with Reference to Selected Eighteenth-Century Sources* (London, 2001)

Cesaratto, Anna, Yan-Bing Luo, Henry D. Smith, and Marco Leona, 'A timeline for the introduction of synthetic dyestuffs in Japan during the late Edo and Meiji periods', *Heritage Science* 6.1 (2018), pp. 1–12

Cobbold, Carolyn, *A Rainbow Palate: How Chemical Dyes Changed the West's Relationship with Food* (Chicago, 2020)

Cook, E.T. and Alexander Wedderburn, eds., *The Complete Works of John Ruskin*, 39 vols (London, 1903–12)

Cook, Thomas, *Cook's Tourists' Handbook for Egypt, the Nile and the Desert* (London, 1869)

Cowie, Helen, *Victims of Fashion: Animal Commodities in Victorian Britain* (Cambridge, 2022)

Crace, J. Gregory, 'On the Decoration of the International Exhibition Building', *Journal of the Society of Arts*, vol. 10, no. 490 (1862)

Cruise, Colin, '"Sick-sad dreams": Burne-Jones and Pre-Raphaelite Medievalism', *The Yearbook of English Studies* 40 (2010), pp. 121–40

Dadd, Richard, *letter to unknown recipient* (24 February 1843). Bethlem Museum of the Mind, 1574

Darwin, Charles, *Journal of Researches into the Natural History and Geology of the Countries Visited During the Voyage of H.M.S Beagle Round the World* (London, 1849)

Darwin, Charles, *On the Origin of Species* (London, 1859)

Darwin, Charles, *The Descent of Man, and Selection in Relation to Sex* (London, 1879)

David, Alison Matthews, *Fashion Victims: The Dangers of Dress Past and Present* (London, 2015)

Davis, John R. et al., eds., 'Almost Forgotten: The International Exhibition of 1862', *Decorative Arts Society Journal* vol. 38 (2014)

Dentith, Simon, 'The Gorgeous Contributions of India: Ruskin, Owen Jones and Oriental Art' *A Journal of Cultural Materialism*, No. 3 (2000), pp. 79–93

Dickens, Charles, 'Hard Times', *Household Words conducted by Charles Dickens*, vol. 9, iss. 211 (8 April 1854)

Dickens, Charles, ed. 'Perkin's Purple', *All the Year Round*, vol. 1 (10 September 1859), pp. 168–71.

Dickens, Charles, 'Ignoramus at the Exhibition', *All the Year Round*, vol VII (23 August 1862), pp. 345–8

Dishon, Dale, 'South Kensington's Forgotten Palace: The Rise and Fall of the 1862 Exhibition Building', *The Journal of the Decorative Arts Society 1850 – the Present* 38 (2014)

Donnelly, Max, '"Rapture and Ridicule": Furniture in the 1862 Medieval Court', *The Journal of the Decorative Arts Society 1850 – the Present*, 38 (2014)

Dootson, Kirsty, *Industrial Color: Chromatic Technologies in Britain, 1856–1969* (PhD dissertation, Yale University, 2018)

Dootson, Kirsty, *The Rainbow's Gravity: Colour, Materiality, and British Modernity* (PMC/Yale, 2023)

Dorment, Richard G., '"A Roman Lady" by Frederick Leighton', *Philadelphia Museum of Art Bulletin* 73 (June 1977), p. 5

Dowling, 'Ruskin's Pied Beauty and the Construction of a "Homosexual" Code', *Victorian Newsletter* 75 (1989), pp. 1–8

Dresser, Christopher, *Principles of Decorative Design* (London, 1873)

Dresser, Christopher, *Principles of Decorative Design* (London, New York, 1873)

Driver, Felix and Sonia Ashmore, 'The Mobile Museum: Collecting and Circulating Indian Textiles in Victorian Britain', *Victorian Studies*, vol. 52, no. 3 (2010), pp. 353–85

Droth, Martina, and Michael Hatt, '*The Greek Slave* by Hiram Powers: A Transatlantic Object', *Nineteenth-Century Art Worldwide* 15, no. 2 (Summer 2016), http://www.19thc-artworldwide.org/summer16/droth-hatt-intro-to-the-greek-slave-by-hiram-powers-a-transatlantic-object (accessed January 11, 2023)

Droth, Martina, Jason Edwards and Michael Hatt, eds., *Sculpture Victorious: Art in an Age of Invention, 1837–1901*, exh. cat., Yale Centre for British Art (London and New Haven, 2014)

Duret, Théodore, 'Expositions de la Royal Academy et de la Grosvenor Gallery', *Gazette des Beaux-Arts*, vol. 1 (1881), pp. 549–56

Eastlake, Charles, *Materials for a History of Oil Painting* (London, 1847)

Eastlake, Elizabeth, *Life of John Gibson, R.A.* (London, 1870)

Eaton, Natasha, *Colour, Art, and Empire: Visual Culture and the Nomadism of Representation* (London, 2013)

Eliason, Chad M. Rafael Maia, Juan L. Parra and Matthew D. Shawkey, 'Signal evolution and morphological complexity in hummingbirds (Aves: Trochilidae)', *Evolution* vol. 74, no. 2 (February 2020)

Ellmann, Richard, *Oscar Wilde* (Harmondsworth, 1988)

Ellis, Havelock, *Sexual Inversion* (Philadelphia, 1915)

Elyse, Nelson, and Wendy S. Walters, *Fictions of Emancipation: Carpeaux's Why Born Enslaved! Reconsidered* (New York, 2022)

Evangelista, Stefano, 'Symphonies in Haze and Blue: Lafcadio Hearn and the Colours of Japan', in ed. Charlotte Ribeyrol, *The Colours of the Past in Victorian England* (Oxford, 2016)

Faxon, Alicia, 'The Influence of Christine de Pisan on Dante Gabriel Rossetti and Elizabeth Siddal' in ed. Liana De Girolami Cheney, *Pre-Raphaelitism and Medievalism in the Arts* (Lewiston, 1992), pp. 93–108

Ferry, Kathryn, 'Printing the Alhambra: Owen Jones and Chromolithography' *Architectural History* 46 (2003), pp. 175–88

Field, George, *Chromatography; or, A Treatise on Colours and Pigments, and of Their Powers in Painting* (London, 1835)

FitzHugh, Elisabeth West, ed., *Artists' Pigments Vol. 3: A Handbook of Their History and Characteristics* (Washington, 1997)

Flints, Kate, book review, *Sarah Angelina Acland: First Lady of Colour Photography, by Giles Hudson* in *Victorian Studies* vol. 58, no. 1 (autumn 2015), p. 179

Fuller, Loïe, *Fifteen Years of a Dancer's Life* (London, 1913)

Gage, John, *J.M.W. Turner: A Wonderful Range of Mind* (London, 1987)

Gange, David and Michael Ledger-Lomas, eds., *Cities of God: The Bible and Archaeology in Nineteenth-Century Britain* (Cambridge, 2013)

Garelick, Rhonda K., *Electric Salome: Loie Fuller's Performance of Modernism* (Princeton, 2009)

Garascia, Ann, '"Impressions of Plants Themselves": Materializing Eco-Archival Practices with Anna Atkins's *Photographs of British Algae*' in *Victorian Literature and Culture* vol. 47, no. 2, (2019), pp. 267–303

Garcia, Bibiana, 'The Nature and Science of the Victorian Era' *OpenMind BBVA* (2019), https://www.bbvaopenmind.com/en/science/scientific-insights/the-nature-and-science-of-the-victorian-era/ (accessed 1 March 2023)

Garfield, Simon, *Mauve: How One Man Invented a Colour That Changed the World* (London, 2000)

Garnier, Bénédicte, 'Tel un dieu antique', in eds. Bénédicte Garnier and Dominique Viéville, *Rodin, Freud Collectionneurs, La passion à l'oeuvre* (Paris, 2008), pp. 67–91

Gaskill, Nicholas, *Chromographia: American Literature and the Modernization of Color* (Minneapolis, 2018)

Gere, Charlotte and Judy Rudoe, 'Jewellery at the 1862 Exhibition', in eds. John R. Davis et al., *'Almost Forgotten': The International Exhibition of 1862, Decorative Arts Society Journal* 38 (2014), pp. 83–105

Gere, Charlotte and Lesley Hoskins, *The House Beautiful: Oscar Wilde and the Aesthetic Interior* (London, 2000)

Gettens, Rutherford John, and George Leslie Stout, *Painting Materials* (New York, 1966)

Gilbert, W.S., *Patience, or, Bunthorne's Bride: A Comic Opera in Two Acts* (London, 1881)

Gladstone, William E., 'The Colour-Sense', *The Nineteenth Century* no.8 (October 1877), pp. 366–88

Goethe, Johann Wolfgang von, *Theory of Colours*, trans. Charles Lock Eastlake (New York, 2006)

Goncourt, Edmond and Jules de Goncourt, *Journal: mémoires de la vie littéraire*, ed. Robert Ricatte (Paris, 1989)

Gould, John, *An Introduction to the Trochilidae, Or Family of Humming-birds* (London, 1861)

Gowing, Lawrence, *Turner: Imagination and Reality*, exh. cat., Museum of Modern Art, New York (New York, 1966)

Greville, Violet, 'The Devonshire House ball', *The Graphic* (10 July 1897), p. 78.

Harvey, John, *Men in Black* (Chicago, 1995)

Harvey, Mark, 'Slavery, Indenture and the Development of British Industrial Capitalism', *History Workshop Journal* 88 (Autumn 2019)

Haslam, Ray, '"According to the requirements of his scholars": Ruskin, drawing and art education' in ed. Robert Hewison, *Ruskin's Artists: Studies in the Victorian Visual Economy* (Aldershot, 2000), pp. 147–65

Hatt, Michael, 'Transparent Forms: Tinting, Whiteness and John Gibson's Venus', *The Sculpture Journal* 23.2 (2014)

Hatt, Michael, 'Sculpture, Chains, and the Armstrong Gun: John Bell's *American Slave*', *Nineteenth-Century Art Worldwide* 15, no. 2 (Summer 2016) http://www.19thc-artworldwide.org/summer16/hatt-on-sculpture-chains-and-the-armstrong-gun-john-bell-american-slave (accessed 11 January 2023)

Havelock, Ellis, *Sexual Inversion* (Philadelphia, 1915)

Haweis, Mary Eliza, *The Art of Dress* (London, 1879)

Haweis, Mary Eliza, *The Art of Decoration* (London, 1881)

Hawksley, Lucinda, *Bitten by Witch Fever: Wallpaper & Arsenic in the Nineteenth-Century Home* (London, 2016)

Haydon, Benjamin Robert, *The Autobiography and Memoirs of Benjamin Robert Haydon 1786–1846 Compiled from his "Autobiography and Journals" and "Correspondence and Table-Talk"*, ed. Alexander P.D. Penrose (New York, 1929)

Hearn, Lafcadio, *Exotics and Retrospectives* [1898] (Boston, 1905)

Hewison, Robert, ed., *Catalogue of the Rudimentary Series in the arrangement of 1873 with Ruskin's comments of 1878* (London, 1984)

Hewison, Robert, *Ruskin's Venice* (London, 2000)

Hewitson, Madeline, 'Victorian Exodus: Visualising the Old Testament in the *Dalziels' Bible Gallery* (1881)' in eds. Sheona Beaumont and Madeleine Emerald Thiele, *John Ruskin, the Pre-Raphaelites, and Religious Imagination: Sacre Conversazioni* (London, 2023)

Hichens, Robert, *The Green Carnation* (New York, 1894)

Hindson, Catherine, 'Interruptions by inevitable petticoats: Skirt Dancing and the Historiographical Problem of Late Nineteenth-century dance', *Nineteenth Century Theatre and Film*, 35(2) (2008), pp. 48–64

Hofmann, A.W., 'Report on The Chemical And Pharmaceutical Products And Processes Exhibited In Class II. Section A. of the International Exhibition held at London in 1862', *Reports by the Juries on the Subjects in the Thirty-six Classes into which the Exhibition was divided* (London, 1863)

Holbrook, Richard Thayer, *Portraits of Dante from Giotto to Raffael: A Critical Study with a Concise Iconography* (London, 1911)

Holman Hunt, William, 'The Present System of Obtaining Materials in Use by Artist Painters, as Compared with that of the Old Masters', *The Journal of the Society of Arts*, vol. 28, no. 1431 (23 April 1880), p. 495

Holmes, John, *Temple of Science: the Pre-Raphaelites and Oxford University Museum of Natural History* (Oxford, 2020)

Holmes, John, *The Pre-Raphaelites and Science* (London and New Haven, 2018)

Hudson, Giles, *The Feminization of Photography and the Conquest of Colour: Sarah Angelina Acland.* (unpublished DPhil Thesis, University of Oxford, 2012a)

Hudson, Giles, *Sarah Angelina Acland: First Lady of Colour Photography* (Oxford, 2012b)

Hughes, Thomas, 'The Human Landscape: John Ruskin, Drawing, and Colour', in eds. Charlotte Gould and Sophie Mesplède, *British Art and the Environment: Changes, Challenges, and Responses since the Industrial Revolution* (London, 2021)

Huish, Marcus B., 'Tanagra Terra-Cottas', *The Studio* 14/64 (1898), pp. 97–104

Humphreys, Henry Noel, *Illuminated Books of the Middle Ages* (London, 1849)

Hutton, Caroline Amy, *Greek Terracotta Statuettes* (London, 1899)

Huysmans, Joris-Karl, *Against the Grain*, trans. John Howard [1884] (New York, 1922)

Jacklin, Elizabeth, 'Study of Fish: Two Tench, a Trout and a Perch c.1822–4 by Joseph Mallord William Turner' in ed. David Blayney Brown, *J.M.W. Turner: Sketchbooks, Drawings and Watercolours* (London, 2017)

Jackson, Holbrook, *The Eighteen Nineties: A Review of Art and Ideas at the Close of the Nineteenth Century* [1913] (London, 1922)

Jacobi, Carol, *William Holman Hunt – Painter, Painting, Paint* (Manchester, 2007)

Jeammet Violaine, ed., *Tanagra, mythes et archéologie* (Paris, 2003)

Jenkins, Ian, 'G.F. Watts' Teachers: George Frederic Watts and the Elgin Marbles', *Apollo* 120, (1984), pp. 176–81

Jenkins, Ian, 'Highlight: An Informed Inventiveness', in eds. Elizabeth Prettejohn and Peter Trippi, *Lawrence Alma-Tadema, At Home in Antiquity* (London, 2016), pp. 50–1

Jockey, Philippe, *Le mythe de la Grèce blanche: Histoire d'un rêve occidental* (Paris, 2013)

Jones, Owen, *The Influence of Religion Upon Art* (London, 1845)

Jones, Owen, ed., *An Apology for the Colouring of the Greek Court in the Crystal Palace* (London, 1854)

Jones, Owen, ed., *The Grammar of Ornament* (London, 1856)

Kalba, Laura, *Color in the Age of Impressionism: Commerce, Technology, and Art* (University Park, PA, 2017)

Katz, Melissa R., 'William Holman Hunt and the Pre-Raphaelite Technique', in eds. Arie Wallert, Erma Hermens and Marja Peek, *Historical Painting Techniques, Materials, and Studio Practice: Preprints of a Symposium* (Los Angeles, 1995)

Keats, John, *Lamia, Isabella, The Eve of St. Agnes and Other Poems* (London, 1820)

Kelvin, Norman, ed., *The Collected Letters of William Morris* vol. 2 (Princeton, 1988)

Lafont, Anne, 'How Skin Colour Became a Racial Marker: Art Historical Perspectives on Race', *Eighteenth-Century Studies* vol. 51, no. 1 (Fall 2017), pp. 89–113

Landow, George P., 'William Holman Hunt's "Oriental Mania" and his Uffizi Self-Portrait' *The Art Bulletin* 64 (1982), pp. 646–55

Lanman, Susan W., 'Colour in the Garden: 'Malignant Magenta', *Garden History* vol. 28, no. 2 (Winter, 2000), pp. 209–221

Lazarus, Emma, 'A Day in Surrey with William Morris', *Century Magazine* 32 (July 1886), pp. 388–97

Le Gallienne, Richard, *Prose Fancies (Second Series)* (London and Chicago, 1896)

Levi, Donata and Paul Tucker, '"J after J. Ruskin": Line in the Art Teaching of John Ruskin and Ebenezer Cooke', *Journal of Art Historiography* 22 (2020), pp. 1–16

Llewellyn, Briony, *John Frederick Lewis: Facing Fame* (Compton, 2019)

Loske, Alexandra, 'Mary Philadelphia Merrifield: Color History as Expertise', *Visual Resources* 33 (2016), pp. 1–16

Mann, Fiona, 'Brushing the Surface: The Practice and Critical Reception of Watercolour Techniques in England, 1850–1880', 2 vols. (unpublished PhD Thesis, Oxford Brookes University, 2011)

Mantz, Paul, 'Exposition de Londres. Peinture et Sculpture. Ecoles française et étrangères (suite)', *Gazette des Beaux-Arts*, 1862, pp. 365–77. Google Books. Free Ebook (accessed 5 June 2018)

Marsh, Jan et al., *Pre-Raphaelite Sisters* exh. cat., National Portrait Gallery (London, 2019)

Marshall, Nancy Rose, *Victorian Science and Imagery* (Pittsburgh, 2021)

Martin, Emily, 'The Tintometer, Anthropology and the Science of Colour', *Anthropology Now* (3 May 2016)

Mason, Frederick Alfred, 'The Influence of Research on the Development of the Coal-Tar Industry, Part II', *Science Progress in the Twentieth Century (1906–1916)* vol. 10, no. 39 (1916), pp. 412–22

Matthews David, Alison, 'Tainted Love: Oscar Wilde's Toxic Green Carnation, Queerness and Chromophobia', in eds. Jonathan Faiers and Mary Westerman Bulgarella, *Colors in Fashion* (London, 2022), pp. 127–43

Matthews David, Alison, *Fashion Victims: The Dangers of Dress Past and Present* (London, 2015)

Matthews, Alison Victoria, 'Aestheticism's True Colors: The Politics of Pigment in Victorian Art, Criticism and Fashion', in eds. Talia Schaffer and Kathy Alexis Psomiades, *Women and British Aestheticism* (Charlottesville, 1999), pp. 172–89

Matthews, T. and John Gibson, *The Biography of John Gibson, R.A., Sculptor, Rome* (London, 1911)

Maxwell, Catherine, 'Whistlerian Impressionism and the Venetian Variations of Vernon Lee, John Addington Symonds, and Arthur Symons', *Yearbook of English Studies* 40/1 and 2 (2010), pp. 217–45

Merrifield, Mary P., *Original Treatises: Dating from the XIIth to XVIIIth Centuries on the Arts of Painting, in Oil, Miniature, Mosaic, and on Glass; of Gilding, Dyeing, and the Preparation of Colours and Artificial Gems* (London, 1849)

Merrifield, Mary Philadelphia, 'The Harmony of Colors as Exemplified in the Exhibition', in *The Art Journal Illustrated Catalogue: The Industry of All Nations* (London, 1851), pp. i–viii

Millais, John Guille, *The Life and Letters of Sir John Everett Millais* (London, 1899)

Morris, William, *William Morris by Himself: Designs and Writings*, ed. Gillian Naylor (London, 1988)

Moser, Stephanie, *Designing Antiquity: Owen Jones, Ancient Egypt and the Crystal Palace* (London and New Haven, 2012)

Moser, Stephanie, *Painting Antiquity: Ancient Egypt in the Art of Lawrence Alma-Tadema, Edward Poynter and Edwin Long* (Oxford, 2020)

Mosley, Stephen, *The Chimney of the World: A History of Smoke Pollution in Victorian and Edwardian Manchester* (Cambridge, 2001)

Nadri, Ghluam A., *The Political Economy of Indigo in India, 1580–1930: A Global Perspective* (Leiden, 2016)

Nichols, Kate, 'Greece and Rome at the Crystal Palace', *Classical Sculpture and Modern Britain, 1854–1936* (Oxford, 2015)

Nietzsche, Friedrich, *The Birth of Tragedy from the Spirit of Music* (Berlin, 1872)

Nochlin, Linda, *The Politics of Vision* (Boulder, 1989)

Nordau, Max, *Degeneration* (London 1895)

Pastoureau, Michel, *Vert. Histoire d'une couleur* (Paris, 2013)

Pater, Walter, *The Renaissance: Studies in Art and Poetry. The 1893 Text*, ed. Donald L. Hill [1893] (Berkeley and Los Angeles, 1980)

Patmore, Coventry, 'Walls and Wall Painting at Oxford', *Saturday Review* 4/113 (26 December 1857), pp. 583–4

Peterson, S. William, ed., *The Ideal Book: Essays and Lectures on the Arts of the Book by William Morris* (Berkeley, 1982)

Phillips, Clare, 'Jewellery', in eds. Stephen Calloway and Lynn Federle Orr, *The Cult of Beauty, The Aesthetic Movement, 1860–1900* (London, 2011), pp. 208–11.

Poliquin, Rachel, *The Breathless Zoo* (Philadelphia, 2012)

Potolsky, Matthew, *The Decadent Republic of Letters: Taste, Politics, and Cosmopolitan Community from Baudelaire to Beardsley* (Philadelphia, 2013)

Potts, Alex, 'Colors of Sculpture', in ed. Roberta Panzanelli, *The Color of Life: Polychromy in Sculpture from Antiquity to the Present* (Los Angeles, 2008), pp. 78–97

Pratt, Mary Louise, 'Arts of the Contact Zone', *Profession* (1991), pp. 33–50

Prettejohn, Elizabeth, *The Art of the Pre-Raphaelites* (Princeton, 2000)

Prettejohn, Elizabeth, 'Between Homer and Ovid: metamorphoses of the "grand style" in G.F. Watts' in ed. Colin Trodd and Stephanie Brown, *Representations of G.F. Watts, Art Marking in Victorian Culture* (Aldershot, 2004), pp. 49–64

Prettejohn, Elizabeth, 'Lawrence Alma-Tadema, Phidias showing the Frieze of the Parthenon to his friends, 1868' in ed. Penelope Curtis, *On the Meanings of Sculpture in Painting* (Leeds, 2009), pp. 106–7

Prettejohn, Elizabeth, *The Modernity of Ancient Sculpture: Greek Sculpture and Modern Art from Winckelmann to Picasso* (London, 2012)

Prettejohn, Elizabeth, 'Visions of ancient Egypt in nineteenth-century painting' in ed. Anna Ferrari and Benjamin Hinson, *Visions of Ancient Egypt* (Norwich, 2022), pp. 65–77

Prettejohn, Elizabeth and Peter Trippi, *Lawrence Alma-Tadema: At Home in Antiquity* (London, 2016)

Pugin, Augustus Welby Northmore, *The True Principles of Pointed or Christian Architecture: Set Forth in Two Lectures Delivered at St. Marie's, Oscott* (London, 1853)

Queen Victoria, *Queen Victoria's Journals* RA VIC/MAIN/QVJ (W) 10 June 1851, http://www.queenvictoriasjournals.org/search/displayItemFromId.do?FormatType=fulltextimgsrc&QueryType=articles&ItemID=18510610 (accessed 1 March 2023)

Reinach, Theodore, 'Un Temple élevé par les femmes de Tanagra', *Revue des études grecques* 12/45 (1889), pp. 53–115

Rhys, Ernest, *Sir Frederic Leighton Bart. PRA, An Illustrated Chronicle* (London, 1895)

Ribeyrol, Charlotte, '"Strange dyes": the colour that dare not speak its name', in ed. Frédéric Ogée, *Definition(s) of Color, Interfaces* 33 (2013), pp. 229–42

Ribeyrol, Charlotte, ed., *The Colours of the Past in Victorian England* (Oxford, 2016)

Ribeyrol, Charlotte, 'The Changing Colours of Nineteenth-Century Art and Literature', *Word & Image* 36, no. 1 (2 January 2020), pp. 1–6

Ribeyrol, Charlotte, *William Burges's Great Bookcase & The Victorian Colour Revolution* (London and New Haven, 2023)

Riggs, Miss., 'Miss Riggs's Travel Diary' (1869) *Thomas Cook Archive*, Record Office for Leicestershire, Leicester and Rutland (uncatalogued)

Roberts, Mary, *Istanbul Exchanges: Ottomans, Orientalists and Nineteenth-Century Visual Culture* (Oakland, California, 2015)

Roget, John Lewis, *History of the Old Watercolour Society* (London, 1891)

Ronetti, Alessandra, '"Chromo-culture." Les danses de la nature de Loïe Fuller et la force énergétique de la lumière', *Romantisme* 193 (2021/3), pp. 84–95

Roque, Georges, *Art et science de la couleur: Chevreul et les peintres, de Delacroix à l'abstraction* (Paris, 2009)

Ross, Iain, *Oscar Wilde and Ancient Greece* (Cambridge, 2013)

Rudoe, Judy 'The Curator, the Manufacturer, Collecting and Connoisseurship: Charles Hercules Read, William Burton and Justus Brinckmann', *The Journal of the Decorative Arts Society 1850 – the Present* 41 (2017), pp. 50–75

Rudoe, Judy, and Charlotte Gere, *Jewellery in the Age of Queen Victoria: A Mirror to the World*, exh. cat, British Museum (London, 2010)

Ruskin, John, *Fors Clavigera* (1871–84), letter 79, 18 June 1877

Ruskin, John, *The Complete Works of John Ruskin*, eds. E.T. Cook and Alexander Wedderburn, 39 vols (London, 1903)

Russell, William Howard, *A Diary in the East During the Tour of the Prince and Princess of Wales* (London, 1869)

Said, Edward, *Orientalism* (London, 2003)

Salter, Thomas W., ed., *Field's Chromatography* (London, 1871), pp. 162–3

Sattin, Anthony, *A Winter on the Nile: Florence Nightingale, Gustave Flaubert and the Temptations of Egypt* (London, 2010)

Schaaf, Larry, 'The First Photographically Printed and Illustrated Book', *The Papers of the Bibliographical Society of America* vol. 73, no. 2, Second Quarter (1979), pp. 209–24

Schaaf, Larry, *Sun Gardens: Cyanotypes by Anna Atkins* (New York, 2018)

Schaffer, Talia, *The Forgotten Female Aesthetes, Literary Culture in Late-Victorian England* (Charlottesville, 2000)

Scharf, George, *The Pompeiian Court in the Crystal Palace* (London, 1854)

Singletary, Suzanne, *James McNeill Whistler and France: A Dialogue in Paint Poetry and Music* (London and New York, 2017)

Smiles, Sam, *The Late Works of J.M.W. Turner: the Artist and his Critics* (London and New Haven, 2020)

Smith, Alison, *The Victorian Nude: Sexuality, Morality and Art* (Manchester, 1996)

Smith, Amy C., 'Winckelmann's influence on the Neoclassical reception of Greek vases', *Journal of Art Historiography* 25 (December 2021), pp. 1–22

Smith II, Henry D., 'Hokusai and the Blue Revolution in Edo Prints', in John T. Carpenter, ed., *Hokusai and His Age: Ukiyo-e Painting, Printmaking, and Book Illustration in Late Edo Japan* (Amsterdam, 2005), pp. 234–69

Smith, Jonathan, *Charles Darwin and Victorian Visual Culture* (Cambridge, 2006)

Spies, Martin, 'Late Victorian aristocrats and the racial other: the Devonshire House ball of 1897', *Race & Class* 57, no. 4 (2016), pp. 95–103

Swift, Anthony, '"The Arms of England that Grasp the World": Empire at the Great Exhibition', *exPLUSultra* vol. 3 (April 2012)

Swinburne, Algernon Charles, 'Notes on Some Pictures of 1868', in *Essays and Studies* (London, 1875), pp. 358–80

Syme, Patrick, *Werner's Nomenclature of Colours* (Edinburgh, 1814)

Symonds, John Addington, *In the Key of Blue and Other Prose Essays* (London, 1893)

Symonds, John Addington, *The Letters of John Addington Symonds*, in eds. Herbert M. Schueller and Robert L. Peters, 3 vols (Detroit, 1967–69)

Taine, Hippolyte, *Taine's Notes on England*, trans. Hyams Edward (London, 1957)

Tennyson, Alfred, *Idylls of the King* (New York, 1892)

Tennyson, Alfred, 'To the Queen', in ed. Christopher Ricks, *The Poems of Tennyson* (Harlow, 1987)

Thackeray, William Makepeace, *Notes of a Journey From Cornhill to Grand Cairo* (London, 1888)

Thistlewood, Jevon, 'An Examination of William Burges's Great Bookcase', *The Journal of the Decorative Arts Society 1850 – the Present* 41 (2017), pp. 26–33

Timbs, John, *The Industry, Science, & Art of the Age: Or, The International Exhibition of 1862 Popularly Described from Its Origin to Its Close: Including Detail of the Principal Objects and Articles Exhibited* (London, 1863)

Tolini, Michelle, '"Beetle Abominations" and Birds on Bonnets: Zoological Fantasy in Late-Nineteenth-Century Dress', *Nineteenth-Century Art Worldwide* 1, no. 1 (Spring 2002), http://www.19thc-artworldwide.org/spring02/206-qbeetle-abominationsq-and-birds-on-bonnets-zoological-fantasy-in-late-nineteenth-century-dress (accessed 1 March 2023)

Townsend, Joyce H., 'The Materials of J.M.W. Turner: Pigments', *Studies in Conservation* 38/4 (1993), pp. 231–54

Townsend, Joyce H., 'Painting Techniques and Materials of Turner and Other British Artists 1775–1875', in eds. Arie Wallert, E. Hermens and Marja Peek, *Historical Painting Techniques, Materials, and Studio Practice: Preprints of a Symposium* (Los Angeles, 1995)

Townsend, Joyce H., 'The Materials Used by British Oil Painters throughout the Nineteenth Century', *Studies in Conservation* 47/1 (2002), pp. 46–55

Townsend, Joyce H., Jacqueline Ridge and Stephen Hackney, eds., *Pre-Raphaelite Painting Techniques, 1848–56* (London, 2004)

Townsend, Joyce H., Leslie Carlyle, Narayan Khandekar and Sally Woodcock, 'Later Nineteenth Century Pigments: Evidence for Additions and Substitutions', *The Conservator* 19/1 (London, 1995), pp. 65–78

Travis, Anthony S., 'The Accidental Discovery of Mauve', *Victorian Review* 40.2 (2014), p. 38

Tree, Isabella, *The Ruling Passion of John Gould: A Biography of the Bird Man* (London, 1991)

Tupper, John Lucas, 'Extracts from the Diary of an Artist', *The Crayon* 3 (1856)

Turnbull, Geoffrey, *A History of the Calico Printing Industry of Great Britain* (Altrincham, 1951)

Vettese Forster, Samantha and Robert M. Christie, 'The significance of the introduction of synthetic dyes in the mid 19th century on the democratisation of western fashion', *JAIC – Journal of the International Colour Association* 11 (2013)

Wakefield, Priscilla, *Introduction to Botany: In a Series of Familiar Letters* (Boston, 1811)

Wallace, Alfred R., 'Hummingbirds' in *Frasers* 28 (1877), pp. 784–6

Wallace, Jennifer, *Shelley and Greece: Rethinking Romantic Hellenism* (London, 1997)

Waring, J.B., and Stephen Thompson, *Masterpieces of Industrial Art & Sculpture at the International Exhibition, 1862: Selected and Described* (London, 1863)

Warrell, Ian, *Turner and Venice* (London, 2003)

Warren, Jeremy, 'A Daughter of Eve', *National Trust Collections* (March 2022), https://www.nationaltrustcollections.org.uk/object/1228372 (accessed 1 March 2023)

Westmacott, Richard, 'On Polychromy in Sculpture, or Colouring Statues', *Journal of the Society of Arts* (4 March 1859), pp. 225–35

Whistler, James McNeill, 'Ten O'Clock Lecture', in *The Gentle Art of Making Enemies* (New York, 1967)

Whistler, James McNeill, letter to Marcus Bourne Huish, 21/26 January 1880. Glasgow University Library, MS Whistler LB 3/8.

Whistler, James McNeill, letter to Matthew Robinson Elden, 15/30 April 1880. Glasgow University Library, MS Whistler E61.

Whistler, James McNeill, *The Gentle Art of Making Enemies* [1890] (New York, 1967)

Wilcox, Scot, *Edward Lear and the Art of Travel* (Yale, 2001)

Wilde, Oscar, 'L'Envoi' [1882] in Rennell Rodd, *Rose Leaf and Apple Leaf* (Portland, 1906), pp. 3–21

Wilde, Oscar, *Poems* [1908] (London, 1913)

Wilde, Oscar, 'The Critic as Artist', in ed. Josephine M. Guy, *The Complete Works of Oscar Wilde: Historical Criticism, Intentions, The Soul of Man*, vol. 4 (Oxford, 2007), pp. 123–206.

Wilde, Oscar, *The Complete Works of Oscar Wilde*, III: *The Picture of Dorian Gray, The 1890 and 1891 Texts*, ed. Joseph Bristow (Oxford, 2005)

Wildman, Stephen, *An Instinct to Draw: John Ruskin's Drawings in the Ashmolean Museum* (Oxford, 2021)

Wilton, Andrew, *The Life and Work of J.M.W. Turner* (London, 1979)

Winckelmann, Johann J., *History of the Art of Antiquity*, trans. H.F. Mallgrave (Los Angeles, 2006)

Winterbottom, Matthew, 'Not Acceptable to Present Taste: William Burges's Great Bookcase', *The Journal of the Decorative Arts Society 1850 – the Present* 41 (2017), pp. 14–25

Wright, Reverend William, 'Lord Leighton in Damascus and After', *The Bookman* IX (March 1896), pp. 183–5

Yan-Bing Luo, Elena Basso, Henry D. Smith II, and Marco Leona, 'Synthetic arsenic sulfides in Japanese prints of the Meiji period', *Heritage Science* 4:17 (2016)

Image Credits

All images © Ashmolean Museum, University of Oxford, with the following exceptions

Fig. 1 Photo: Tate; **Fig. 2** Collection Christophel / Alamy Stock Photo; **Fig. 3** Science Museum Group; **Fig. 4** © National Railway Museum / Science & Society Picture Library – All rights reserved; **Fig. 5** Historic Royal Palaces; **Fig. 6** Royal Collection Trust / © His Majesty King Charles III, 2023 / Bridgeman Images; **Fig. 7** The Devonshire Collections, Chatsworth; **Fig. 8** Reproduced by permission of Chatsworth Settlement Trustees / Bridgeman Images; **Fig. 9** Philadelphia Museum of Art, Pennsylvania, PA, USA / Gift of Mr. and Mrs. W. W. Keen Butcher, 1997 / Bridgeman Images; **Fig. 10** © National Science & Media Museum / Science & Society Picture Library – All rights reserved; **Fig. 11** © National Science & Media Museum / Science & Society Picture Library – All rights reserved; **Fig. 12** The Bodleian Libraries, University of Oxford ((Vet) 1856 d. 10 (Atlas), title page); **Fig. 13** Hanna Holborn Gray Special Collections Research Center, University of Chicago Library; **Fig. 14** © Victoria and Albert Museum, London; **Fig. 15** The Bodleian Libraries, University of Oxford (Fiedler J. 11.20. title page); **Fig. 16** Photo: Tate; **Fig. 17** City of London Corporation; **Fig. 18** The Metropolitan Museum of Art, New York. Gift of Friends of the Thomas J. Watson Library. www.metmuseum.org; **Fig. 19** The Bodleian Libraries, University of Oxford (Johnson b.66. frontispiece); **Fig. 24** Photo: Tate; **Fig. 25** The Metropolitan Museum of Art, New York. Bequest of Cornelius Vanderbilt, 1899. www.metmuseum.org; **Fig. 26** Photo: Tate; **Fig. 27** Phoebe Ann Traquair – Two Pages, Illuminated, 'Sonnets from the Portugese' by Elizabeth Barrett Browning, National Galleries of Scotland. Phoebe Anna Traquair Bequest 1936; **Fig. 28** Getty Research Institute (via Internet Archive); **Fig. 29** By Kind Permission of the Warden, Fellows, and Scholars of Keble College, Oxford / Bridgeman Images; **Fig. 31** Photo: Tate; **Fig. 33** The British Library Board; **Fig. 34** Bridgeman Images; **Fig. 36** Photo by Birmingham Museums Trust, licensed under CC0; **Fig. 37** The British Library Board; **Fig. 38** Photo: Tate; **Fig. 39** Bridgeman Images; **Fig. 40** The Bodleian Libraries, University of Oxford (257735 b. 39, plate XVIII); **Fig. 41** The Bodleian Libraries, University of Oxford (137 c. 13m, untitled illustration); **Fig. 42** © Victoria and Albert Museum, London; **Fig. 43** Royal Collection Trust / © His Majesty King Charles III, 2023 / Bridgeman Images; **Fig. 45** © Victoria and Albert Museum, London; **Fig. 46** © Victoria and Albert Museum, London; **Fig. 47** The Bust of a King, Soissons © The Stained Glass Museum; **Fig. 48** Image © the Whitworth, The University of Manchester. Photography by Michael Pollard; **Fig. 53** Dante Alighieri. Colour lithograph, 1859, after S. Kirkup after a fresco attributed to Giotto. Wellcome Collection. Public Domain Mark; **Fig. 54** Phoebe Ann Traquair – Two Pages, Illuminated, 'Sonnets from the Portugese' by Elizabeth Barrett Browning, National Galleries of Scotland. Phoebe Anna Traquair Bequest 1936; **Fig. 57** Image courtesy of The Potteries Museum & Art Gallery, Stoke-on-Trent. 2002.C.454 (158/20612); **Fig. 58** Punch Cartoon Library / TopFoto; **Fig. 59** Photo © Fine Art Images / Bridgeman Images; **Fig. 60** © Manchester Art Gallery / Bridgeman Images; **Fig. 63** The Bodleian Libraries, University of Oxford (Arts b.110. pl. XL); **Fig. 65** © Victoria and Albert Museum, London; **Fig. 66** From The New York Public Library, https://digitalcollections.nypl.org/items/510d47d9-4b42-a3d9-e040-e00a18064a99; **Fig. 67** From The New York Public Library,https://digitalcollections.nypl.org/items/d3a80cb0-0743-0135-1499-55ea61f610a9; **Fig. 68** From The New York Public Library, https://digitalcollections.nypl.org/items/510d47d9-4adb-a3d9-e040-e00a18064a99; **Fig. 69** Private collection, courtesy of Hans P. Kraus Jr., New York; **Fig. 70** © Museum of the History of Science, Oxford, inv. 16181; **Fig. 71** © Museum of the History of Science, Oxford, inv.27301; **Fig. 72** © Museum of the History of Science, Oxford, inv. 29265; **Fig. 73** Image © National Museums Scotland; **Fig. 74** © Museum of the History of Science, Oxford, inv.17957; **Fig. 75** © Manchester Art Gallery; **Fig. 76** © The Trustees of the British Museum; **Fig. 77** The Bodleian Libraries, University of Oxford (CR. D. 14/2. pl. 67); **Fig. 78** © The Trustees of the British Museum; **Fig. 79** © Illustrated London News Ltd/Mary Evans; **Fig. 80** © Manchester Art Gallery; **Fig. 81** © National Portrait Gallery, London; **Fig. 82** The Bodleian Libraries, University of Oxford (MS. Douce 59. fol. 4r); **Fig. 83** Photo: Tate; **Fig. 84** The Bodleian Libraries, University of Oxford (JJC Soap 1 (41). Recto); **Fig. 85** © Museum of the History of Science, Oxford, inv.76705; **Fig. 86** © Manchester Art Gallery; **Fig. 87** Fashion Museum Bath; **Fig. 88** © Manchester Art Gallery; **Fig. 89** © Manchester Art Gallery; **Fig. 90** Punch Cartoon Library / TopFoto; **Fig. 92** © Science Museum / Science & Society Picture Library – All rights reserved; **Fig. 93** © Victoria and Albert Museum, London; **Fig. 94** World History Archive / Mary Evans Picture Library; **Fig. 95** Courtesy National Museums Liverpool, Walker Art Gallery; **Fig. 96** The Metropolitan Museum of Art, New York. Gilman Collection, Museum Purchase, 2005. www.metmuseum.org; **Fig. 97** RIBA Collections; **Fig. 98** Photo by Birmingham Museums Trust, licensed under CC0; **Fig. 99** The Metropolitan Museum of Art, New York. Gilman Collection, Museum Purchase, 2005. www.metmuseum.org; **Fig. 100** The Devonshire Collections, Chatsworth; **Fig. 101** © Manchester Art Gallery; **Fig. 102** Hulton Archive / Getty Images; **Fig. 103** © Illustrated London News Ltd/Mary Evans; **Fig. 110** BnF; **Fig. 111** Copyright Pitt Rivers Museum, University of Oxford. Accession number: 1998.211.9; **Fig. 112** © National Trust / Andrew McGregor; **Fig. 113** © Victoria and Albert Museum, London; **Fig. 114** RIBA Collections; **Fig. 115** © The Trustees of the British Museum; **Fig. 116** © The Trustees of the British Museum; **Fig. 117** The Faringdon Collection Trust, Buscot Park; **Fig. 119** Getty Research Institute; **Fig. 120** City of London Corporation; **Fig. 121** City of London Corporation; **Fig. 122** Bridgeman Images; **Fig. 123** The Bodleian Libraries, University of Oxford (902.8 Art.10); **Fig. 124** © Image; Crown Copyright: UK Government Art Collection; **Fig. 125** New Art Gallery Walsall Permanent Collection; **Fig. 130** Photo by Birmingham Museums Trust, licensed under CC0; **Fig. 132** The Metropolitan Museum of Art, New York. Bequest of Mrs. Charles Wrightsman, 2019. www.metmuseum.org; **Fig. 133** The Metropolitan Museum of Art, New York. Gift of Kenneth Jay Lane, 2014. www.metmuseum.org; **Fig. 134** The Bodleian Libraries, University of Oxford ((OC) 170 n.81, Cover); **Fig. 135** The Bodleian Libraries, University of Oxford ((OC) 170 n.81, Unfoliated plate); **Fig. 136** © Victoria and Albert Museum, London; **Fig. 137** The Bodleian Libraries, University of Oxford ((OC) 170 n.81, Unfoliated plate); **Fig. 139** The Bodleian Libraries, University of Oxford ((OC) 170 n.81, Unfoliated plate); **Fig. 140** © UIG History / Science & Society Picture Library – All rights reserved; **Fig. 141** © National Science & Media Museum / Science & Society Picture Library – All rights reserved; **Fig. 142** Joan Hart Collection; **Fig. 143** © British Library Board. All Rights Reserved / Bridgeman Images; **Fig. 144** Private Collection; **Fig. 145** Private Collection; **Fig. 146** © Detroit Institute of Arts/ Bridgeman Images; **Fig. 147** The Hunterian, University of Glasgow; **Fig. 150** Albert Moore – Beads. National Galleries Scotland. Purchased 1910; **Fig. 151** Private Collection, Photo © Christie's Images / Bridgeman Images; **Fig. 152** Copyright Pitt Rivers Museum, University of Oxford. Accession number: 1998.99.3; **Fig. 153** Copyright Pitt Rivers Museum, University of Oxford. Accession number: 1998.99.4; **Fig. 155** © Victoria and Albert Museum, London; **Fig. 156** The Metropolitan Museum of Art, New York. Marguerite and Frank A. Cosgrove Jr. Fund, 2017. www.metmuseum.org; **Fig. 157** The Hunterian, University of Glasgow; **Fig. 158** The Hunterian, University of Glasgow; **Fig. 159** Punch Cartoon Library / TopFoto; **Fig. 160** Photo: Tate; **Fig. 162** A skeleton gentleman at a ball asks a skeleton lady to dance; representing the effect of arsenical dyes and pigments in clothing and accessories. Wood engraving, 1862. Wellcome Collection. Public Domain Mark; **Fig. 163** Courtesy of the National Library of Medicine; **Fig. 163** Courtesy of the National Library of Medicine; **Fig. 164** © The Trustees of the British Museum; **Fig. 165** Granger / Bridgeman Images; **Fig. 166** Museu de Monserrat. Donated by Josep Sala Ardiz 1980; **Fig. 167** By Permission of the President and Fellows of Trinity College Oxford; **Fig. 168** The Bodleian Libraries, University of Oxford (Windows and Bills Advertisement Folder 1 (38)); **Fig. 169** The Bodleian Libraries, University of Oxford (Windows and Bills Advertisement Folder 1 (3)); **Fig. 170** © Victoria and Albert Museum, London; **Fig. 171** © NATIONAL MUSEUM OF WALES; **Fig. 172** Mary Evans Picture Library; **Fig. 173** Collection Raimondo Biffi; **Fig. 174** From the collection of Prof. Shane Butler. Photo: Ashmolean Museum, University of Oxford; **Fig. 175** By Permission of the President and Fellows of Trinity College Oxford; **Fig. 176** © The Trustees of the British Museum; **Fig. 177** © The Trustees of the British Museum; **Fig. 178** © Art Gallery of Ontario / Gift from the Junior Women's Committee Fund, 1969 / Bridgeman Images; **Fig. 179** The Stapleton Collection / Bridgeman Images; **Fig. 180** City of London Corporation; **Fig. 181** Photo: Tate; **Fig. 182** The Hunterian, University of Glasgow; **Fig. 185** © Victoria and Albert Museum, London; **Fig. 186** © Indianapolis Museum of Art / Robertine Daniels Art Fund in memory of her husband & son / Bridgeman Images; **Fig. 187** The Cleveland Museum of Art, Gift of Ralph King 1925.1202; **Fig. 188** Hopkins, Albert A. Magic; Stage Illusions and Scientific Diversions, including Trick Photography. Comp. and Ed. by Albert A. Hopkins ... with an Introduction by Henry Ridgely Evans ... With Four Hundred Illustrations. England: Low, 1897, 1897. Web; **Fig. 189** © Look and Learn / Bridgeman Images; **Fig. 190** Theatre Collection Allard Pierson University of Amsterdam; **Fig. 191** © Victoria and Albert Museum, London; **Fig. 192** The Bodleian Libraries, University of Oxford (John Johnson, Soap 1 (74). Recto)

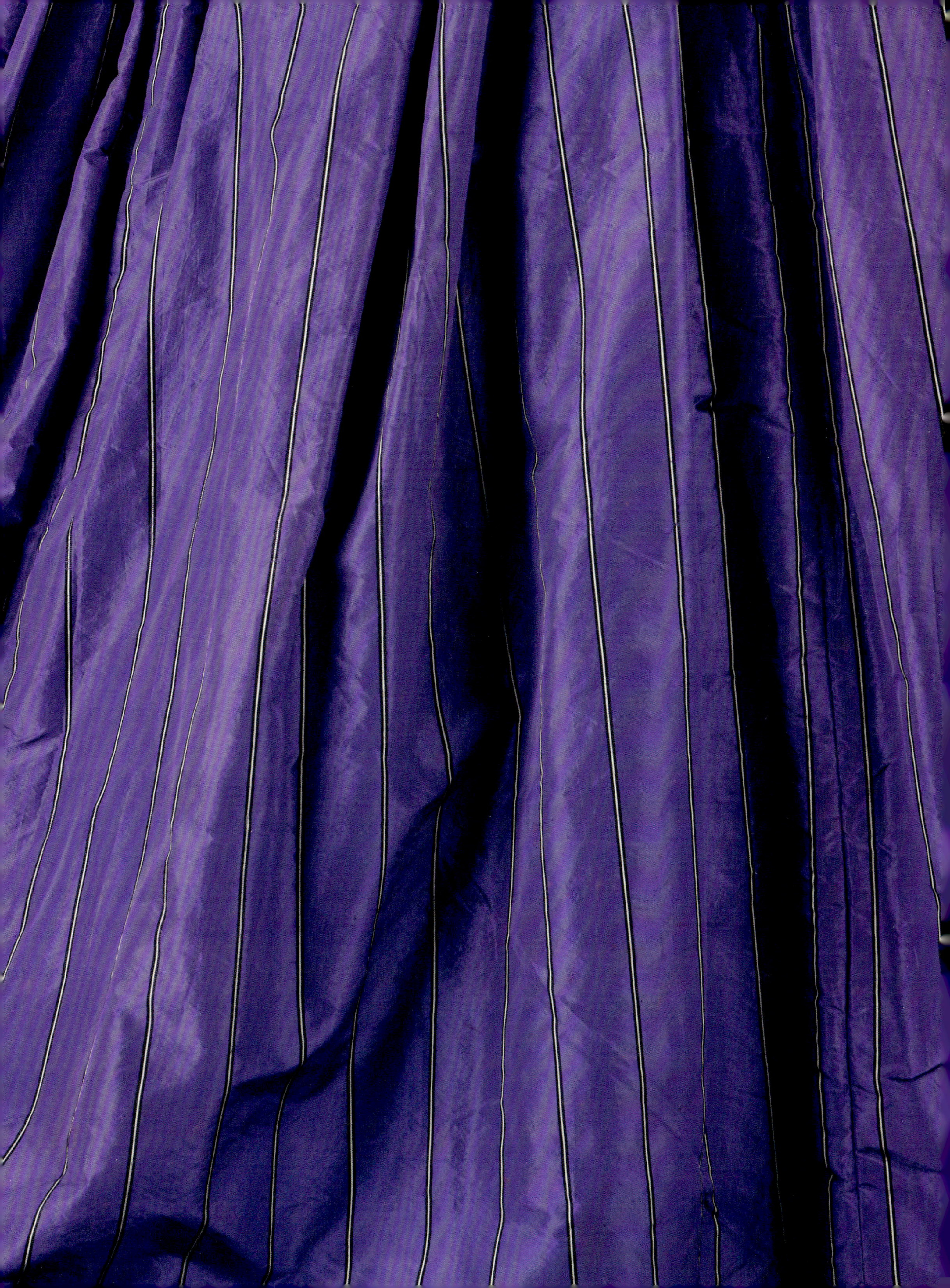

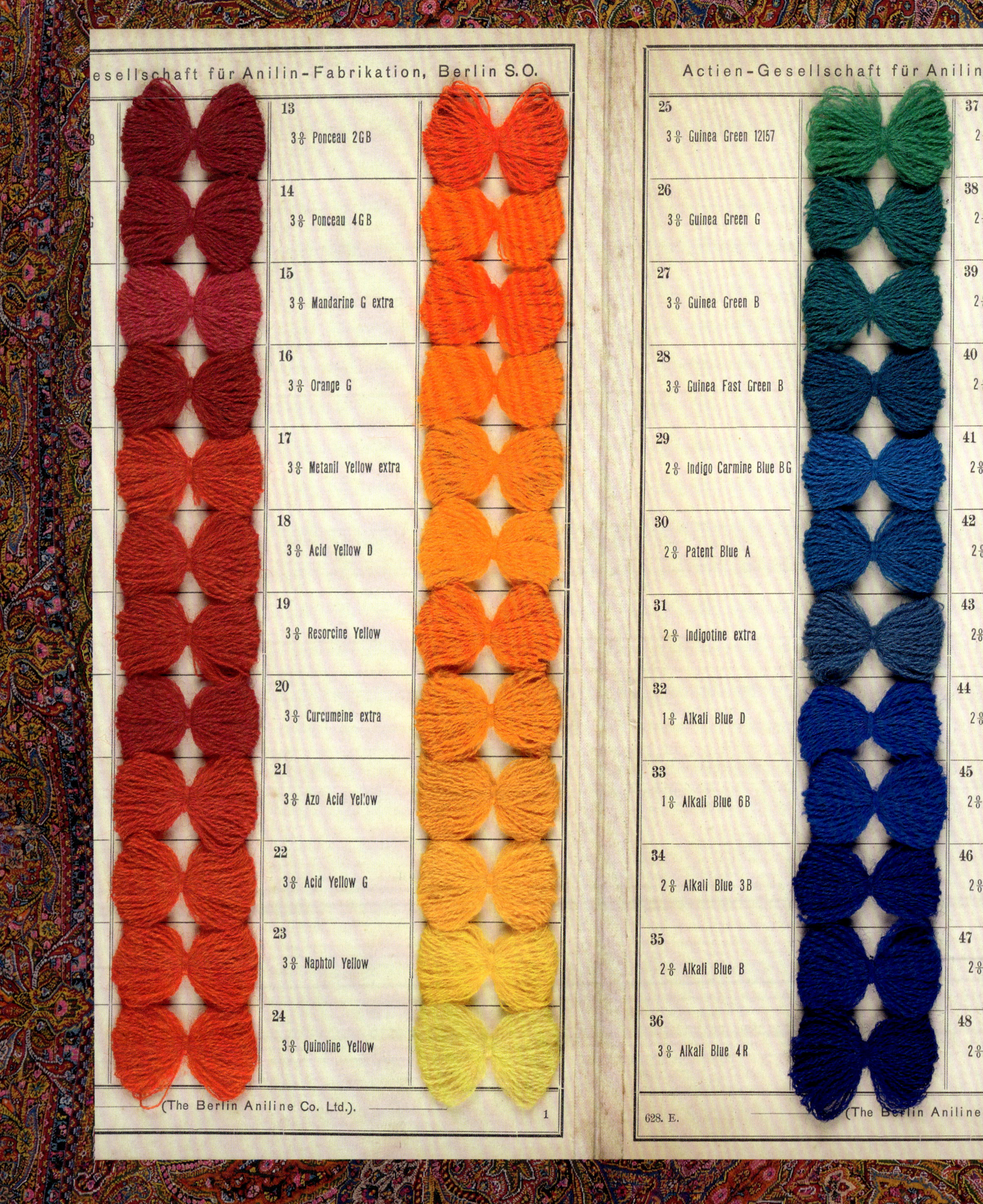
esellschaft für Anilin-Fabrikation, Berlin S.O.
13
3 % Ponceau 2GB
14
3 % Ponceau 4GB
15
3 % Mandarine G extra
16
3 % Orange G
17
3 % Metanil Yellow extra
18
3 % Acid Yellow D
19
3 % Resorcine Yellow
20
3 % Curcumeine extra
21
3 % Azo Acid Yellow
22
3 % Acid Yellow G
23
3 % Naphtol Yellow
24
3 % Quinoline Yellow
(The Berlin Aniline Co. Ltd.).
1
Actien-Gesellschaft für Anilin-
25
3 % Guinea Green 12157
26
3 % Guinea Green G
27
3 % Guinea Green B
28
3 % Guinea Fast Green B
29
2 % Indigo Carmine Blue BG
30
2 % Patent Blue A
31
2 % Indigotine extra
32
1 % Alkali Blue D
33
1 % Alkali Blue 6B
34
2 % Alkali Blue 3B
35
2 % Alkali Blue B
36
3 % Alkali Blue 4R
37
38
39
40
41
42
43
44
45
46
47
48
628. E.
(The Berlin Aniline